John Hawkins has long been a trail-blazer in the attempt to re̲ ̲
of formal and functional linguistics. *Efficiency and Complexity in Grammars*
charts new territory in this domain. The book argues persuasively that a small
number of performance-based principles combine to account for many grammatical constraints proposed by formal linguists and also explain the origins
of numerous typological generalizations discovered by functionalists.

Frederick J. Newmeyer, *University of Washington.*

The central claim in Hawkins's new book is that grammar facilitates language
processing. This rather natural idea is by no means novel: attempts to explain
aspects of linguistic structure on the basis of processing considerations go back
at least to the 1950s. But such attempts have characteristically been little more
than "just so stories" – that is, post hoc accounts of isolated observations. What
has been lacking until now is anything that could be called a theory of how
constraints on the human processor shape grammatical structure.

Hawkins has filled this lacuna. Starting with three very general and intuitive
principles about efficient processing of language, he derives a rich array of
predictions about what kinds of grammatical structures should be preferred.
He then adduces a wealth of evidence to demonstrate that his predictions hold.
His data are of a variety of types, including grammatical patterns in particular languages, typological tendencies, usage statistics from corpora, historical
changes, and psycholinguistic findings. The phenomena he deals with are similarly varied, including word order, case making, filler-gap dependencies, island
constraints, and anaphoric binding.

Efficiency and Complexity in Grammars is a landmark work, setting a new
standard in the study of the relationship between linguistic competence and
performance.

Tom Wasow, *Stanford University.*

Hawkins argues that grammars are profoundly affected by the way humans
process language. He develops a simple but elegant theory of performance
and grammar by drawing on concepts and data from generative grammar, linguistic typology, experimental psycholinguistics and historical linguistics. In
so doing, he also makes a laudable attempt to bridge the schism between the
two research traditions in linguistics, the formal and the functional. *Efficiency
and Complexity in Grammars* is a major contribution with far-reaching consequences and implications for many of the fundamental issues in linguistic
theory. This is a tremendous piece of scholarship that no linguist can afford to
neglect.

Jae Jung Song, *University of Otago.*

Efficiency and Complexity in Grammars

JOHN A. HAWKINS

OXFORD
UNIVERSITY PRESS

OXFORD

UNIVERSITY PRESS

Great Clarendon Street, Oxford OX2 6DP

Oxford University Press is a department of the University of Oxford.

It furthers the University's objective of excellence in research, scholarship, and education by publishing worldwide in

Oxford New York

Auckland Bangkok Buenos Aires Cape Town Chennai
Dar es Salaam Delhi Hong Kong Istanbul Karachi Kolkata
Kuala Lumpur Madrid Melbourne Mexico City Mumbai Nairobi
São Paulo Shanghai Taipei Tokyo Toronto

Oxford is a registered trade mark of Oxford University Press
in the UK and in certain other countries

Published in the United States
by Oxford University Press Inc., New York

A catalogue record for this title is available from the British Library.

Library of Congress Cataloging in Publication Data
Data available

ISBN 0–19–925268–8 (hbk.)
ISBN 0–19–925269–6 (pbk.)

Typeset by Newgen Imaging Systems (P) Ltd., Chennai, India
Printed in Great Britain on acid-free paper by
Biddles Ltd., King's Lynn

To Kathryn and Kirsten,
who delayed this book beautifully

Contents

Preface

Has performance had any significant impact on the basic design features of grammars? Putting this another way: do the variation patterns that we observe in the world's 6,000 languages point to a causal role for principles of processing and use? One tradition of research, following Chomsky's theory of an autonomous and ultimately innate grammar, answers this question in the negative. Other researchers, some following Greenberg's early work on performance and cross-linguistic markedness hierarchies, answer it in the affirmative. These two research traditions, the formal and the functional, use different methodologies and they formulate different kinds of linguistic generalizations, and this makes it hard for an uncommitted observer to assess their respective arguments. Compounding this difficulty has been the absence for many years of systematic data from performance, on the basis of which we could test whether principles of structural selection and processing have left any imprint on grammars and grammatical variation. The field of experimental psycholinguistics has now reached the point, however, where we have a growing body of performance data from English and certain other languages, and the advent of corpora has made available large quantities of usage data that can be accessed in the pursuit of theoretical questions.

The time has come when we can return to the big question about the role of performance in explaining grammars and give some answers based not on philosophical speculation but on the growing body of empirical data from grammars and from performance. Do these two sets of data correspond or do they not? Are distributional patterns and preferences that we find in the one found in the other? If such correspondences can be found, this will provide evidence against the immunity of grammars to performance. If, moreover, the properties of grammars that can be linked to patterns and preferences in performance include the very parameters and constraints of Chomskyan Universal Grammar, then we will have evidence for a strong causal role for performance in explaining the basic design features of grammars.

I argue in this book that there is a profound correspondence between performance and grammars, and I show this empirically for a large number of syntactic and morphosyntactic properties and constructions. Specifically the data of this book support the following hypotheses and conclusions:

- Grammars have conventionalized syntactic structures in proportion to their degrees of preference in performance, as evidenced by patterns of selection in corpora and by ease of processing in psycholinguistic experiments (the 'performance–grammar correspondence hypothesis').
- These common preferences of performance and grammars are structured by general principles of efficiency and complexity that are clearly visible in both usage data and grammatical conventions. Three of these principles are defined and illustrated here: Minimize Domains, Minimize Forms, and Maximize On-line Processing.
- Greater descriptive and explanatory adequacy can be achieved when efficiency and complexity principles are incorporated into the theory of grammar; stipulations are avoided, many exceptions can be explained, and improved formalisms incorporating significant generalizations from both performance and grammars can be proposed.
- Psycholinguistic models need to broaden the explanatory basis for many performance preferences beyond working-memory load and capacity constraints. The data presented here point to multiple factors and to degrees of preference that operate well within working memory limits, while some preferred structures actually increase working memory load as currently defined.
- The innateness of human language resides primarily in mechanisms for processing and for learning. The innateness of grammar is reduced to the extent that efficiency and complexity provide a more adequate description of the facts, in conjunction with a theory of adaptation and change and the performance–grammar correspondence proposed here.
- The language sciences are currently fragmented into often mutually indifferent subdisciplines: generative grammar, typology, psycholinguistics, and historical linguistics. It is important, if we are to advance to the next stage of descriptive adequacy and if we are to make progress in understanding why grammars are the way they are, that we try to integrate key findings and insights from each of these areas.

I realize that these conclusions will be unwelcome to many, especially those with philosophical commitments to the status quo. But the current compartmentalization in our field and the absence of any real exchange of ideas and generalizations between many of the research groups is not satisfactory. Peer-group conformist pressures also encourage acceptance rather than critical assessment and testing of ideas that have become almost dogmatic. There needs to be a reassessment of the grammar–performance relationship at this point. And in particular somebody needs to juxtapose the kinds of data and generalizations that these different fields have discovered and see whether there is, or is not, some unity that underlies them all. My primary goal is to attempt to do this. And my finding is that there is a deep correspondence between performance data and grammars and that grammatical theorizing needs to take account of this, both descriptively and at an explanatory level.

There are so many people that I am indebted to for ideas and assistance in writing this book that I have decided not to list names at the outset but to make very clear in the text whose contributions I am using and how. I have been fortunate over the years to have had colleagues and mentors in typology, formal grammar, psycholinguistics, and historical linguistics without whom I could not have undertaken the kind of synthesis I am attempting here. At an institutional level I must mention the German Max Planck Society which has generously supported my work over a long period, first at the psycholinguistics institute in Nijmegen and more recently at the evolutionary anthropology institute in Leipzig. Most of this book was written in Leipzig and I am grateful to this institute, and to its co-director Bernard Comrie in particular, for the opportunity to complete it there. The University of Southern California in Los Angeles has also supported me generously over many years.

Leipzig 2003   JAH

Abbreviations

A	appositive
Abs	absolutive
Acc	accusative
Accus	accusative
Adj	adjective
AdjP	adjective phrase
Adjwk	weak adjective
AdvP	adverb phrase
Agr	agreement
AH	accessibility hierarchy
Anaph	anaphor
Ant	antecedent
C	complementizer
CL	classifier
Classif	classifier
CNPC	complex noun phrase constraint
Comp	complementizer
CRD	constituent recognition domain
CV	consonant-vowel (syllable)
CVC	consonant-vowel-consonant (syllable)
Dat	dative
Def	definite determiner
Dem	demonstrative determiner
Det	determiner
DO	direct object
DP	determiner phrase
EIC	early immediate constituents
Erg	ergative
F	form
Fams	families (of languages)
Fem	feminine
FGD	filler–gap domain
F : P	form–property pairing

Fut	future
G	genitive
Gen	genitive
HPD	head–pronoun domain
IC	immediate constituent
IO	indirect object
IP	inflection phrase
L	lenition
LD	lexical domain
Lgs	languages
L to R	left to right
M	mother node
m (mXP/XPm)	a mother-node-constructing category on the left/right periphery of XP
Masc	masculine
MaOP	maximize on-line processing
MHG	Middle High German
Mid.	middle
MiD	minimize domains
Mod.	modern
MiF	minimize forms
N	noun
Neut	neuter
NHG	New High German
Nom	nominative
Nomin	nominative
NP	noun phrase
NRel	noun before relative clause
O	object
OBL	oblique
OCOMP	object of comparison
OHG	Old High German
OP	on-line property
Op	operator
OP/UP	on-line property to ultimate property (ratios)
OT	optimality theory
OV	object before verb
OVS	object before verb before subject
P	preposition or postposition

P	property
Part	particle
PCD	phrasal combination domain
Pd	dependent prepositional phrase
Perf	perfect(ive)
PGCH	performance–grammar correspondence hypothesis
Pi	independent prepositional phrase
Pl	plural
Plur	plural
Poss	possessive
Possp	possessive phrase
PP	prepositional phrase
Prep	preposition
Pro	pronoun
P-set	pragmatic set
Qu	quantifier
R	restrictive
R-agr	rich agreement
R-case	rich case marking
Rel	relative (clause)
RelN	relative clause before noun
RelPro	relative pronoun
Relv	relativizer
R-pronoun	reflexive pronoun
RQ	requires
R to L	right to left
S	sentence
S	subject
S′	sentence bar
Sg	singular
Sing	singular
SOV	subject before object before verb
SVO	subject before verb before object
SU	subject
TDD	total domain differential
θ	theta (role)
UG	universal grammar
UP	ultimate property
V	verb

VO	verb before object
VOS	verb before object before subject
VP	verb phrase
VSO	verb before subject before object
XP	an arbitrary phrase

1

Introduction

An interesting general correlation appears to be emerging between perform-ance and grammars, as more data become available from each. There are patterns of preference in performance in languages possessing several struc-tures of a given type. These same preferences can also be found in the fixed conventions of grammars, in languages with fewer structures of the same type. The performance data come from corpus studies and processing experiments, the grammatical data from typological samples and from the growing number of languages that have now been subjected to in-depth formal analysis.

The primary goal of this book is to explore this correlation in a broad range of syntactic and morphosyntactic data. I will argue that many of these common preferences of performance and grammars can be explained by efficiency and complexity, and some general and predictive principles will be defined that give substance to this claim. In this introductory chapter I define my goals and show how they are relevant to current issues in linguistics and psycholinguistics.

1.1   Performance–grammar correspondences: a hypothesis

An early example of the correlation between grammars and performance data can be found in Greenberg's (1966) book on feature hierarchies such as Singular > Plural > Dual and Nominative > Accusative > Dative. Morpho-logical inventories across languages, declining allomorphy and increased formal marking all provided evidence for the hierarchies, while declining frequencies of use for lower positions on each hierarchy, in languages like Sanskrit with productive morphemes of each type, showed a clear performance correlation with the patterns of grammars.

Another early example, involving syntax, was proposed by Keenan & Comrie (1977) when motivating their Accessibility Hierarchy (SU>DO>IO/OBL> GEN) for cross-linguistic relativization patterns. They argued that this gram-matical hierarchy correlated with the processing ease of relativizing on these different positions and with corpus frequencies in a single language (English) with many relativizable positions (Keenan & S. Hawkins 1987, Keenan 1975). This correlation was extended to other relativization patterns beyond the Accessibility Hierarchy in Hawkins (1999).

Givón (1979: 26–31) observed that selection preferences in one language, in favor of definite rather than indefinite clausal subjects, e.g. in English, corresponded to a categorical requirement for definite subjects in another (Krio).

The preferred word orders in languages with choices have been argued in Hawkins (1994) to be those that are productively grammaticalized in languages with fixed orders, and in almost exact proportion to their degree of preference.

More recently Bresnan et al. (2001) compared the usage preference for subjects obeying the Person Hierarchy (1st, 2nd > 3rd) in English with its conventionalized counterpart in the Salish language Lummi, in which sentences corresponding to *The man knows me* are ungrammatical and must be passivized to *I am known by the man* (Jelinek & Demers 1983, 1994, Aissen 1999).

But apart from examples such as these, there has been little systematic juxtaposition of single-language performance variation data with cross-linguistic grammatical patterns and parameters. There has been no shortage of studies of performance, in English and certain other languages. Much of psycholinguistics is in essence concerned with patterns of preference in performance (faster reaction times, fewer errors, higher frequencies, etc.). But psycholinguists are not primarily interested in the conventionalized knowledge systems that we call grammars, or in grammatical variation. They are interested in the performance mechanisms that underlie comprehension and production in real time. Conversely it has been widely assumed in linguistics, since Chomsky (1965), that grammars have not been shaped by performance to any significant extent. Grammars, according to this view, are predetermined by an innate language faculty, and they stand in an asymmetrical relationship to language performance. Grammatical rules and principles are constantly accessed in processing, but processing has not significantly impacted grammars. Hence there would be no reason to look for a correlation.

The alternative to be pursued here is that grammars have been profoundly shaped by language processing. Even highly abstract and fundamental properties of syntax will be argued to be derivable from simple principles of processing efficiency and complexity that are needed anyway in order to explain how language is used. As I see it, the emerging correlation between performance and grammars exists because grammars have conventionalized the preferences of performance, in proportion to their strength and in proportion to their number, as they apply to the relevant structures in the relevant language types.

Grammars are 'frozen' or 'fixed' performance preferences. I shall refer to this as the Performance–Grammar Correspondence Hypothesis (PGCH). It is defined in (1.1).

(1.1) *Performance–Grammar Correspondence Hypothesis* (PGCH)
Grammars have conventionalized syntactic structures in proportion to their degree of preference in performance, as evidenced by patterns of selection in corpora and by ease of processing in psycholinguistic experiments.

This hypothesis formed the basis for the parsing explanation for word order universals in Hawkins (1990, 1994). It is supported by a number of other parsing explanations for grammars that were summarized in Hawkins (1994), including Kuno (1973a, 1974) and Dryer (1980) on center embedding avoidance in performance and grammars; Janet Fodor's (1978, 1984) parsing explanation for the Nested Dependency Constraint; and Bever's (1970) and Frazier's (1985) explanation for the impossibility of *that* deletion in English sentential subjects in terms of garden path avoidance. I also summarized morphological studies such as Hawkins & Cutler (1988) and Hall (1992) on the processing of suffixes versus prefixes in lexical access and on the cross-linguistic suffixing preference, and phonological work by Lindblom et al. (1984) and Lindblom & Maddieson (1988) on the perceptual and articulatory basis for cross-linguistic hierarchies of vowel and consonant inventories.

The PGCH has received further support during the last few years. Haspelmath (1999a) has proposed a diachronic theory in which usage preferences in several grammatical areas lead to changing grammatical conventions over time. Bybee & Hopper (2001) document the role of frequency in the emergence of grammatical structure. There have been intriguing computer simulations of language evolution, exemplified by Kirby (1999), which incorporate processing preferences of the kind assumed here for linear ordering and which test the assumption that the observed grammatical types will emerge over time from such preferences. There have also been developments in Optimality Theory, exemplified by Haspelmath (1999a) and Aissen (1999), in which functional motivations are provided for many of the basic constraints of that theory. Some of these motivations are of an explicitly processing nature. For example, STAY, or 'Do not move' (Grimshaw 1997, Speas 1997), is considered by Haspelmath to be 'user-optimal' since 'leaving material in canonical positions helps the hearer to identify grammatical relationships and reduces processing costs for the speaker'. A further development within this theory, Stochastic Optimality Theory (Bresnan et al. 2001, Manning 2003) is also relevant to the PGCH since it is an explicit attempt to generate the preferences of performance ('soft constraints') as well as the grammatical conventions ('hard constraints') using the formal machinery of Optimality Theory, appropriately extended.

But despite this growing interest in performance–grammar correspondences, Chomsky's (1965) assumption that performance has not significantly shaped grammars is still widely held in linguistics and in psycholinguistics. One reason for this is the success of much descriptive work in autonomous formal syntax and semantics. This work is philosophically grounded in the innateness hypothesis (see e.g. Chomsky 1968, 1975, Hoekstra & Kooij 1988). The belief that one could be contributing to the discovery of an innate language faculty and of the child's initial cognitive state through detailed formal analysis of certain structures and languages, is very appealing to many linguists and psycholinguists. Another reason for resisting the PGCH is that theories of processing and use are still in their relative infancy, and many basic issues, including the nature of working memory, production versus comprehension differences, and the processing of many non-European linguistic structures, have not yet been resolved in the theoretical psycholinguistic literature. This makes an explicit comparison of grammatical and performance theories difficult.

My personal view is that work in formal syntax and semantics has now reached the point where it must take account of the kinds of processing motivations to be proposed here, for at least two reasons. First, if there are systematic correspondences between grammars and performance, a theory that accounts only for grammars is not general enough and misses significant generalizations that hold for both conventionalized and non-conventionalized data. And second, principles of performance offer a potential explanation for why grammars are the way they are, and they can help us decide between competing formal models.

There is currently a lot of stipulation in formal grammar. Principles are proposed because they handle certain data in certain languages. Questions of ultimate causation are rarely raised other than to appeal to a hypothesized, but independently unsupported, innateness claim, and this has consequences for descriptive adequacy. I am regularly finding universals and patterns of cross-linguistic variation that are predicted by performance patterns and by the principles derived from them, and that are not predicted by current formal models. Formal grammars have been remarkably successful at describing many syntactic and semantic properties of sentences, and the performance data to be given here support their psychological reality. But if there is a functional grounding to formal grammatical properties, then it is counterproductive to ignore it when formulating the best general principles and predictions, and this is, I believe, what motivates the kind of functionally based Optimality

Theory advocated by Haspelmath (1999*a*) and the Stochastic OT of Bresnan et al. (2001). There are different ways of incorporating functionalism, as argued by Bresnan & Aissen (2002) v. Newmeyer (2002), but it should not be ignored altogether. To do so puts us in the position a biologist would be in if he or she were asked to come up with a theory of species diversity and evolution while paying no attention whatsoever to Darwin's functional ideas on natural selection. Such a theory would be partial at best.

1.2   Predictions of the PGCH

The PGCH makes predictions, which we must define. In order to test them we need performance data and grammatical data from a range of languages involving the same grammatical structures. Throughout this book I will proceed as follows. First, find a language whose grammar generates a plurality of structural alternatives of a common type. They may involve alternative orderings of the same constituents with the same or similar domination relations in the phrase structure tree, e.g. different orderings of NP and PP constituents in the free-ordering post-verbal domain of Hungarian, or [PP NP V]vp v. [NP PP V]vp in a verb-final language like Japanese. Or they may involve alternative relative clauses with and without an explicit relativizer, as in English (*the Danes whom/that he taught* v. *the Danes he taught*). Or alternations between relativizations on a direct object using a gap strategy v. the resumptive pronoun strategy, as in Hebrew. Or even relativizations on different Accessibility Hierarchy positions using the same common (e.g. gap) strategy in a given language.

Second, check for the distribution of these same structural patterns in the grammatical conventions across languages. The PGCH predicts that when the grammar of one language is more restrictive and eliminates one or more structural options that are permitted by the grammar of another, the restriction will be in accordance with performance preferences. The preferred structure will be retained and 'fixed' as a grammatical convention, the dispreferred structures will be removed. Either they will be eliminated altogether from the output of the grammar or they may be retained in some marginal form as lexical exceptions or as limited construction types. So, for example, if there is a general preference in performance for constituent orderings that minimize the number of words on the basis of which phrase structure groupings can be recognized, as I argued in Hawkins (1994), then I expect the fixed word orders of grammars to respect this same preference. They should permit rapid immediate constituent (IC) recognition in the normal case. Numerous adjacency effects are thereby predicted between sister categories in grammars, based on their (average) relative weights and on the information that they provide about phrase structure on-line (through e.g. head projection). Similarly, if the absence of the relativizer in English performance is strongly associated with adjacency to the head noun, while its presence is productive under both adjacency and non-adjacency, then I expect that grammars that actually remove the zero option altogether will also preferably remove it when non-adjacent before or at the same time as they remove it under adjacency. And if the gap relativization strategy in Hebrew performance provides evidence for a structural proximity preference to the head noun, compared with the resumptive pronoun strategy, then it is predicted that the distribution of gaps to pronouns across grammars should be in this same direction, with gaps being more or equally proximate to their head nouns.

These are illustrations of the research strategy that lies ahead. The grammatical predictions of the PGCH can be set out more fully as follows:

(1.2) *Grammatical predictions of the PGCH*

   (a) If a structure A is preferred over an A′ of the same structural type in performance, then A will be more productively grammaticalized, in proportion to its degree of preference; if A and A′ are more equally preferred, then A and A′ will both be productive in grammars.

   (b) If there is a preference ranking A>B>C>D among structures of a common type in performance, then there will be a corresponding hierarchy of grammatical conventions (with cut-off points and declining frequencies of languages).

   (c) If two preferences P and P′ are in (partial) opposition, then there will be variation in performance and grammars, with both P and P′ being realized, each in proportion to its degree of motivation in a given language structure.

For someone who believes in the PGCH, principles of performance should be reflected in the conventionalized rules of grammars and in grammatical variation, and hence performance data can help us discover and formulate the most adequate grammars. Throughout this book I will suggest that many current grammatical generalizations for e.g. adjacency, subjacency, asymmetry, and other phenomena are not quite correctly formulated. Processing and performance data can lead to new descriptive generalizations and to a new understanding of why grammars are the way they are. And if there are systematic correspondences between performance and grammars, then any model of grammar will lack generality if it does not incorporate in some way the explanatory primitives that underlie performance preferences.

Conversely, grammars should enable us to predict the preferences that will be found in performance variation, and hence grammatical conventions can be of interest to performance theorists beyond the fact that they are sources of knowledge that are activated in processing. So, for example, in Hawkins (1990) I argued that the Greenbergian word order correlations pointed to a principle of efficient parsing, E(arly) I(mmediate) C(onstituents), whose preferences appeared to be conventionalized in grammars in proportion to the degrees defined by the associated metric. I subsequently set about testing this on performance data from different languages with the help of many collaborators, and in Hawkins (1994) I could report that there was indeed strong evidence for EIC in the performance preferences of languages with choices. In a similar vein, Keenan & Comrie's (1977) Accessibility Hierarchy was first formulated on the basis of relativization data across grammars, for which they hypothesized an ease-of-processing explanation, and this was then supported by corpus studies and psycholinguistic experiments using English (Keenan & S. Hawkins 1987, Keenan 1975).

Patterns across grammars can also shed light on general issues in psycholinguistics. In Hawkins (1994, 1998a) I argued that head-final grammars suggested a rather different prediction for weight effects in performance than is found in current production models, namely heavy constituents before lighter ones in head-final languages, with the reverse pattern in English and head-initial languages. Performance data were given supporting this (see also Yamashita & Chang 2001 for further evidence), and this point will be developed further in §5.1.2.

It should become clear that there is a strong empirical basis to the PGCH. Performance preferences will be supported by extensive data. When trying to predict and account for these data I shall cast a wide theoretical net. The present work draws on insights from psycholinguistic models of production (Levelt 1989) and comprehension (J. A. Fodor et al. 1974) and from metrics of complexity such as Miller & Chomsky (1963), Frazier (1985), and Gibson (1998), all of which are tied to models of formal syntax. It incorporates connectionist insights (MacDonald et al. 1994). It draws on the kinds of functional ideas proposed by Haiman (1983, 1985), Givón (1979, 1995), and Newmeyer (1998), and on applications of these ideas in language typology by e.g. Bybee (1985), Comrie (1989), and Croft (2003). It also draws on neo-Gricean work by Levinson (2000) and Sperber & Wilson (1995), and argues, with them, that the syntax and conventionalized meaning of many constructions is enriched through inferences in language use, and that a proper analysis of these constructions must include an account of these pragmatic enrichments in addition to their syntax and semantics. I also cast a wide net in the formulation of grammatical generalizations in this book, and make use of typologists' generalizations and language samples as well as different formal descriptions and models.

There is a strong cross-linguistic emphasis as well. Performance and grammatical data are taken from many different language types. Current processing models in psycholinguistics are, unfortunately, still heavily oriented towards English and other European languages, and this means that I am often forced to make hypotheses about the processing of non-European structures, which I hope that psycholinguists around the world will want to test. Sometimes I have to rely on suggestive but insufficient data from certain languages, and I hope that others will want to remedy this through more extensive data collection and testing. Current grammatical models are, fortunately, much more compatible with cross-linguistic diversity than they used to be.

1.3   Efficiency and complexity

The correlating patterns of preference in performance and grammars that are the focus of this book will be argued to be structured by efficiency and complexity. The principles that will give substance to this claim are formulated at a very general level and they predict a wide range of data.

My ideas about complexity have been strongly influenced by Miller & Chomsky's (1963) original metric of syntactic complexity in terms of the ratio of non-terminal to terminal nodes, and by the extensions of it in Frazier (1985). The basic insight that Miller & Chomsky gave us was this. Complexity is a function of the amount of structure that is associated with the terminal elements, or words, of a sentence. More structure means, in effect, that more linguistic properties have to be processed in addition to recognizing or producing the words themselves. In a clause with a sentential subject in English, such as *that John was sick surprised Sue*, the non-terminal to terminal node ratio is higher than it is in the extraposed counterpart, *it surprised Sue that John was sick*, in which there is an additional terminal element (*it*) but the same amount of higher structure, and this results in a lower ratio of structure to words. Frazier (1985) and Gibson (1998) have modified this metric, and refined its predictions, by defining it locally on certain subsets of the terminal elements and their dominating nodes, rather than globally throughout a sentence. My theory of Early Immediate Constituents (EIC) in Hawkins (1990, 1994) was also a local complexity metric (for alternative linear orderings).

I now want to extend Miller & Chomsky's insight into other areas of grammar, such as syntactic properties going beyond phrase structure nodes and dominance relations. I want to make it applicable also to morphology and to morphosyntax. I also want to include semantics. The basic idea to be developed is this. Complexity increases with the number of linguistic forms and the number of conventionally associated (syntactic and semantic) properties that are assigned to them when constructing syntactic and semantic representations for sentences. That is, it increases with more forms, and with more conventionally associated properties. It also increases with larger formal domains for the assignment of these properties.

Efficiency, as I see it, may involve more or less complexity, depending on the syntactic and semantic representations to be assigned to a given sentence and on their required minimum level of complexity. But some structures can be more efficient than others relative to this minimum. Specifically I shall propose three very general principles of efficiency that are suggested by the preferences of performance and grammars.

Efficiency is increased, first, by minimizing the domains (i.e. the sequences of linguistic forms and their conventionally associated properties) within which certain properties are assigned. It is increased, secondly, by minimizing the linguistic forms (phonemes, morphemes, etc.) that are to be processed, and by reducing their conventionally associated properties, maximizing in the process the role of contextual information (broadly construed), including frequency effects and various inferences. Third, efficiency is increased by selecting and arranging linguistic forms so as to provide the earliest possible access to as much of the ultimate syntactic and semantic representation as possible. In other words, there is a preference for 'maximizing on-line property assignments'.

These principles are simple and intuitive, there is a lot of evidence for them, and they subsume ideas that many others have proposed. The devil lies in the details, as usual. By defining them the way I do I hope to subsume more data under fewer principles, to account for interactions between different efficiency preferences in a principled way, and to see some familiar data in a new and more explanatory light. I also hope to convince the reader that general considerations of efficiency do indeed motivate what might seem to be irreducible and abstract properties of the innate grammatical core.

These principles will be justified on the basis of sample performance and grammatical data and, once formulated, they will structure the predictions for further testing, following the ideas in (1.2). They predict productive versus less productive language types, in accordance with (1.2a). They predict the existence of grammatical hierarchies, in accordance with (1.2b). And they predict grammatical variation when preferences are in competition, in accordance with (1.2c). They also make predictions for language change and evolution and for the relative chronology of language acquisition in different language types. Acquisition is not the major focus of this book; but this theory does make predictions for it; they need to be tested, and if they are correct a lot of learning theory will be reducible to more general considerations of processing ease that are as relevant for mature speakers as they are for language acquirers. I will also suggest that this processing-based approach to acquisition provides a potential solution to the learnability or 'negative evidence' problem (Bowerman 1988).

1.4   Issues of explanation

There is clearly a biological and an innate basis to human language. That much is obvious. The issue is: precisely what aspects of language and of language use are innately determined? Our species has grammars and others don't, so it is tempting to assume simply that grammar is innate, and this is what Chomskyan linguistics standardly does. Innateness inferences are drawn from grammatical principles, in conjunction with the claim that these principles could not be learned from the (limited) 'positive data' to which the child is exposed (cf. Hoekstra & Kooij 1988). The learnability argument is controversial, however, since it is not clear that principles of U(niversal) G(rammar) actually solve the problem (cf. Bowerman 1988), and since children do learn intricate and language-particular grammatical details from positive data that pose learnability problems for which UG can no longer be invoked as a solution (cf. Hawkins 1988, Arbib & Hill 1988, Culicover 1999). In addition, because the innateness claim is not currently supportable by any independent evidence, such explanations run the risk of circularity. Innateness inferences drawn exclusively from grammatical principles are claimed to give an innateness explanation for the grammars they are derived from, and the back-up argument about (un)learnability is unsupported and weak.

Consider, for example, the contrast between grammatical and ungrammatical subject-to-subject raisings in English, e.g. *John is likely to pass the exam* v. **John is probable to pass the exam*. It poses a learning problem that involves idiosyncratic facts of English, rather than principles of UG. Some adjectives (and verbs) behave like *likely* and permit raising, others behave like *probable* and do not. The child hears the former but not the latter, and evidently succeeds in learning the grammaticality distinction based on positive evidence alone. The negative evidence problem here is so similar to that for which UG has been offered as a solution (e.g. for subjacency violations in Hoekstra & Kooij

1988), and the number of negative evidence problems that reduce to language-particular idiosyncrasies is so overwhelming (see Culicover 1999), that the whole relevance of UG to learnability must be considered moot. There is a real issue here over how the child manages to infer ungrammaticality from the absence of certain linguistic data, while not doing so for others, i.e. there is a negative evidence problem, as Bowerman (1988) points out. But UG cannot claim to be the solution.

It is important for these reasons that alternative explanations for fundamental principles of grammar should be given serious attention. For if grammatical universals can emerge from performance preferences, then cross-linguistic generalizations and parameters can no longer be automatically assumed to derive from an innate grammar. Performance considerations and processing mechanisms may provide the explanation, and the ultimate explanation for grammars shifts to whatever explains performance and to considerations of language change and evolution. Some of the processing mechanisms that have been proposed for performance are quite plausibly the result of a neural architecture for language use that is at least partially domain-specific and innate (J. A. Fodor 1983). There is clearly a strong innate basis to the physiological aspects of speech and hearing. Much of meaning and cognition is presumably innate. But whether, and to what extent, the universals of syntax are also innately determined now becomes a more complex, and I believe more interesting, question. The kinds of data from performance and grammars to be considered in this book are relevant to its resolution. They suggest that even abstract and non-functional-looking grammatical constraints, such as the head-ordering parameter and subjacency, are grounded more in the 'architectural innateness' of language use, to quote Elman's (1998) useful term, than in the 'representational innateness' of the kind advocated by Chomsky.

I do not currently know how far the PGCH can be taken and to what extent it can replace proposals for an innate grammar. We need to keep an open mind on this whole issue and avoid dogmatic commitments to uncertainty. What I do know is that empirical support for the PGCH is growing and that it makes sense of a number of grammatical facts that have been mysterious or stipulated hitherto or that have gone unnoticed. It can account for cross-categorial word order universals (§5.3) and adjacency effects (Chapters 5 and 6). It can explain numerous hierarchies in filler–gap dependencies, and it can motivate reverse hierarchies for fillers co-indexed with resumptive pronouns (§7). It can make predictions regarding symmetries and asymmetries (§8). It can motivate the very existence and nature of fundamental syntactic properties such as the 'head of phrase' generalization (Chapter 5 and Hawkins 1993, 1994).

And it can account for cross-linguistic hierarchies in morphology (§§4.1–2) and for numerous aspects of 'grammaticalization' in the evolution of morphosyntax (§§4.3–4).

If we assume an innate architecture underlying language processing, as we surely must, we also have to keep an open mind about the precise form that it takes, given the state of the art in psycholinguistics and the unresolved issues in this field. We must keep an open mind too on the precise causality of the efficiencies and preferences to be discussed here and on the manner in which they emerge from this architecture. In Hawkins (1994, 2001) I appealed to increasing working memory load in progressively larger domains for phrase structure processing as an explanation for linear ordering preferences and adjacency effects. Gibson (1998) builds on this same working memory idea to explain locality preferences in integration (and memory) domains when processing combinatorial relations and dependencies. His work has inspired me to generalize my own discussion of domain minimization beyond phrase structure processing and filler–gap dependencies. At the same time I shall suggest that these preference patterns of performance and grammars point to the need for a more general and more multi-faceted theory of efficiency, within which working memory load is just one causal factor. We will see evidence for preferred reductions in articulatory effort in production, and for principles of least effort that are fine-tuned to frequency effects, discourse accessibility, and knowledge-based inferencing. Some preferences point to on-line error avoidance and to 'look-back' rather than 'look-ahead' effects, which avoid delays in property assignments on-line. I will argue that some of these efficiencies actually increase working memory load, as currently defined, whereas others decrease it, and that once we have a broad set of (cross-linguistic) preference data we can tease apart the respective roles of working memory load and of other causes. Speed of communication and less processing effort can also emerge as preferences from models with very different working memory architectures and indeed without any working memory as such (e.g. MacDonald & Christiansen 2002).

It is important that we think about these deeper causalities and that we try to resolve general issues of processing architecture. But in the present context my goal is to show that there are profound correspondences between performance and grammars, and to do this I must formulate generalizations and predictions at a level that can apply to a broad range of facts and in a way that does not make premature commitments to just one causal type or architecture. That is why performance preferences and grammatical principles will be formulated here in terms that are compatible with numerous different psycholinguistic and grammatical models, and they are general enough to potentially contribute to issues within each. Three principles will be proposed: Minimize Domains, Minimize Forms, and Maximize On-line Processing. The first of these is an extension of the Early Immediate Constituents idea of Hawkins (1994). Increasing the basic principles like this is potentially more explanatory, but it can also introduce the kinds of problems that Newmeyer (1998: 137–53) discusses in his critique of all competing motivation theories.

1.5   The challenge of multiple preferences

The dangers to which Newmeyer draws our attention are these. First, theories with multiple motivations (or constraints or preferences) are often too 'open-ended', proposing principles when they are convenient and apparently required by the data, but in the absence of independent support. Second, no independent support is given for the relative strengths of principles, and hence there is no explanation for why one should be stronger than another when they compete. And third the interaction of principles often results in vacuous predictions: nothing is really ruled out by their collective application.

These points need to be heeded, as do his criteria (p. 127) for the very existence of a valid external functional motivation for grammars.[1] In the present work the constraints are not open-ended. I limit my basic functional motivations to just three: Minimize Domains, Minimize Forms, and Maximize On-line Processing.

Independent support for the relative strengths of these principles comes, in the first instance, from actual performance data taken from languages with choices, as explained in §1.2. These data sometimes reveal principles in conflict and sometimes they reveal principles reinforcing each other. The present theory, in contrast to many others, makes predictions for relative quantities and gradedness effects that should emerge from this interaction of principles. It also predicts the degree to which a preference defined by a single principle should exert itself in a sentence of a given type, as a function of the degree of e.g. domain minimization distinguishing competing versions of this sentence (alternative orderings, more versus less explicit counterparts, and so on). It does not just observe a frequency effect, it tries to derive it. One principle may be stronger than another in a given construction and language type (e.g. Minimize Domains over Maximize On-line Processing), or one processing relation (phrase structure recognition) may be stronger than another

---

[1] Newmeyer (1998: 127) proposes three criteria for a convincing external explanation for linguistic structure: 'First, it must lend itself to precise formulation. . . . Second, we have to be able to identify a *linkage* between cause and effect. . . . And third, any proposed external motivation must have measurable typological consequences.'

(verb–complement processing) in a given construction, because the degree of preference for the one exceeds that of the other according to the quantitative metrics proposed. The extent of the overall preference will then be reflected in quantities of selections in performance, and derivatively in grammars. On other occasions different principles and different processing relations will define the same preferences and there will be no or very limited variation.

These collective predictions will be shown to be far from vacuous: structural competitors are predicted to occur in proportion to their degrees of preference, preference hierarchies are definable among structures of a common type, and when the preferences converge on a given structural type, there should be no variation.

Moreover, we don't actually have a choice, in the current state of the art, between single preference theories and multiple preference theories or between syntax-only theories and broader theories. There are multiple constraints that are clearly relevant in performance, as MacDonald et al. (1994) have shown in their work on syntactic ambiguity resolution. Structural misassignments and garden path effects depend not just on structural factors but on semantics and real-world knowledge, on discourse context effects and on frequencies as well. Linear ordering choices in free word order structures similarly reflect syntactic and semantic relations of different types (Chapters 5 and 6). These multiple constraints have left their imprint in grammars. So, whatever the dangers are here, we have simply got to deal with them, and the present book tries to do this in a way that minimizes the problems Newmeyer discusses by maximizing the generality of principles, supporting them with quantitative data from performance, and by trying to motivate and derive their interaction in a principled way.

2

Linguistic Forms, Properties, and Efficient Signaling

In §1.3 I proposed an efficiency–complexity hypothesis and I referred to three general principles that will give substance to it: Minimize Domains, Minimize Forms, and Maximize On-line Processing. In this chapter and the next I shall define these principles and associated sub-principles, discuss their respective motivations, and illustrate the kinds of preferences and dispreferences that they predict. The current chapter will introduce background assumptions, before giving more detailed definitions in Chapter 3. Chapter 4 will elaborate on and test one principle in particular (Minimize Forms) and Chapters 5–8 will test the individual and combined predictions of all three predictions on data from performance and grammars.

I need to proceed gradually in presenting this approach since this way of looking at grammars, which is heavily influenced by processing, is quite alien to linguists unfamiliar with psycholinguistics. It also takes some getting used to for many psycholinguists, whose primary interest is performance and whose training in linguistics has often been limited to generative grammar. It is my hope that the present book, which draws on formal grammar, language typology, historical linguistics, and language processing, will foster greater mutual awareness and will encourage specialists in each to take account of the work of others.

2.1 Forms and properties

Let us begin with some basics about language and grammar. I shall refer frequently to 'linguistic forms' and their associated 'properties'.

Forms will be understood here to include the phoneme units, morpheme units, and word units of each language, as defined in standard linguistics text-books (e.g. O'Grady et al. 2001). I shall also include word sequences or phrases under the 'forms' of a language, as described in phrase structure grammars and construction grammars (see Jackendoff 1977, Gazdar et al. 1985, Pollard & Sag 1994 for phrase structure, and Goldberg 1995 and Croft 2001 for constructions). With the exception of the phonemes, all these forms can be said to 'signal' certain semantic and/or syntactic properties. There are, to use the basic insight from the theory of linguistic signs (J. Lyons 1968: 404), certain conventionalized and arbitrary associations between forms and meanings, and between forms and syntactic properties such as syntactic category status. A given form in a language, F, will be said to signal a given property, P, just in case F has the conventionally associated syntactic or semantic property P.

What are some of the major types of properties that are signaled by linguistic forms? Let us start with meanings. Associated with each word in a language, such as *student* in English, is a certain lexical-semantic content of the kind defined in dictionaries. A derivational morpheme like *-er*, which converts *sing* to *singer*, also has lexical-semantic content and results in a composite meaning of the type 'one who does the activity in question', here singing. Some words, such as verbs, are also associated with semantic requirements of co-occurrence, called 'selectional restrictions' in Chomsky (1965). The verb *drink* takes an animate subject and a liquid object. Some word sequences or combinations have an associated meaning that goes beyond the meanings of their parts and that is not compositional. The sequence *count on* in English, as in *I counted on my father in my college years*, has a meaning that is quite different from 'counting' by itself and from 'location *on* something'. This combinatorial meaning (roughly that of 'I depended on X') has to be listed in a dictionary. This example reveals why word sequences must also be regarded as basic forms in a language, in addition to single words: there are properties that are uniquely associated with the sequence itself.

Some semantic properties are associated with sequences of whole phrases or constructions, not just with sequences of individual words. Consider English clauses consisting of a subject NP and a sister VP, i.e. [NP vp[V X]]. The subject NP receives very different 'theta-roles' (Chomsky 1981, Dowty 1991), depending on the contents of the VP. If the verb is intransitive the subject theta-role can be 'agent' or 'patient'. Contrast *The boy ran* (agent) with *The boy fell* (patient). There is a sensitivity to the verb here.[1] Transitive VPs can be associated with a wide variety of theta-role assignments to the subject and to the object. Compare *the boy hit the dog*, *the runner hurt his leg*, *the key opened the door*, and *this tent sleeps four* (Fillmore 1968, Rohdenburg 1974, Hawkins

---

[1] Notice that it isn't just the verb that determines the appropriate theta-role in intransitive clauses. Sometimes the whole VP does. Compare *the man fell upon his enemies* (agent) with *the man fell upon hard times* (patient), in which the verb–preposition sequence is identical and it is the sister NP of the preposition, *his enemies* v. *hard times*, that ultimately determines the subject's theta-role.

1986). The subject *the boy* is an agent, *the runner* is an experiencer, *the key* is an instrument, and *this tent* is a locative. More complex structures of the 'control' and 'subject-to-object raising' types (Rosenbaum 1967, Postal 1974), which are identical or similar in surface structure, e.g. *I persuaded John to be nice* v. *I believed John to be nice*, are also associated with different theta-role assignments. *John* is assigned a theta-role by *persuaded* but not by *believed*.

Different verb positions in a clause can signal different constructional meanings. Finite verb inversion in English and verb-first in German are associated with various non-declarative meanings, such as questioning or commanding (Hawkins 1986). The immediately pre-verbal position of many verb-final languages is associated with a 'focus' interpretation (Kim 1988, Kiss 2002). A topic-marked NP in Japanese (Kuno 1973*b*) or an initially positioned NP in Kannada (Bhat 1991) carries a topic + predication interpretation that includes definiteness or genericness of the topic, 'aboutness' (Reinhart 1982) for the predication, and numerous subtle semantic relations between topic and predication of the kind exemplified for Mandarin Chinese in Tsao (1979). Different linear orderings of quantifiers and operators can also be associated with different logical scopes, with the leftmost quantifier/operator generally receiving the wide scope interpretation (Allwood et al. 1977). All these grammatical meanings are associated with, and signaled by, their respective syntactic structures.

Words and derivational morphemes signal syntactic properties as well as semantic ones. *Student* is a noun in English and this fact is listed in dictionaries along with its meaning. The derivational morpheme *-er* converts the verb *sing* into the noun *singer*, while inflectional morphemes like the plural *-s* in *singers* preserve the syntactic category status of the stems to which they attach. Mirroring the semantic co-occurrences of words like *drink* are syntactic requirements of co-occurrence, labeled 'strict subcategorization' restrictions in Chomsky (1965). A verb like *hit* is transitive and requires a direct object NP, the verb *run* has both transitive and intransitive uses (*John ran/John ran the race*), and two syntactic co-occurrence frames are given in its lexical entry. The noun *reliance* takes a   lexically listed complement PP with the preposition *on* in English (*reliance on this information*), not *of* or *from*. And so on.

In addition to these lexically specific syntactic co-occurrences of *hit*, *run*, and *reliance*, there are general syntactic properties associated with categories and phrases that do not need to be listed in the lexicon. Any noun, like *student* and *singer*, will 'project to' or 'construct' a dominating noun phrase mother node, by virtue of the fact that nouns are head categories (Jackendoff 1977, Corbett et al. 1993, Pollard & Sag 1994). The word *student* therefore signals 'noun' based on its lexical entry, and this in turn signals 'noun phrase mother' by general syntactic principles holding for all nouns, which are in turn subsumed under general principles for all head categories. The word combination *smart student*, consisting of the adjective *smart* in a left-adjacent position to the noun *student* signals, by general syntactic principles of English, that *smart* is a syntactic sister of *student* within the mother noun phrase constructed by the latter, i.e. np[adj[smart] n[student]]. More precisely, this relative positioning coupled with the syntactic category status of *smart* as an adjective signals that the sisterhood relation is of a particular type, an adjunct rather than a specifier or complement (Jackendoff 1977, Corbett et al. 1993, Pollard & Sag 1994). Depending on one's syntactic theory this may have consequences for the attachment site of *smart* in the phrase-internal branching structure of the NP. In Jackendoff's theory specifiers are highest, adjuncts lower, and complements lowest in the internal branching structure of each 'maximal projection' for a phrase. These syntactic differences are then associated with corresponding semantic differences between specifiers, adjuncts, and complements. For more classical theories of syntax with flatter phrase structures, based on Chomsky (1965), there would be semantic differences only.

2.2   Property assignments in combinatorial and dependency relations

It should be clear from these examples that some syntactic and semantic properties are associated with, and signaled by, individual words or morphemes, while others result from combinations of words and of phrases. Our concept of the 'forms' of a language must therefore be broad enough to include combinations of smaller forms that signal properties over and above those that could be assigned to their parts in isolation. We therefore need a working definition of 'combination', and for present purposes I propose (2.1):

(2.1) *Combination*
       Two categories A and B are in a relation of combination iff they occur within the same mother phrase and maximal projections (phrasal combination), or if they occur within the same lexical co-occurrence frame (lexical combination).

Smart is in phrasal combination with *student*, by this definition, since both are in the same mother phrase (NP), *opened* combines with *the door* in the same VP, and the subject *the key* combines with this VP within S. These phrasal combinations are defined by general phrase structure rules. Subject and object arguments of a verb are in lexical combination with that verb and with one another, and more generally the so-called 'complements' of a verb are listed alongside that verb in its lexical entry. Complements are subject to the selectional restrictions and strict subcategorization requirements illustrated above and they may receive theta-roles from their verbs.

Some words or morphemes across languages actually signal the existence of a phrasal combination within a common mother phrase. Agreement morphemes on noun modifiers, as in Latin (Vincent 1987), or case copying in Australian languages (Blake 1987, Plank 1995), signal what is plausibly co-constituency even when modifier and head noun are discontinuous. The particle *de* in Mandarin Chinese and *ve* in Lahu signal attachment of a left-adjacent modifier to a right-adjacent head noun within the NP (Hawkins 1994: 389, C. Lehmann 1984). The linkers or 'ligatures' of Austronesian function similarly (Foley 1980). In the absence of such morphemes and words the combination in question can be signaled by tight adjacency and linear ordering, as in *smart student* and *opened the door* in English.

Similarly, case assignment by verbs can be viewed as the surface expression of a lexical relation of combination between a verb and its arguments. The verb *sehen* ('see') in German assigns nominative case to its (VP-external) agent NP and accusative to the (VP-internal) patient, *helfen* ('help') assigns nominative to the agent and dative to the recipient. The selection of a case template for a given verb can vary both diachronically and across languages (see Primus 1999, Blake 2001), and it is for this reason that the co-occurrences of a verb have to be listed lexically and are not always predictable by general rules. Verb agreement can also signal lexical co-occurrence structure (Primus 1999). In the absence of case marking and verb agreement, tight adjacency and linear ordering can distinguish the NP arguments of a given verb from one another, as in English *The man gave the boy the book.*

The various properties that are assigned in these combinations (sister of P, adjunct of N, object complement of V, etc.) will be called 'combinatorial properties'. Much of syntactic theory is devoted to a specification and description of their precise nature. Despite many differences between models, e.g. over the amount of phrase-internal branching or over the respective roles of general syntactic rules versus lexical regularities, there is a large element of agreement, and much insight has been gained since Chomsky (1957).[2]

There is a second general relation that is often invoked in syntax on which there is much less agreement, however, and this is the relation of dependency (see Tesnière 1959, Hays 1964 for early proposals). The intuition to be captured

---

[2] See Brown & Miller (1996) for a concise comparison of many different grammatical models and approaches.

here is that one category depends on another for the assignment of a particular property. Dependencies include cases where the categories are already in a relation of combination with one another, as this term is defined here. They also include more distant dependencies between categories that are neither sisters nor in a lexical co-occurrence relation with one another.

It is not my intention to review the large research literature on dependency since Tesnière and Hays, because I believe there is an important processing aspect to it that has been neglected and that one cannot actually give a consistent and cross-linguistically valid definition in purely grammatical terms. When we add processing to grammar, on the other hand, dependencies become more empirically verifiable, the original intuition is easier to define, and we also make some new predictions for cross-linguistic variation which we can test.

In the definition to be given here I shall take the perspective, initially at least, of a parser receiving terminal elements one by one in a parse string.[3] When the parser receives the first two words of a sentence, e.g. *the boy* in English, it can recognize the categories determiner + noun, it can attach them to a mother noun phrase, it can assign lexical-semantic content to *boy* and a uniqueness semantics to the definite determiner (Hawkins 1978, 1991), but it cannot yet assign a theta-role. If the third and final word of the sentence is *ran*, then the theta-role agent can be assigned to *the boy* (in addition to nominative case). If the third and final word is *fell*, a patient theta-role is assigned. I shall say that the subject NP 'depends on' the following intransitive VP for this theta-role assignment. Similarly *the key* depends on the following transitive VP *opened the door* for assignment of the instrument role, and *this tent* depends on *sleeps four* for its locative. In these examples the NPs are 'zero-specified' with respect to theta-roles, and also with respect to case (in contrast to the case-marked pronouns *he* v. *him*), and these properties are assigned by a dependency relation in the absence of explicit signaling in the noun phrase itself.

Conversely, the verbs and VPs in these examples can be said to depend on the choice of NP for selection of their appropriate lexical co-occurrence frame and for selection of their appropriate meaning from the often large set of dictionary entries with respect to which a verb is ambiguous or polysemous. *Run* is syntactically ambiguous in English between intransitive and transitive uses (*the boy ran/the boy ran the race*), and it is semantically ambiguous or polysemous between a whole range of interpretations depending on the choice

---

3 Later in this section I shall suggest that considerations of production are closely aligned with those of comprehension and parsing with respect to the processing of dependencies. Their parsing is clearer, however, and I shall focus on that in this presentation.

of subject (*the water ran/the stocking ran/the advertisement ran*) or object (*the boy ran the race/ran the water/ran the advertisement*) (cf. Keenan 1979). I shall say that *run* depends on the relevant NPs for selection of its syntactic co-occurrence frame and meaning from the total set listed in its lexical entry. The verb *open* likewise has several syntactic co-occurrence frames (*John opened the door with a key/the key opened the door/the door opened*) and several meanings as well, and it depends on its accompanying NPs and PPs for disambiguation and polysemy reduction. These reductions in meaning brought about by the arguments of transitive and intransitive verbs are systematic and extensive, and a parser must constantly access its arguments when assigning the appropriate meaning to a verb.

Co-indexation is another type of dependency. A co-indexation relation between a pronoun or anaphor and its antecedent requires that the parser copy the antecedent's index onto the pronoun/anaphor. The pronoun/anaphor depends on the antecedent for assignment of its index, therefore, and the parser must have access to the antecedent in order to fully process the pronoun/anaphor. Similarly, a gap or subcategorizor co-indexed with a given filler involves a dependency on the filler, and the parser needs to access this latter when copying the index.

In all these examples the parser has to access one category when making a property assignment to another. Much variation between structures and across languages can now be viewed in terms of the greater or lesser exploitation of such dependency relations as a way of assigning properties to categories. In *the boy ran* there is a nominative case dependency on the finite verb (and an accusative case dependency in the topicalized *the boy I saw*), but there is no nominative case dependency in *he ran*, since *he* is intrinsically nominative and the parser does not need to access the finite verb in order to assign it (even though this is a combinatorial property listed in the lexical co-occurrence frame for *run*). Explicitly case-marked NPs in verb-final languages such as Japanese and Kannada do not involve a dependency on the following verb for case assignment and theta-role assignment, by this logic, since the parser can assign these properties prior to the verb in whose lexical co-occurrence frame they are actually listed. The verb, on the other hand, will be dependent on preceding case-marked NPs for selection of its appropriate syntactic co-occurrence frame and for semantic disambiguation and polysemy reduction. These examples reveal how a processing approach to dependency can result in partially different dependency relations from those defined by a purely grammatical approach. Case assignment to an NP is independent of a verb if it can be assigned without accessing that verb, and whether this can be done will reflect the richness and uniqueness of its morphological marking.

Languages with flexible syntactic categories and with regular ambiguities even between noun and verb, such as the Polynesian language Tongan (Broschart 1997), make use of nominal and verbal particles and of other contextual clues for category disambiguation, and I shall say that the ambiguous predicates are dependent on such particles for category assignment. A huge number of predicates in English are actually category-ambiguous and dependent on (often immediately) preceding closed-class words or other contextual indicators for category assignment (*a run* v. *to run*; *a play* v. *to play*; etc.). Other languages have nouns and verbs that are inherently distinct from one another, morphosyntactically or lexically, and their category status can be assigned without any such dependency (Schachter 1985, Hengeveld 1992, Anward et al. 1997).

More generally, languages with rich inflections (Latin) or agglutinative morphology (Turkish) will permit more processing and property assignments within words and phrases themselves, whereas isolating languages with impoverished morphologies (Chinese, Vietnamese, and to a considerable extent English) will involve more dependency assignments and will exploit neighboring and co-occurring words to a greater extent. This will have important consequences for adjacency (Chapters 5–6) and for linear precedence (Chapter 8). Tighter adjacency relations will be predicted for isolating languages as a result. Languages with widespread category ambiguity can be further predicted to prefer disambiguating particles in a position prior to, rather than after, their category-ambiguous predicates, since category assignments can then be made immediately on-line without having to wait for, and leave unassigned, this important syntactic decision (§4.4.2). This approach will also make predictions for the typological distribution of rich case marking and rich verb agreement across languages (§8.5).

I shall define dependency as follows:

(2.2) *Dependency*

Two categories A and B are in a relation of dependency iff the parsing of B requires access to A for the assignment of syntactic or semantic properties to B with respect to which B is zero-specified or ambiguously or polysemously specified.

If we compare this definition for dependency with the definition of combination in (2.1), it will be clear that many relations between a given A and B can be both, and I shall refer to these as 'combinatorial dependencies'. Theta-role assignment to *the door* in *opened the door* is an example. But a filler–gap dependency like *where_i did you ask the question O_i?*, in which the co-indexed categories are not in a relation of phrasal combination and do not co-occur within the same lexical co-occurrence frame (*where* being an adjunct to *ask the question*), is a dependency but not a combinatorial one. In general, when I talk about the 'dependency' of B on A I will mean that B depends on A in the sense of (2.2) and that it may or may not combine with it. And when I talk about A 'combining' with B as in (2.1) I will mean that there may or may not be simultaneous dependencies.

The properties that are assigned by dependency relations will be called 'dependency assignments', defined in (2.3):

(2.3) *Dependency assignment*
   If the parsing of a word or phrase B requires access to another A for the assignment of property P to B, B being zero-specified or ambiguously or polysemously specified with respect to P, then P is a *dependency assignment* and B is dependent on A with respect to P.

Co-indexation (P) is a dependency assignment to a pronoun or anaphor (B) from its antecedent (A). So is theta-role assignment (P) to a subject NP (B) from an intransitive verb or transitive VP (A). The appropriate lexical-semantic content (P) is a dependency assignment to transitive *run* (B) when the parser accesses *the water* (A) as opposed to *the race* (A). And the selection of the syntactic category noun (P) in Tongan is a dependency assignment to an ambiguous or polysemous predicate (B) when the parser accesses an NP-constructing particle or function category (A).

Dependency assignments are made within 'domains' of terminal elements in surface structure together with their associated syntactic and semantic properties. I shall understand a domain to be the smallest connected sequence of forms and properties that is sufficient for the processing of the dependency relation in question. The same notion of domain will also be invoked for combinatorial relations.

(2.4) A *combinatorial or dependency domain* consists of the smallest connected sequence of terminal elements and their associated syntactic and semantic properties that must be processed for the production and/or recognition of the combinatorial or dependency relation in question.

The domains in which immediate constituent (IC) relations of combination can be processed are called 'constituent recognition domains' in Hawkins (1994). The domain sufficient for processing the VP and its three immediate constituents (V, PP1, PP2) in the following sentence is shown in bold: *the old lady **counted on him** in her retirement*. The domain sufficient for processing the lexical meaning of the verb is ***counted on him***, and (in an appropriate context) possibly just ***counted on***. The dependency domain for co-indexation in the following sentence involves only the set of connected words shown in bold and their associated properties, since the other words are not relevant for index copying and do not need to be accessed: *in his youth **the boy**i **chastised himself**i quite often.* The domain for theta-role assignment to the subject NP is shown similarly: *yesterday **the key opened the door** with ease.* And so on.[4]

This parsing approach to dependency captures the original intuition in a way that is now easier to test. We can examine individual words or phrases and ask whether a given property can be assigned to them based on their explicit forms and corresponding lexical entries and grammar, independently of their syntactic or semantic context, or whether a particular property assignment does depend crucially on some other word or phrase that must be accessed within a given domain, as in the examples I have given. In §5.2.1 I will suggest that the verb–preposition sequence *count on* in English differs from *play on* since the verb *count* is dependent on the preposition *on* for its lexical-semantic selection, whereas *play* is not; and I shall propose some entailment tests that discriminate between dependent and independent verbs (*I counted on my son* does not entail *I counted*, whereas *I played on the tennis court* does include the meaning of, and entails, *I played*). Empirical predictions for syntactic positioning and adjacency will then be made on the basis of such dependency differences, which are in turn derived from independent tests for dependency like the entailment test just illustrated.

Contrary to Tesnière (1959), who insisted that dependencies between A and B are always asymmetric, dependency relations in this approach can be symmetrical or asymmetric, and this will have important consequences for the explanation of symmetries and asymmetries across languages (Chapter 8). Whether there is a dependency relationship or not can be impacted by surface morphosyntax, such as case marking and agreement, and more generally by the inherent richness of words and phrases in on-line processing and by the extent to which properties can be assigned to them independently of their syntactic and semantic context. When dependencies are symmetrical, we see symmetrical orderings, and when they are asymmetric, we see asymmetries (§8.4).

A brief word, before I turn to efficiency itself, about parsing and production. Notice that I formulate the definition of dependency in (2.2) and (2.3) in terms of parsing (i.e. comprehension). The language producer uttering *the boy fell* could potentially assign a patient theta-role to *the boy* prior to the production of *fell* by accessing the lexical entry for this latter in the Formulator (Levelt 1989). And quite generally there are numerous forms and properties

---

4 Again I am glossing over differences between production and comprehension, to which I return.

that the speaker could have some inner representation of, in the Conceptualizer and the Formulator, prior to their articulation. The hearer cannot assign the patient role to *the boy* prior to hearing the verb and VP that determine their assignment, however. Dependencies are easier to define and discuss from the hearer's perspective, and yet production data also provide clear evidence for them, for example in the adjacency data of §§5.1–2. The speaker can assign the appropriate meaning to *count* on-line, without waiting for the preposition *on*, yet production data indicate a clear preference for *on* to occur immediately after *count* in sequences like this. This might be taken to suggest that speakers are being altruistic and packaging their sentences so as to speed up on-line processing for hearers, even when there is no obvious speaker benefit. Alternatively production and comprehension may employ a common mechanism from which both can benefit from the adjacency of *count* and *on*. Speaker altruism is not a generally attractive basis for a production model (cf. Kirby 1999 for discussion), and the common mechanism idea is currently being developed in work by Gerard Kempen.[5] I make no attempt to try to solve this problem here, but I will provide data that may contribute to its solution.

2.3   Efficiency and complexity in form–property signaling

Efficiency is a more difficult concept to define than complexity. Let us assume, following the discussion in §1.3 and incorporating the basic notions introduced in the present chapter, that complexity is a function of the number of formal units and conventionally associated properties that need to be processed in domains relevant for their processing. Efficiency may therefore involve more or less complexity, depending on the proposition to be expressed and the minimum number of properties that must be signaled in order to express it. Crucially, efficiency is an inherently relative notion that compares alternative form–property pairings for expressing the same proposition, and the (most) efficient one is the one that has the lowest overall complexity in on-line processing. Fewer forms and properties and smaller domains need to be processed, while still communicating the same proposition. The (most) efficient structure will also be argued to be the one that provides the earliest possible access to properties in the ultimate proposition to be communicated.

   We can summarize these ideas with the slogans 'Express the most with the least' and 'Express it earliest'. Our principles Minimize Domains and Minimize Forms follow from the former, while Maximize On-line Processing follows from the latter. Often these efficiency considerations will overlap. When there

---

[5] See e.g. Kempen (2003).

is less to be processed, the relevant properties can be assigned earlier. But sometimes they pull in different directions, as we shall see.

As an illustration of the Minimize Domains principle, compare the basic vp[V NP PP] structure of *Mary gave the book she had been searching for since last Christmas to Bill*, containing a 'heavy' NP, with its shifted vp[V PP NP] counterpart, *Mary gave to Bill the book she had been searching for since last Christmas*. The combinatorial domain (cf. (2.4)) that needs to be parsed in order to recognize these three ICs of the VP is much larger in the former example than it is in the latter. Compare the italicized portions of (2.5a) and (2.5b):

(2.5) a. Mary vp[*gave* np[*the book she had been searching for since last Christmas*] pp[*to* Bill]]

b. Mary vp[*gave* pp[*to Bill*] np[*the* book she had been searching for since last Christmas]]

A full twelve words (and their associated properties) must be parsed in (2.5a) in order to recognize the three sisters of the VP phrase, whereas only four words need be parsed in (2.5b), assuming that the preposition constructs the PP and the definite article the NP (see Hawkins 1994 and §4.4.2). (2.5b) is more efficient, therefore, since it permits recognition of the same phrase structure information as (2.5a) on the basis of much less form–property processing (eight fewer words and their properties). This intuition about relative efficiency can be supported by showing that the performance preference for (2.5b) over (2.5a) increases in direct proportion to the difference between domain sizes in alternative pairs. When the difference is only four words rather than eight (as in *Mary gave to Bill the book she was searching for*) the preference for the shifted structure is less. The greater the efficiency of one structure over another by this criterion, the more frequently it should, and does, occur in corpora (§5.1.1) and the more it is preferred in production experiments (Stallings 1998).

Similarly, the domain for parsing the lexical combination and dependency between *count* + *on* is more efficient if these two words are adjacent to one another (*count on my father in my college years*) rather than separated (*count in my college years on my father*), since the combinatorial dependency can then be parsed on the basis of just two words. Again the degree of preference for their adjacency in performance should be, and is, directly proportional to the degree of difference between competing domains (which ultimately reflects the size of any constituent intervening between *count* and *on*) (cf. §5.2.1).

The clear intuition that emerges from these examples is that when some property is assigned within a combinatorial or dependency domain, the size of that domain should be as small as possible. In other words, parse the fewest possible forms and their associated properties in order to assign the property in question. This is the essence of Minimize Domains. This principle will also assert that this is a quantitative preference. When there is a large difference between competitors, the more efficient one is selected more frequently, often exceptionlessly. When the difference is smaller, it is selected less often. Domain minimization will also reflect the number of syntactic and semantic properties whose processing domains can be minimized in a given order: the more processing operations (as in the example of *count* plus a PP headed by *on*), the more adjacency. Some dependencies will necessarily apply to non-adjacent elements for expressive reasons, such as the co-indexing dependencies of many anaphors and gaps. The application of Minimize Domains will then result in 'proximity' effects, rather than strict adjacency.

Minimize Domains is a simple principle of least effort, therefore. If a particular property can be derived from a smaller rather than a larger domain, then less effort will be expended in its processing, and processing can be faster. One way of capturing this insight is to appeal to psycholinguistic models of working memory, such as Just & Carpenter (1992) or Gibson (1998). Simultaneous processing and working-memory loads are reduced when domains are small. Fewer forms and properties need to be held active in memory while the relevant combinatorial and dependency relation is being processed. On the other hand, processing at all levels, from sound recognition through word recognition and structural processing, is extremely fast, and this is something that both modular (J. A. Fodor 1983) and non-modular theorists (Marslen-Wilson & Tyler 1980, 1987) are agreed on. The ultimate explanation for the efficiency differences to be discussed here, and for the theory of efficiency itself, will depend on a resolution of general issues in psycholinguistics, such as the nature of working memory and other properties of the human processing architecture. Minimize Domain effects may ultimately follow from fewer working memory demands and from less simultaneous processing, though other possible explanations can be offered as well and there are also preferences to be documented here that *increase* working memory load, as currently defined (see §8.2.2).

The principle of Minimize Forms follows from the same logic as Minimize Domains. If formal units and their associated properties are preferably reduced in the domains that must be accessed for combinatorial and dependency relations, then why not reduce the individual linguistic forms themselves, i.e. the phonemes, morphemes and words? And why not reduce their associated linguistic properties to the minimum point at which communicative goals can be met? I shall argue that there is evidence for exactly this preference.

The reduction in phonemes and morphemes is what underlies George Zipf's (1949) brilliant observations about the correlations between brevity of form and frequency of use in English. The more common a word is, the shorter it is in general, and hence the more reduced its phonological and morphological structure. The same correlation was proposed by Greenberg (1966) in relation to markedness hierarchies such as Singular > Plural > Dual (§4.1). Grammatical morphemes for singularity are often zero whereas plurality has an explicit form (as in English), and dual is often more complex than plural. At the same time, the frequency of singularity is greater than plurality and that of plurality is greater than dual. Rosch's (1978) 'basic level categories' are also relevant here. These are categories such as *dog* that carry the most information, have high cue validity, and high frequency of occurrence compared with other (subordinate and superordinate) categories. They are also signaled by more reduced linguistic forms (e.g. *dog* v. *golden retriever*).

There is a second aspect to Minimize Forms that applies to properties rather than to the forms themselves. The intuition that needs to be captured is that it is preferable to reduce the number of distinct form–property pairs in a language as much as possible, as long as the intended contextually appropriate meaning can be recovered from reduced linguistic forms with more general meanings. A minimal 'intension' (J. Lyons 1977: 158–9), i.e. semantic and syntactic generality compatible with a large set of 'extensional' possibilities, can often be reduced to very particular semantic and syntactic properties in performance by exploiting discourse, real-world knowledge, and accessible linguistic structure (see §§3.2.2–3 for detailed discussion).

Our first efficiency slogan above was 'Express the most with the least', i.e. minimize domains and minimize forms. The second was 'Express it earliest'. This is a more radical proposal, in the context of grammars at least, which will be captured by the principle of Maximize On-line Processing.

The central idea is this. It is inefficient to delay the assignment of properties in the on-line parse string. Speech is a linear sequence of forms and properties, each of which contributes to the ultimate syntactic and semantic representation for a sentence. The distribution of 'on-line properties' to 'ultimate properties' should favor earlier rather than later property assignments, whenever possible. When domains are minimal, property assignments will also be early. But often non-minimal domains seem to be good for early property assignments, in the event that earliness and minimization compete.

Consider just an abstract illustration of the earliness idea at this point. Let us say that there are five words in a parse string, and twenty properties to be assigned to the ultimate syntactic and semantic representation of the sentence in the string. If properties are evenly distributed, there would be a cumulative addition to the ultimate property total of $4 + 4 + 4 + 4 + 4$. If the distribution were skewed towards late property assignments, e.g. $2 + 2 + 3 + 3 + 10$, then the parser would experience a substantial delay in building these ultimate representations and hence in comprehension. But if the distribution is skewed towards earliness, e.g. $8 + 5 + 3 + 2 + 2$, then the parser can build its ultimate representations sooner. I will say that early property assignments within a common domain are more efficient than later ones and we will see clear structural preferences and dispreferences that reflect this on-line distribution of properties to forms (§3.3.3, §7.5, and §8).

3

Defining the Efficiency Principles and their Predictions

In the last chapter I introduced the basic logic of the efficiency principles to be proposed, Minimize Domains, Minimize Forms, and Maximize On-line Processing, and gave some informal examples of their application. These principles and their predictions must now be defined. Various subsidiary principles will also be introduced in this chapter.

3.1 Minimize Domains (MiD)

This principle is defined in (3.1):

(3.1) *Minimize Domains* (MiD)
> The human processor prefers to minimize the connected sequences of linguistic forms and their conventionally associated syntactic and semantic properties in which relations of combination and/or dependency are processed. The degree of this preference is proportional to the number of relations whose domains can be minimized in competing sequences or structures, and to the extent of the minimization difference in each domain.

The definitions for 'combination' and 'dependency' were given in the last chapter in (2.1) and (2.2) and are repeated here for convenience:

(2.1) *Combination*
> Two categories A and B are in a relation of combination iff they occur within the same mother phrase and maximal projections (phrasal combination), or if they occur within the same lexical co-occurrence frame (lexical combination).

(2.2) *Dependency*
> Two categories A and B are in a relation of dependency iff the parsing of B requires access to A for the assignment of syntactic or

semantic properties to B with respect to which B is zero-specified or ambiguously or polysemously specified.

The definition of a 'domain' for processing combinatorial and dependency relations was given in (2.4) and is also repeated:

(2.4) A *combinatorial or dependency domain* consists of the smallest connected sequence of terminal elements and their associated syntactic
and semantic properties that must be processed for the production
and/or recognition of the combinatorial or dependency relation in
question.

MiD defines a preference for the most minimal surface structure domains sufficient for the processing of each combinatorial and dependency relation. Some illustrations were given in §2.2–3.

MiD subsumes my earlier principle of Early Immediate Constituents (EIC) (Hawkins 1994), which defined a preference for minimal Constituent Recognition Domains (CRDs). These were surface domains sufficient for the recognition of phrase-internal sisterhood combinations, as exemplified by the Heavy NP Shift alternation of (2.5) in §2.3. A CRD is defined in (3.2) and EIC in (3.3):

(3.2) *Constituent Recognition Domain* (CRD)
The CRD for a phrasal mother node M consists of the smallest set
of terminal and non-terminal nodes that must be parsed in order to
recognize M and all I(mmediate) C(onstituent)s of M.

(3.3) *Early Immediate Constituents* (EIC)
The human parser prefers linear orders that minimize CRDs (by
maximizing their IC-to-nonIC [or IC-to-word] ratios), in proportion
to the minimization difference between competing orders.

IC-to-nonIC and IC-to-word ratios measure the number of categories, phrases and/or words that need to be parsed in order to recognize the imme-diate constituents of a phrase.[1] For example, in the sequence *John vp[went ppi[to London] pp2[in the late afternoon]]* there are three ICs in the VP

---

[1] IC-to-word ratios are simplified procedures for quantifying what is technically an IC-to-nonIC ratio, which measures the ratio of ICs to all other terminal and non-terminal nodes in the domain. The goal is to capture how much other material needs to be processed in order to recognize phrasal groupings and IC structure, and hence how much other material needs to be processed simultaneously with IC recognition. For explicit comparison of the two metrics, see Hawkins (1994: 69–83); for empirical testing of word-based and various (structural) node-based complexity metrics, see Wasow (1997, 2002). Wasow found no statistically significant differences between the predictions of the different metrics.

(V, PP1, and PP2), and four words in the CRD that suffice for their recognition (shown in bold), given the parsing principles of Hawkins (1994). This makes an IC-to-word ratio of $3/4 = 75\%$. The IC-to-non-IC ratio divides the number of ICs by the total number of non-terminal and terminal nodes in the CRD, other than the ICs themselves. The higher these ratios, the more minimal is the CRD, since the phrasal groupings of words (i.e. the IC structure of a given mother node M) can be recognized on the basis of less material in the parse string. When CRDs are longer, as in *John vp[went pp2[in the late afternoon] pp1[to London]]*, the ratios are lower. The CRD now contains more words (six) that are required for recognition of the same three ICs, and the IC-to-word ratio is $3/6 = 50\%$, which is lower than the 75% for the reverse ordering of PPs. Relevant examples testing EIC's predictions for performance and for the conventionalized orderings of grammars will be given in Chapter 5.

MiD is a much more general principle than EIC. It predicts that *all* syntactic and semantic relations between categories will prefer minimal domains for processing, and it defines a degree of preference that is the collective product of several possible relations between categories. The more syntactic and semantic relations linking two categories, and the more minimal their domains can be in the processing of each, the more adjacent or proximate these categories should be. For example, when two sisters contract an additional relation over and above sisterhood, such as a head–complement relation, I expect the processing domain for this relation to be preferably minimal. If there is a lexical-semantic dependency between e.g. *count* and the PP headed by *on* in *count [on my son] [in my later years]*, the domain in which this can be processed should be minimal, and we should see this preference reflected in the ordering of the two PPs. In this example we will need to consider both the phrasal combinatorial domain for recognizing sisters ([V PP PP]) and the lexical domain (of combination and dependency) that preferably positions *on my son* next to *count.* When both favor the same ordering in their respective domains, namely when a short PP precedes a longer one and is in a lexical relationship with the verb, the ordering should be clear and consistent. When the preferences pull in different directions, i.e. when the longer PP is in the relationship of lexical combination and dependency, we expect performance variation, with each preference asserting itself in proportion to its degree (see prediction (1.2c) of the Performance–Grammar Correspondence Hypothesis in §1.2). We will see in §5.2.1 that this prediction is confirmed.

The principle of MiD offers a potential explanation for adjacency in syntax. Adjacency has always been a fundamental relation between categories. Rules of phrase structure define the co-occurrence of some and the non-co-occurrence of others. They also define relative degrees of adjacency between heads and their subcategorized complements, restrictive adjuncts and appositive adjuncts (Jackendoff 1977, Pollard & Sag 1987). But why are these patterns found rather than others?

MiD provides the following answer. Since each relation of combination or dependency prefers a minimal domain in which it can be processed, then the more relations there are between two categories, the more processing domains there will be that exert a preference for the minimal separation of categories, with adjacency being the ultimate minimization. If there are multiple processing relations favoring the adjacency of heads and complements, for example, more than between heads and adjuncts, as I shall argue there are, then we expect stronger adjacency effects in performance. By the PGCH (§1.1) we then predict that these same preferences should be visible in grammatical rules.

Data from performance and grammars will be presented in Chapter 5 that test the MiD prediction for individual syntactic and semantic relations, as well as the hypothesized cumulative effect for categories linked by multiple relations. One way to make the cumulative hypothesis precise is to focus on head categories in conjunction with a plurality of phrases, each of which is potentially adjacent to the head, and to define the following prediction:

(3.4) *Adjacency to Heads*
Given a phrase {H, {X, Y}}, H a head category and X and Y phrases that are potentially adjacent to H, then the more combinatorial and dependency relations whose processing domains can be minimized when X is adjacent to H, and the greater the minimization difference between adjacent X and adjacent Y in each domain, the more H and X will be adjacent.

Chapter 5 is devoted to this prediction. It also introduces (in §5.2.3) a new metric for calculating the cumulative efficiency of a given structural variant and it predicts when that variant will actually be selected over its competitors. This metric defines the 'total domain differential' between competing sequences or structures, as a function of the collective minimization difference across all processing domains. Some of its predictions are quite novel, and they appear to be supported. This metric also defines the relative strengths and weightings of different syntactic and semantic relations, not by stipulating them, but by examining their associated processing domains and by quantifying the minimization preferences of different relations across competing structures. It therefore takes us some way towards a solution for the relative strength problem raised by Newmeyer (1998) (see §1.5).

Chapter 6 examines the impact of minimal formal marking on domain minimization. Phrases that are minimally marked syntactically or morpho-syntactically will be compared with their more explicit counterparts. The minimal forms involve more dependencies on their heads in processing in order to assign the properties that are signaled explicitly by fuller and more independently processable forms. The more dependent phrases should exhibit tighter adjacency by this logic, for the same reason that semantically dependent categories prefer adjacency: there are more relations to be processed between them, each of which prefers a minimal domain.

Relevant data will include relative clause adjuncts with and without explicit relativizers (*the students (whom) he teaches*), complement clauses with and without explicit complementizers (*She realizes (that) he's a nice guy*), adject-ives with and without explicit agreement markers (e.g. Latin v. English), and NP-internal constituents with and without case copying (e.g. Kalkatungu v. Warlpiri). In all these data, from performance and grammars, the zero-marked phrases are more dependent on the head and they do indeed exhibit tighter adjacency to it. The total domain differential metric (cf. §5.2.3) makes some fine-tuned predictions that are tested in this chapter.

I will also consider 'control' structures in Chapter 6, such as *John promised to go to the doctor* and *I persuaded/promised John to go to the doctor*, in which the subordinate subcategorizer *go* must satisfy its subcategorization and semantic processing requirements by accessing an argument in the matrix clause, the syntactic domain for which has long been known to be a 'Minimal Distance' one in general (Rosenbaum 1967). The infinitival verb depends on the controller for its (subject) argument, whereas the co-occurrence requirements of corres-ponding finite verbs can be satisfied locally within the subordinate clause in non-control counterparts with co-indexed pronouns such as *I persuaded John*i *that he*i *should go to the doctor*. Raising structures will also be considered from this perspective.

Chapter 7 considers relative clause and *wh*-movement universals across grammars from the perspective of MiD (3.1). The larger the separation between a filler and its subcategorizer or gap, and the more properties that must be processed in the domain linking filler and gap, the less minimal will be the relevant processing domains. Such long-distance dependencies are motiv-ated by expressive considerations (speakers do want to say things like *the students*i *that you believe that Harry saw*i), but processing demands increase as domains increase, and we expect to see consequences of this. Corpus fre-quencies and processing ease under experimental conditions should decline as domains become longer and more internally complex in terms of syntactic structure and semantic content. And grammars should exhibit patterns of conventionalization that are sensitive to these increases, resulting in hierarchies in which some languages cut off at each lower position, as in the Keenan & Comrie (1977) Accessibility Hierarchy. Several increasing complexity hierarchies of this type will be presented, with correlating performance data involving frequencies and processing ease (cf. §7.3). These data will enable me to test the following prediction for 'filler–gap domains' (FGDs).[2]

(3.5) *Filler–Gap Complexity Hypothesis*
       If an FGD of complexity n on a complexity hierarchy H is grammatical, then FGDs for all less complex variables on H (n − 1) will also be grammatical; if an FGD of complexity n is ungrammatical, then FGDs for all more complex variables on H (n + 1) will also be ungrammatical.

Resumptive pronouns are a type of copy that can be used in lieu of a gap, and they diminish the subcategorizer's dependence on the head noun filler. In Hebrew relative clauses corresponding to *the students that I taught them*, the subcategorizer's co-occurrence requirements can be processed locally in the same way that they would be in a normal (main or subordinate) clause. Chapter 7 will accordingly test prediction (3.6), as well as other more specific predictions related to (3.5):

(3.6) *Resumptive Pronoun Hierarchy Prediction*
       If a resumptive pronoun is grammatical in position P on a complexity hierarchy H, then resumptive pronouns will be grammatical in all lower and more complex positions that can be relativized at all.

When discussing all of these structures we will need to make explicit the precise syntactic and semantic relations that are involved in each, and their respective domains of processing. In the case of relative clauses the reference of the head is semantically reduced by a restrictive relative clause, while the semantic interpretation of this latter as an adjunct is defined by reference to the head. The head noun is co-indexed with some category or position within the relative (the 'position relativized on'), either a subcategorizor (*the Danes*i *you taught*i), a relative pronoun (*the Danes*i *whom*i *you taught*), a resumptive pronoun (*the Danes*i *that you taught them*i), or a gap (*the Danes*i *you taught* Oi), depending on the precise structure (and on one's theory of co-indexing). The subcategorizor, in turn, must satisfy its lexical co-occurrence requirements by accessing various argument positions that are either internal to the relative

---

[2] A 'filler–gap' structure can be defined for present purposes as a nominal head or *wh*-word plus clausal sister in which there is a gap or subcategorizor co-indexed with the head/*wh*, but no overt co-indexed copy of it; see (7.8) in §7.1.

clause or external to it in the form of the nominal head. In the Hebrew relative clause with in situ resumptive pronouns these lexical co-occurrences are satisfied locally. A displaced *Wh*-relative pronoun in English is also within the relative clause. But in a zero-relative (*the students*i *I taught*i) the head itself must be accessed when processing the verb, and the verb's subcategorization domain therefore extends outside the relative clause. This additional dependency on the head should result in a smaller distance between head and subcategorizor compared with corresponding relative pronoun and resumptive pronoun structures.

These considerations reveal that the predictions of MiD (3.1) can be tested not only on competing orderings of the same categories relative to a head, as in (3.4), but on competing variants of one and the same category as well, such as relative clauses with different levels of explicitness, or finite v. infinitival complement phrases. When these competitors involve different domain minimizations we can test the following prediction:

(3.7) *Proximity Hypothesis*
       Given a structure {A, X, B}, X a variable for a phrase or phrases intervening between A and B, then the more relations of combination or dependency that link B to A, the smaller will be the size and complexity of X.

(3.7) predicts that relative clauses with zero relativizers and without resumptive pronouns will prefer closer proximity to the head. The verb or other subcategorizor in the zero relative corresponds to B in (3.7) and it is dependent on the nominal head (A) for the processing of its lexical co-occurrence requirements. In a relative clause with a resumptive pronoun or relative pronoun the subcategorizor does not depend on the head (A) for these co-occurrences, but on local pronouns within the relative clause. Hence the processing domains linking A and B are fewer when relative pronouns or resumptive pronouns are present. Separating a zero-marked relative from its head noun should accordingly be dispreferred, while separation of the explicitly marked counterpart should be much more productive (§6.1.1). Across languages we expect to find that the degree of formal marking for dependencies should increase (when grammars permit more v. less explicitly marked dependencies) in proportion to the surface distance between the interdependent categories (§6.2). And any structural and semantic complexity within the intervening phrases of X should increase the proportion of e.g. resumptive pronouns to gaps in relative clauses (§7.2 and §7.4).

3.2   Minimize Forms (MiF)

The principle of Minimize Forms was introduced in §2.3 and is defined in (3.8):

> (3.8)   *Minimize Forms* (MiF)
>
> The human processor prefers to minimize the formal complexity of each linguistic form F (its phoneme, morpheme, word, or phrasal units) and the number of forms with unique conventionalized property assignments, thereby assigning more properties to fewer forms. These minimizations apply in proportion to the ease with which a given property P can be assigned in processing to a given F.

The processing of linguistic forms and of their properties requires effort. This effort is minimized by reducing the set of units in a form that need to be articulated and processed, i.e. the phonemes, morphemes, words, or phrases in question. It is also minimized by reducing the number of conventionalized properties that are assigned to forms in the grammar or lexicon and that need to be activated in processing. Choices have to be made over which properties get priority for unique assignment to forms, and the remaining properties are then assigned to more general forms that are ambiguous, vague, or zero-specified with respect to the property in question. It is up to the 'context', broadly construed, to permit assignment of the intended P to a form F that is compatible with a larger set of properties {P}.

(3.8) is inspired by Haiman's (1983, 1985) principle of 'economy' and by the supporting data that he summarizes from numerous languages. It builds on discussions of ambiguity, vagueness, and zero specification in semantics and grammatical theory (e.g. J. Lyons 1977, Kempson 1977). It also incorporates Grice's (1975) second Quantity maxim for pragmatic inferencing ('Do not make your contribution more informative than is required') and more specifically Levinson's (2000: 114) Minimization principle derived from it ('"Say as little as necessary", that is, produce the minimal linguistic information sufficient to achieve your communicational ends').

3.2.1   *The logic of MiF*

There are four interconnected aspects to this principle that are captured in (3.8).

First the minimization preference applies to the set of formal units that comprise a given F. A long word, *television*, can be reduced to a shorter form, *TV*. Number marking can be expressed by an explicit morpheme (singular marking on nouns in Latvian) or by zero (English singulars). A phrasal type, like an NP, can be realized by a full form, *the doctor*, by a pronoun *he*, or (in appropriate

environments) by a zero pronominal. A VP can have full and reduced counterparts as well: *Mary will [pay the bill]/[do so]/[O]*. Letting small letters stand
for arbitrary formal units of a given form F signaling a property P (with Fo
standing for zero formal marking), MiF defines an increasing preference for
minimality in formal marking, ultimately for zero.

(3.9) REDUCE THE FORMAL UNITS IN {F}
        $Fo : P_1 > Fa : P_1 > Fab : P_1 > Fabc : P_1$

MiF applies, secondly, to the properties that are assigned to linguistic forms.
It is not efficient to have a distinct F for every possible P, e.g. a distinct color
word for every shade of red, a distinct syntactic or semantic category for every
real-world distinction that can be observed between physical entities, a distinct
transitive sentence pattern for all the myriad ways in which two entities can
interact in a two-argument clause, or a distinct number inflection for every
numerical value between one and a million. Choices need to be made, and
MiF asserts that it is preferable to minimize these choices, thereby minimizing
the number of unique form–property pairings in a language. Certain shades
of red are lexicalized (*crimson, scarlet,* etc.), most are not; a limited number
of distinct syntactic categories are grammaticalized, as is a limited set of two-
argument transitive sentence types, each argument of which is compatible with
several theta-roles from among Dowty's (1991) proto-agent and proto-patient
possibilities (the selection between them being dependent on the particular
verb); certain numerical values are assigned to unique inflections (singular,
dual, trial, etc.). And so on. We can summarize this as follows:

(3.10) MINIMIZE UNIQUE {$F_1 : P_1$} PAIRS

When form–property pairs are minimized, more properties must be
expressed by fewer forms, and many forms expand their compatibility with
a larger set of properties. Inflectional plurality has to cover all numbers for
which there is no uniquely distinctive dual or trial or paucal. In languages with
small inventories of basic color terms, the semantic coverage of the terms that
do exist has to be greater. This expansion in property assignments to forms is
accomplished in different ways. A form F that has a unique value (P_1) in one
language may be ambiguous in another (it signals P_1 or P_2 or P_3, etc). F may be
vague: for example inflectional plurality is vague with respect to all numbers
larger than one in English, and English *red* is vague with respect to all the
different shades of red. When there is vagueness F has a general and minimal
'intension' P: (J. Lyons 1977: 158–9) that is compatible with a large ('extensional') set of possibilities, {$P_1, P_2, P_3, \ldots, P_n$}. An extreme form of vagueness
is zero specification, P_0, as exemplified by theta-role assignments to full NPs in

English (*the boy ran/the boy fell*). Plurality is positively specified for a numerical value, albeit a very general one, and *red* has a certain color meaning that is compatible with numerous shades, but *the boy* is completely neutral to any kind of theta-role. We can summarize this aspect of the MiF preference in (3.11):

(3.11) ASSIGN MORE PROPERTIES {P} TO FEWER FORMS {F} THROUGH

$$F : P_1 \text{ v } P_2 \text{ v } P_3, \text{ etc (ambiguity)}$$
$$F : P_i\{P_1, P_2, P_3, \dots, P_n\} \text{ (vagueness)}$$
$$F : P_0 \text{ (zero specification)}$$

In the three cases shown the property alternatives compatible with a given F are expanded relative to $F_1 : P_1$, and the need for a unique form–property pairing is reduced. Vagueness is intermediate between ambiguity and zero specification, since compatible properties like P_1 are not conventionalized and may not be activated in processing if they are not contextually required. Ambiguities, such as the lexical ambiguity of *bank* or the grammatical ambiguity of *the shooting of the hunters*, are conventionalized form–property pairings that are listed in dictionaries and grammars. Experimental findings indicate that ambiguous property assignments are activated in processing and resolved in context (e.g. Swinney 1979, MacDonald et al. 1994). Vagueness involves activation of some general meaning, with possible contextual reduction (it may or may not matter which shade of red the speaker has in mind or which particular plural number is at issue). And zero specification involves full reliance on context for any additional meaning or syntactic property that is assigned to the zero-specified form.

(3.11) is a corollary of (3.10). Minimizations in unique form–property pairings are accomplished by expanding the compatibility of certain forms with a wider range of properties. Ambiguity, vagueness, and zero specification are efficient, inasmuch as they reduce the total number of forms that are needed in a language. The opposite asymmetry between forms and properties is synonymy, whereby two distinct forms convey one and the same property, e.g. $F_1 : P_1$ and $F_2 : P_1$. Synonymy is highly inefficient, since it increases the number of forms in a language, at no extra benefit in terms of property signaling, and it is for this reason that pure synonyms are quite rare. Synonymy avoidance is a much discussed principle in lexicography (J. Lyons 1977, 1995), and in language change and evolution (Hurford 2000). The ultimate explanation is, I believe, MiF (3.8). Synonyms do not minimize unique $F_1 : P_1$ pairs, they increase them, contra (3.10). They assign more forms to fewer properties, rather than more properties to fewer forms, contra (3.11). And the properties that they do convey are signaled by some other form–property pairing, which makes them one of the first targets for removal by MiF.

Ambiguity, vagueness and zero specification are, by contrast, efficient in a second respect as well. The multiple properties that are assignable to a given form can generally be reduced to a specific P in actual language use by exploiting 'context' in various ways. I will refer to such reductions in performance as 'enrichments', and this is the fourth aspect of MiF that needs to be commented on. More specific properties can, and often must, be so assigned, in effect reducing ambiguous P_1 v. P_2 v. P_3 to an unambiguous P_1, or a vague $\{P_1, P_2, P_3, \ldots, P_n\}$ or zero-specified P_0 to a specific P_1. Enrichments can also apply to unambiguous P_1 properties, such as an agent theta-role, resulting in a particular type of agentive interpretation from among a set of alternatives once the verb is processed (cf. Dowty 1991, Primus 1999). This is summarized in (3.12):

(3.12) ENRICH TO A SPECIFIC P IN PERFORMANCE

Since the knowledge sources and inferences that lead to enrichment are already accessible and active in language use, exploiting them by reducing the set of forms and properties in the linguistic code is efficient: see §3.2.3 below.

3.2.2 *Form minimization predictions*

Both formal units and unique property assignments can be minimized in the ways we have seen: see (3.9) – (3.11). One cannot minimize everything, however, and assign all properties through a performance enrichment of very general properties: see (3.12). This would reduce human languages to a few highly polysemous grunts beyond the capacity of the processor to provide the necessary enrichment. There has to be a balance and a trade-off between conventionalized form–property pairings on the one hand and on-line enrichment on the other. How is this balance achieved? The principle of MiF leads to the following predictions:

(3.13) *Form minimization predictions*

    a. The formal complexity of each F is reduced in proportion to the frequency of that F and/or the processing ease of assigning a given P to a reduced F (e.g. to zero).

    b. The number of unique $F_1 : P_1$ pairings in a language is reduced by grammaticalizing or lexicalizing a given $F_1 : P_1$ in proportion to the frequency and preferred expressiveness of that P_1 in performance.

(3.13) asserts that frequency and processing ease regulate reductions in form, while frequency and preferred expressiveness regulate grammaticalization and lexicalization preferences. The result in both cases will be fewer forms to convey the intended properties, in conjunction with enrichment.

Why should frequency be such an important predictor, and why should it result both in reductions in form and in preferred property assignments? Consider the former first (3.13a). By assigning reduced forms to high-frequency properties, and by reserving more complex forms for lower-frequency properties, the overall number of formal units that need to be articulated and processed, in a given sentence and in a lifetime of sentence usage, is smaller. By contrast, if reduced forms systematically conveyed low-frequency properties and more complex forms high-frequency properties, or if reduced forms were neutral to frequency with the result that some reduced forms expressed frequently used properties while others did not, then more processing of formal units would be required in performance overall. Frequency effects in form reduction therefore accomplish an overall minimization in articulation and processing.

I referred above to Zipf's (1949) correlation between word size and frequency in English: short words are more frequent than longer ones in general; and as lexical meanings gain in frequency of usage their formal expression will often become shorter (*TV* for *television*). In grammars, high-frequency closed-class grammatical categories are typically more minimal than their lower-frequency counterparts. Auxiliary verbs are often reduced and contracted in comparison with lexical verbs, each of which has a frequency that is significantly less than that of each auxiliary. Pronouns are generally shorter than full NPs containing lexical nouns, each of which will be less frequent than a grammaticalized pronoun. When definite and indefinite articles emerge historically from demonstratives and from the numeral 'one' respectively, the greater frequency of the articles is matched by a reduction in phonological and/or morphological structure (*the* v. *that*, *a(n)* v. *one* in English, etc.). High-frequency syntactic patterns are also more minimal than lower-frequency patterns. Intransitive clauses are much more frequent than transitive clauses and are less internally complex. Relative clauses on subject position are more frequent than relativizations on objects, and in languages like Hebrew the former is more minimal (the underlying subject is a gap) than the latter (which can contain either a gap or an explicit pronoun in the object position relativized on).

Turning to (3.13b), there are numerous semantic and syntactic properties that are frequently occurring in performance and that have priority for conventionalization across grammars. The property of causation is invoked often in everyday language use and is regularly conventionalized in the morphology, syntax, or lexical meanings of words across languages (Comrie 1989: 165–84, Shibatani 1976). Agenthood and patienthood are frequently expressed and are given systematic (albeit partially different) formal expression in ergative–absolutive, nominative–accusative, and active languages (Dixon 1994, Primus 1999). Reference to nominal entities is highly frequent and the category NP appears to be universal, though not perhaps the noun–verb distinction itself (Schachter 1985, Sasse 1993, Broschart 1997). The very frequent speech acts (asserting, commanding, and questioning) are each given distinct formal expression across grammars, whereas less frequent speech acts, such as baptizing or bequeathing, are assigned separate lexical items, but not a uniquely distinctive construction in the syntax (Sadock & Zwicky 1985). In general, lexicalization responds to much lower levels of frequency, as in this example, compared to morphology and syntax, whose grammatical meanings are more general and abstract and subsume propositional and referential possibilities that are compatible with numerous lexical items and numerous usage instances. Within the lexicon the property associated with *teacher* is frequently used in performance, that of *teacher who is late for class* much less so. The event of *X hitting Y* is frequently selected, that of *X hitting Y with X's left hand* less so. The more frequently selected properties are conventionalized in single lexemes or unique categories, phrases, and constructions in all these examples. Less frequently used properties must then be expressed through word and phrase combinations, and their meanings must be derived by a process of semantic composition.

It is this last point that holds the key to the explanatory question raised above: why are frequently used properties given priority when assigning properties to forms uniquely? The answer is plausibly the same as we gave for form reduction and Zipfian effects. Sensitivity to high frequency results in more minimal forms within a sentence and in a lifetime of sentence usage. If less frequently used properties were given priority for unique $F_1 : P_1$ assignments, or if these assignments were neutral to frequency with the result that some were high-frequency and some were low-frequency properties, then more word and phrase combinations would be needed overall whenever the enrichment to P_1 was not contextually guaranteed. If *teacher* meant 'teacher who is late for class', then the meaning of *teacher* would need to be expressed by semantic composition through appropriate word and phrase combinations (e.g. by *someone who gives instruction at school level*), since the closest single word would be preempted by its low-frequency property assignment. If dual number had priority for a grammatical number system, then singularity and plurality would need to be expressed by alternative and less grammaticalized forms or they would need to be derived by appropriate combinations (two minus one, two and more, etc.). In languages like Tongan in which lexical categories are highly ambiguous between noun and verb, there has to be an accompanying particle that unambiguously constructs NP v. VP/S, i.e. the combination here does what unambiguous and unique category assignments to single predicates achieve in other languages that avoid this plurality of forms. The conventionalization of high-frequency properties in unique $F_1 : P_1$ pairings minimizes the overall number of forms that need to be articulated and processed, therefore.

One of the best-documented and cross-linguistically researched set of examples supporting both (3.13a) and (3.13b) comes from the 'feature hierarchies' or 'markedness hierarchies' of Greenberg (1966) and Croft (1990, 2003). These authors proposed hierarchies such as Singular > Plural > Dual > Trial/Paucal and used them to structure a number of generalizations pertaining both to grammar and to performance. These generalizations are directly relevant for the predictions in (3.13) and I shall return to them in §§4.1–2. 'Grammaticalization' phenomena in language change are also relevant to (3.13a) and (3.13b) and I shall return to them in §§4.3–4.

3.2.3 *Maximize the ease of processing enrichments*

MiF asserts that minimal formal complexity and increased generality in content will be efficient in proportion to the ease with which enrichments can be made in performance, converting a set of compatible properties to a particular P, cf. (3.12). The existence of a convention pairing some F with the relevant P enables the hearer to recognize this property by virtue of knowing the convention itself. But when there is no convention, the hearer needs help. We can define the following sub-principle of MiF:

(3.14) *Maximize the ease of processing enrichments*
The human processor prefers to maximize the ease with which a set of property alternatives {P} can be reduced to a particular P in performance.

In (3.15) I enumerate some major factors that facilitate enrichments in processing.

(3.15)   a. High entity or event accessibility in the current discourse.
b. High frequency of P assignments in previous discourses.
c. Default or stereotypic correlations between P_1 and a second property P_2, permitting P_1 to be inferred from P_2.

d. Relevance or enrichment implicatures based on real-world knowledge.
e. Structural identity between a phrase or clause containing an F signaling P and another phrase or clause to which P is assigned.
f. An accessible linguistic category A on the basis of which a combinatorial property or dependency assignment P can be made to B.

The accessibility of entities in discourse (i.e. 3.15a) and its impact on the choice of appropriate referring expressions has been much discussed in pragmatic studies of reference within linguistics and psycholinguistics. Entities that have been recently mentioned are more accessible than those mentioned further back in time (Prince 1981, Ariel 1990). Entities that have been mentioned explicitly (*a house* : *the house/it*) are also more accessible than those whose existence is derived by an associative or bridging inference or by a general knowledge 'frame', such as *a house* : *the roof* (Minsky 1975, Clark & Haviland 1977, Hawkins 1978, Clark & Marshall 1981, Matsui 2000). The general performance pattern that emerges from quantitative studies of the selection of different definite NP types in English and other languages is that more accessible entities are referred to by shorter and more reduced forms, e.g. by pronouns (*it*) rather than full NPs (*the house*); cf. Ariel (1990), Brizuela (1999). Pronouns typically have minimal formal complexity and a semantic content that is highly vague with respect to the choice of referents, whereas full NPs are semantically richer and much less vague. When the context makes an entity highly accessible, the semantic generality of a minimally complex form suffices to pick out the intended referent for the hearer (*it*), and the extra semantic richness of more complex forms is unnecessary. The set of entities within the current universe of discourse and their accessibility ranking provides the potential for enrichment that can lead to the selection of a unique referent from among many possible referents compatible with the semantics of the NP. The high accessibility of a referent is available for free, so to speak, and not to exploit it and to use additional formal units with richer semantic content is inefficient by MiF.

Zero pronominal forms require an even more accessible antecedent than explicit pronouns, typically one that involves some constrained syntactic environment that 'licenses' the zero form. Linguistic theories differ over the number of such empty elements that they postulate, Government-Binding theory being one of the more generous (Chomsky 1981), but whenever they are postulated there is always a highly accessible antecedent within the sentence itself that makes a referent available for the empty pronominal. A nice illustration of the accessibility correlate of explicit v. zero anaphora can be seen in the data first discussed by Hankamer & Sag (1976) for VP anaphora. An explicit VP anaphor, as in *It's not clear that you will be able to **do it***, can have either a textual antecedent (*I'm going to **stuff this ball through this hoop***) or a situational one (in which someone is trying to stuff the ball through the hoop). The zero form, *It's not clear that you will be able to,* can have only the textual antecedent and cannot (in general!) refer directly to the situation in which someone is trying to stuff the ball through the hoop. The textual antecedent is already available for free, by virtue of the parser having just processed the previous discourse. But recognition of a situational antecedent requires additional attention to, and processing of, what is going on visually, making it less accessible at the moment of utterance, and the zero form requires the higher accessibility of the textual antecedent. And quite generally the higher the accessibility of an entity or event in the current discourse, the more minimal its form and the more compatible its content can be with multiple entities and events, since accessibility provides the enrichment.

High frequency is another major source of property enrichments in performance (3.15b) and is relevant once again to MiF: see (3.13a, b). This can be seen clearly in ambiguity and polysemy reductions. MacDonald et al. (1994) provide a particularly insightful summary of much of the experimental research on both lexical and syntactic ambiguity resolution, and the pattern that emerges from this is that the frequency with which a particular meaning or grammatical property is assigned to a form F is positively correlated with its preferential selection in on-line processing. For example, all things being equal (in neutral or unbiased contexts) listeners will preferably assign the more frequent meaning to a lexically ambiguous noun like *port* (a type of wine or a harbor) and the more frequent grammatical category to a word like *bluff*, which can be both a noun and a verb. The theoretical presumption here is that listeners will have encountered the preferred assignments of properties to forms in their previous discourses (in proportion to the kinds of frequency biases that researchers find in sample corpora such as Francis & Kučera 1982), and they will access this frequency information when making an enrichment to P1. Such frequency effects have to be considered alongside the biasing effect of the current discourse, however. In the context of wines, *port* is preferably a type of wine rather than a harbor. The strength of a frequency effect and its ability to resist a discourse accessibility effect is, in the theory of MacDonald et al. (1994), a function of the difference in frequency between competing property assignments: 'Biasing contexts produce selective access when the alternative meanings are similar in frequency and when they are consistent with the higher frequency meaning of biased words, but not when they favor lower frequency meanings.' (MacDonald et al. 1994: 679).

Frequency also plays a role in the third factor listed in (3.15c): default or stereotypical correlations between properties permitting an enrichment to P1 from a given P2. An example can be seen in the alternation between zero and explicit case marking in certain languages. For example, grammatical subjects are more frequently animate than inanimate and definite rather than indefinite across languages; direct objects have the opposite default values. In response to this, certain patterns of differential case marking have evolved, whereby inanimate and indefinite objects can be zero-marked while (the more subject-like) animate or definite objects have an explicit accusative case marker, e.g. in Turkish and Persian (Comrie 1989). Conversely, subject marking can be zero for animates and definites and non-zero for the more object-like inanimates and indefinites (Aissen 1999). The generalization that suggests itself here is that inanimacy and indefiniteness permit the inference to 'objecthood', because of their frequent association, and this inference permits zero object marking, by MiF. There is no such inference, however, when a (direct object) NP is animate or definite and does not match the default. Conversely, subjects can be zero-marked when their stereotypic inferences go through and NPs are animate and definite.

The fourth factor listed in (3.15d) involves enrichment through relevance (Sperber & Wilson 1995) or other implicature types that access real-world knowledge, such as Levinson's (1983, 2000) 'Informativeness' principle and the comprehension principles of Gernsbacher (1990) and Sanford & Garrod (1981). An example that I find particularly compelling is that of noun–noun compounds, like *paper factory, paper plate, paper clip, paper money*. One can classify these pre-modifying compounds into different semantic types, as Quirk et al. (1985) do, and one can derive them transformationally from semantically more explicit post-modifiers, as Levi (1978) does. But the most important point about meanings such as 'factory that makes paper', 'plate that is made of paper', 'clip for use on paper', etc. is that they derive crucially from our knowledge of the world and are, in effect, conversational inferences or 'implicatures' that make sense of these minimal forms. All that the grammar really encodes here is that the rightmost element is the syntactic and semantic head and *paper* is the syntactic and semantic modifier. These minimal grammatical specifications are then enriched by language users with whatever meanings match the world (a factory makes paper, a plate does not, but it can be made of paper, and so on). Similarly the range of meanings associated with the so-called possessive construction, *Wendy's children* ('those to whom she is a parent'), *Wendy's house* ('the one she lives in'), *Wendy's theory* ('the one she originated'), is also the product of an inference applied to a minimally specified grammatical form (Sperber & Wilson 1995). Linguists are really classifying the world when they define semantic types here, and these constructions can mean whatever the world allows them to mean, as long as this is compatible with their minimally specified conventional meanings.

The fifth and sixth factors (3.15e, f) provide enrichment through a conventionalized exploitation of structural features within a sentence, rather than through the wider context. Structural identity and parallelism are a major source of inferential enrichment, for example in co-ordinate deletion structures. Several examples will be discussed in the next chapter (§4.5). Minimally specified meanings and syntactic properties can also be enriched through dependency assignments to a form B by exploiting some neighboring or proximate form A whose inherent and conventionalized properties will result in reduced ambiguity or polysemy or other enrichment to B, as in the examples of §2.2: a patient theta-role and nominative case can be assigned to *the boy* in combination with *fell*; a category-ambiguous predicate can be assigned the category N(oun) in combination with an NP-constructing particle in Tongan; and so on. The grammatical conditions constraining dependency assignments include a 'constituent-command' regularity (Reinhart 1983), and a possible motivation for this in terms of the current theory will be provided in §4.6.

The production and comprehension of linguistic forms can be minimized by exploiting sentence-external and sentence-internal clues in the ways we have just seen. As a result, the processor avoids the articulation and processing of explicit linguistic material that is derivable or inferable from the linguistic or larger context. MiF (3.8) defines a preference for the smallest (but still rather large) set of form–property pairs in a language, and this is made possible by expanding the set of properties {P} assignable to the set of forms {F}, subject to the ease of enriching each set of property alternatives to a particular P in performance, based on sentence-external or sentence-internal clues. Levinson (2000) discusses an important truth about the exploitation of such clues, namely 'Inference is cheap', which I understand to mean that these inferences take place anyway, and this is what underlies the minimization efficiencies considered here. It is inefficient to undertake additional processing of forms and properties when the relevant properties are already inferable contextually or are readily accessible structurally through parallelism or through already existing combinatorial relations.

Complexity in this context means that a sentence employs more forms, with more conventionalized property assignments, than it needs to, relative to these easy-to-process enrichments: a fuller NP type rather than a pronoun; a sentence without co-ordinate deletion when deletion could have occurred; a resumptive pronoun within a relative clause in lieu of a gap; and so on.

Work in grammatical analysis has traditionally paid insufficient attention to how phrases and constructions actually receive the properties they do, simply taking the end product as a grammatical fact. We need to look more closely at the differences between minimal and explicit forms and ask how properties are assigned in processing. We need to distinguish between properties that are inherent in given words and phrases, properties that are assigned in combinatorial and dependency domains, and properties that are contextual inferences of different types. When we do this I believe we can achieve greater clarity on fundamental notions in linguistic theory like dependency and underspecification and we can make better predictions both for performance and for grammars.

3.3   Maximize On-line Processing (MaOP)

Minimize Domains (3.1) and Minimize Forms (3.8) provide definitions for the efficiency slogan 'Express the most with the least' that was introduced in §2.3. The third principle, which captures the 'Express it earliest' intuition, must now be defined.

Notice by way of introduction that there can be efficiency differences between alternative orderings of sister PPs to an intransitive verb, even when there is no absolute reduction in the size of the processing domain for one ordering compared with the other, i.e. even when they do not differ in domain minimization. In §3.1 I compared *John vp[went [to London] [in the late afternoon]]* with *John vp[went [in the late afternoon] [to London]]*. The former had a four-word Constituent Recognition Domain (CRD) for the VP, the latter a six-word CRD, making the former more minimal (with a higher IC-to-word ratio of 3/4 = 75% v. 3/6 = 50%). But let us now add a third postverbal PP: *John vp[went [to London] [in the late afternoon] [after a long siesta]]* v. *John vp[went [in the late afternoon] [to London] [after a long siesta]]*. In earlier work I argued that there was still evidence for a short-before-long preference in cases such as this, i.e. a preference for *[to London]* to precede the longer *[in the late afternoon]*, even when there could be no overall reduction in CRD size, and I proposed an on-line metric for measuring IC-to-word ratios that would capture this. The on-line metric revealed that there was a stronger preference when one of the competing CRDs was actually reduced compared with the other. But it also showed that an internal arrangement alone, within competing CRDs of the same word length, could still result in preferences.[3]

The on-line metric illustrated in fn. 3 predicts different preferences for alternative orderings. But when we look at other syntactic and semantic processing operations, it becomes clear that there is a much more general principle here involving efficiency in on-line property assignments. In order to capture it I propose the formulation given in (3.16), together with a new associated metric in terms of On-line Property to Ultimate Property ratios (OP-to-UP ratios). (3.16) refers to the 'unassignment' and 'misassignment' of properties in on-line processing, which will be explained immediately in §3.3.1. The basic intuition that (3.16) tries to capture is that many preferences appear to be correlated with the earlier assignment of common properties, in one ordering or structural variant, v. their later assignment in another.

---

[3] The on-line metric of Hawkins (1994: 82) is defined as follows. First count the ICs in the domain from left to right (starting with 1). Then count the non-ICs (or words alone) in the domain (again starting with 1). The first IC is then divided by the total number of non-ICs that it dominates (e.g. 1/2). The second IC is divided by the highest total for the non-ICs that it dominates (e.g. if this IC dominates the third through seventh non-IC in the domain, then 2/7 is the ratio for the second IC); and so on for all subsequent ICs. The ratio for each IC is expressed as a percentage, and these percentages are then aggregated to achieve a score for the whole CRD. For the competing orders discussed in the main text, this defines the following efficiency differences (the slightly different on-line metric of Hawkins 1990 makes fundamentally similar predictions). CRDs are shown in bold.

(1) John vp[**went** [**to London**] [in the late afternoon]]
(2) John vp[**went** [**in the late afternoon**] [to London]]
(1′)   VP: IC-to-word ratio = 3/4 or 75%
(2′)   VP: IC-to-word ratio = 3/6 or 50%
(1″)   VP: on-line IC-to-word ratio:

   1/1   2/3   3/4
   100%   67%   75% = 81% (aggregate)

(2″)   VP: on-line IC-to-word ratio:

   1/1   2/5   3/6
   100%   40%   50% = 63% (aggregate)

(3) John vp[**went** [**to London**] [in the late afternoon] [after a long siesta]]
(4) John vp[**went** [**in the late afternoon**] [to London] [after a long siesta]]
(3′)   VP: IC-to-word ratio = 4/8 or 50%
(4′)   VP: IC-to-word ratio = 4/8 or 50%
(3″)   VP: on-line IC-to-word ratio:

   1/1   2/3   3/7   4/8
   100%   67%   43%   50% = 65%

(4″)   VP: on-line IC-to-word ratio:

   1/1   2/5   3/7   4/8
   100%   40%   43%   50% = 58%

The preference for (1) over (2) is revealed both by the simpler IC-to-word ratios (75% v. 50%) and by the on-line ratios (81% to 63%). The preference for (3) over (4) is less strong, and is not revealed by the simple domain minimization metric of (3′) and (4′), but it is revealed by the on-line metric (65% v. 58%).

(3.16) *Maximize On-line Processing* (MaOP)
> The human processor prefers to maximize the set of properties that are assignable to each item X as X is processed, thereby increasing O(n-line) P(roperty) to U(ltimate) P(roperty) ratios. The maximization difference between competing orders and structures will be a function of the number of properties that are unassigned or misassigned to X in a structure/sequence S, compared with the number in an alternative.

3.3.1 Unassignments and misassignments

The notion of an unassignment is a relative one: a particular syntactic or semantic property which could be assigned earlier in a structure/sequence S is assigned later in an alternative S′. In *John vp[went [in the late afternoon] [to London] [after a long siesta]]* recognition of the second PP daughter of VP is delayed compared with *John vp[went [to London] [in the late afternoon] [after a long siesta]]*. On other occasions syntactic or semantic property assignments to a category X may require a 'look ahead' (Marcus 1980) to a later category in the parse string, Y, resulting in fewer property assignments to X as X itself is processed, and this look ahead can be avoided in the alternative Y X ordering or in an alternative structure. The theoretical problem posed by any attempt to define such unassignments precisely is, however, that an alternative S′ that avoids the late assignment of property P1 might itself result in the later assignment of P2, compared with structure S, with the result that the processor is no better off with S′ than it is with S. What the associated metric has to capture, therefore, is a quantification of the overall advantage of S over S′ with respect to early on-line property assignments.

Consider some of the properties that are assigned in the on-line processing of a complement clause for the verb *realize*, and let us examine the impact that the presence or absence of an explicit complementizer *that* has on the timing of these property assignments.

(3.17) a. I vp[realize s2[the boy knows the answer]]
     b. I vp[realize s2[that the boy knows the answer]]

The lexical co-occurrence frame for *realize* includes the S-complement option, and this option can be assigned immediately when *that* is parsed. In the absence of *that*, the immediately following *the boy* does not match the direct object co-occurrence possibilities of *realize* (one can *realize this fact*, but one cannot **realize the boy*), and hence no case or theta-role is assigned to *the* *boy* by *realize*. But nor is the subordinate S2 recognizable at *the boy* either, according to the parsing principles of Hawkins (1994), since this NP does not uniquely construct it.[4] Hence the recognition of S2 is delayed until the first word that does uniquely construct a clause, namely the finite verb *knows* (by Grandmother Node Construction in Hawkins 1994: 361), which then delays attachment of S2 to the matrix VP, recognition of S2 as an (accusative) direct object of *realize*, and the attachment of *the boy* to S2. The competing structure with a *that* complementizer (3.17b) permits earlier recognition of many of these nodes and relations, according to these parsing assumptions, and will often be preferred over structures without *that* by the metric to be proposed here. It is important, therefore, to examine the precise distribution of all relevant on-line property assignments to forms, in order to make empirical predictions that test MaOP's preferences.

MaOP predicts that a structure or sequence S will be dispreferred in proportion to the number of properties that are unassignable to it on-line, compared with the number (un)assigned in an alternative structure or sequence. The following factors will all lower the O(n-line) P(roperty) to U(ltimate) P(roperty) ratios for sentence types to which they apply:

(3.18) *Unassignment factors*

> a. the number of words and phrases that undergo some temporary unassignment of properties on-line, compared with an alternative structure/sequence in which the relevant properties are immediately assignable;
>
> b. the number of any mother–daughter attachments that are temporarily unassignable to the words and phrases in (a);
>
> c. the number of any relations of combination or dependency that are temporarily unassignable to the words and phrases in (a).

A quantification of the impact of such unassignments in the on-line processing of (3.17a) v. (3.17b) will be illustrated in §3.3.2.

Corresponding to the pair (3.17a, b) is a very similar pair of competing structures with the matrix verb *believe*:

(3.19) a. I vp[believe s2[the boy knows the answer]]
         b. I vp[believe s2[that the boy knows the answer]]

---

[4] *The boy* might eventually be a left-branching NP within a pre-nominal possessive phrase, e.g. *I realize the boy's uncle knows the answer*, which means that construction of a grandmother S over *the* in np[*the boy*] is not guaranteed in on-line processing.

There is one difference, however. The lexical co-occurrence frame for *believe* does include an animate NP argument to which case and a theta-role can be assigned (i.e. one can *believe someone*), and since the immediately following *the boy* is compatible with these structural and semantic properties it is assigned to *believe* as an argument on-line, creating a so-called 'garden path' (Frazier 1985, MacDonald et al. 1994). The terminology to be used here is 'misassignment'. Not only are certain properties of the ultimate syntactic and semantic representation not assignable on-line, but erroneous properties are assigned that will eventually be expunged from the ultimate representation. Such misassignments arise precisely when (a) certain properties are unassigned on-line (e.g. the construction of S2 is not assigned at its onset in (3.17a) and (3.19a)) and (b) some ultimately erroneous co-occurrence possibilities are activated for categories and phrases in the unassignment period prior to a clarification of their eventual property assignments (*the boy* in (3.19a) will eventually receive its case and theta-role from the subordinate verb *knows*, not from *believe*). It is very often the case that there are unassignment structures for each misassignment type in a language (e.g. (3.17a) corresponding to (3.19a)), the difference being that co-occurrence possibilities and structural compatibilities that produce the misassignment (one can *believe the boy*) do not hold in the unassignment structure (one cannot *realize the boy).

Some additional misassignments are given in (3.20):

(3.20) a. *The horse raced past the barn* fell.
      b. While Mary was *reading the book* fell down.

In (3.20a), for example, the words and phrases italicized are parsed as a simple main clause on-line, and are then reanalyzed as a head plus reduced relative clause (i.e. *the horse that was raced past the barn*) once the predicate *fell* is encountered. All these misassignments are inefficient since the misassigned properties make no contribution to the ultimate syntactic and semantic representation of the sentence, and their repair also requires processing effort. We can give a grammatically based quantification of misassignment inefficiencies by adding up the factors listed in (3.21):

(3.21) *Misassignment factors*

      a. the number of words and phrases that undergo some temporary misassignment of properties on-line;

b. the number of any additional dominating nodes that must be introduced into the syntactic tree when correcting the misassignments in (a);

c. the number of any mother–daughter attachments that are temporarily misassigned to the words and phrases in (a);

d. the number of any relations of combination or dependency that are temporarily misassigned to the words and phrases in (a);

e. the number of mother–daughter attachments that replace those misassigned in (c);

f. the number of relations of combination or dependency that replace those misassigned in (d).

When these factors are applied to different misassignment types it can be shown that *I believe the boy knows the answer* (3.19a) is a less severe garden path than *The horse raced past the barn fell* (3.20a). Fewer words and phrases are misrecognized on-line in the former (3.21a), fewer additional nodes must subsequently be introduced (3.21b), there are fewer misassigned relations of attachment (3.21c), combination, and dependency (3.21d), and the number of such relations replacing those misassigned is less (3.21e) and (f).

This is shown in (3.22) and (3.23), in which misassigned entities, relations, and properties have been quantified according to the criteria (a–f) in (3.21). The misassignment total for (3.22) is significantly less than for (3.23). (vp1[NP2] means that NP2 is attached as an immediate daughter to VP1, etc.).

(3.22)

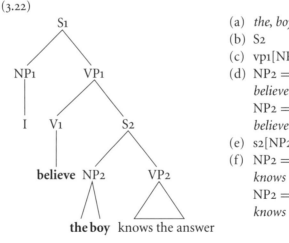

(a) *the, boy,* NP2   [3]
(b) S2   [1]
(c) vp1[NP2]   [1]
(d) NP2 = Accus of
     believe
     NP2 = θ-object of [2]
     believe
(e) s2[NP2], vp1[S2]   [2]
(f) NP2 = Nomin of
     knows
     NP2 = θ-subject of [2]
     knows
                 TOTAL =   11

(3.23)

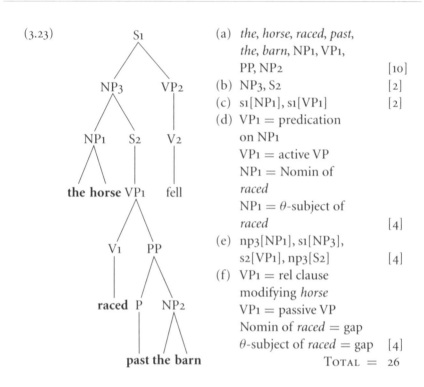

(a) *the, horse, raced, past,* *the, barn,* NP1, VP1, PP, NP2	[10]
(b) NP3, S2	[2]
(c) s1[NP1], s1[VP1]	[2]
(d) VP1 = predication on NP1	
VP1 = active VP	
NP1 = Nomin of *raced*	
NP1 = θ-subject of *raced*	[4]
(e) np3[NP1], s1[NP3], s2[VP1], np3[S2]	[4]
(f) VP1 = rel clause modifying *horse*	
VP1 = passive VP	
Nomin of *raced* = gap	
θ-subject of *raced* = gap	[4]
TOTAL =	26

3.3.2   *The quantitative metric*

Any delay in on-line processing through unassignment, with or without an additional misassignment, reduces the OP-to-UP ratio of a sentence. This ratio is calculated according to the procedure set out in (3.24):

(3.24) *On-line property to ultimate property ratio*

The OP-to-UP ratio is calculated at each word X within a connected set of words ⟨... X ...⟩ whose property assignments differ between two competing structures S and S′. The cumulative number of properties assignable at each X is divided by the total number of properties to be assigned in the connected set in the ultimate representation of each structure, and the result is expressed as a percentage (e.g. 4/20 = 20%, 8/20 = 40%, 10/20 = 50% for successive words, etc.). The higher these on-line percentages, the more efficient is structure S or S′, since more properties are assigned earlier.

This metric captures the on-line efficiency differences between competing structures S and S′, by quantifying how many of the ultimate properties to be assigned to each X can actually be assigned earlier rather than later. An **Unassignment Difference** between the two can then be quantified by summing up OP-to-UP ratios for all words being compared and assessing whether S or S′ has the higher overall score.

Let us illustrate how this works. (3.25a) and (b) show on-line property assignments to sentences (3.17a) and (b) respectively, for a significant subset of syntactic and semantic properties grouped according to type: syntactic category (e.g. N or Det); phrasal type constructed at the relevant point in the parse (principally mother nodes or grandmother nodes: see Hawkins 1994); mother–daughter attachments made at the relevant point; and various argument structure relations of combination and dependency (case and theta-role assignment) which will be subsumed here, for simplicity, under a single grammatical relations characterization (e.g. $NP_2 = SU\text{-}V_2$ means that NP_2 is the subject of V_2). The words whose property assignments are common to (3.25a) and (b) are given in parentheses (these properties are shown for (3.25a) and not repeated in (3.25b)). The smallest connected set of words whose property assignments differ are *the boy knows* in (3.25a) and *that the boy knows* in (3.25b). The number of properties assigned on-line is given under each word, and the corresponding OP-to-UP ratio is calculated as a percentage.

(3.25) a.	(I	realize)		the	boy	knows	(the answer)
Categories	Pro	V_1		Det	N	V_2	
Phrases	NP_1, S_1	VP_1		NP_2		VP_2, S_2	
Attachments	$np_1[Pro]$	$vp_1[V_1]$		$np_2[Det]$	$np_2[N]$	**$vp_2[V_2], s_2[VP_2]$**	
	$s_1[NP_1]$	$s_1[VP_1]$				**$vp_1[S_2], s_2[NP_2]$**	
Relations		$NP_1 = SU\text{-}V_1$				**$S_2 = OBJ\text{-}V_1,$**	
						$NP_2 = SU\text{-}V_2$	
				3	2	9	
OP/UP ratio:				$3/14 = 21\%$	$5/14 = 36\%$	$14/14 = 100\%$	

(3.25) b.	(I	realize)	that	the	boy	knows	(the answer)
Categories			**Comp**	Det	N	V_2	
Phrases			**S_2**	NP_2		VP_2	
Attachments			**$s_2[Comp]$**	$np_2[Det]$	$np_2[N]$	$vp_2[V_2]$	
			$vp_1[S_2]$	$s_2[NP_2]$		$s_2[VP_2]$	
Relations			**$S_2 = OBJ\text{-}V_1$**			$NP_2 = SU - V_2$	
			5	4	2	5	
OP/UP ratio:			$5/16 = 31\%$	$9/16 = 56\%$	$11/16 = 69\%$	$16/16 = 100\%$	

Property assignments whose timing differs on-line are shown in larger type and in bold. It is visually apparent that (3.25a) involves a significant delay in property recognition during its first two words compared with (3.25b) and is skewed towards later property assignments, as shown in the OP-to-UP ratios

(21% v. 31% for the first word, and 36% v. 56% for the second). But (3.25a) needs fewer words overall for the assignment of shared properties than (3.25b), three v. four, and by the third word all relevant properties have been assigned, whereas (3.25b) has only reached 69% at word three and 100% at word four. The Unassignment Difference between (3.25a) and (b) turns out to be almost equal as a result, as shown in (3.26).

(3.26)	Unassignment Difference:	Word #1	#2	#3	#4
	ZERO (3.25a)	21%	36%	100% ($\rightarrow$)	
	THAT (3.25b)	31%	56%	69%	100%
		-10	-20	$+31$	0

i.e. ZERO and THAT are almost equally preferred ($+31/-30$)

When subordinate NP subjects are longer and more complex than *the boy*, the skewing towards late property assignments in the zero structure becomes that much greater, and MaOP (3.16) predicts a preference for *that*, in direct proportion to the length of the subordinate subject, in fact. This is illustrated in (3.27a, b), in which two extra words have been added to *the boy*. The Unassignment Difference is calculated in (3.28).

(3.27) a.	(I realize)		the	small	young	boy	knows	(the answer)
Categories			Det	Adj	Adj	N	V2	
Phrases			NP2				VP2,S2	
Attachments			np2[Det]	np2[Adj]	np2[Adj]	np2[N]	vp2[V],s2[VP2]	
							vp1[S2],s2[NP2]	
Relations							S2 = OBJ-V1,	
							NP2 = SU−V2	
			3	2	2	2	9	
OP/UP ratio:			3/18 = 17%	5/18 = 28%	7/18 = 39%	9/18 = 50%	18/18 = 100%	

(3.27) b.	(I realize) that	the	small	young	boy	knows	(the answer)
Categories	Comp	Det	Adj	Adj	N	V2	
Phrases	S2	NP2				VP2	
Attachments	s2[Comp]	np2[Det]	np2[Adj]	np2[Adj]	np2[N]	vp2[V2]	
	vp1[S2]	s2[NP2]				s2[VP2]	
Relations	S2 = OBJ-V1					NP2 = SU − V2	
	5	4	2	2	2	5	
OP/UP ratio:	5/20 = 25%	9/20 = 45%	11/20 = 55%	13/20 = 65%	15/20 = 75%	20/20 = 100%	

(3.28)	Unassignment Difference:	Word #1	#2	#3	#4	#5	#6
	ZERO (3.27a)	17%	28%	39%	50%	100% ($\rightarrow$)	
	THAT (3.27b)	25%	45%	55%	65%	75%	100%
		$+8$	$+17$	$+16$	$+15$	-25	

i.e. THAT preferred by $56 - 25 = 31$

Misassignments to *I believe the boy knows the answer* (3.19a) compared to *I believe that the boy knows the answer* (3.19b) would involve the same OP-to-UP ratio differences as (3.25a) and (3.25b), since this metric measures the number of ultimately correct properties that are assigned at each word on-line. The erroneous on-line attachments and relations shown in (3.22) are corrected later in the parse, at the verb *knows*, which is also the point at which the unassigned properties are assigned in (3.25a). The misassignments are hypothesized here to require further processing effort in proportion to their number (see the factors listed in (3.21)), while both they and the unassignments delay the recognition of a sentence's ultimate properties, as reflected in the OP-to-UP ratios.

3.3.3   *Predictions for performance and grammars*

One general prediction that is made for the NP1-V-NP2-VP structural type in English, and for its alternation with an unassignment-reducing or garden-path-avoiding NP1-V-*that*-NP2-VP sequence, is the following. In the event that (i) NP2 is not compatible with the lexical co-occurrence requirements of the matrix V (e.g. *realize the boy*) and (ii) NP2 is not a nominative case-marked NP that can construct a clause on-line (like *that*) by Grandmother Node Construction (Hawkins 1994: 361), then the longer the NP2, the worse the unassignments will be by (3.18) and the lower the OP-to-UP ratio. The longer the NP2, the worse the misassignments are by (3.21) as well when NP2 is compatible with the lexical co-occurrence requirements of a matrix verb such as *believe*. Either way, the longer a non-case-marked NP2, the worse the unassignments or misassignments, and the more we predict the alternative structure with *that*.

The corpus data in (3.29) are taken from Rohdenburg (1999: 102) and all involve the matrix verb *realize* with a complement clause containing zero or *that*.[5] These data test (and support) MaOP's predicted preference for *that* as more and more property assignments are delayed in the zero structure compared with *that*. They show that when NP2 is a personal pronoun (most of which are case-marked in English) the distribution of zero to *that* is random (48% to 52%). Personal pronouns and *that* are equally efficient constructors of S. But as the length and complexity of a full NP2 subject increases from 1–2 words to 3+ words, the distribution of zero to *that* declines from 26% to 10%, as OP-to-UP ratios decline.

---

[5] Rohdenburg's corpus for these data comes from *The Times* and *Sunday Times* of London (first quarter of 1993).

(3.29) *Matrix verb:*
realize

	Zero complement S	THAT complement S
Personal pronoun NP2 subject	48% (127)	52% (37)
1–2 word full NP2 subject	26% (32)	74% (89)
3+ word full NP2 subject	10% (15)	90% (130)

Further predictions are tested in §6.1.2.

Experimental evidence in psycholinguistics has repeatedly shown that mis-assignments are hard to process (cf. Frazier 1985 and MacDonald et al. 1994 for an extensive literature review). The grammatically based metric of (3.21), derived from MaOP (3.16), defines degrees of processing difficulty for different garden path sentences, and these degrees need to be tested on performance data from various languages.

Syntactic and semantic complexity are not the only factors that determine the severity of a garden path, however. Discourse context and frequency effects associated with particular verbs can bias the parser towards the ultimately correct representation at a point of temporary ambiguity and can avoid a potential garden path altogether. The metric of (3.21) is just one of several factors determining degree of processing difficulty through misassignment, therefore, and these other factors must be controlled for during testing.

My central claim about grammars will be that they too have responded to the efficiency differences predicted for performance by MaOP (3.16) and its associated OP-to-UP metric (3.24). I will argue in Chapter 8 that grammatical conventions reveal dispreferences for unassignments and misassignments (in proportion to their degree), and that these dispreferences are what explain the absence of symmetry and the existence of numerous asymmetries. Symmetry is observed when categories A and B are found productively in A + B and B + A orders across languages: both Verb + Object (VO) and Object + Verb (OV) are productive. Asymmetry occurs when only A + B is attested or is significantly preferred, either in all languages or in a subset for which independent empirical evidence suggests that symmetry could have occurred. For example, displaced *wh*-elements almost always stand to the left of their sister clauses, rarely to the right (A + B/*B + A). I will argue that such asymmetries avoid regular unassignments or misassignments that would arise in the *B + A order and are motivated by MaOP.

Many unassignments arise when a form B cannot receive its full set of properties on-line because some property of B, P, is dependent for its assignment on the properties of form A which follows B (B + A). The reverse ordering (A + B) may permit a full assignment of properties to B on-line, including P, since the parser now has access to A in the parse string. In the event that dependencies are asymmetrical, i.e. B depends on A for the assignment of P whereas A does not depend on B for any assignments, then an asymmetrical A + B ordering is predicted.

Co-indexation of an anaphor with its antecedent can serve as an example. In a VSO language the relative ordering of *chastised John*i *himself*i makes it possible for the parser to assign the appropriate index to *himself* immediately as this direct object is parsed, by accessing the preceding antecedent, *John*i. In a VOS language, however, the index cannot be assigned on-line and this parsing decision has to wait until the following subject has been parsed, whereupon it can be assigned retrospectively. There are a number of such asymmetric dependencies between what we loosely call 'subjects' and 'objects' (cf. Primus 1999) and it is no accident, as I see it, that there is a strong preference for subjects to precede objects in the languages of the world (Greenberg 1963). Many properties of objects cannot be assigned on-line when they precede subjects, and it is to this that I attribute the asymmetry. More generally, when dependencies between two forms are asymmetrical, we see regular linear-precedence asymmetries across languages (§8.2).

For many pairs of categories A and B, however, there is symmetry in the dependency relations that link them: B is dependent on A for some properties, and A on B for others. A verb like *run* is dependent on co-occurring NPs for the selection of its appropriate transitive or intransitive lexical co-occurrence frame and for its meaning assignment (*run the race/run the water/run the ad*, etc). A direct object NP like *the race* is dependent on *run* for its theta-role and for providing the mother node VP to which NP is attached. Dependencies are symmetrical here and so are the orderings VO and OV. Each avoids some potential unassignments (or misassignments) on-line, while introducing others.

The role of morphosyntax now appears in a new light. Dependencies that are forward-looking to categories that have not yet been parsed are inefficient from the perspective of MaOP, since the relevant properties cannot be assigned on-line. When the verb precedes its NP arguments, a rich verb agreement system enables the parser to access the lexical co-occurrence structure of the verb at the verb and to immediately select the appropriate intransitive, transitive, or ditransitive co-occurrence frame, and appropriate lexical-semantic content, without having to wait for the arguments on which these property assignments depend. When NP arguments precede the verb, a rich morphological case system can give on-line information about syntactic cases and their associated theta-roles prior to the verb. Rich verb agreement should be most productive in verb-early languages, therefore, and rich case marking in NP-early (and verb-late) languages: i.e. both verb agreement and case marking should be skewed to the left of the clause. §8.5 tests these and related predictions for morphosyntax.

4

More on Form Minimization

In the last chapter I defined the principle of Minimize Forms (3.8) and formulated some form minimization predictions (3.13):

(3.8) *Minimize Forms* (MiF)

The human processor prefers to minimize the formal complexity of each linguistic form F (its phoneme, morpheme, word or phrasal units) and the number of forms with unique conventionalized property assignments, thereby assigning more properties to fewer forms. These minimizations apply in proportion to the ease with which a given property P can be assigned in processing to a given F.

(3.13) *Form Minimization Predictions*

a. The formal complexity of each F is reduced in proportion to the frequency of that F and/or the processing ease of assigning a given P to a reduced F (e.g. to zero).
b. The number of unique $F_1 : P_1$ pairings in a language is reduced by grammaticalizing or lexicalizing a given $F_1 : P_1$ in proportion to the frequency and preferred expressiveness of that P_1 in performance.

In this chapter I first illustrate and test these predictions using some of Greenberg's (1966) markedness hierarchies (§4.1). The next section (§4.2) tests the same hierarchies on diachronic data from an evolving language family (Germanic). I then consider 'grammaticalization' phenomena in relation to MiF and processing (§4.3). In §4.4 I illustrate the general points made about grammaticalization with a brief case study involving definiteness marking. In §4.5 I consider how forms can be minimized on the basis of processing enrichments through structural parallelism, continuing the general discussion of processing enrichment that was initiated in §3.2.3. In §4.6 I consider enrichments made on the basis of dependency assignments, as this term was defined in (2.3) of §2.2. This leads to a discussion of the constituent-command constraint on many dependencies and to a general principle of Conventionalized Dependency.

4.1   Greenberg's markedness hierarchies

Greenberg (1966) proposed 'feature' or markedness hierarchies such as those in (4.1) and used them to structure a number of generalizations pertaining both to grammars and to performance.[1]

(4.1) a. Nom > Acc > Dat > Other (for case marking)
       b. Sing > Plur > Dual > Trial/Paucal (for number)
       c. Masc > Fem > Neut (for gender)
       d. Positive > Comparative > Superlative

The grammatical evidence came from morphological inventories of different sizes across grammars, from declining allomorphy, and from increased formal marking. Declining frequencies of use in sample texts from different languages pointed to an intriguing correlation with performance. For the number hierarchy (4.1b), for example, Greenberg gave the following figures from Sanskrit:

(4.2) Sanskrit noun inflection frequencies:
       Singular = 70.3%
       Plural = 25.1%
       Dual = 4.6%

The other hierarchies had similar frequency correlates.

Based on this evidence we can hypothesize that markedness hierarchies are conventionalizations of **performance frequency rankings** defined on entities within common grammatical and/or semantic domains. Singular nouns are more frequent than plurals, which are more frequent than duals. The ultimate causes of these different frequencies appear to be quite diverse. They may result from the fact that the relevant entities occur with different frequencies in the real world (there are more plural groups than duals, for example), or they

---

[1] I shall use 'feature hierarchies' and 'markedness hierarchies' interchangeably when discussing morphosyntax in this book.

Some refinements have been proposed in the hierarchies of (4.1) since Greenberg's (1966) discussion of them. See e.g. the following overview articles and monographs: Primus (1993, 1995, 1999) and Dixon (1994) for case systems; Corbett (2000) on number; Corbett (1991) on gender. See also Croft (1990, 2003) for updated discussion of the hierarchies themselves and of their correlating properties. It remains to be seen to what extent the MiF predictions of (3.8) and (3.14) are still correct in relation to these refinements, and to what extent performance preferences can actually motivate the necessary changes in detail. Haspelmath (2002), in one of the most recent general overviews of morphology, confirms the close correlation between morphological marking and frequency and the role of frequency in explaining what are otherwise exceptions to purely grammatical regularities in cases such as 'markedness reversals'. In this context I shall preserve Greenberg's formulations, since it was these formulations that he used when illustrating and testing the correlations with performance. None of the hierarchies in (4.1) appears to be defective in any serious or major way.

might reflect social and communicative biases when describing entities in the world (in favor of animates rather than inanimates, for example in the gender hierarchy). Syntactic and semantic complexity differences between clause types to which the relevant morphemes are assigned are also relevant. The increasing complexity of ditransitive over transitive over intransitive clauses is matched by the increasing *in*frequency of the morphological cases that are unique to each, datives being typically associated with ditransitives, and accusatives with transitives, while nominatives occur with all clause types and are generally the sole arguments of intransitives: see Primus (1999) for a quantification of case assignment by verbs in a language (German) with several case distinctions.[2] But whatever the precise causality of these frequency asymmetries is for a given hierarchy, it appears to be reflected in cross-linguistic grammatical patterns that conventionalize morphosyntax and allomorphy in accordance with MiF. The form minimization predictions of (3.13) predict a performance frequency correlate both with form reductions in grammars and with preferred patterns of conventionalization.

For form reductions we can state Greenberg's cross-linguistic generalization as follows:

(4.3) *Quantitative Formal Marking Prediction*
       For each hierarchy H the amount of formal marking (i.e. phonological and morphological complexity) will be greater or equal down each hierarchy position.

(4.3) follows from (3.13a). Its effects can be seen especially clearly in the distribution of zero allomorphs, which almost always include the highest position(s) on each hierarchy, if they occur at all. The singular morpheme on English nouns is systematically zero (*student*) whereas plurality generally has non-zero allomorphs (e.g. *students*). The highest case on the case hierarchy of (4.1a) and on the corresponding hierarchy for ergative languages (Abs > Erg > Dat > Other) is often zero, whereas the accusative (or ergative) is generally non-zero (Dixon 1994, Primus 1999); and if a lower case is zero, higher one(s) will be as well. Positive adjectives in English are not formally marked, whereas comparatives and superlatives are (*big/bigger/biggest*), in accordance with (4.1d).

Non-zero forms also reveal greater or equal complexity down the hierarchy positions. The third person plural suffix in the Austronesian language Manam is *di* (contrasting with a third person singular zero form). The dual

---

[2] Primus (1999) gives the following case assignment figures for verbs in German, based on a count of 17,500 verbs listed in Mater (1971): Nom 17,500; Acc 9,700; Dat 5,450; Gen 40. These figures follow the case hierarchy of (4.1a).

incorporates the plural and adds a dual suffix to it, -*ru*, with an intervening buffer, *di-a-ru*. The paucal suffix -*to* also incorporates the plural and the buffer, -*di-a-to* (Lichtenberk 1983).

A second cross-linguistic generalization from Greenberg (1966) can be captured as follows:

(4.4) *Morphological Inventory Prediction*
       For each hierarchy H if a language assigns at least one morpheme uniquely to a given position, then it assigns at least one uniquely to each higher position.

This follows from (3.13b). For example, if a language like Latin has a distinct oblique or non-dative case in its morphological system (like an ablative), as it does, it is predicted to have a distinct dative, a distinct accusative, and a distinct nominative. If a language has a distinct dative, then no predictions are made for any lower cases, but a distinct accusative and nominative are predicted as before.[3] For the number hierarchy, if a language has a distinct paucal form, as Manam does (Lichtenberk 1983), then it should have a distinct dual, a distinct plural and a distinct singular, which it does.[4] These predictions are formulated at the level of the grammatical system of a language and not on individual declensional classes or paradigms, for reasons that are discussed in Hawkins (1998*b*, *c*).[5]

A third cross-linguistic generalization from Greenberg (1966) can be formulated as the 'declining distinctions prediction':

(4.5) *Declining Distinctions Prediction*
       For each hierarchy H any combinatorial features that partition references to a given position on H will result in fewer or equal morphological distinctions down each lower position of H.

---

[3] For ergative languages the hierarchy Abs > Erg > Dat > Other needs to be proposed (see e.g. Primus 1999); hence a unique dative could imply either distinctive ergative and absolutive cases or distinctive accusative and nominative.

[4] The Cushitic language Bayso (Corbett & Hayward 1987) is a rare exception to this prediction since it has a paucal category in addition to singular and plural, but no dual.

[5] These markedness predictions are straightforwardly counterexemplified if they are applied to individual morphological paradigms or individual grammatical categories. They have to be applied to the underlying morphological system as a whole, and to the categories that are motivated for the grammar of each language. For example, neuter nouns of the *bellum* class in Latin collapse nominative and accusative forms in both singular and plural, but have a distinct dative. A separate dative implies a separate accusative according to the morphological inventory prediction (4.4), and this prediction does not hold for *bellum* but does hold for Latin case-marking as a whole (there are distinct dative, accusative, and nominative forms in the *dominus* paradigm, for example). More generally, case syncretisms in paradigms often apply to adjacent positions on these hierarchies (nominative and accusative, accusative and dative, dative and other), with the result that some paradigms would be exceptions to

This also follows from (3.13b). For example, in Modern English singular pronouns are partitioned for gender (*he*/*she*/*it*), resulting in unique gender-specific forms, whereas plural pronouns are not so partitioned and the corresponding forms (e.g. *they*) are vague or ambiguous with respect to gender. In Old High German both singular and plural were partitioned for gender. Both systems are compatible with (4.5). What is ruled out is the inverse of English in which there are more gender distinctions in the plural than in the singular. More generally, the singular should exhibit more or equal case distinctions than the plural and more or equal case and gender combinations throughout each grammar. The different cases and genders in turn should exhibit more or equal partitionings and more allomorphy in their higher hierarchy positions as well.

The frequency rankings exemplified by (4.2) can make sense of the grammatical generalizations here. The properties that are conventionalized as unique or unambiguous property assignments to forms (i.e. F1 : P1 in (3.13b)) are preferably those that can be used most frequently in performance. And quite generally, properties and property combinations are conventionalized in proportion to their performance frequency. The following principle of morphologization follows from (3.13b):

(4.6) *Morphologization*
   A morphological distinction will be grammaticalized in proportion to the performance frequency with which it can uniquely identify a given subset of entities {E} in a grammatical and/or semantic domain D.

If a less frequently used property such as dual number receives distinctive morphology, i.e. a unique pairing of some F1 with duality (P1), then so do the more frequently used plural and singular properties. If the less frequently used dative receives distinctively unique morphology in a case system, so do the more frequently used accusative and nominative (or ergative and absolutive— see fn. 3). The principle of (4.6) (ultimately (3.13b)) leads to the morphological inventory predictions of (4.4), once the frequency rankings are known for the respective properties in each domain D.

Correspondingly, as the overall frequency of a hierarchy position declines, so too the frequencies of the various subsets of uses within each position that are potentially available for allomorphic partitionings decline also. The set of entities referred to by Plur+Masc can be no greater than, and will generally

predictions that are valid for the grammatical system as a whole. We can say that a particular morphological feature M exists in the grammatical system of a language if and only if M is morphologically distinguished in at least one productive paradigm and category. See §4.2 for further illustration of this partial tension between adjacent syncretisms in individual paradigms and predictions for the underlying system.

be much less than, the set of all plurals, and plurals are used for reference less frequently than singulars. As a result, fewer allomorphic distinctions are predicted down each hierarchy, as stated in the declining distinctions prediction of (4.5). Allomorphic combinations of features such as Plur+Masc and Plur+Fem also prefer to be used as frequently as possible, and they should be present or absent across languages in direct proportion to their combinatorial potential for use.

These performance and grammatical data associated with markedness hierarchies illustrate the testing of PGCH hierarchy prediction (1.2b) in §1.2: if there is a preference ranking A>B>C>D among structures of a common type in performance, then there will be a corresponding hierarchy of grammatical conventions (with cut-off points and declining numbers of grammars).

This kind of performance-based approach to markedness can also make sense of 'markedness reversal' phenomena, when for example singularity is more marked than plural for certain classes of collective nouns that occur more frequently in the plural such as 'beans' and 'leaves' (cf. Haspelmath 2002: 244, Croft 1990: 145).[6]

More generally, this approach provides an explanation for the hierarchy rankings themselves, it can motivate what would be unmotivated exceptions from the perspective of an autonomous grammar, and it makes predictions for variation across and within grammars. The effect of the quantitative formal marking prediction in (4.3) is to reduce articulatory effort for the speaker as well as the associated processing of formal units in both production and comprehension, down hierarchies such as (4.1). The morphological inventory prediction (4.4) and the declining distinctions prediction (4.5) reduce the number of conventionalized properties that need to be assigned in production and comprehension down these hierarchies. The hierarchies, in turn, are correlated with frequencies of occurrence, real-world knowledge, discourse accessibility, and with preferred expressiveness. The data summarized here point to an efficient needs-based fine-tuning with respect to processing effort and articulatory effort, exploiting already existing activation levels resulting from such frequencies, etc. (cf. §§3.2.2–3). This explains structural choices in performance and the preferred grammatical patterns across languages.

4.2   Markedness hierarchies in diachrony

The form minimization predictions of (3.13) can be tested on comparative grammars synchronically, as Greenberg (1966) did. They can also be tested

---

[6] For example, in certain nouns in Welsh whose referents are much more frequently plural than singular, like 'leaves' and 'beans', it is the singular form that is morphologically more complex than the plural, e.g. *deilen* ('leaf') v. *dail* ('leaves'), *ffäen* ('bean') v. *ffa* ('beans'); cf. Haspelmath (2002: 244).

on diachronic data. In fact, evolving grammars within a family of related languages provide a particularly subtle test since morphological differences between the dialects are at first quite small and they increase over centuries to fill the variation space that is observable across different genetic groups. It is instructive to consider whether such gradual changes proceed in accordance with (3.13). In this section I shall examine noun phrase morphology in the history of Germanic. This language family has undergone considerable changes in case marking, number marking and gender marking, for which hierarchies (4.1a, b, c) make clear predictions in combination with (3.13). I shall focus here on the morphological inventory prediction (4.4) and the declining distinctions prediction (4.5).

4.2.1 *Morphological inventory predictions*

Consider the first three positions on the case hierarchy (4.1a), Nom > Acc > Dat. The morphological inventory prediction (4.4) predicts that if a language possesses a separate dative case, and hence has at least one set of uniquely dative forms, then it must also possess separate and unique accusative and nominative forms as well, i.e. Nom/Acc/Dat as in Modern German. If this three-case system merges into a two-case system, as happened in the history of English, the case that must go is the lowest one, dative, and this case must merge with the next lowest one, accusative, i.e. Nom/AccDat, resulting in a nominative v. non-nominative (or objective) system.[7]

This follows from the implicational structuring of the hierarchy. Nom/AccDat is compatible with 'if unique Dat, then unique Acc' (there are neither), with 'if unique Acc, then unique Nom' (the consequent holds, but not the antecedent, which is compatible with the truth of an implicational statement), and with 'if unique Dat, then unique Nom' (again the consequent holds, but not the antecedent). There is no instance here of the antecedent being satisfied while the consequent is not, which is what these implications rule out. Hence this two-case system is predicted to be a possible diachronic development out of the three-case Nom/Acc/Dat.

There are two other ways in which this system could have been reduced to two cases, *NomAcc/Dat and *NomDat/Acc, but both are ruled out. *NomAcc/Dat is incompatible with (4.4) because (4.4) requires that a separate dative co-occur with a separate accusative and a separate nominative, and the collapsing of nominative and accusative and the resulting dative/non-dative

---

7 Again these predictions hold at the level of the grammar, cf. fn. 5. To lose a separate dative means that this case is lost in the grammatical system, in the now merged AccDat case. Surface morphological forms of the erstwhile dative case could be preserved meanwhile as the surface expression of this collapsed AccDat, rather than accusative forms, as happened in pronominal forms such as Old English Acc *hine*/Dat *him* which became Modern English AccDat *him*.

opposition offends the prediction 'if unique Dat, then unique Acc and unique Nom'. Similarly, *NomDat/Acc and the resulting accusative v. non-accusative opposition would offend 'if unique Acc, then unique Nom', since nominative and dative are collapsed. It does not offend 'if unique Dat, then unique Acc', since there is no longer a unique dative and hence the antecedent of the implication is not satisfied even though the consequent is (there is a unique accusative). Nor does *NomDat/Acc offend 'if unique Dat, then unique Nom' (by transitivity of implication), since neither the antecedent nor the consequent is now satisfied. But it does violate 'if unique Acc, then unique Nom'.

The only permissible two-case reduction is to Nom/AccDat. The remaining option is for all three cases to be collapsed, which is also permitted by these implications. The full predictions made by (4.4) are summarized in (4.7):

(4.7) Case Hierarchy: Nom > Acc > Dat
       Permitted: Nom/Acc/Dat
                     Nom/AccDat
                     NomAccDat
  Non-permitted: *NomAcc/Dat
                     *NomDat/Acc

In Old English there were separate Nom/Acc/Dat cases, as in German. The reduction to a two-case system in Modern English has, of course, been to the predicted Nom/AccDat. But there are some more subtle aspects of this change that we now see in a new light. The predictions of (4.4) apply at the level of the grammatical system (recall fn. 5), and do not rule out syncretisms such as NomAcc/Dat within individual paradigms and categories. Indeed, syncretisms of all adjacent positions on the case hierarchy, NomAcc/Dat, Nom/AccDat and NomAccDat are attested in the three-case system of Modern German: NomAcc/Dat in e.g. third-person plural pronouns *sie* (3rdPlur-NomAcc) v. *ihnen* (3rdPlur-Dat); Nom/AccDat in e.g. first person plural pronouns *wir* ('we-Nom') v. *uns* ('us-AccDat'); and NomAccDat in many singular nouns, e.g. *Wasser* ('water-NomAccDat'). But as soon as the three-case system was reduced to two cases, the Nom/Acc/Dat system had to change to Nom/AccDat, and this had consequences for those individual paradigms and categories that were syncretized in a way that was at variance with the new system.

Nom/AccDat syncretisms in Old English were already identical in their distribution to the new system and could remain (Old English *wē* ['we-Nom'] v. *ūs* ['us-AccDat'], Modern English *we* v. *us*). But NomAcc/Dat syncretisms like the Old English *hīe* (3rdPlur+NomAcc) v. *him* (3rdPlur+Dat) were incompatible with the new system and had to be reanalyzed. The originally ambiguous *hīe* in Old English could translate both Modern English *they* in *they killed the king's men* and *them* in *the king's men killed them*, but it was reduced to an exclusively nominative interpretation when the system changed. The originally uniquely dative *him* replaced *hīe* in its accusative function, bringing this particular paradigm into line with the new Nom/AccDat system.[8]

The important point here is that this reanalysis is predicted by (4.4) and by the distribution of permitted v. non-permitted case systems shown in (4.7). A NomAcc/Dat syncretism for an individual paradigm cannot coexist within a two-case Nom/AccDat system, because it would provide at least one productive instance of a separate dative, and this is at variance with the systematic collapsing of Acc and Dat. An overall system of the type NomAcc/Dat is impossible for the reasons discussed above. Hence, a separate dative within certain paradigms can exist only within the context of a three-case system, and this reduction in the system forces the reanalysis of NomAcc/Dat syncretisms to Nom/AccDat, by reassigning the accusative from the nominative to the dative.[9]

This discussion of the case hierarchy has made no reference to the fourth productive case in Germanic morphological paradigms, the genitive. The full form of the case hierarchy in (4.1a) is Nom > Acc > Dat > Other, and this suggests that the genitive should be regarded as the lowest case, i.e. Nom > Acc > Dat > Gen. This makes a number of correct predictions, but one has to be careful when analyzing the genitive in Germanic since it is a multi-functional category that is used most frequently as a possession marker within the NP (German *der Hut des Mannes* 'the man's hat'). The case hierarchy of (4.1a), by contrast, refers to arguments of the verb and the cases they assign. Hence the correctness or otherwise of Nom > Acc > Dat > Gen must be established by looking at clause-level arguments only. The prediction to be derived from (4.4) for the genitive is: if at least one uniquely genitive morpheme is assigned by a verb to a verbal argument, then at least one uniquely dative morpheme will be as well; if at least one uniquely dative morpheme is assigned, so is at least one uniquely accusative; etc. This prediction is clearly satisfied in Modern German (*der Mann* [Nom], *den Mann* [Acc], *dem Mann(e)* [Dat], *des Mannes* [Gen]). Similarly the declining distinctions predictions of the next section are compatible with this ranking as well: see fn. 13 below. And it is further supported by the valency data for German verbs cited in fn. 2, in which genitive case assignments by verbs are significantly less frequent than all other case assignments.

---

[8] *Hīe* and *him* were subsequently replaced in Middle English by the Scandinavian and now Modern English forms *they* and *them*.

[9] Another logically possible outcome would have been a completely collapsed NomAccDat.

Similar diachronic predictions are made by (4.4) in relation to the number hierarchy (4.1b), Sing > Plur > Dual. The distinction between singular and plural has been completely productive throughout all stages of Germanic, but separate dual forms are also found in first and second person pronouns in a number of dialects, e.g. Gothic, Old Norse, Modern Icelandic, Old English, Old Saxon, and North Frisian. For example, the Old English first person forms were *ic* [Sing], *wē* [Plur], and *wit* [Dual].

The prediction we make here is that the dual will be the first category to lose its unique and distinctive expression (and the last to develop it in the reverse process of language evolution), and that it will merge with the plural, i.e. we will have Sing/PlurDual, rather than *SingPlur/Dual or *SingDual/Plur. The reasoning is parallel to Nom/AccDat v. *NomAcc/Dat and *NomDat/Acc. Most of the modern Germanic languages do in fact have Sing/PlurDual, and Germanic as a whole exhibits both this permitted two-number system and the three-number system Sing/Plur/Dual.

Greenberg's gender hierarchy (4.1c) Masc > Fem > Neut is actually counter-exemplified in this formulation by the Scandinavian languages that have collapsed masculine and feminine into a common gender opposed to the neuter (e.g. modern Danish *mand-en* 'man-the' and *kon-en* 'woman-the', but *hus-et* 'house-the') and by Dutch, which does the same. A MascFem/Neut system offends the prediction 'if unique neuter, then unique feminine and unique masculine'. In fact, Greenberg's formulation needs to be weakened anyway (and rendered more politically correct!) in order to accommodate languages in which the feminine is the unmarked form.[10] This can be done by collapsing the first two positions, making it compatible with systems in which either the masculine is the highest position, or the feminine is highest, or they are equal:

(4.1′) c. Masc, Fem > Neut (for gender)

Equality can be interpreted here as equal distinctiveness (both genders are distinguished in the grammar, and they have the same amount of allomorphy) or as equal non-distinctiveness, making this hierarchy compatible with the collapsed common gender v. neuter marking of Scandinavian and Dutch.[11]

---

[10] Languages with unmarked feminines include Diyari, and most of the Omotic languages, e.g. Dizi, cf. Corbett (1991: 30). Languages of the Arawá family also have unmarked feminine gender (Dixon 1999: 298).

[11] Both (4.1c) and (4.1′c) are compatible with developments in the Romance languages, in which the neuter was regularly lost and masculine and feminine were preserved (French *le garçon* 'the boy [Masc]', *le bâtiment* 'the building [Masc]', *la fille* 'the girl [Fem]'). In both formulations the neuter is the ultimate antecedent property and feminine and masculine are consequent properties which can exist in the absence of the antecedent.

4.2.2 *Declining distinctions predictions*

Prediction (4.5) refers to the combinations of features that partition categories on a hierarchy. For example, on the number hierarchy (4.1b) singular combines with masculine in German to yield uniquely distinctive Sing+Masc forms (*der Mann* 'the man-NomSgMasc', *er* 'he-NomSgMasc'), but there are no uniquely distinctive Plur+Masc forms. Plural *sie* 'they' is ambiguous between masculine, feminine, and neuter; and *die Männer* 'the men' is not morphologically distinguishable from *die Frauen* 'the women' and *die Häuser* 'the houses', and is recognizably masculine only on the basis of a lexical property of *Mann*, which is, in turn, realized solely on the basis of singular uses. The result of this combinatorial asymmetry is that there is less allomorphic variation in the plural of the definite article, and in plural adjective inflections, noun inflections, and pronouns. Putting this another way, there is less morphological partitioning of the plural, and fewer morphological distinctions are expressed in this number than in the singular.

Prediction (4.5) claims that distinctions should decline down all of these performance-derived hierarchies. In a diachronic context these declines should be respected for each hierarchy at each successive stage of a language. The total number of distinctions made by the grammar can be larger or smaller, and can increase or decrease over time. What should be preserved is the relative asymmetry in numbers of distinctions down the hierarchies. In order to test this we need to do some counting.

Let us begin by illustrating abstractly the richest possible morphological system that could result from the combination of features shown in (4.8). All of these features are found in the early Germanic dialects and most (all but the accusative/dative distinction) are found in all the modern dialects as well.

(4.8) Sing/Plur; Nom/Acc/Dat; Masc/Fem/Neut; and III

	Sing			Plur			
	Masc	Fem	Neut	Masc	Fem	Neut	
Nom	a	d	g	j	m	p	
Acc	b	e	h	k	n	q	18-item system
Dat	c	f	i	l	o	r	

In this diagram each lower-case letter represents a uniquely distinctive morphological form for the relevant feature combination, or a uniquely distinctive syntagmatic sequence of morphological forms (e.g. the definite article *den* in Modern German is unambiguously Sing+Masc+Acc with a singular noun *den Mann*, and unambiguously Plur+Dat with a (dative) plural *den Männern*).

Thus, 'a' has the unique value Sing+Masc+Nom+III, 'b' has the unique value Sing+Masc+Acc+III, etc. The largest number of such unique combinations for this set of features is eighteen. Hence, Germanic languages that distinguish Sing/Plur, Nom/Acc/Dat, and Masc/Fem/Neut in the third person could, in principle, dispose of as many as eighteen feature combinations in their morphological systems (for the noun phrase).

The most conservative dialects, Gothic, Old Norse, and Modern Icelandic, approach this richness, as we shall see. But the distinctiveness of the feature combinations in the other dialects has been substantially reduced. Even when three cases and three genders are preserved, as in Modern German, the number of formal distinctions made is substantially less, as shown in (4.9):

(4.9) Modern Standard German NP system (third person)

	Sing			Plur			
	Masc	Fem	Neut	Masc	Fem	Neut	
Nom	a	d	f	g	g	g	
Acc	b	d	f	g	g	g	8-item system
Dat	c	e	c	h	h	h	

a = der Mann; er
b = den Mann; ihn
c = dem Mann(e); ihm
d = die Frau; sie

e = der Frau; ihr
f = das Haus; es
g = die Männer, Frauen, Häuser; sie
h = den Männern, Frauen, Häusern; ihnen

The shared lower-case letters indicate the systematic collapsing of potentially distinctive combinations that could have been expressed with this feature set, as in (4.8). Modern German makes only eight distinctions in its full NPs and pronouns, some of them unambiguous in their combinatorial product ('a' has the unique value Sing+Masc+Nom+III), others ambiguous ('c' is ambiguous between Sing+Masc+Dat+III and Sing+Neut+Dat+III).

(4.5) makes a prediction for each hierarchy in relation to all the other features with which the ranked categories of that hierarchy can combine. For number we can test it by asking: how many case and gender distinctions are made in the singular v. the plural? The singular makes three case distinctions in (4.9) (Nom/Acc/Dat exemplified by a/b/c), but the plural makes only two (NomAcc/Dat, cf. g/h). The singular makes three gender distinctions (Masc/Fem/Neut, e.g. a/d/f), the plural collapses them into one undifferentiated form (e.g. g). Overall the singular makes six case and gender partitionings (a–f), the plural only two (g and h).

For the case hierarchy (4.1a) we do the same. The nominative makes three gender distinctions (cf. a/d/f), the accusative three (b/d/f), and the dative at most two (c/e). The nominative also makes two number distinctions (e.g. a/g),

TABLE 4.1   Testing the Declining Distinctions predictions on Modern German third person NPs (full NPs and pronouns), cf. (4.9)

Cases distinguished in each number	Genders distinguished in each number	Case and gender partitionings (total)
Sing ≥ Plur 3 2	Sing ≥ Plur 3 1	Sing ≥ Plur 6 2 a/b/c/d/ g/h e/f
Genders distinguished in each case Nom ≥ Acc ≥ Dat 3 3 2	Numbers distinguished in each case Nom ≥ Acc ≥ Dat 2 2 2	Gender and number partitionings (total) Nom ≥ Acc ≥ Dat 4 4 3 a/d/f/g b/d/f/g c/e/h
Cases distinguished in each gender Masc v. Fem ≥ Neut 3 2 2	Numbers distinguished in each gender Masc v. Fem ≥ Neut 2 2 2	Case and number partitionings (total) Masc v. Fem ≥ Neut 5 4 4 a/b/c/ d/e/g/ f/c/g/ g/h h h

the accusative two (e.g. b/g), and the dative two (e.g. c/h). Overall the nominative makes four gender and number partitionings (a/d/f/g), the accusative four (b/d/f/g), and the dative three (c/e/h). For the gender hierarchy (4.1′c) we predict Masc v. Fem ≥ Neut with respect to case and number partitionings. This method applied to the Modern German system of (4.9) is summarized in Table 4.1.[12]

---

[12] The quantification method in Table 4.1 counts both unambiguous and ambiguous feature combinations. Lower-case 'a' is counted as one of the entries for Nom and so is 'g', even though 'a' is unambiguously Nom while 'g' is ambiguous between Nom and Acc. The intuition that this method captures is this: how many forms or form combinations are available in the morphological system of the language that can express nominative case, either unambiguously or ambiguously? One could limit these calculations to feature combinations that are unique to the category whose predicted ranking is being tested on each hierarchy. Thus, 'g' would not be counted for either Nom or Acc in the case hierarchy prediction. This alternative method gives the same relative ranking for (4.9), though with lower absolute scores:

Sing ≥	Plur	Nom ≥	Acc ≥	Dat	Masc v.	Fem ≥	Neut
6	2	1	1	1	2	2	1
a/b/c/d/e/f	g/h	a	b	e	a/b	d/e	f

There is no good theoretical reason for excluding the ambiguous feature combinations in this way, however, and for making a systematic distinction between unambiguous and ambiguous feature combinations with respect to prediction (4.5). What is at issue is the size of the set of distinctions made within the grammar and their relationship to hierarchies such as (4.1) This relationship is tested most straightforwardly, and with less unjustified data exclusion, by the method illustrated in Table 4.1.

The crucial column is the rightmost one. The quantity of morphological partitionings for each higher hierarchy position should always be greater than or equal to each lower position. For Sing ≥ Plur the totals are 6 and 2 respectively, for Nom ≥ Acc ≥ Dat they are 4 and 4 and 3 respectively, and for Masc v. Fem ≥ Neut they are 5 and 4 and 4 respectively. These declining totals are in accordance with (4.5).[13]

We can now conduct a more ambitious test of (4.5) by examining the combinatorial morphological systems found in the other Germanic dialects. In the following diagrams, (4.10)–(4.16), I give the major system types that are attested for third person NPs (including pronouns) in fourteen Germanic dialects. These diagrams have been established using the same criteria that were used for Modern German in (4.9): is there at least one category, or syntagmatic combination of categories, that uniquely distinguishes the feature combination in question?

For each dialect I examined the following: all definite determiner forms; nouns of the *a-*, *ō-*, *i-*, and *n-* declensions (where they are still distinguished); strong adjective inflections; weak adjective inflections; and definite pronouns. If any feature combination was uniquely represented in any one of these paradigms or by paradigms in combination, a separate lower-case letter was assigned. If not, the syncretisms and collapsings at the level of the system were indicated by shared lower-case letters. For example, Gothic quite productively distinguishes Masc/Fem/Neut in the plural, in its definite determiner (*Þái* Nom+Masc+Plur, *Þōs* Nom+Fem+Plur, *Þō* Nom+Neut+Plur), in weak adjectives, strong adjectives, and definite pronouns. The three-way gender distinction in the plural is made only in the nominative and accusative, however. In the dative plural all three genders are regularly collapsed, in the definite determiner (*Þáim*), the definite pronoun (*im*), and strong adjectives (*blindáim*). Weak adjectives do preserve a two-way gender distinction here, however, between MascNeut (*blindam*) and Fem (*blindōm*). Hence, a two-gender distinction in the dative plural exists in the morphological system

---

[13] Notice that if we add the genitive to the case hierarchy, Nom > Acc > Dat > Gen, as discussed in §4.2.1, then the genitive will have equal combinatorial expressiveness to the dative, and less than the accusative and nominative. The genitive collapses masculine and neuter in the singular (*des Mannes* and *des Hauses* v. *der Frau*), just like the dative, and in contrast to the nominative and accusative, which preserve the distinction. The genitive collapses all three genders in the plural (*der Männer, Häuser, Frauen*), like the other cases. The genitive, like the other cases, also makes a Sing/Plur distinction. Hence adding genitive to the case hierarchy would give a total partitioning for that hierarchy of Nom = 4, Acc = 4, Dat = 3, Gen = 3, and the relative quantities for the other hierarchies would remain constant, though with higher absolute numbers on account of the additional genitive cases. This is all in accordance with the declining distinctions prediction.

overall, and will be carried by all Gothic NPs in the syntagmatic sequence Det + Adj$_{wk}$ + N. Proceeding on this basis we arrive at the different Germanic systems shown in (4.10)–(4.16). The forms on the left are in the singular, those on the right in the plural. All forms are third person.[14]

(4.10) Gothic

	Masc	Fem	Neut		Masc	Fem	Neut	
Nom	a	d	g		h	k	n	
Acc	b	e	g		i	l	n	14-item system
Dat	c	f	c		j	m	j	

(4.11) Old Norse, Mod. Icelandic

	Masc	Fem	Neut		Masc	Fem	Neut	
Nom	a	d	g		i	l	m	
Acc	b	e	g		j	l	m	13-item system
Dat	c	f	h		k	k	k	

(4.12) Old High German, Old Saxon, Old English

	Masc	Fem	Neut		Masc	Fem	Neut	
Nom	a	d	g		h	j	k	
Acc	b	e	g		h	j	k	11-item system
Dat	c	f	c		i	i	i	

(4.13) Middle High German

	Masc	Fem	Neut		Masc	Fem	Neut	
Nom	a	d	g		h	h	j	
Acc	b	e	g		h	h	j	10-item system
Dat	c	f	c		i	i	i	

(4.14) New High German (see (4.9))

	Masc	Fem	Neut		Masc	Fem	Neut	
Nom	a	d	f		g	g	g	
Acc	b	d	f		g	g	g	8-item system
Dat	c	e	c		h	h	h	

(4.15) Mid. English, Mod. English, Mod. Danish, Mod. Dutch, North Saxon

	Masc	Fem	Neut		Masc	Fem	Neut	
Nom	a	c	e		f	f	f	
Acc	b	d	e		g	g	g	7-item system
Dat	b	d	e		g	g	g	

[14] For a summary of basic morphological paradigms in these Germanic dialects, see Russ (1990) and König & van der Auwera (1994) and the references cited therein.

(4.16) North Frisian[15]

	Masc	Fem	Neut		Masc	Fem	Neut	
Nom	a	c	e		f	f	f	
Acc	b	d	b		g	g	g	7-item system
Dat	b	d	b		g	g	g	

What is immediately striking about these summaries is that they confirm the intuition behind the declining distinctions prediction. In each system we see lower positions on the hierarchies collapsing distinctions before (or at the same time as) all higher positions. In Gothic the neuter collapses case distinctions before the masculine and feminine, and the dative collapses gender distinctions before the nominative and accusative. Singular and plural have identical partitionings in this system. In Old Norse and Modern Icelandic neuter consistently syncretizes nominative and accusative, while masculine consistently preserves this distinction and the feminine preserves it in the singular. The dative syncretizes all genders in the plural, whereas the nominative and accusative preserve them in both singular and plural. Overall the plural is now considerably more reduced compared to the singular.

As we progress through historical time down to the modern west and north Germanic dialects it is clear that more and more distinctions are being collapsed, but that these collapsings preserve the relative rankings of their respective hierarchy positions: there are always more (or equal) syncretisms in lower positions. We can test this impression precisely by quantifying the number of partitionings down each hierarchy within each system, as we did for Modern German in Table 4.1. This is done in Table 4.2. For each hierarchy, each quantity on the left should be greater than, or equal to, each quantity on the right. It can be seen that all the predictions are correct.

I conclude that the explanatory forces that underlie Minimize Forms (3.8) operate at successive historical stages in closely related languages. In particular,

---

[15] The distribution of morphological forms in the North Frisian dialects is more complex than in New High German (4.14) and in English (4.15). For the Mooring dialect of Bökingharde, Walker (1990: 17) lists a uniquely distinctive Sing+Nom+Neut pronoun *hat* ('it'), i.e. 'e' in (4.16), distinct from Sing+Nom+Masc *hi* ('he') and Sing+Nom+Fem *jü* ('she'), 'a' and 'c' respectively. But Mooring, in contrast to English *it*, collapses the accusative and dative masculine singular *ham* with the neuter, and hence this form, i.e. 'b', covers all of Sing+Acc+Masc, Sing+Dat+Masc, Sing+Acc+Neut and Sing+Dat+Neut. In addition, Mooring has case-neutral Sing+Neut forms *dåt* and *et*, which co-exist in the nominative with *hat* and in the accusative and dative with *ham*, but do not add any uniquely distinctive feature combinations of their own. In the plural Mooring has a gender-neutral and also case-neutral *ja*, i.e. 'f' (corresponding to both *they* and *them* in English) as well as *jam* for accusative and dative uses only, i.e. 'g' (corresponding just to *them*). The *ja* form is the sole bearer of the Plur+Nom combination, and *jam* is uniquely non-nominative. Mooring has more pronominal forms than both English and German, but it is still a 7-item system like English. The pronominal forms of Modern English, *he/him/she/her/it/they/them*, are the exclusive carriers of the seven distinctions a/b/c/d/e/f/g respectively. The seven forms of Modern German, *er/ihn/ihm/sie/ihr/es/ihnen*, are distributed as shown in (4.9) in the main text. Mooring has 9 forms in all, *hi/ham/jü/har/hat/dåt/et/ja/jam*, with the values a/b/c/d/e/b&e/b&e/f&g/g/ respectively.

TABLE 4.2　Testing the Declining Distinctions predictions on Germanic third person NPs (full NPs and pronouns), cf. (4.10)–(4.16)

	Case and gender partitionings (total) in each number Sing ≥ Plur		Gender and number partitionings (total) in each case Nom ≥ Acc ≥ Dat			Case and number partitionings (total) in each gender Masc v. Fem ≥ Neut		
Gothic (4.10)	7	7	6	6	4	6	6	4
Old Norse etc. (4.11)	8	5	6	6	4	6	5	4
OHG etc. (4.12)	7	4	6	6	3	5	5	4
MHG (4.13)	7	3	5	5	3	5	5	4
NHG (4.14)	6	2	4	4	3	5	4	4
Mid. Eng. etc. (4.15)	5	2	4	[4	4]	4	4	3
North Frisian (4.16)	5	2	4	[3	3]	4	4	4

the progressive loss of feature combinations in these morphological systems is highly correlated with frequency of use. Psycholinguistic experiments have confirmed the reality of frequency sensitivities in lexical access and in ambiguity resolutions on-line (cf. e.g. MacDonald et al. 1994). It is therefore plausible to assume that performance preferences operate at each historical stage and exert a selective pressure in favor of the retention or loss of certain distinctions. If the dative plural is far less frequent than the dative singular and than other cases, as it is, then each gender-distinctive dative plural would be less frequent still and the performance pressure in favor of its retention, by the morphologization principle (4.6), would be much less than it is for a gender-distinctive nominative and accusative singular. The progressive syncretisms visible in (4.10)–(4.16) and in Tables 4.1 and 4.2 support this performance-driven approach to morphological restructuring. The ultimate reasons for these performance frequency asymmetries can be quite diverse, as I pointed out in §4.1. What is significant in this context is simply their existence and the fact that native speakers are unconsciously aware of them. It is this awareness, I believe, that ultimately underlies the kinds of historical changes we have seen in this chapter. Current grammatical models of morphology do not have a good explanation for them, precisely because they are performance-driven.

4.3　Grammaticalization and processing

The term 'grammaticalization' was first introduced by Meillet (1912), and refers to the diachronic progression from a lexical item to a grammatical form or from one grammatical form to another. Examples are future *will* in English, which developed out of a corresponding verb meaning 'want' (cf. German *will* '(he/she) wants'), and the English definite article *the*, which emerged from a demonstrative. There has been much research into grammaticalization phenomena in different languages in recent years, whose fruits are summarized in e.g. Heine & Reh (1984), Traugott & Heine (1991), Hopper & Traugott (1993), Christian Lehmann (1995), Heine & Kuteva (2002), and in historical linguistics textbooks such as Campbell (1998).

Grammaticalization has been described as a 'weakening' in both form and meaning. Heine & Reh (1984: 15) define it as 'an evolution whereby linguistic units lose in semantic complexity, pragmatic significance, syntactic freedom, and phonetic substance'. With respect to form, grammaticalization does very often result in a reduction in phonological units and/or in morphological and syntactic structure, for example when independent words lose certain sounds and become cliticized or affixed. This is exemplified by English *will*, which can attach to a preceding subject, *I'll*, *he'll*, etc., and which loses its first two phonemes when it does so. Similarly *the* is phonologically reduced compared with *that* and *this*, etc., both in segments and in stress, and *a(n)* is reduced compared with the numeral *one* from which it developed.

As for the properties that are assigned to grammaticalized forms, they always play a productive role in the grammars of the relevant languages. *Will* joins the system of finiteness marking in English syntax and the tense system of English semantics. The definite article becomes an important part of noun phrase (or determiner phrase—see Abney 1987) syntax and semantics. The precise relationship between the 'donor' or source property P1 and the grammaticalized property P2 can vary, but there is always some natural and plausible link between P1 and P2 such that the one can merge gradually into the other over time. One's wishes and wants generally relate to the future, so future tense is a plausible semantic extension from wishing and wanting. The definite article also emerges via gradual and plausible stages from a demonstrative, as we shall see in §4.4. In fact, most of the research on grammaticalization has been devoted to these P1 → P2 pathways or 'clines' and to a linguistic analysis of the different relations between P1 and P2 and the types of semantic and syntactic changes that they exemplify (see Traugott & König 1991 for summary and discussion).

But there is also a performance and processing aspect to grammaticalization. Campbell (1998: 239–40) summarizes thirty grammaticalization clines, and in all of them the P2 property appears to be more productive in the grammars containing them than P1, with the result that F2 : P2 forms will be used more frequently than F1 : P1.[16] This is straightforwardly the case when a grammatical

---

[16] For the benefit of readers who are less familiar with the grammaticalization literature, the first 10 grammaticalization clines summarized by Campbell (1998: 239–40) are: (1) auxiliary < main verb; (2) case suffixes < postpositions; (3) case-marking < serial verbs; (4) causatives < causal verb;

form develops out of a lexical one, e.g. when the verb 'give' provides the source for a dative case marker, since the lexical semantics of 'give' limits its applicability to a narrower range of sentences than does the corresponding syntax and semantics of dative case. But there appear to be regular expansions as well when one grammatical form (e.g. a demonstrative) gives rise to another (*the*).[17] This means that grammaticalization becomes relevant to the form minimization predictions of (3.8) and (3.13).

Greater frequency of use predicts reductions of form in grammaticalized F2 : P2 pairs. This is not something that is unique to grammaticalization: it follows from MiF and from the general principle of least effort that motivates it. Moreover, the greater productivity and frequency of F2 : P2 is in accordance with the generalization captured in (3.13b) to the effect that form–property pairings are preferred in proportion to their potential for use. These regular grammaticalization clines are conventionalizing more frequently usable, not less frequently usable, and more preferred properties at successive historical stages.

There are actually three issues and questions that are raised by the grammaticalization literature when viewed from a processing perspective, and I believe that processing can contribute to their resolution.

First, why do we find *both* reductions in form *and* expansions in F2 : P2 usage relative to F1 : P1? Why not just P2 expansions without the formal reductions? Why aren't there *increases* in form co-occurring with property expansions? MiF and (3.13a) provide a general answer.

Second, can we predict, and limit, the set of regular grammaticalization clines that we will find evidence for in language history? The performance generalization which appears to be consistent with the literature is that the changes must result in an *increase* in frequency of usage. You cannot have P1 being more preferred and more frequent than P2 when P1 $\rightarrow$ P2. This generalization follows from (3.13b), since if universal diachronic changes were in the direction of less frequent and less preferred properties, or were indifferent to frequency and preference, then we would not see the kinds of priorities in favor of high frequency and preferred properties that we do see in cross-linguistic universals like the markedness hierarchies of §4.1. It remains to be seen whether this increasing frequency prediction is always correct. It also remains to be seen

(5) complementizer/subordinate conjunction < 'say'; (6) coordinate conjunction ('and') < 'with'; (7) copula ('to be') < positional verbs 'stand', 'sit' or 'give', 'exist'; (8) dative case marker < 'give'; (9) definite article < demonstrative pronoun; (10) direct object case markers < locatives or prepositions.

[17] English frequency counts such as Francis & Kučera (1982) show that the definite article is more frequently used than demonstrative determiners. Frequency data for P1 and P2 properties need to be collected from a range of languages for the other grammaticalization clines in order to test the relative frequency prediction made here.

whether the set of grammaticalization clines currently proposed in the literature is well defined. Some grammatical forms will lose in productivity as others gain. If a definite article develops out of a demonstrative, other forms of definiteness marking in a language may decline and the demonstrative determiners that overlap in usage with the definite article will also decline. The point about grammaticalization pathways is that they have the status of diachronic universals and laws, which should hold regardless of language type and regardless of the idiosyncrasies of particular languages. The processing approach advocated here incorporates a hypothesis for constraining these universals of change.

There is a third puzzle about grammaticalization that has not received the attention it deserves. Why is it that grammaticalization clines are set in motion in some languages and not in others, or set in motion at some stage of a language and not at another? Why or when does *want* get recruited for a future tense marker, if at all? Why or when does *give* become a dative marker, or a demonstrative a definite article, again if at all? The intuition that underlies discussions of this point, when they are discussed, is that there is some structural pressure or need for the relevant grammatical category (F2 : P2) and that this motivates its expansion out of an earlier F1 : P1. It is difficult to give precision and content to this claim. But a processing approach to grammar can clarify some of the intuitions here and come up with new generalizations that help us explain these expanding P1 → P2 properties. We need to look at the semantics/pragmatics and at the syntax of each historical stage, and we need to consider how the relevant properties are processed, in order to formulate these generalizations.

In the next section I illustrate these three potential advantages of a processing approach to grammaticalization with a brief case study.

4.4   The grammaticalization of definiteness marking

The definite article, in languages that have one, is almost always descended from a demonstrative morpheme with deictic meaning (C. Lyons 1999: 331), and specifically from a demonstrative determiner (Diessel 1999*a*, *b*). The precise nature of this deictic meaning is discussed at length in J. Lyons (1977: vol. ii) and can be roughly paraphrased as follows: *that book = the book (which is) there; this book = the book (which is) here* (p. 646). Anderson & Keenan (1985) survey demonstrative systems in a broad range of languages, and point out that they almost always involve a deictic contrast between at least two locations defined either with respect to the speaker alone or with respect to the speaker and the hearer. Their meaning involves a restrictive modification of a pragmatic nature that identifies which referent of the head noun is intended, and it is this restriction that is made explicit in John Lyons's paraphrases. The deictic restriction identifies the referent for the hearer by indicating that it exists and is unique within the appropriate subset of entities in the visible situation or previous discourse. By searching in this subset, the hearer can access it.

What we see in the evolution of definite determiners out of demonstratives, and in their further syntacticization, is a set of changes that are directly relevant for the three points raised in §4.3.

First, definite articles involve either less or equal formal marking compared with demonstrative determiners, not more: in English *the* has fewer and more reduced segments (CV rather than CVC, and a schwa vowel) and less stress. There are languages in which the erstwhile demonstrative and definite forms have evolved further into cliticized NP particles compatible with indefiniteness as well as definiteness (e.g. Tongan *e*, Broschart 1997, and Maori *te*, Bauer 1993). Such items have also been reconstructed as the source of affixal agreement markers on adjectives (in Lithuanian, C. Lyons 1999: 83), as the source of noun class markers (in Bantu, Greenberg 1978), gender markers (in Chadic, Schuh 1983), and gender and case markers (in Albanian, C. Lyons 1999: 71). Formal reduction and loss of syntactic and morphological independence go hand in hand here with increasing grammaticalization.

Second, the properties associated with later forms in this cline involve a gradual expansion in the set of NPs that are compatible with the erstwhile demonstrative marking. Definite articles have semantic/pragmatic and syntactic properties that permit their attachment to more NPs than do demonstrative determiners and are used more frequently. Expansion to indefiniteness, as in Polynesian, permits more attachments still and even greater frequency of usage. Further syntacticization as agreement, noun class, gender markers, etc. permits usage of the relevant cliticized or affixal forms regardless of their original semantic/pragmatic properties. We can hypothesize that these final stages of grammaticalization will also be accompanied by increasing frequency of usage, until the cycle is complete. They can then be removed from the language altogether, as the reverse process of morphological reduction and syncretism sets in of the kind we have witnessed in the once richly inflected Indo-European. As this happens, new grammaticalization clines are set in motion, such as demonstrative → definite article in the recorded Germanic and Romance languages.

Third, a processing approach to these historical expansions leads to new hypotheses about why these originally demonstrative forms should be recruited for property extensions. It has been commonplace to focus on the expanded semantics and pragmatics of the definite article compared with the demonstrative (e.g. Hodler 1954). But this is a consequence, as I see it, not a cause of the grammaticalization. There is no compelling semantic/pragmatic reason why the definite article should emerge out of a demonstrative to express meanings that are perfectly expressible in languages without definite articles. But there are some compelling reasons, involving the processing of grammar, that can motivate an expansion of the determiner category, and that can motivate it in language types and at historical stages at which it appears to happen. And these reasons can also make sense of a number of properties in the grammar of definiteness that would otherwise be mysterious.

4.4.1   *Semantic/pragmatic extensions*

The typology of definiteness marking across languages (C. Lyons 1999) and the history of the evolution of the definite article in well-described Germanic languages (Heinrichs 1954, Hodler 1954) give a converging picture of the gradual semantic/pragmatic progression in the evolution of definite determiners. Using the theory of definiteness presented in Hawkins (1978, 1991) I would identify the major stages as follows.[18]

Stage 1. The deictic restriction is abandoned, and with it the explicit or implicit contrast between entities near the speaker and far from the speaker. As a result the identifiability of referents is now defined relative to the whole (visible) situation or the whole previous text (within memory), and uniqueness (more generally, inclusive reference—see Hawkins 1978) within these parameters is what makes identifiability possible. *The book* succeeds as an appropriate definite NP when there are no other books in the visible situation or in the previous text.[19] At this initial stage the definite article is limited to anaphoric references to the previous text and/or to objects existing in the immediate situation of utterance. Examples are the 'anaphoric' articles of early Germanic, such as Gothic *sa* (Hodler 1954), the Lakhota *k'u* article (C. Lyons 1999: 54, Buechel 1939), and Hausa *din* (C. Lyons 1999: 53, Jagger 1985). North Frisian *D*

---

[18] A convenient summary of the major ideas in Hawkins (1978, 1991) that are relevant for this section can be found in C. Lyons (1999: 3–13) and in Haspelmath (1999*b*). The semantic/pragmatic part of Hawkins (1978, 1991) is essentially a synthesis of the appropriateness conditions for definiteness, as presented in Christophersen (1939), with Russell's (1905) theory of definite descriptions and its existence, uniqueness, and predication semantics (*the present king of France is bald* asserts existence (there is a present king of France), uniqueness (there is only one present king of France), and a predication (this individual is bald)). Hawkins (1991) recasts the 1978 theory in neo-Gricean terms, following Levinson (1983) and Sperber & Wilson (1986).

[19] There are some appropriate uses of singular definites (e.g. *pass me the spanner, close the door*) in which uniqueness is not always required: see C. Lyons (1999: 14) and Birner & Ward (1994). This is generally because it is either irrelevant which (spanner) is selected or because uniqueness is provided by a 'processing enrichment' from context (there is only one door that is open), cf. §3.2.3.

is basically at Stage 1, with some incipient movement to Stage 2 (C. Lyons 1999: 162–5, Ebert 1971*a*, *b*).

Stage 2. The pragmatic sets ('P-sets' in Hawkins 1991) within which unique-ness/inclusiveness of definite reference can be defined now expand from visible (*mind the step*) to non-visible and larger situations (*the king has abdicated*), and from anaphoric references based on previous mention (*a house : the house*) to general-knowledge-based inferences and stereotypic 'frames' (*a house : the door*)—cf. Minsky (1975), Clark & Marshall (1981). The definite article covers a broader range of P-sets at this stage, including the original visible situation and previous discourse sets. The Hausa definite suffix -*n* is an early Stage 2 article with considerable optionality of occurrence and with a clear sensitivity to degree of accessibility of the referent (C. Lyons 1999: 52–3, Jagger 1985). The Old High German definite article also expands step by step from more to less accessible P-sets and inferences (Hodler 1954).

Stage 3. NPs with the definite article extend their usage possibilities to generic references that signal inclusiveness only, with little or no pragmatic delimitation (*the lion is a mammal, the Italians eat pizza*). The level of access-ibility that is required at the end of Stage 2 has become so weak that it can be abandoned and the definite article can be used with semantic and truth-conditional content only. At the same time, pragmatic conditions of appropriateness still apply to NPs that are not used generically, and hearers must disambiguate between generic and non-generic, find the intended P-set when this is required, and assign a pragmatically unrestricted inclusive inter-pretation when it is not. The middle and modern periods of the Germanic languages exemplify this stage (Hodler 1954). German has gone further than English and regularly uses the definite article with generic plurals where Eng-lish does not: *er zieht den Rosen die Nelken vor* (he prefers Def+Dat+Pl roses Def+Acc+Pl carnations) 'he prefers carnations to roses'. He prefers *the carna-tions* to *the roses* in English suggests pragmatically identifiable sets of each. Both languages have a productive definite singular generic. French has also extended its generic plural usage further than English (C. Lyons 1999: 51): *elle adore les romans policiers* (she adores DEF novels detective) 'she adores detective stories'.

Stage 4. NPs with the definite article are extended to specific indefinite ref-erences in addition to definiteness. We can account for this by saying that the definite article has abandoned uniqueness/inclusiveness, in certain uses, while maintaining the existence claim. The range of possible uses is now very large, spanning pragmatically identifiable references at one end, inclusive and generic references, and purely existential claims at the other. Polynesian lan-guages exemplify this stage, e.g. *e* in Tongan (Broschart 1997) and *te* in Maori (Bauer 1993).

We can summarize this progression as follows. Stage 1 abandons the implicit deictic contrast between degrees of proximity to the speaker and/or hearer and defines uniqueness/inclusiveness relative to some whole P-set, primarily the visible situation or previous discourse set shared by the interlocutors. Stage 2 abandons this limitation to highly accessible P-sets and generalizes the pragmatic parameters of existence and uniqueness/inclusiveness, i.e. more P-sets. Stage 3 abandons pragmatic delimitation altogether and permits NPs to simply refer inclusively, i.e. universally and generically. And Stage 4 abandons inclusiveness and permits NPs to simply assert existence. Each stage maintains the usage possibilities of the previous one and introduces more ambiguity and polysemy, but expands the grammatical environments and the frequency of usage of the definite article. There are then further extensions still as the definite/indefinite particle is recruited for purely syntactic purposes, agreement and noun class marker, etc., and eventually loses all connection to definiteness and indefiniteness. In order to understand these extensions we will need to examine more formal and syntactic aspects of definiteness, and their processing.

Meanwhile the definite article may be omitted throughout Stages 1–4 from NPs that are inherently definite, such as proper names, and from NPs with possessives. Haspelmath (1999*b*) attributes the absence of definiteness marking here to 'economy', following Haiman (1983, 1985). In the present context I would derive this Haspelmath–Haiman generalization from MiF (3.8). Proper names are inherently definite, and possessed NPs are generally definite.[20] Hence definiteness meaning is a readily inferable processing enrichment (§3.2.3), which motivates its expression by zero (cf. (3.13a)), for the same reason that zero forms are widespread in the high positions of markedness hierarchies (§4.1). Zero marking at the early stages of definite article expansion accordingly covers both intrinsically or regularly definite NPs, and NPs that can be *either* definite *or* indefinite semantically/pragmatically and to which the definite article has not yet expanded.

4.4.2   *Syntactic extensions*

As the definite article expands its semantic and pragmatic range, more NPs can and do contain a definite article in performance. At the same time the definite article becomes more productive in the syntactic rules of the grammar. It may be generated in combination with certain head noun types, like proper names, or with certain modifiers like adjectives and relative clauses, with which it could

---

[20] See Haspelmath's (1999*b*) text counts from different languages for justification of the claim that possessed NPs are generally definite.

not co-occur in earlier stages of the language. In the 'determiner phrase' (DP) theory of Abney (1987), an expanding number of DP types will be generated with an overt determiner head. In the theory assumed here I will keep the traditional NP analysis, for reasons discussed in Hawkins (1993, 1994: 352–3, 403–6). Within an associated syntactic parser or processor, the expanding definite article joins the set of categories that can 'construct' or 'project to' NP (cf. §5.1.1), i.e. N, pronouns, other determiners, even inflected adjectives (cf. Hawkins 1993, 1994). These syntactic categories are generally uniquely dominated by NP, not by VP, PP, or AdjP, etc., and they can act as unambiguous signals, in both comprehension and production models, to construct it. In the early Germanic languages this NP was also richly case-marked (cf. §4.2.2). One syntactic processing function of the expanding definite article can be defined as NP Construction, therefore:

(4.17) *NP Construction*
        The definite article constructs a (case-marked) NP.

Increased definite article usage means greater activation of NP Construction in performance. The expanding semantic and pragmatic uses have a syntactic processing correlate, therefore, and this correlate, in the form of (4.17), incorporates a prediction. Nouns can always construct NP, with or without accompanying sisters. If we assume that the definite article also constructs NP, then it should be possible to find NPs with definite articles and without nouns. We do not expect to find NPs consisting of a definite article alone, on account of the second processing principle to be presented in (4.18) below, but we do predict a possible complementarity between definite articles and nouns, given that both can construct the same mother phrase, NP.[21]

Notice that English permits omission of nouns with restrictive adjectives plus the definite article, *the rich, the poor, the good, the bad*, etc. Spanish (C. Lyons 1999: 60) has expanded this option (cf. *lo difícil* 'the difficult thing') to other categories such as the infinitival VP in *el hacer esto fue fácil* (DEF to-do this was easy) 'doing this was easy'. Malagasy has expanded it to locative adverbs, as in *ny eto* (DEF here), meaning 'the one(s) who is/are here' (Anderson & Keenan 1985: 294). There are numerous languages in which the definite article signals a nominalization of some kind, as in Lakhota *ktepi kį wąyake* (kill DEF he-saw) 'he saw the killing' (C. Lyons 1999: 60), or in which it constructs

---

[21] In Hawkins (1993, 1994: 379) I formulated an Axiom of Constructability which requires that a phrase, e.g. NP, must always be recognizable on the basis of at least one uniquely constructing category dominated by NP. This axiom explicitly allows for a possible plurality of constructors, and this contrasts with the bi-uniqueness between a projecting daughter and its mother that is assumed in most current theories of phrase structure. The functional equivalence of Def and N therefore leads us to expect NPs with np{N}, with np{Def, N}, and with np{Def, X} where X ≠ N.

a subordinate clause in a noun phrase position, e.g. as subject or object, for example in Huixtan Tzotzil and Quileute (C. Lyons 1999: 60–61).

The precise values of X (X $\neq$ N) within np{Def, X} can vary in these different languages, i.e. there are different grammatical conventions for the precise set of NPs within which the definite article does the constructing of NP. But the very possibility and cross-linguistic productivity of omitting the noun and of still having the phrase recognized as NP, in so-called 'nominalizations' and other structures in which the definite article combines with a variety of categories, follows from (4.17).

There is a related set of phenomena in languages whose lexical items are highly ambiguous with regard to syntactic category, even for the major parts of speech like noun and verb. Such languages seem to require immediate disambiguation of noun and verb, by a functional particle adjacent or proximate to the ambiguous category, on the basis of which the intended category can be recognized by a dependency assignment (as defined in (2.3) of §2.2). The Polynesian languages are often discussed in this context (see e.g. Broschart 1997). Disambiguating particles appear to play a crucial role in Cayuga as well (Sasse 1988).

It is no accident, as I see it, that one of the major disambiguators in Polynesian is the expanded definite/indefinite article. Tongan *e* and Maori *te* have become general NP constructors and in the process they convert ambiguous predicates into nouns within the NP constructed. Other (tense and aspect) particles construct a clause (IP) or VP and convert ambiguous lexical predicates into verbs (cf. Broschart 1997). English also has a large number of words that are ambiguous between noun and verb, and there are many minimal pairs such as *they want to run/the run* and *to film/the film is fun*. The article constructs NP here and disambiguates between N and V.

The general prediction we make for cross-linguistic variation is that the amount of noun/verb ambiguity in the lexicon should be correlated with more extensive and obligatory use of the definite article or of other NP-constructing particles.[22] We have a potential motivation here for the expanded grammaticalization of the definite article in Polynesian. We also have a further motive for its retention in English, beyond the reason for its original expansion that I shall argue for below.

---

[22] It should be possible to test this prediction for cross-linguistic variation by quantifying numbers of lexical items that are category-ambiguous within the lexicon of a language (or within a subset), numbers of syntactic environments that require the definite article or other NP constructors, and corpus frequencies for these, in a sample of languages on the continuum from highly ambiguous to highly unambiguous lexical categories. The more lexical ambiguity, the more syntactic environments and higher frequencies are predicted for the articles.

There is a further prediction that can be made. On-line processing efficiency (cf. MaOP (3.16) and §3.3) is improved when the definite article or other NP-constructor precedes the lexically ambiguous predicate. If it follows, syntactic category status will be indeterminate at the time the predicate is recognized, and this will delay important aspects of both syntactic and semantic interpretation. When the phrasal constructor and disambiguator precedes, as in English *the run* v. *to run*, and as in Polynesian, then all these components of word grammar can be assembled immediately upon recognition of the word.[23]

Christopher Lyons (1999: 64) points out that 'there is a strong tendency for the definite article, if a free form, to occur initially in the noun phrase, independently of a language's general constituent-order pattern', and cites examples such as Lakhota *wowapi waste kį* (book good DEF) 'the good book' as very much the exception. The majority of languages with phrasal clitic articles that he discusses (pp. 72–9) also prefer attachment to a left-peripheral category, namely Kwakw'ala, Nootka, Amharic, Bulgarian, Rumanian and Albanian; only Basque prefers the right periphery.

There is a second processing function of the definite article:

(4.18) *NP Attachment*
The definite article attaches specified categories to the (case-marked) NP that it constructs.

An NP constructed by the definite article is a 'Construction Domain' (Hawkins 1994: 355) within which co-occurrence requirements and options can be defined, as is usual for other constructing (and 'head'-like) categories (Hawkins 1993, 1994: §6). A category C that constructs a higher phrase P can require the attachment of other categories to P precisely because the existence of P as an attachment site is always guaranteed by the occurrence of C.

This attachment function of the definite article is fundamental to an understanding of numerous grammatical properties that go beyond NP construction itself. It explains interesting parallels between the definite article and other phrasal combining devices such as the 'nominalizing' particles *de* in Mandarin, *ge* in Cantonese, and *ve* in Lahu (C. Lehmann 1984: 61–2, Li & Thompson 1981, Matthews & Yip 1994, Hawkins 1994: 388–9). These parallels extend to the ligatures of Austronesian (Foley 1980), and to agreement phenomena in dependent- and head-marked languages (Nichols 1986). These devices all signal attachment of constituents to a common mother phrase, and there are cross-linguistic patterns that reflect the degree of functional motivation for

---

[23] For evidence supporting the immediacy of lexical access and processing, see Marslen-Wilson (1989) and Tyler (1989).

signaling the attachment.[24] The particular attachment functions of the definite article appear to be diachronic expansions of its earlier demonstrative meaning, which is equivalent to a restrictive relative clause or adjective with deictic content modifying a noun (*that book* = *the book (which is) there*). This content expands first to include any kind of restrictive modifier plus noun, then restrictive or appositive modifiers, and eventually NPs with a variety of co-occurring categories other than N, as in the 'nominalizing' and other examples above.

It is because of (4.18) that definite articles are especially productive in NPs containing adjectives and relative clauses whose attachment to NP is not guaranteed by their own projection properties (an adjective is the head of an adjective phrase, not of an NP, etc.). Thus, when there are proper name heads of NP in English an accompanying restrictive relative or adjective takes a definite article, *the Mary that you know, the clever Mary*. Proper names alone generally do not in English, *Mary*, and nor do appositive relatives and adjectives, *Mary(,) who you know, clever Mary*. In German, by contrast, restrictively modified names take the definite article, and so can appositively modified names (*die kluge Maria* 'clever Mary'). Other modifiers of N also trigger an obligatory definite article in English. 'Predicational' modifiers such as *the color azure* (azure is a color) and *the name Algernon* (Algernon is a name) are ungrammatical without *the*: **(a) color azure, *a name Algernon*. So are many 'NP complement clauses' such as *the (*a) fact that Alzheimer's is an age-linked dementia* (Hawkins 1978, 1991).

Himmelmann (1998) discusses numerous prepositional phrases in Rumanian and Albanian in which the NP sister to P omits the (affixed) definite article when the NP contains N alone but keeps it when the noun is modified by an additional category such as an adjective or relative clause. Compare Rumanian *intrat în casă* (entered in house) 'entered the house' and *intrat în case mare* (entered in house-DEF big) 'entered the big house' (Mallinson 1986: 55). Some languages have special definite determiners that perform a 'cataphoric' function with relative clauses, e.g. English plural *those* in *those students that pass the exam* (will receive a diploma) and German *diejenigen* in *diejenigen*

---

[24] For example, the nominalizing particles of Mandarin (*de*) and Cantonese (*ge*), which serve to attach many adjectives, relative clauses, and possessive phrases to N within NP, exhibit a clear sensitivity to the strength of the bond between modifier and head. Matthews & Yip (1994: 159) point out that *ge* is omitted from adjective–noun pairs when the adjective denotes an inherent characteristic of the noun, e.g. *baahk jáu* ('white wine'). Definite articles are also frequently omitted when the strength of the bond itself can signal the attachment. Adjectives with a strong inherent link to the noun in Swedish, for example, can omit the preposed definite article, which can be argued to signal attachment in advance, e.g. *vita hus-et* (white house-DEF) 'the White House'. Adjectives with a less inherent link to a following noun require the preposed article, e.g. *det pigga murmeldjur-et* (DEF alert marmot-DEF) 'the alert marmot' (Börjars 1994).

Studenten, die das Examen bestehen (DEF students RELPRO DEF exam pass)
'those students who pass the exam'. North Frisian uses its (more restricted
and more deictic) D-article as opposed to the (more general and more genuinely definite) A-article (Ebert 1971*a*, *b*) for this purpose: *det buk, wat hi tuiast
skrewen hee, dochts niks* (DEF book RELPRO he first written has is worthless)
'the book that he wrote first is worthless'. Early definite articles are used very
productively in this cataphoric or determinative function, according to Diessel
(1999*a*, *b*), and (4.18) provides a reason why.

In a number of languages the attachment is signaled within the modifier
itself by an affix or particle that either continues to function or used to function as a definite article. The agreement affixes on Albanian adjectives are
derived historically from the definite article (C. Lyons 1999: 79): *i mir-i djalë*
(DEF good-AGR boy) 'the good boy'. The Baltic languages Lithuanian and
Latvian have definite adjective declensions that are the result of an affixed
demonstrative stem with 'j', and the South Slavic languages Serbo-Croat and
Slovenian show relics of a system of similar origin (C. Lyons 1999: 82–4). Arabic
has a definite prefix on adjectives in definite NPs: *al-bustān-u l-kabīr-u* (DEF-
garden-NOM DEF-big-NOM) 'the big garden' (C. Lyons 1999: 91). In Tigre
a prenominal adjective modifier is marked with *la*, as are relative clauses e.g.
la-tənaddeqq-a bet (RELV-you.build-FEM house) 'the house that you build',
and this *la* is identical to the definite article clitic that attaches to nouns, *la-bāb*
(DEF-gate); see Tosco (1998) for extensive discussion.

Modern Greek presents us with some minimal pairs that shed light on this
attachment function of the definite article. Normally the adjective precedes the
noun in Greek and when the NP is definite the definite article occurs only once
and in leftmost position. But the adjective can also follow, and when it does so
a second definite article is required in order to signal co-constituency within
the NP, as in the following example from Joseph & Philippaki-Warburton
(1987: 51):

(4.19) Mu   arésun   i   fústes   i   kondés (Greek)
       Me-GEN please-3PL DEF skirts-FEM+PL DEF short-FEM+PL
       'I like the short skirts.'

If the second article is absent (*i fústes kondés*) the interpretation is that of a
secondary predication, i.e. 'I like skirts to be short', in which *kondés* is not
NP-attached.

The explanatory question that all of this raises is: why should the definite
article be recruited for more and more NPs in performance and grammar
and gradually jettison the semantic-pragmatic conditions of its deictic source?

I believe that the processing of grammar is in the driving seat and that it motivates this gradual bleaching of definite article meaning. There is no compelling semantic reason for why the definite article should expand to generic NPs and indefinites, when there are expressive alternatives for these meanings and when the result is considerable polysemy requiring disambiguation and enrichment. But there are compelling processing reasons for recruiting more definite articles into languages in which expanded NP construction is functionally motivated, e.g. those with ambiguous lexical categories or with regular noun omissions and nominalizations. Structures in which the explicit signaling of NP attachment is advantageous, as in (4.19), also motivate more definite articles.

These processing principles incorporate testable predictions for the language types and historical stages at which grammaticalized definiteness marking will emerge or expand (see fn. 22). I have argued (Hawkins 1994: 405) that the emergence and expansion of the definite article in early Germanic, and its further expansion in Modern German compared with Modern English, can be explained in terms of processing. There is an interesting asymmetry in German inflectional marking within NPs, which seems quite arbitrary from a purely grammatical perspective but which makes sense in processing terms. In the sequence np[Det Adj N X] determiners are the most differentiated categories with respect to on-line case assignment to NP, adjectives next, nouns least, and postnominal X categories not at all.[25] The form of the determiner permits case to be assigned to the NP, either on its own (in conjunction with default preferences for nominative over accusative or for agent over patient, etc.—cf. §8.2.2) or in combination with a typically immediately following adjective or noun. When a determiner is absent, np[Adj N X], adjectives have distinctive 'strong' inflection and they take on this primary case-assignment function—cf. Hawkins (1986). Nouns have least differentiation for case, and postnominal categories have none (a relative pronoun within a relative clause takes the case of the position relativized on, not the case that is appropriate for the mother of the head noun). The determiner is not only the first constructor of NP in on-line processing, it is the primary case assigner. NP construction and case assignment are therefore generally simultaneous (and most on-line assignments are ultimately correct in conjunction with performance defaults). When the NP consists of a pronoun, np[Pro], case can again be assigned simultaneously with NP construction, on account of rich case marking. It is the

[25] When a determiner precedes, adjective inflections in German are either exclusively 'weak' (after the definite article) with considerable syncretism, or primarily 'weak' with occasional 'strong' and distinctive forms (after the indefinite article); see Hawkins (1986: 15). In the absence of a determiner, adjective inflections are strong. Case marking on nouns is reduced to an optional -*e* on masculine and neuter singular datives and an -(*e*)*n* on dative plurals.

first item in the NP that both constructs the NP and assigns the relevant case to it. But the category that was systematically losing its inflectional distinct-iveness in the older periods of Germanic was the noun. The expansion of the definite article succeeded in converting many NPs of the form np[N] into np[Def N], thereby preserving a processing regularity that was threatened by case syncretisms on nouns.

Case-disambiguating definite articles in German generic plurals such as *er zieht den Rosen die Nelken vor* 'he prefers carnations to roses' (cf. §4.4.1) illus-trate a Middle High German extension of this motivation which was without parallel in Middle English, since case distinctiveness had been lost on full NPs in English at that point and vp[V NP PP] sequences were required instead. The extensive ambiguity in the English lexicon between noun and verb provides a continued motivation, among others, for the retention of an article category to this day.

These are some (partial) particulars from Germanic. The details will vary from language to language, but the functional motivation for NP Construc-tion and Attachment are universal, and the pressure to recruit and expand the demonstrative determiner for this purpose will reflect the availability or loss of other devices in the life cycle of grammatical categories that can perform these functions. The precise role of these processing principles in relation to the typology and evolution of a language needs to be modeled within a multi-factor complex adaptive system of the kind described by Gell-Mann (1992). For Germanic, construction of a case-marked NP has been a signific-ant motivation. For Bantu, construction of an NP of a certain class is a general typological regularity within the language, and this has plausibly provided the motivation for definiteness expansion in these languages (Greenberg 1978). In other languages, attachment marking will be the primary motivation. The approach to grammaticalization illustrated here makes many predictions for cross-linguistic variation. It also helps us to understand why there are reduc-tions in both form and meaning, why changes are in the direction of increased productivity, and why the emergence of new syntactic units is expected in some languages and not others, and at some historical stages and not oth-ers. The processor is in the driving seat, and by defining processing functions and motivations explicitly, we can capture intuitions that have been implicit hitherto and make explicit predictions for variation and change.

4.5   Processing enrichments through structural parallelism

In §3.2.3 I gave a summary of some major ways in which a given form F (including zero) that is compatible with many properties {P} can be enriched in performance to a specific P. The enrichments in these examples were made possible by inferences resulting from the current discourse, from frequency effects derived ultimately from all prior discourses, and from real-world knowledge. Enrichment can also be based on an exploitation of structural cues within the sentence being processed. One such cue involves structural identity and parallelism. There are several relevant phenomena here that have not yet, to my knowledge, been interconnected in quite the way they can be. The crucial point is that syntactic and semantic content that is absent from a clause can often be inferred by being copied from a parallel form or structure in which the missing content is present. The inferences that make possible such minimal forms can then be conventionalized in grammatical rules, and have been conventionalized in ways that make sense from a processing perspective.

Let us define the following preference:

(4.20) *Maximize Parallelism*
        The human processor prefers to maximize parallelism when copying syntactic and semantic content from a target onto a minimal form.

Targets are forms or form sequences and their properties that are accessed in the relevant processing domains when copying syntactic and semantic content from an explicit form onto a minimal form. The minimal form is dependent on the target for its enrichment, and the dependency domain for the enrichment consists of the smallest structural sequence sufficient for its processing. Principle (4.20) is motivated by general considerations of efficiency in conjunction with the general logic of MiF (3.8) and Maximize the Ease of Processing Enrichments (3.14) (see §3.2.3). The copying of properties from a target onto a minimal form is easiest when there is maximal parallelism between target and minimal form.

Co-ordinate deletions reveal the role of parallelism especially clearly, and it is this parallelism that renders the so-called deletion recoverable. In a sentence like *John angered O and Fred amused the woman* the target phrase, *the woman*, is copied onto the gap site. Target and gap receive an identical semantic interpretation here, while the structure of the sentence that contains the target is parallel to the structure containing the gap, except for the gap site itself, i.e. [NP vp[V O]] AND [NP vp[V NP]]. Since other terminal elements in the target and gap sentences are overt (and often non-identical, as in this example), this makes it possible for the parser to recognize the gap. The target and gap site are calculated from the right edge of the right conjunct here to the first overt and structurally matching categories on the left, namely *amused* and *angered*. That the two sentences must indeed be structurally parallel and co-ordinate can be seen in the contrast with *John angered O while Fred amused the woman*, in which the potential (but impossible) target on the right is in a subordinate, not a co-ordinate clause. It is this parallelism in the comparison of the two surface sequences that permits the gap site to be recognized and filled in processing (in addition to possibly assisting factors such as the transitivity of *angered*, which requires a direct object, a factor that would not be as strong with ambiguously transitive and intransitive verbs). As a result parallelism facilitates the enrichment of a minimal form.

Van Oirsouw (1987) provides a detailed discussion of co-ordinate deletion rules that is very compatible with the approach outlined here and that accounts readily for mirror image effects in the direction of 'deletion' across structures and languages. If the target is on a right branch, the gap is to the left (as in the example above), but if the target is on a left branch, the gap is on the right (as in *The priest preached water and O drank wine*). Gap sites must, he argues, be readily inferable from the left or right edges of co-ordinate structures. These conditions on co-ordinate deletion follow naturally from ease of processing and can be argued to have shaped the performance preferences that preceded conventionalization in different languages. The precise manner of this conventionalization can be expected to exhibit 'parameters' such as directionality, depending on the structure of the containing clauses and phrases. We can also predict variation in the degree of parallelism that is required across languages and structures. Complete parallelism makes processing easiest, but partial parallelism (as in *John angered O while Fred amused the woman*) could be permitted as well, in grammars in which deletion under complete parallelism is also possible, resulting in a hierarchy structured by efficiency and complexity. This needs systematic investigation.

Ambiguity tests using VP anaphors or empty VPs provide a further example of the role of parallelism in assigning content from a target to a minimal form. Kempson (1977) discusses sentences like *One day I will vp[kick the bucket] and you will vp[do so] too* and *One day I will vp[kick the bucket] and you will vp[O] too*. She points out that if *kick the bucket* receives its idiomatic meaning ('to die') in the first conjunct, then it must receive it in the anaphoric and empty VPs as well, and if the bucket is being kicked literally in the interpretation of the first conjunct, then this same meaning is assigned to the anaphoric and empty VPs. Enrichment of the minimal forms vp[*do so*] and vp[O] is made on the basis of the target VP here, and it is obviously easiest for the hearer to infer what the enrichment is supposed to be if the semantics of the target is preserved identically in the structure to be enriched. This results in parallelism effects, and in the availability of these constructions as tests for ambiguity v. vagueness. Under ambiguity, at most one reading can be selected in the target clause and this same reading must be assigned to the anaphor or gap. With vagueness, a single linguistic meaning is compatible with different states of affairs (e.g. in *John hit Bill* the hitting could be with the left hand or the right hand) and the target and the anaphor/empty category sentences could potentially be linked to different states of affairs in a given universe of discourse while receiving the same general meaning in both conjuncts. Hence so-called 'crossed readings' are possible for vagueness, but not for ambiguity.

Filler–gap dependencies provide further examples of parallelism. Parallelism can be seen when properties of a filler and its gap are shared (cf. §7.1). For *Wh*-fillers there are extensive parallelisms between the displaced *Wh* phrase and the empty position (or subcategorizor) with which it is linked, including theta-role and case in addition to the shared referential index. This is because the *Wh*-phrase is moved to a clause-peripheral position where it preserves the same syntactic and semantic relations with categories in the clause that it would have had in situ (and that it does have in languages and structures without such displacements). But so too for the head noun filler of a relative clause, whose matrix grammatical relation is in principle quite distinct from that of the position relativized on. Processing and acquisition studies have nonetheless noticed the existence of 'parallel function' effects (Sheldon 1974, MacWhinney 1982, Clancy et al. 1986), whereby the grammatical relation of the filler is preferably identical to that of the position relativized on. This results in a preference for relatives that combine matrix subject with relativization on an underlying subject (*the student [who studied linguistics] passed the exam*) and matrix object with underlying object relativization (*I know the student [that you know]*).

There is a reflection of this preference in the grammars of certain languages. In Persian, for example, the case of the position relativized on can be carried into the matrix filler, making the two positions superficially parallel in morphosyntax, even when their underlying grammatical relations are distinct, as in (4.21) (from Comrie 1989: 154). The accusative marker *ra* reflects the position relativized on here, not the grammatical relation of *Zan-i* in the matrix, which is a subject.

(4.21) Zan-i-ra   [ke didid] inja-st   (Persian)
       woman-the-ACC that you-saw here is
       'The woman that you saw is here.'

In Ancient Greek a similar attraction usually works the other way around with the case of the filler being copied onto the relative pronoun within the relative clause (Comrie 1989).

Relative clauses with pronominal heads provide extensive examples, in English and other languages, of parallel function effects (e.g. *I went where he went*). And the number of languages with relative clauses whose nominal heads have a conventionalized parallel function requirement with the matrix is, according to Aldai (2003), greater than is currently realized (contra Kirby 1999), especially in the lower positions of the Keenan & Comrie (1977) Accessibility Hierarchy (cf. §7.2). Aldai focuses on relative clauses in Basque from this perspective: cf. Cole (1976: 244–5) for Hebrew.

4.6   The principle of conventionalized dependency

Parallelism is not the only structural basis for property enrichments to minimal forms. Dependency assignments can be made productively to a given form B when a second form A can be accessed in a variety of other structural positions. Often A and B will be syntactic sisters and in a combinatorial relation in these cases (cf. (2.1)). An object NP zero-specified for case and theta-role can receive these properties by accessing an accompanying sister verb. Intransitive *count* can receive its appropriate interpretation by accessing a sister PP (*on my son* v. *in the evening*). On other occasions there is structural asymmetry between A and B. A reflexive anaphor is generally lower and more deeply embedded in clause structure than the antecedent from which it derives its index, and cannot be higher. Compare *John$_i$ vp[washed himself$_i$]* with **Heself$_i$ vp[washed John$_i$]*. A gap within a relative clause is also lower than its head noun filler.

There is a major constraint on such dependencies that has assumed increasing importance in grammatical theorizing since it was first proposed by Reinhart (1983): constituent-command (or c-command$'$). Reinhart defined it as follows (p. 18):

(4.22)   *C-command*
Node A c(onstituent)-commands node B iff the branching node most immediately dominating A also dominates B.

A necessary condition for B to depend on A, according to this theory, is that A must c-command B. The antecedent (A) of a co-indexation relation must c-command its anaphor (B). A filler (A) must c-command its dependent gap or subcategorizor (B). An NP zero-specified for case (B) is c-commanded by the verb (A) on which it is dependent for case assignment, in accordance with the definition in (4.22). The verb, in turn, is c-commanded by the NP(s) on which it depends for ambiguity and polysemy reduction. An ambiguous or polysemous predicate (B) in Tongan is c-commanded by the particle or function category (A) on the basis of which an unambiguous syntactic category is assigned to it, e.g. N. And so on.

C-command appears to be a powerful constraint on dependencies. It limits the domains in which dependencies can hold, and their directionality: the anaphor must be c-command*ed*, while the antecedent c-commands, not the other way round. But why can't it be the other way round? More generally, why is there a c-command constraint at all? Considerations of processing efficiency suggest an answer.

Reference to branching nodes and immediate domination in (4.22) indicates that there is an intimate link between c-command and the notion of phrasal combination that was defined in (2.1), namely A combines with B iff A and B are dominated by the same syntactic mother phrase M. A and B c-command each other when they are syntactic sisters, both being dominated by M. A and B may depend on each other in this case. But when a category B depends on some A which is not a sister of B, and does not strictly combine with it according to (2.1), there is nonetheless an extended form of combination between them. In *John washed himself*, *washed* combines with *himself* to make a VP, and this whole VP then combines with the NP subject *John* to make a clause (S). Though *himself* does not combine with *John*, therefore, the VP within which it is a sister of the verb does combine with, and is a sister of, *John*. We can say that *John* is in an 'extended combination domain' for *himself* within the clause S, therefore.

Consider the nodes in (4.23).

(4.23)

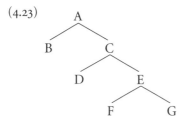

G combines with F here to make E, E combines with D to make C, and so on. Let us define an (extended) combination domain of a node α, i.e. an (E)CD, so as to include both sisters and possible extended sisters of α as follows:

(4.24) *The (extended) combination domain of a node α in X*
consists of any sister β of α, and of any sisters of all nodes dominating α, within a containing node X.

The (E)CD of node G within A in (4.23) consists of F, D, and B. The (E)CD of E consists of D and B, the (E)CD of C consists of B only, and so on.

An interesting asymmetry now emerges. Whereas D is in the (E)CD of G, G is not in the (E)CD of D, nor is F; whereas B is in the (E)CD of e.g. D and of E, D and E are not in the (E)CD of B. In other words, a node β cannot be in the (E)CD of a node α if β is properly contained within a sister γ of α. *John* is in the (E)CD of *himself* in *John washed himself*, but *himself* is not in the (E)CD of *John*. *John* combines with the whole VP, not with a proper subpart of VP. Since combinations by definition create larger units out of smaller units, the relations of extended combination will always be defined on sisters of the larger units, and these sisters will be in the (extended) combination domains of the smaller subunits, and not vice versa.

I therefore propose the following constraint:

(4.25) *Dependency Domain Constraint*
Node B can be dependent on node A if A is in an (extended) combination domain of B within some X.

Seen from this perspective, dependencies between categories are parasitic on the combinatorial relations that hold between them. This is why dependent elements (gaps and anaphors etc.) can look up the tree, but not down it, in order to satisfy their dependency relations.

In *John washed the boy* the subject is in the (E)CD for the direct object, and not vice versa, and there is no co-indexation. When there *is* a co-indexation dependency, it goes from the object to the subject, mirroring the asymmetrical combination that holds in all cases, in accordance with (4.25). When two categories are sisters, like V and a direct object, they are in each other's combinatorial domains and the dependencies can go in both directions.

We can now link c-command and (4.25) to considerations of processing efficiency. When a dependency is conventionalized between an anaphor (B) and an antecedent (A), c-command guarantees that the category A which the parser must access in order to process B will be in an (extended) combination domain of B—cf. (4.24). Why is this important? It is important because it provides a structural basis for the accessibility of A to B, and this structural basis is the grammatical counterpart of contextual accessibility and of the other extragrammatical factors that lead quite generally to processing enrichments in performance (cf. (3.15) in §3.2.3). A is accessible to B by virtue of the independent grammatical relation of (extended) combination linking them. The direct object can be dependent on the subject since it combines with the verb to make VP, and VP combines with the subject. Hence the subject is accessible to the object on the basis of these (extended) combinations. But the subject cannot be made dependent on the object since the subject combines with the whole VP, not with a proper subpart of it. Hence there is no combinatorial basis for the accessibility of the object to the subject in processing.

One consequence of this asymmetry in (extended) combinations is that clauses with objects always have subjects that can potentially provide the antecedents for anaphors. Clauses with subjects will always have a sister VP, but this VP may or may not contain a direct object (and frequently does not). Hence it will regularly not contain an antecedent that a subject anaphor would need.

I suggest that there is a principle of 'grammatical accessibility' that operates when dependency assignments are conventionalized in grammars. When a reduced B (including zero) is made dependent on A for some property assignment P, A must be grammatically accessible to B. This can be done by positioning A within an (extended) combination domain of B. Alternatively, as in the examples of §4.5, accessibility can be accomplished through structural parallelism. Syntactic and semantic content is copied from a target onto a minimal form, and the parallelism between the containing (co-ordinate) clauses is what renders the target recognizable and easy to process. The 'deletion' is recovered in this way. Hence the A phrase on which B is dependent in conventionalized rules must be grammatically accessible to B through structural relations that include (extended) combination and parallelism.

The examples of §4.5 revealed a second desideratum for rules of conventionalized dependency. Not only is A grammatically accessible to B, but the property P that constitutes the dependency assignment ((2.3) in §2.2) must be assignable with ease, in accordance with the predicted ease of processing enrichments ((3.14) in §3.2.3). Maximal parallelism in deletion structures makes processing easiest, though I hypothesized that we should expect structured hierarchies here incorporating different degrees of parallelism between the target clause and the deletion clause. Similarly, there are structured hierarchies for filler–gap and anaphoric binding dependencies in (extended) combination domains, in accordance with Minimize Domains (3.1). Filler–gap hierarchies are illustrated in §7.2 and §7.4. Anaphoric binding hierarchies are summarized in Huang (2000: 93). Reflexive anaphors are optional in English environments such as *John$_i$ saw a snake near him(self)$_i$* but obligatory in the smaller and less complex domain involving a subject and a direct object, e.g. *John$_i$ defended himself$_i$ (*him$_i$)*. More generally, if an anaphor is possible or required in a complex environment, its occurrence in smaller and easier-to-process environments will be at least as productive as, and possibly more productive than, in the more complex environments. A long-distance anaphor occurs in the embedded environment of an infinitival complement in Russian, and in non-embedded environments as well (Rappaport 1986).

These considerations lead to the following principle:

(4.26) *Principle of Conventionalized Dependency*
　　　　If a grammar conventionalizes a dependency of B on A with respect
　　　　to P, then

　　　(i)　A must be grammatically accessible to B through an independent
　　　　　　structural relation;
　　　(ii)　P must be assignable to B with ease.

Forms can be minimized by exploiting both sentence-internal and sentence-external clues (see §3.2.3), therefore. When the enrichments are closely tied to structural properties, in the ways we have just seen, then grammatical accessibility and maximal ease of assignment are natural grammatical correlates of the sentence-external factors that facilitate processing enrichments, such as discourse accessibility, frequency and relevance, etc. (cf. (3.15) in §3.2.3). As a result, the processor avoids the articulation and processing of explicit linguistic material that is derivable or inferable from the linguistic or larger context. As I mentioned in §3.2.3, quoting from Levinson (2000), 'inference is cheap', and this is what underlies these minimization efficiencies. It would be inefficient to undertake additional processing of forms and properties when the relevant properties are already inferable contextually or are readily accessible structurally through parallelism or through already existing combinatorial relations.

5

Adjacency Effects Within Phrases

The present chapter examines patterns of adjacency and relative ordering in performance data and across grammars. The goal will be to show that there are clear preferences in the selections that are made from options available in performance, and that the same preferences can be found in the grammatical conventions of languages with fewer options. The data will mainly involve lexical head categories, such as verbs, in combination with various sister phrases. The particular efficiency principle at issue is Minimize Domains, which was defined in §3.1 as follows:

> (3.1) *Minimize Domains* (MiD)
>
> The human processor prefers to minimize the connected sequences of linguistic forms and their conventionally associated syntactic and semantic properties in which relations of combination and/or dependency are processed. The degree of this preference is proportional to the number of relations whose domains can be minimized in competing sequences or structures, and to the extent of the minimization difference in each domain.

My earlier principle of Early Immediate Constituents (EIC, see Hawkins 1990, 1994) is now subsumed under MiD. The following adjacency prediction was also formulated in §3.1:

> (3.4) *Adjacency to Heads*
>
> Given a phrase {H, {X, Y}}, H a head category and X and Y phrases that are potentially adjacent to H, then the more combinatorial and dependency relations whose processing domains can be minimized when X is adjacent to H, and the greater the minimization difference between adjacent X and adjacent Y in each domain, the more H and X will be adjacent.

I begin by illustrating in §5.1 some of the predictions made by EIC for adjacency in performance, followed in §5.2 by performance data that test the more general hypothesis of (3.4) involving multiple adjacency preferences.

I then show that these same preferences can be seen in the fixed conventions of grammars: grammaticalized adjacencies predicted by EIC are illustrated in §5.3, and grammaticalizations of multiple adjacency preferences in §5.4. Some competitions between domain minimization efficiencies, in different phrases and domains, are then illustrated in §5.5.

5.1   EIC preferences for adjacency in performance

5.1.1   *EIC in head-initial structures*

In a head-initial language like English there is a clear preference for short phrases to precede longer ones, the short ones being adjacent to the head of the relevant phrase. This preference appears to be directly proportional to their relative weight.

In §2.3 I compared the heavy-NP-shifted [V PP NP] structure of *Mary gave [to Bill] [the book she had been searching for since last Christmas]* with its corresponding basic order [V NP PP], *Mary gave [the book she had been searching for since last Christmas] [to Bill]*. The shifted structure has been shown by Wasow (1997, 2002) to be preferred in performance data in proportion to the weight difference between the heavy NP and a lighter PP sister, where relative weight is measured either by word numbers or by numbers of nodes. In Hawkins (1994: 183) corpus each additional word of relative weight resulted in a higher proportion of shifting, culminating eventually in 100% for large word differentials between the NP and the PP. Overall a short NP or PP was adjacent to V and preceded its longer sister in 89% of these data (365/412). Degrees of relative weight in heavy-NP shifting preferences have also been corroborated experimentally in the production tasks conducted by Stallings (1998).

Consider the alternation between two prepositional phrases (PPs) in English following an intransitive verb. In the corpus of Hawkins (2000) short PPs were systematically preferred before longer PPs when PPs were permutable with truth-conditional equivalence, i.e. when the speaker had a choice, as in (5.1a) and (b).

(5.1) a. The man vp[waited pp1[for his son] pp2[in the cold but not unpleasant wind]]

b. The man vp[waited pp2[in the cold but not unpleasant wind] pp1[for his son]]

Overall 82% of the sequences that involved a length difference were ordered short before long (265/323), the short PP being adjacent to V, and the degree of

TABLE 5.1   English prepositional phrase orderings by relative weight
(Hawkins 2000: 237)

n = 323	PP2 > PP1 by 1 word	by 2–4	by 5–6	by 7+
[V PP1 PP2]	60% (58)	86% (108)	94% (31)	99% (68)
[V PP2 PP1]	40% (38)	14% (17)	6% (2)	1% (1)

PP2 = longer PP; PP1 = shorter PP.
Proportion of short-long to long-short given as a percentage; actual numbers of
   sequences in parentheses.
An additional 71 sequences had PPs of equal length (total n = 394).

the weight difference correlated precisely with the degree of preference for the
short before long order, as shown in Table 5.1.

In Hawkins (1994) I argued for an explanation of these relative weight effects
in terms of the efficiency with which syntactic structure could be parsed. The
immediate constituents (ICs) of a phrase can typically be recognized on the
basis of less than all the words dominated by that phrase, and some orderings
reduce the number of words needed to recognize these ICs compared with
others. The result is faster and more efficient constituent structure recognition.
Compare (5.1a) and (b) from this perspective:

(5.1) a. The man vp[waited pp1[for his son] pp2[in the cold but not
unpleasant wind]]

        1   2 3 4   5

        -

    b. The man vp[waited pp2[in the cold but not unpleasant wind] pp1[for
    his son]]

        1   2 3   4 5 6   7   8   9

        -

Five connected words in (5.1a) can construct VP and its three ICs, V, PP1, and
PP2, compared with nine in (5.1b), assuming that head categories like P (or
other constructing categories) immediately project to mother nodes such as
PP and render them predictable on-line.[1] The greater efficiency of (5.1a), in
which the same structure can be derived from less input, can then be captured
in terms of its higher IC-to-word ratio within the VP Constituent Recognition

---

[1] For detailed discussion of node construction and an Axiom of Constructability for phrase structure,
see Hawkins (1993) and (1994: ch. 6). See also Kimball (1973) for an early formulation of the basic insight
about phrasal node construction in parsing (his principle of New Nodes).

Domain (CRD) (see (3.2) and §3.1 for definition of a CRD and illustration of this quantification procedure):

(5.1′) a. VP: IC-to-word ratio = 3/5 or 60%
        b. VP: IC-to-word ratio = 3/9 or 33%

The higher ratio of (5.1a) captures its greater efficiency.[2]

We must now generalize and relabel this domain in order to capture what are plausibly parallel benefits for the speaker. These benefits have been confirmed in the preferences elicited in production experiments (Stallings 1998) and in data from written and spoken production. The quantification procedure illustrated in (5.1′) is also most plausible from the speaker's perspective. It assumes that the second PP in (5.1a) and (b) is recognizable as a VP constituent as soon as the P is parsed that constructs it, rather than as a PP complement or adjunct of the immediately preceding noun. This makes sense for the speaker since the speaker knows the meaning and structure of the terminal string that he/she is producing item by item. From the hearer's perspective, structural, semantic, and discourse considerations will also often permit the correct attachment to be made at the second P, but there will be some on-line ambiguities whose resolution will require access to more of the internal structure of the second PP than the P itself. If *his son* in (5.1) had been previously referred to as *his son in distress*, then there would be a context effect in favor of low attachment of the PP constructed by *in* as *in* is parsed in (5.1a) and more of the internal structure of this PP would have to be read in order to assign high attachment. From the hearer's perspective the efficiency difference between (5.1a) and (b) is less systematic than it is from the speaker's, therefore, and the precise advantage of one order over the other will depend on how much of the second PP needs to be parsed for correct attachment.[3]

I shall accordingly relabel a CRD as a Phrasal Combination Domain (PCD), making it compatible with both production and comprehension. Essential aspects of the definition remain unchanged from (3.2). The contents of this domain are determined by the grammar of phrase structure and by the combinatorial relations holding between members of each phrase, in conjunction with a fairly standard assumption about unique projection, the particular version

---

[2] In the event that one or both of the PPs is clause (S- or IP-) dominated, rather than VP-dominated, EIC makes the same short before long prediction, see Hawkins (1994: 123–6) for detailed quantification.

[3] In Hawkins (2000) I examined whether there was evidence for on-line ambiguity avoidance in the selection of the PP orderings themselves. This was done by inspecting those sequences of PPs that are semantically compatible with a (truth-conditionally distinct) high and low attachment in one order, but not in the other, and seeing whether there was a preference for the unambiguous order. Ambiguity avoidance appeared to have no statistically significant effect.

of which I have argued for elsewhere (cf. the references in n. 1).[4] A PCD is, in effect, the smallest domain that permits a phrasal node to be constructed along with its daughter ICs.

(5.2) *Phrasal Combination Domain* (PCD)
   The PCD for a mother node M and its I(mmediate) C(onstituent)s consists of the smallest string of terminal elements (plus all M-dominated non-terminals over the terminals) on the basis of which the processor can construct M and its ICs.

EIC can be generalized to make it compatible with production and comprehension as follows:

(5.3) *Early Immediate Constituents* (EIC)
   The human processor prefers linear orders that minimize PCDs (by maximizing their IC-to-nonIC [or IC-to-word] ratios), in proportion to the minimization difference between competing orders.

Comparable data to those of Table 5.1 have been presented for numerous other head-initial structures in various languages in Hawkins (1994). For example, data were collected from the post-verbal domain of Hungarian by Stephen Matthews, i.e. from a free-ordering domain in which constituents are permutable (according to Kiss 1987, 2002). One set of data involved the relative ordering of two NPs with left-peripheral NP construction, by a head noun or determiner as shown in (5.4), i.e. these NPs involved no left-branching genitives or relative clauses and are abbreviated here as mNP (for left-peripheral mother node construction):

(5.4) a. [Döngetik np[facipöink]   np[az utcakat]] (Hungarian)
         batter   wooden shoes-1Pl the streets-ACC
         'Our wooden shoes batter the streets'
      b. Döngetik np[az utcakat] np[facipöink]]

Each additional word of relative weight resulted in a stronger preference for the short before long orders, i.e. for those with smaller PCDs and higher IC-to-word ratios in this clausal domain, as shown in Table 5.2. And 89%

---

4 One important respect in which my approach to headedness and projection differs from standard assumptions involves bi-uniqueness v. uniqueness of the mother–head relation. It is sufficient for processing that a category C should project to a unique mother M, and it is not necessary that this should be a bi-uniqueness relation, as in X-bar theory (see e.g. Jackendoff 1977). My theory is accordingly compatible with a plurality of categories {C} capable of constructing the same M (e.g. a pronoun, a proper name, a noun, and a determiner can all construct NP; see §4.4.2), but it is not compatible with a plurality of different mothers constructed by the same C (since this would make abstract structure unrecognizable in performance).

TABLE 5.2   Hungarian noun phrase orderings by relative weight
(Hawkins 1994: 133; data collected by Stephen Matthews)

n = 85	mNP2 > mNP1 by 1 word	by 2	by 3+
[V mNP1 mNP2]	85% (50)	96% (27)	100% (8)
[V mNP2 mNP1]	15% (9)	4% (1)	0% (0)

mNP = any NP constructed on its left periphery.
NP2 = longer NP; NP1 = shorter NP.
Proportion of short-long to long-short given as a percentage; actual numbers
    of sequences in parentheses.
An additional 21 sequences had NPs of equal length (total n = 116).

were ordered short-before-long overall (85/95) compared with 11% long before
short (10/95).

5.1.2   *EIC in head-final structures*

Performance data from Japanese reveal an equally principled set of preferences, but for the mirror-image long-before-short pattern. This is predicted
by EIC. Postposing a heavy NP or PP to the right in English shortens PCDs
and increases IC-to-word ratios. Preposing heavy constituents in a head-final
language has the same effect, since the relevant constructing categories (V for
VP, P for PP, etc) are now on the right (which is abbreviated here as VPm,
PPm, etc). In a structure like [{1PPm, 2PPm} V] the PCD for VP will proceed
from the first P(ostposition) encountered to the verb, and will be smaller if
the shorter 1PPm is adjacent to the verb than if the longer 2PPm is adjacent.
The preferred pattern overall should be long before short in Japanese, therefore, and the degree of this preference should increase with increasing weight
differentials. In this way the time course from recognition and production of
the first PP to the VP-final verb will be faster than if the long PP is adjacent to
V and follows the shorter PP.[5]

Consider some illustrative data collected by Kaoru Horie and involving
orderings of [{NPo, PPm} V], where NPo stands for a direct object NP containing an accusative case particle *o*, in combination with a postpositional
phrase, i.e. with right-peripheral construction of PP by P (PPm). I assume here
that the *o* is the constructing category for this case-marked NP, paralleling the

---

[5] For quantification of this long-before-short preference in head-final languages, see Hawkins
(1994: 80).

final postposition in PP and the final V in VP, and that the processing of VP proceeds bottom-up in an order such as [PPm NPo V]: daughter constituents of PPm are processed before the PP itself is recognized (by projection from P). The distance and time course from the first constructing category (P or *o*) to V is then shorter when the longer phrase precedes the shorter one— i.e. [PPm NPo V] is preferred when PPm > NPo, and [NPo PPm V] is preferred when NPo > PPm. An example of the relevant sentence type is given in (5.5):

(5.5) a. Tanaka ga   [[Hanako kara] [sono hon   o]   katta]
       Tanaka NOM   Hanako from   that   book ACC bought
       'Tanako bought that book from Hanako' (Japanese)
    b. Tanaka ga [[sono hon o] [Hanako kara] katta]

Table 5.3 presents the relative weights of the two non-subject phrases and their correlated orderings. NPo and PPm are collapsed together for present purposes. The data for [PPm NPo V] v. [NPo PPm V] orders are presented in Table 5.6 below. Table 5.3 reveals that each additional word of relative weight results in a higher proportion of long before short orders, mirroring the short before long preferences of Tables 5.1 and 5.2. The overall preference for long before short in Table 5.3 is 72% (110/153) and 28% (43/153) short before long. This long-before-short effect in Japanese has been replicated in Yamashita & Chang (2001). It can also be seen in the widespread *preposing* preference for subordinate clauses with final complementizers in this and other head-final languages, and in many other long-before-short structures in these languages (cf. §§5.3–4).

TABLE 5.3   Japanese NPo and PPm orderings by relative weight (Hawkins 1994: 152; data collected by Kaoru Horie)

n = 153	2ICm > 1ICm by 1–2 words	by 3–4	5–8	by 9+
[2ICm 1ICm V]	66% (59)	72% (21)	83% (20)	91% (10)
[1ICm 2ICm V]	34% (30)	28% (8)	17% (4)	9% (1)

NPo = direct object NP with accusative case particle *o*.
PPm = PP constructed on its right periphery by a P(ostposition).
ICm = either NPo or PPm.
2IC = longer IC; 1IC = shorter IC.
Proportion of long-short to short-long orders given as a percentage; actual numbers of sequences in parentheses.
An additional 91 sequences had ICs of equal length (total n = 244).

The preference for long before short in Japanese is not predicted by current models of language production, all of which are heavily influenced by English-type postposing effects. Yet it points to the same minimization preference for PCDs that we saw in head-initial languages. For example, according to the Incremental Parallel Formulator of De Smedt (1994), syntactic segments are assembled incrementally into a whole sentence structure, following message generation within a Conceptualizer. The relative ordering of these segments is predicted to reflect both the original order of conceptualization and the processing time required by the Formulator for more complex constituents. Short constituents can be formulated with greater speed in the race between parallel processes and should accordingly be generated first, before heavy phrases.

The theory of EIC, by contrast, defines a general preference for minimal PCDs in all languages. This minimization is accomplished through the close and efficient positioning of categories that construct the immediate constituents of phrases. The result: heavy ICs to the left and short ICs to the right in head-final languages. This preference is evident in performance and has been systematically conventionalized in grammars. Production modelers need to rethink their weight predictions in the light of this cross-linguistic regularity.

I suggest that the relationship between the Conceptualizer and the Formulator is somewhat less parallel than in De Smedt's model. The Conceptualizer can be cognitively aware that some NP or clause being generated will eventually be contained within a semantic phrasal type whose surface expression is head-final, before the Formulator has actually constructed the P and PP in its syntactic representation. In other words, the production of head-final phrases in the Japanese Formulator is most plausibly bottom-up, and the conceptual structure that is produced on-line can be richer than the corresponding syntactic structure that has been generated at a given moment within the Formulator. Preference data such as those of Table 5.3 point to the reality of domains defined by constructing categories within phrases, and these data would look very different if ICs such as PP could be constructed in advance of their heads. In fact, we *would* then predict short-before-long effects in both head-initial and head-final languages, since each phrase would be constructible at or near its left periphery by an immediate translation of conceptual structure into syntactic structure. Since the preferences of production look instead much like those we expect for comprehension (the Japanese hearer does not know on-line that an initial NP or clause will eventually be PP-dominated, rather than VP- or AdjP-dominated, and his/her parsing of left-branching PPs is of necessity bottom-up), and since we have no reason to expect complete altruism on the speaker's part (see Kirby 1999 for discussion), I conclude that domain minimization benefits for the speaker are indeed very similar to those of the hearer. This in turn leads to a theory of the Formulator that is fine-tuned to the phrase structure grammar of the language in question and that generates an efficient syntactic structure after prior conceptualization. Specifically, formulation proceeds in accordance with minimization benefits that operate within the Formulator itself, and in a manner that can apply both for the speaker and for the hearer.

5.2   Multiple preferences for adjacency in performance

The adjacency hypothesis of (3.4) predicts a preference for adjacency that is proportional to the number of combinatorial and dependency relations whose domains can be minimized in competing orders, and in proportion to the extent of the minimization difference in each domain. This can be tested by re-examining data from the last section to see whether the processing of additional relations between a head and its sisters has the predicted effect on adjacency. Some of these data went against weight alone and had non-minimal PCDs. Such orders deserve special scrutiny, since they are predicted here to involve some other syntactic or semantic link whose processing prefers a minimal domain.

5.2.1   *Multiple preferences in English*

For Heavy NP Shift Wasow (1997) has shown that it is not just (relative) heaviness of the NP that motivates the selection of [V PP NP] over [V NP PP]. If there is what he calls an 'opaque collocation' between V and PP such that the meaning of one cannot be processed without access to the other, then there is significantly more adjacency between them. A relevant example is *take into account X*. This lexically listed word combination has a meaning that is non-compositional, and it requires a processing domain that includes both V and PP for meaning assignment. These collocations had a 60% shifting ratio in his data, compared with only 15% for V-PP sequences such as *take to the library X* that are not lexically listed and whose meanings are fully compositional (i.e. X is literally taken and X does go to the library).

In between opaque collocations (*take into account X*) and non-collocations (*take to the library X*) Wasow proposed an intermediate category of 'transparent collocations', i.e. those that 'should be comprehensible to a speaker who knows the literal meaning of each of the words in it, but has never before encountered them in this combination' (Wasow 1997: 96). An example is *bring to someone's attention X.* The shifting ratio for these was lower than the 60% for opaque collocations, at 47%, but still significantly higher than the 15% for non-collocations. Wasow's 'collocations' correspond to what I am calling here a 'lexical combination' (cf. (2.1) in §2.2), and the transparency or opacity of the collocation seems to reflect whether there is an additional dependency between the V and the PP, as this was defined in (2.2) of §2.2. The high shifting ratio for opaque collocations is therefore a product both of this semantic dependency and of their lexical collocational status. This latter alone brought about three times as many Heavy NP Shifts compared with non-collocations (47% v. 15%), and the additional dependency resulted in four times as many shifts (60% v. 15%).

Heavy NP Shift can apparently minimize surface domains for the processing of lexical combinations and dependencies within what I will call a 'Lexical Domain' (LD), i.e. the smallest domain sufficient for the processing of lexically listed combinations and dependencies (cf. (5.6) below). The theory presented here makes a prediction for all such lexical co-occurrences and dependencies. They should all prefer adjacency. The syntactic phrases listed among the co-occurrence requirements or options for a given head category should prefer adjacency to that head. The selectional restrictions imposed by a verb should prefer the adjacency of phrases mentioned in these restrictions to that verb. The lexically sensitive theta-roles assigned to NPs by a given verb will prefer adjacency between these NPs and V. And the range of meanings assigned to a 'function' category by reference to its 'argument' (a transitive V in relation to a direct object NP, *run the race/the ad/the water,* and an adjective in relation to a noun, *flat beer/road/tire*: see Keenan 1979) should prefer adjacency between function and argument.

The data of Table 5.1 involving two PPs following an intransitive verb provide a test case for the role of such lexical combinations in predicting adjacency. Many of these PPs involve strong lexical relations with the verb, others do not, and the former should prefer minimal domains for processing. These preferences should also interact with relative weight in systematic ways. We must first come up with an empirically reliable way of distinguishing different types of PPs. One distinction commonly drawn in the theoretical literature is between 'complement' PPs, which are lexically listed alongside the verbs that govern them, and 'adjunct' PPs, which are not so listed and which are positioned by general syntactic rules. The PP *for John* is a complement in *wait for John,* whereas *in the evening* is an adjunct in *wait in the evening.*[6]

---

[6] See Schütze & Gibson (1999: appendix A) for a summary of the differences between complement (or argument) PPs and adjunct PPs, and an insightful discussion of the difficulties involved in defining necessary and sufficient criteria for this distinction.

The trouble with the complement/adjunct distinction is that there are several more primitive distinctions that underlie it, and there are examples that fall in between. Some complements are obligatorily required, others are optional, like adjuncts. A transitive verb requires its complement object NP, and an intransitive verb like *depend* requires a co-occurring PP headed by *on* (*I depended on John*, cf. **I depended*). The intransitive *wait*, on the other hand, is grammatical without its PP complement (*I waited for John* and *I waited*). The intransitive *count* is also grammatical without its PP complement headed by *on* (*I counted*), but the meaning is different from that which is assigned in the presence of the complement (*I counted on John*). More generally, there can be a semantic dependency between an intransitive verb and its complement PP, as there is in *count on John*, and as there is between transitive verbs and their object complements (*run the race/the ad/the water*, etc). Or there may be no such dependency, as in *I waited for John*, which logically implies *I waited* alone. A dependency relation may or may not join a combinatorial one in the lexical entry for a verb, therefore, and this combinatorial relation may or may not be obligatory. The interpretation of the preposition may also depend on that of the verb, even when the verb's meaning is not dependent on the preposition. *For* in *wait for John* is an example. It does not have the kind of benefactive meaning that one finds in more literal uses such as *I did this for John*.

If some PP is obligatorily required by an intransitive verb or if there is a dependency between V and P in either direction, we might view such properties as sufficient for classification of the relevant PP as a complement. There are only few intransitive verbs like *depend* that actually require a co-occurring PP for grammaticality, but many like *count on* or *wait for* that involve a dependency, so we might use dependency as the major criterion for distinguishing complements from adjuncts. I will propose some dependency tests below. They provide what is arguably a sufficient criterion for complementhood and for the co-occurrence of a PP in the lexical co-occurrence frame of intransitive verbs. The problem with them, and the problem with the whole complement/adjunct distinction, is that there are many intransitive verbs for which accompanying PPs are listed in standard dictionaries, largely for semantic reasons, and yet these PPs cannot be shown to be complements by the usual criteria and tests. Tests such as the dependency test to be offered here appear to correctly identify what others call complements, but the remaining PPs are not necessarily adjuncts and include some PPs that are listed in lexical entries.[7]

---

7 Consider a verb like *follow*. One of its lexical entries in the *American Heritage Dictionary* defines its meaning as 'to come, move, or take place after another person or thing in order or time'. Sequences like *follow behind the car* and *follow in the next century* contain PPs whose semantic content gives further specification to the semantic content of this verb (which is explicitly defined using PPs in the lexical

In Hawkins (2000: 242) I applied two dependency tests to the data of Table 5.1. One test, the Verb Entailment Test, asked: does [V, {PP1, PP2}] entail V alone or does V have a meaning dependent on either PP1 or PP2? For example, if *the man waited for his son in the early morning* is true, then it is also true that *the man waited*, and so the former entails the latter. But *the man counted on his son in his old age* does not entail *the man counted*. Another test, the Pro-Verb Entailment Test, asked: can V be replaced by some general Pro-verb or does one of the PPs require that particular V for its interpretation? For example, *the boy played on the playground* entails *the boy did something on the playground*, but *the boy depended on his father* does not entail *the boy did something on his father*.[8]

When there was a lexical-semantic dependency between V and one of the PPs by these tests, then 73% (151/206) had that PP adjacent to V. Recall that 82% had a shorter PP adjacent to V and preceding a longer one in Table 5.1. For PPs that were *both* shorter *and* lexically dependent, the adjacency rate to V was even higher, at 96% (102/106). The combined adjacency effect exerted by lexical dependency and EIC was statistically significantly higher than for each factor alone.[9]

paraphrase). There is every reason for saying that *behind the car* and *in the next century* 'match' the lexical definition given for *follow*, in a way that a manner expression like *at great speed* or a causal expression like *for obvious reasons* do not, and hence PPs like *behind the car* can be argued to be part of the lexical co-occurrence frame for *follow*. But tests involving obligatory co-occurrence or even lexical-semantic dependency do not always succeed in capturing such semantically based co-occurrences.

[8] These entailment tests distinguished verbs that were independently processable (coded Vi) from those that were dependent on at least one PP for their semantic processing (coded Vd). They also distinguished prepositions that were independently processable (Pi) from those that were dependent on V (Pd). The two tests were defined as follows (Hawkins 2000: 242–3):

   (i) Verb entailment test

      If [X V PP PP] entails [X V], then assign Vi.

      If not, assign Vd, indicating (by a 'v' subscript) which PP(s) is/are
         required in addition to V for an entailment to go through (e.g. [X Vd PPv PP]
         entails [X Vd PPv]).

   (ii) Pro-verb entailment test

      If [X V PP] entails [X Pro-V PP] or [*something* Pro-V PP] for any
         pro-verb sentence listed below, then assign Pi.

      If not, assign Pd.

      Pro-verb sentences: X *did something* PP; X *was* PP; *something happened* PP; *something was the case* PP; *something was done (by X)* PP.

[9] In Hawkins (2000: 249) I also applied a second semantic test to the V-PP-PP sequences, involving lexical matching (see fn. 7), which asked: does one or the other PP give more or equal semantic specification to the semantic content of V, as defined explicitly in any one lexical entry for V in the *American Heritage Dictionary*? So, the PP *behind the car* would be judged lexically matching in *follow behind the car*, whereas *at great speed* would not be judged lexically matching in *follow at great speed*. For a verb like *sit*, *sit in the armchair* would involve a lexically matching PP, whereas *sit in the afternoon* would not. When one PP was lexically matching and the other was not, the lexically matching one was adjacent to V in 76% of the relevant sequences (172/225). This effect was just as strong as that defined by

The processing of a lexical combination, as revealed through these entail-ments, evidently prefers a minimal domain, just as the processing of phrase structure information and of phrasal combining does. This can be explained as follows. Any separation of *count* from *on his son* and of *wait* from *for his son* delays both recognition and production of the lexical co-occurrence frame intended for these predicates by the speaker, and it delays assignment of the verb's dependent properties by the hearer. A verb can be, and typically is, asso-ciated with several lexical co-occurrence frames, all of which may be activated when the verb is processed (cf. Swinney 1979, MacDonald et al. 1994). Accom-panying PPs will select between them, and in the case of verbs like *count* they will resolve a semantic garden path. For dependent prepositions, increasing separation from the verb also expands the lexical processing domain and the working memory demands that are required for interpreting the preposition.

When lexical processing and phrasal processing reinforce one another, i.e. when the lexically listed PP is also the shorter PP, we have seen that adjacency to the verb is almost perfect, at 96%. This is predicted by MiD (3.1) and by (3.4). When the two processing domains pull in different directions, i.e. when the complement PP is longer, we expect variation. What is predicted here is a stronger effect within each processing domain in proportion to the minimiza-tion difference between competing sequences. For phrasal combinations this difference will be a function of the weight difference between the two PPs, as measured by EIC ratios. For lexical domains it will be a function of the absolute size of any independent PP (Pi) that intervenes between the verb and an interdependent PP. Let us abbreviate a PP judged interdependent by one or both entailment tests as Pd. In the event that Pi is a short two-word phrase, the difference between, say, [V Pd Pi] and [V Pi Pd] will be just two words. But as Pi gains in size, the processing domain for the lexical dependency between V and Pd grows, and the minimization preference for [V Pd Pi] grows accordingly.

EIC's graded weight preferences and predictions were confirmed in the data of Table 5.1. For lexical dependency it is indeed the absolute size of the poten-tially intervening Pi that determines the degree of the adjacency preference between V and Pd, as shown in Table 5.4. As Pi grows in size, its adjacency to V declines.[10]

the dependency tests (at 73%). For PPs that were *both* lexically matching *and* shorter the adjacency rate to V was again 96% (105/109), which was statistically significantly higher than for lexical matching and EIC alone. The reason for the similar results is that there was a high correlation between PPs judged to be dependent by the dependency tests and those judged to be lexically matching (see Hawkins 2000: 249–50). This correlation is expected on the assumption that both tests are diagnostics for PPs that contract a relation of co-occurrence with the relevant verb and are in lexical combination with it.

[10] In corresponding tables given in Hawkins (2000) and (2001) I included five additional sequences, making 211 in all, in which both PPs were interdependent with V, but one of them involved more

TABLE 5.4   English lexically dependent prepositional phrase orderings (data from Hawkins 2000)

n = 206	Pi = 2–3 words	:4–5	:6–7	:8+
[V Pd Pi]	59% (54)	71% (39)	93% (26)	100% (32)
[V Pi Pd]	41% (37)	29% (16)	7% (2)	0% (0)

Pd = the PP that is interdependent with V by one or both entailment tests.
Pi = the PP that is independent of V by both entailment tests.
Proportion of adjacent V-Pd to non-adjacent orders given as a percentage; actual numbers of sequences in parentheses.

TABLE 5.5   Weight and lexical dependency in English prepositional phrase orderings (Hawkins 2000: 247)

n = 206	Pd > Pi by			Pd = Pi	Pi > Pd by		
	5+	2–4	1	1	1	2–4	5+
[V Pd Pi]	7% (2)	33% (6)	74% (17)	83% (24)	92% (23)	96% (49)	100% (30)
[V Pi Pd]	93% (28)	67% (12)	26% (6)	17% (5)	8% (2)	4% (2)	0% (0)

Pd = the PP that is interdependent with V by one or both entailment tests.
Pi = the PP that is independent of V by both entailment tests.
Proportion of adjacent V-Pd to non-adjacent orders given as a percentage; actual numbers of sequences in parentheses.

Multiple preferences therefore have an additive adjacency effect by increasing the number of processing domains that prefer minimization. They can also result in exceptions to each preference when they pull in different directions. Most of the fifty-eight exceptional long-before-short sequences in Table 5.1 do indeed involve a dependency or lexical match between V and the longer PP (Hawkins 2000), applying in proportion to the kind of domain minimization preference shown in Table 5.4. Conversely, V and Pd can be pulled apart by EIC, in proportion to the weight difference between Pd and Pi. This is shown in Table 5.5.

When Pi > Pd and both weight (minimal PCDs) and lexical dependency prefer Pd adjacent to V, there is almost exceptionless adjacency (in the righthand columns). When weights are equal and exert no preference, there is a strong (83%) lexical dependency effect. When the two preferences

dependencies than the other. I have excluded these five here, resulting in a total of 206 sequences, in all of which one PP is completely independent while the other PP is interdependent with V by at least one entailment test.

conflict and the dependent Pd is longer than Pi (in the left-hand columns) EIC asserts itself in proportion to its degree of preference: for one-word differentials lexical dependency still claims the majority (76%) adjacent to V; for 2–4-word differentials the short-before-long preference wins by 67% to 33%; and for 5+ word differentials it wins by a larger margin of 93% to 7%. EIC therefore asserts itself in proportion to its degree of preference for minimal PCDs. I shall return to a further discussion of these data in §5.2.3.

Let us conclude this section by defining a Lexical Domain:

(5.6) *Lexical Domain* (LD)
The LD for assignment of a lexically listed property P to a lexical item L consists of the smallest possible string of terminal elements (plus their associated syntactic and semantic properties) on the basis of which the processor can assign P to L.

I make fairly standard assumptions about the properties that are listed in the lexicon. They include: the syntactic category or categories of L (noun, verb, preposition, etc.); the syntactic co-occurrence frame(s) of L, i.e. its 'strict subcategorization' requirements of Chomsky (1965) (e.g. V may be intransitive or transitive, if intransitive it may require an obligatory PP headed by a particular preposition, or there may be an optionally co-occurring PP headed by a particular preposition, etc.); 'selectional restrictions' imposed by L (Chomsky 1965) (e.g. *drink* requires an animate subject and liquid object); syntactic and semantic properties assigned to the complements of L (e.g. the theta-role assigned to a direct object NP by V); the different range of meanings assignable to L with respect to which L is ambiguous or polysemous (the different senses of *count* and *follow* and *run*); and frequent collocations of forms, whether 'transparent' or 'opaque' in Wasow's (1997, 2002) sense. Some of these properties are necessarily combinatorial and their processing prefers a minimal domain linking the items combined (e.g. the subcategorizor and its subcategorized phrase(s)). Others may be combinatorial in some languages and structures only. Syntactic category assignment may require access to a co-occurring item (*a run* v. *to run*, etc., see §2.2, §4.4.2) or it may be unique to the lexical item in question (*student* is a noun only and not a verb in English). The meaning of a particular verb may not vary in combination with a direct-object NP or a PP. Whenever there is a relation of lexical combination and/or dependency, however, the present theory defines a minimization preference for the domain within which the lexically listed property is assigned.

5.2.2   *Multiple preferences in Japanese*

For the Japanese data of Table 5.3 I predict a similar preference for complements and other lexically co-occurring items adjacent to the verb, and a similar (but again mirror-image) interaction with the long-before-short weight preference. The verb contracts more syntactic and semantic relations with a direct object NP as a second argument or complement than it does with a PP, many or most of which will be adjuncts rather than complements. Hence a preference for NP adjacency is predicted, even when the PP is shorter and will then precede the longer NP, though this preference should decline with the increasing (relative) heaviness of the NP and with the increasing EIC pressure in favor of long before short phrases. This is confirmed in Table 5.6, where NP-V adjacency stands at 69% overall (169/244) and is as high as 62% for NPs longer than PP by 1–2 words and 50% for NPs longer by 3–4 words, yielding to the (overall preferred) long before short pattern only for 5+ word differentials (21%).

When EIC and complement adjacency reinforce each other in favor of [PPm NPo V] in the right-hand columns, the result is significantly higher NP adjacency (of 80%, 84%, and 100%). When weights are equal there is a strong (66%) NP adjacency preference defined by the complement-processing preference alone. And when EIC and complement adjacency are opposed in the left-hand columns, the results are split and EIC applies in proportion to its degree of preference. Table 5.6 is the mirror image of Table 5.5 with respect to the interaction between EIC and lexical domain processing, the former for a head-initial language, the latter for a head-final one.

One further prediction that remains to be tested on Japanese involves the PP-V adjacencies, especially those in the right-hand columns in which adjacency is not predicted by weight. These adjacencies should be motivated by strong lexical dependencies, i.e. they should either be complements or lexical

TABLE 5.6   Weight and direct object adjacency in Japanese (Hawkins 1994: 152; data collected by Kaoru Horie)

n = 244	NPo > PPm by			NPo = PPm	PPm > PPo by		
	5+	3–4	1–2		1–2	3–8	9+
[PPm NPo V]	21% (3)	50% (5)	62% (18)	66% (60)	80% (48)	84% (26)	100% (9)
[NPo PPm V]	79% (11)	50% (5)	38% (11)	34% (31)	20% (12)	16% (5)	0% (0)

NPo = see Table 5.3.
PPm = see Table 5.3.
Proportion of adjacent NPo-V to non-adjacent orders given as a percentage; actual numbers of sequences in parentheses.

collocations in Wasow's (1997, 2002) sense, and more fine-tuned testing should be conducted in order to distinguish the different PP types of Japanese here.

5.2.3   *Total domain differentials*

The existence of multiple domains and preferences for the processing of syntactic and semantic properties requires a metric that can assess their combined effect within a given structure. The principle of MiD (3.1) predicts tighter adjacency, the more combinatorial and dependency relations there are, and in proportion to the difference between competing domains in the processing of each relation. For the English V-PP-PP sequences, both of these (essentially relative) predictions were confirmed, in the data of Tables 5.1, 5.4, and 5.5. But can we make any more absolute predictions for when e.g. the [V Pi Pd] variant will actually be selected over [V Pd Pi], as a function of its overall efficiency?

In the data of Table 5.5 there is a revealing conflict in the left-hand columns between relative weight (or phrase structure combination and the resulting short-before-long preference) and the preferred adjacency of lexically dependent PPs (Pd). These data suggest at first that relative weight is the stronger preference, since lexical dependency claims a majority (of 74%) only when the resulting long-before-short ordering involves a one-word difference, and for all other relative weights of 2+ words, the majority of orders are short-before-long with the dependent Pd non-adjacent to V.

But there is another way to view this interaction. Recall that the adjacency preference of Pd is proportional to the size of any intervening Pi (Table 5.4). Every PP, whether Pd or Pi, will be at least two words in length, since it comprises a preposition and at least a one-word NP. Perhaps, therefore, the reason why a relative weight difference of one word cannot generally assert itself in favor of the normally preferred short-before-long order, when the longer PP is a Pd, is because the size of an intervening Pi will be longer (at 2+ words) than a relative weight difference of 1. Hence the LD differential will always exceed the PCD differential in this case, and the overall efficiency of the structure will be greater when Pd is adjacent to V. As the relative weights increase, however, their word differential totals will gradually equal or exceed the absolute size of Pi, and the overall efficiency of the sequence will shift in favor of relative weight and minimal PCDs.

In other words, I suggest that we make predictions for the relative strength of these two factors, the syntactic (phrasal combination) and the lexical, by measuring their respective domain minimizations in terms of words. We can then formulate a prediction for the selection of a particular structural variant based on an assessment of the degree of minimization that can be accomplished in each domain within each competing sequence. Whichever sequence has the highest overall minimization will be more efficient and should be the one selected.

Let us define a Total Domain Differential (TDD) as in (5.7) and an associated prediction for performance as in (5.8):

(5.7)   *Total Domain Differential* (TDD)
       The TDD is the collective minimization difference between two competing sequences measured in words and calculated on the basis of the phrasal combination domains, lexical domains, or other domains required for the processing of syntactic or semantic relations within these sequences.

(5.8)   *TDD Performance Prediction*
       Sequences with the highest collective minimization differences will be those that are preferably selected, in proportion to their relative TDDs.

For the data of Table 5.5 we are dealing with phrasal combination domains (EIC effects) and with lexical domains (using the entailments of §5.2.1 as a diagnostic for lexical combinations—see fn. 8). The TDD predictions can be set out as follows:

(5.9)   *TDD Predictions for Table 5.5*
       For Pi > Pd   Only [V Pd Pi] preferred
       [V Pd Pi]   Both PCDs and LDs prefer
       [V Pi Pd]   Neither prefer
       For Pi = Pd   No PCD preference
       [V Pd Pi]   LD prefers (in proportion to Pi size)
       [V Pi Pd]   LD disprefers (in proportion to Pi size)
       For Pd > Pi   PCD and LD conflict
       [V Pd Pi]   LD preference ≥ PCD preference (i.e. the size of Pi ≥ weight difference)
       [V Pi Pd]   PCD preference ≥ LD preference (i.e. the weight difference ≥ size of Pi)

These predictions are straightforward when Pi > Pd and when weights are equal, since a Pd adjacent to V is always preferred. But matters are more interesting when Pd is the longer phrase, as in *count [on his support] [in warfare]*. The Pd consists of three words here and the Pi of two. The LD prefers [V Pd Pi] over [V Pi Pd] by two words, therefore. The weight difference (Pd > Pi) is one word, so the PCD prefers [V Pi Pd] by one. The LD preference exceeds the PCD preference, so the (long-before-short) [V Pd Pi] is predicted overall. In *count [in old age] [on the lost son of my past]*, on the other hand, the Pd has seven words and Pi has three. The weight difference is now four, which exceeds the size of Pi. The PCD preference for [V Pi Pd] exceeds the LD preference for [V Pd Pi] by 1, so (short-before-long) [V Pi Pd] is predicted overall.

The results are set out in (5.10). I first give the total number correct for the 206 sequences of Table 5.5 (a full 90%), along with the numbers that come within one word per domain of being correct. I then give separate figures for the conflict cases in which Pd > Pi. The success rate here is 83%, and this jumps to 97% for sequences that come within one word per domain of the preferred TDD.

(5.10) *Results for Table 5.5*
   Total with preferred orders = 90% (185/206)
      Additional total within 1 word per domain of preferred TDD = 95% (196/206)
   Total correct in conflict cases = 83% (59/71)
      Additional total within 1 word per domain of preferred TDD = 97% (69/71)

These figures provide encouraging support for a multiple-domain approach to relative ordering and specifically for the predictions of (5.8). A TDD as defined in (5.7) is measured in numbers of words, but this could easily be adapted to quantify a more inclusive node count, or a count in terms of phrasal nodes only. I expect that Wasow's (1997, 2002) demonstration of the high intercorrelation between different units of measurement for EIC will generalize to other domains as well. The predictions of (5.8) also count different domains equally and assess their collective preference in terms of the (minimum) word total required for processing across all domains. I shall comment on this presently.

There is an important general principle that we see in these data, especially when different processing operations make competing demands. Sometimes one of these exerts a stronger preference for ordering and adjacency, and sometimes their relative strength is reversed. We cannot say that one preference is always stronger than the other, therefore. It depends on the particular properties of individual sentences, specifically on the relative weights of the two PPs and on the absolute size of the Pi. This has consequences for any performance model or for a grammatical model like Stochastic Optimality Theory (Bresnan et al. 2001, Manning 2003) that defines relative strengths in advance and that gives not just a ranking but a graded ranking between constraints reflecting these relative strengths. We see here that the relative rankings can change, based on idiosyncrasies in the data. The crucial data sets (the conflict cases) provide no evidence for any inherent ranking between phrasal combination and lexical co-occurrence processing, let alone a graded one.

The theory proposed here predicts relative strengths and rankings on the basis of a single general principle of minimization (5.7). It does not stipulate them, it derives them, and it predicts the degree to which each factor will apply in a given sentence type. Stochastic rankings and ranking reversals follow from (5.7), and by having a general predictor we avoid having to define probabilities for performance selections in certain data sets based only on an observed quantification of these selections.

It may be that (5.7) is unrealistic and that we do need to build in certain inherent strength asymmetries between factors. But if we are going to bias our calculations in some way, we have to have a good theoretical reason for doing so, beyond simple observation of the facts. Can we expect phrasal combination effects to be stronger than lexical co-occurrence effects, in general, even when their potential minimizations are equal? The data of (5.10) suggest not, but other interactions may suggest otherwise. In the absence of a good theory motivating why one processing domain should be inherently stronger or weaker than another, it is worth exploring how far we can go by counting word minimizations across domains equally. In the event that a principled reason can eventually be given for why one domain should exert a stronger influence on structure selection than another, this can easily be factored into the predictions, but in the meantime I shall run the tests assuming equality between different processing domains. The domains themselves are independently motivated by grammatical, lexical, and processing theories, and their respective minimizations in different structural variants will define their different strengths.

Notice finally that the predictions of this section have made no reference to the pragmatic information status of the two postverbal PPs in English, but have been based on syntactic and semantic relations only. In Hawkins (1994: 214–42) I argued that weight effects (short-before-long and long-before-short) are highly correlated with given-before-new and new-before-given orders respectively, and that much of the apparent support for pragmatic theories of word order flexibility could be reanalyzed as an EIC effect, i.e. in terms of syntactic processing efficiency. I suggested that a pragmatic explanation for 'discourse-configurational nodes', such as topic and focus, was convincing, but that a pragmatic explanation for scramblings in free word order structures was much less so, given the correlations with weight. In Hawkins (2000: 255–7) I examined a large subset of the double PP data considered here and classified them according to their given-before-new and new-before-given status, and I compared the pragmatic predictions of Firbas (1966) and Givón (1983,

1988) with those of EIC and lexical adjacency. The preference for given-before-new over new-before-given was significant in these English data. However, the strength of this preference, as measured by the number of sequences correctly predicted, was weaker than that of the other factors, and pragmatics did not appear to play a predictive role in data subsets for which the other factors defined only a weak or no preference, which led me to question its significance again (in free word order structures). Since then, however, Arnold et al. (2000) have shown, for Dative Movement and Heavy NP Shift alternations in English, that there is evidence for pragmatic status as an additional contributing factor, even though pragmatics and weight are correlated. This is an important result. Clearly we need more such studies in which pragmatic factors are included among other determinants of relative ordering, in order to determine the precise role of each. Such studies are particularly vital in head-final languages, in which long-before-short orders should favor a new-before-given pragmatic ordering at variance with given-before-new (cf. Hawkins 1994: 232–42).

5.3   EIC preferences for adjacency in grammars

Grammatical conventions across languages reveal the same degrees of preference for minimal phrasal combination domains that were evident in the performance data of §5.1. The grammatical preferences can be seen in patterns of attested v. non-attested basic word orders, in relative quantities of languages, in distinctions between different types of categories, e.g. between single-word and branching phrasal categories, and in hierarchies of co-occurring word orders. They can also be seen in the different directionalities for rearrangement rules in head-initial and head-final languages.

5.3.1   *The Greenbergian correlations*

The Greenbergian word order correlations provide strong evidence that the adjacency of lexical head categories is massively preferred over non-adjacency. EIC predicts these correlations. Two of them are presented in (5.11) and (5.12), with IC-to-word ratios given for each order in (5.11).[11] (5.11) shows a correlation between verb-initial order and prepositions, and between verb-final and postpositions (i.e. phrases corresponding to [*went* [*to the store*]] v. [[*the*

---

[11] The quantitative data in (5.11) are taken from Matthew Dryer's sample, measuring languages rather than genera (see Dryer 1992, Hawkins 1994: 257). A genus for Dryer is a genetic grouping of languages comparable in time depth to the subfamilies of Indo-European. The quantitative data in (5.12) come from Hawkins (1983, 1994: 259).

store to] went]). (5.12) shows one between prepositions and nouns preceding possessive (genitive) phrases and between postpositions and nouns following (corresponding to [*in*[*books of my professor*]] v. [[*my professor of books] in*]).

(5.11) a. vp[V pp[P NP]] = 161 (41%)   b. [[NP P]pp V]vp = 204 (52%)
            IC-to-word: 2/2 = 100%   IC-to-word: 2/2 = 100%
         c. vp[V [NP P]pp] = 18 (5%)   d. [pp[P NP] V]vp = 6 (2%)
            IC-to-word: 2/4 = 50%   IC-to-word: 2/4 = 50%
            Assume: V = 1 word; P = 1; NP = 2
            EIC-preferred (5.11a) + (5.11b) = 365/389 (94%)

(5.12) a. pp[P np[N Possp]] = 134 (40%)   b. [[Possp N]np P]pp = 177 (53%)
         c. pp[P [Possp N]np] = 14 (4%)   d. [np[N Possp] P]pp = 11 (3%)
            EIC-preferred (5.12a) + (5.12b) = 311/336 (93%)

The adjacency of V and P, and of P and N, guarantees the shortest possible domain for the recognition and production of the two ICs in question (V and PP within VP, P and NP within PP). Two adjacent words suffice, hence 100% IC-to-word ratios. In the non-adjacent domains of the (c) and (d) orders, ratios are significantly lower and exemplifying languages are significantly less. The preferred (a) and (b) structures collectively account for 94% and 93% of all languages respectively.

It is patterns like these that have motivated the head-initial (or VO) and head-final (OV) parameters in both typological and generative research: see e.g. Vennemann (1974), W. Lehmann (1978), Hawkins (1983), Travis (1984, 1989), and Dryer (1992). The two language types are mirror images of one another, and EIC offers an explanation for this: both (a) and (b) are optimally efficient. They are equally good strategies for phrase structure production and recognition, and both are predicted to be productive.

A purely grammatical approach to linear ordering can also capture the preferences of (5.11) and (5.12) by defining a head ordering parameter, as the works just cited do. This parameter is either stipulated, or else some attempt is made to derive it from independent grammatical considerations. In Hawkins (1983) I argued, using an X-bar rule schema of the type introduced in Jackendoff (1977), that grammars with consistent cross-categorial orders of head categories were simpler in proportion to their consistency than grammars with inconsistent head orderings, since fewer ordering rules or statements were needed overall. Category-specific rules could be replaced by general rules valid for all phrases when the internal ordering of daughter categories was consistent. The theory of EIC, by contrast, is a grammar-external explanation. I now believe that it is more explanatory than a grammar-internal theory. It is also descriptively more adequate in relation to the cross-linguistic facts. It makes predictions for typological variation that grammatical considerations alone do not make, and these predictions appear to be supported. The data of (5.11) and (5.12) do not provide conclusive evidence for an EIC-type explanation over a grammar-internal one, therefore, but other considerations do.[12]

For example, Matthew Dryer has shown in his important paper on the Greenbergian correlations (Dryer 1992) that there are systematic exceptions to consistent head ordering when the non-head category is a single-word item such as an adjective in relation to a noun (e.g. *yellow book*) or an intensifying adverb in relation to an adjective (e.g. *very smart*). There are many otherwise head-initial languages with non-initial heads in these constructions (e.g. English), and conversely there are many predominantly head-final languages with head-initial orders such as noun before adjective (e.g. Basque). When the non-head is a branching phrasal category, however, there are good correlations with the predominant head ordering position, exemplified by the position of the verb in relation to its direct object within the VP (i.e. VO v. OV), and Dryer proposes a Branching Direction Theory as an alternative to the head ordering parameter. The reality of this single word/branching phrase difference can be seen in English in the contrast between single-word prenominal adjectives (*yellow book*) and postnominal adjective phrases (*book yellow with age*).

In terms of grammar, single-word adjectives and multi-word adjective phrase sisters are most plausibly of the same grammatical type, namely adjective phrases, i.e. np[adjp[*yellow*] *book*] and np[*book* adjp[*yellow* [*with age*]]]. All things being equal they should pattern the same way with respect to rules that refer to adjective phrases, such as positioning rules. To the extent that they do not, it should be possible, from the perspective of a purely grammatical theory, to find a grammatical basis for distinguishing them. But the

---

[12] Svenonius (2000) argues that the 'headedness parameter' illustrated by these Greenbergian correlations is 'arguably not a function of processing' (p. 7). He may be right, of course, but a purely grammatical approach simply stipulates this parameter, and fails to capture the minimization generalization that is evident both in grammatical rules/principles and in performance data from languages with free orderings. Nor is the headedness parameter descriptively adequate, without further stipulation: there is a systematic difference between heads with branching phrasal sisters (such as NPs or PossPs) and those with non-branching single-word sisters, as discussed in the main text. All of the patterns in this chapter follow from processing ease, specifically from MiD (3.1). There may be a better processing explanation ultimately. There may eventually be less stipulative accounts of the grammatical conventions. But in the meantime we have what appear to be significant generalizations across grammatical and performance data, and various theories of grammar (surveyed in detail in Dryer 1992) whose very autonomy prevents them from capturing these generalizations and from becoming more explanatory. See §9.2 for elaboration of this point.

single-word/multi-word difference is primarily a difference in terminal content among identical phrases. And excluding the unwanted daughter complements of the adjective phrase in prenominal position (i.e. excluding *the yellow with age book*) is not actually straightforward grammatically. Normally if a rule of positioning, rearrangement, deletion, and substitution refers to a mother phrase, the daughters of that mother are automatically positioned, rearranged, etc. along with the mother, but not here.[13] And even if some difference in type can be justified between pre-nominal adjectives and post-nominal adjective phrases, it would need to be shown in a grammar-only theory why the difference in question should correlate with their respective positions. The grammar alone does not predict Dryer's single-word/multi-word distinction, therefore, and stipulations without explanatory motivation are required. EIC, by contrast, explains and predicts the difference as follows.

When a head category like N has a branching phrasal sister like adjp {*yellow, with age*} or possp{*of, the professor*}, the distance from N to the head category P or V that constructs the next higher phrase, PP or VP respectively, will be very long when head orderings are inconsistent. Thus, the IC-to-word ratios for (5.12c) pp[P [Possp N]np] and (5.12d) [np[N Possp] P]pp are significantly lower than for (5.12a) pp[P np[N Possp]] and (5.12b) [[Possp N]np P]pp, since the branching phrasal category Possp intervenes between P and N. But if the intervening category is a non-branching single-word category, like an adjective, then the difference between, say, pp[P np[N Adj]] and pp[P [Adj N]np] is not that great—only one word. Hence the domain minimization preference for noun initiality (and correspondingly for noun finality in postpositional languages) is significantly less than it is for intervening branching phrases like possessive phrases or adjective phrases like *yellow with age*. In fact, when there is only a one-word difference between competing domains in performance data (see the double PP orderings of Table 5.1), both ordering options are generally productive, and so they are too in grammars.[14]

The correlations between head orderings for which branching phrases can potentially intervene, and the lack of correlation for non-branching categories, is consistent with EIC's preferences. EIC predicts consistency in the former case, since domain size differences between adjacent and non-adjacent heads are considerable. It predicts either less consistency or inconsistency in the latter case, when domain size differences are small, which is what we find.

---

[13] See Hawkins (1994: 282–93) for discussion.

[14] See Hawkins (1994: 282–93) for discussion of the discrepancy between prenominal and postnominal modifiers in the grammar of English, in terms of EIC, and for a similar discrepancy between preverbal and postverbal modifying phrases.

5.3.2   *Other ordering universals*

We can make further predictions from EIC that are not predicted by grammatical considerations alone. Consider multiple branching NPs consisting of a head noun (N), a single-word adjective (Adj), and a relative clause (S′) exemplified by (5.13) in English:

(5.13) beautiful sonatas [that Menuhin will perform]

Adjectives and relative clauses are similar categories syntactically in that both are adjunct sisters of a noun. They also have a similar semantic potential for restrictive or appositive modification of the noun. The relative orderings of these three items, and the correlations between these orderings and the relative positioning of items internal to the relative clause such as the verb and the complementizer, are subject to severe universal constraints which are not expected on grammatical grounds alone. Consider the gross structure of (5.13):

(5.13′) np[Adj N s′[C S]]

C stands here for the category that constructs the relative clause (relative pronouns or complementizers in English, a subordination affix attached to a finite verb as in Basque, participial marking on non-finite verbs indicating subordinate status as in Turkish: see C. Lehmann 1984, Hawkins 1994: 387–93). There are twelve logically possible orderings of Adj, N, and S′ (ordered [C S] or [S C]). Only four of these have 100% IC-to-word ratios for the NP PCD (all with adjacent Adj, N, and C), and these four are exactly those found in the vast majority of languages:

(5.14)	Structure	IC-to-word ratio	Attested languages
A	[N Adj [C S]]	3/3 = 100%	Extensive: Romance, Arabic, Ewe
B	[Adj N [C S]]	3/3 = 100%	Extensive: Germanic, Greek, Finnish
C	[[S C] N Adj]	3/3 = 100%	Extensive: Basque, Burmese
D	[[S C] Adj N]	3/3 = 100%	Extensive: Tamil, Turkish, Lahu

The remaining eight orders all have significantly lower ratios and only a small minority of languages are distributed among them, in proportion to their IC-to-word ratios calculated according to the on-line efficiency metric of Hawkins (1990) and (1994: 82) see fn. 3 of Chapter 3. Once again, optimally minimal domains for phrasal combination are found in the great majority of languages, with minor language types attested in proportion to their relative degree of efficiency.

Degrees of preference can be seen especially clearly in hierarchies of co-occurring word orders. These hierarchies are not predicted by grammars, nor are they predicted by the simple dichotomy between branching and non-branching nodes, as in Dryer's (1992) theory. They point instead to the need for graded distinctions between different branching nodes, as a function of their aggregate complexity and its impact on domain size.

It has been well known since Miller & Chomsky (1963), Bever (1970), and Kimball (1973) that center embeddings are hard structures to process. This dispreference follows, in large measure, from EIC. The more complex a center-embedded constituent is (e.g. the heavier an NP in vp[V NP PP]) and the longer the resulting PCD, the greater will be EIC's degree of dispreference.[15] Correlating with this there are hierarchies of tolerance for center embed-dings of different degrees of complexity in the conventions of grammars. For example, in the center-embedded environment between a preposition and a head noun within NP, i.e. pp[P np[__ N]], we find the implicational and dis-tributional patterns shown in (5.15) and (5.16). Prenominal categories lower on this hierarchy generally require the co-occurrence of those higher on it, and are correspondingly less frequent across languages compared with their postnominal counterparts.[16]

(5.15) a. Prep: [NDem, NAdj, NPossp, NRel]   e.g. Arabic, Thai
        b. Prep: DemN   [NAdj, NPossp, NRel]   e.g. Masai, Spanish
        c. Prep: DemN, AdjN   [NPossp, NRel]   e.g. Greek, Maya
        d. Prep: DemN, AdjN, PosspN   [NRel]   e.g. Maung
        e. Prep: DemN, AdjN, PosspN, RelN   e.g. Amharic

(5.16) DemN   49%   NDem   51%
        AdjN   32%   NAdj   68%
        PosspN   12%   NPossp   88%
        RelN   1%   NRel   99%

---

[15] See Vasishth (2002) for discussion and experimental evidence (primarily from Hindi) regarding the role of identical case marking and other factors that contribute to processing difficulty in clausal center embeddings.

[16] The precise implicational statements that structure the Prepositional Noun Modifier Hierarchy of (5.15) are the following (see Hawkins 1983: 75): If a language is prepositional, then if RelN then PosspN (exceptionless in Hawkins (1983: 73)); if PosspN then AdjN (97% of prep lgs are compatible with this implication in Hawkins (1983: 288)); and if AdjN then DemN (exceptionless in Hawkins (1983: 71) but e.g. Sango is a counterexample: see Dryer (1993)). The distributional data of (5.16) come from Hawkins (1983: 96).

TABLE 5.7   A center-embedding hierarchy (Hawkins 1983: 75, 96)

Structure	Modifer ratio preposed	Lg quantity preposed	Modifier ratio postposed	Lg quantity postposed
pp[P np{Dem, N}]	2/2 = 100%	49%	2/2 = 100%	51%
pp[P np{Adj, N}]	2/3 = 67%	32%	2/2 = 100%	68%
pp[P np{Possp, N}]	2/4 = 50%	12%	2/2 = 100%	88%
pp[P np{Rel, N}]	2/6 = 33%	1%	2/2 = 100%	99%

Assume: Dem = 1 word, Adj = 1, Possp = 2, Rel = 4.
Assume: P constructs PP, N or Dem constructs NP.

Relative clauses are on aggregate longer and more complex categories than possessive phrases, which are on aggregate longer than single-word adjectives. If a language permits the relative clause to intervene between P and N, it permits the less complex possessive phrase, and if it permits the latter it generally permits single-word adjectives. Demonstrative determiners construct the same phrase (NP) as head nouns in the theory of Hawkins (1993, 1994) and both [P [DemN]] and [P [NDem]] are therefore equally efficient. The relative IC-to-word ratios for preposed (center-embedded) and postposed orders are calculated in Table 5.7. As center-embedded categories of increasing aggregate length intervene (Adj < Possp < Rel), increasing the size of the PCD for PP, the ratios decline and the number of attested grammars declines. The only center-embedded category that is productive at all is the single-word adjective (at 32%), for the reasons discussed in §5.3.1.[17] Prenominal possessive phrases are found in only 12% of prepositional languages, and prenominal relatives in only 1%.

What Table 5.7 shows is that as domain sizes increase, the minimization preference for head-adjacent over center-embedded orders increases also, and the number of attested grammars declines. This and other center-embedding

---

[17] Given the relative markedness of pre-nominal positioning for adjectives in the head-initial language English, it is interesting to note the following performance statistics from the Longman Spoken and Written English Corpus. Biber et al. (1999: 597) point out that 70–80% of premodified noun phrases in English are limited to a single-word premodifier (which may be a single-word adjective, a participial (-*ed* or -*ing*) adjective, or a noun modifying a head noun). About 20% have two-word premodification, and only about 2% have three or four-word premodification. The potential expansion in the PCD for PP that is permitted by the grammar when premodifiers intervene between P and the head of NP is severely limited in performance, therefore, since the great majority of premodifiers are single words. Moreover, many of these premodifiers will be preceded by determiners which will construct the NP (or DP) in advance of N (Biber et al. do not supply the figures here). The degree of non-minimality that actually occurs in the PCDs for PP in English performance appears to be quite small. It would be interesting to compare premodifier length in English both with and without a preceding determiner, and in preverbal and postverbal position.

hierarchies are structured by degrees of preference for minimal v. non-minimal domains (Hawkins 1994: 315–21). Differences between branching categories such as possessive phrases and relative clauses are not predicted by Dryer's (1992) Branching Direction Theory since they are both simply branching as opposed to non-branching. But the former are significantly shorter on aggregate than the latter, and this predicts a stronger possibility of occurrence in prenominal position within a head-initial language than for relative clauses, which is what we find in Table 5.7 and in languages such as English.[18]

EIC also predicts different directionalities for transformational rules of rearrangement in head-initial and head-final languages. Rules such as Heavy NP Shift, Extraposition, and Extraposition from NP in a language like English are predicted to rearrange complex NPs, VPs, and Ss to the right, since these phrases are constructed by projecting categories such as N, Det, Comp, etc., at or near their left peripheries. PCDs can be shortened by a rightward movement from a basic order for phrases that are unusually long (cf. the supporting performance data summarized in §5.1.1 and in Hawkins 1994, Wasow 1997, 2002). For head-final languages, similar domain minimization benefits are achieved by preposing complex constituents that are constructed at or near their right peripheries. For example, preposing a potentially center-embedded object complement in Japanese with a right peripheral complementizer (i.e. s[NP s′[S C] V] $\Rightarrow$ s[s′[S C] NP V]) results in a much smaller PCD for processing the matrix clause. Matrix and subordinate clauses are each processed in short and efficient domains, just as they are in English, though the relative ordering is now subordinate before matrix v. matrix before subordinate in English.

This processing theory motivates rightward movements for complex constituents in head-initial languages, therefore, contra the stipulations of current antisymmetry theories deriving from Kayne (1994) (cf. §8.6). Head-final languages with head-final projecting categories in complex constituents are predicted to rearrange them to the left.

These EIC effects in grammars support the Performance–Grammar Correspondence Hypothesis (PGCH) of §1.1. The preferred PCDs in the performance

---

[18] The Longman Spoken and Written English Corpus provides striking support for the markedness of prenominal *s*-genitives in English v. the postnominal *of*-genitive. Biber et al. (1999: 304) show that the former is in the majority only for one-word genitives (*Bill's dog*), and that the majority shifts to the *of*-phrase for 2+words, attaining almost 100% for 4+words. Their (approximated) figures are:

1-word genitive:	65% -s	35% *of*
2-word genitive:	35% -s	65% *of*
3-word genitive:	5% -s	95% *of*
4-word genitive:	< 2.5% -s	almost 100% *of*

The potential distance permitted by the grammar of English between P and N when an *s*-genitive intervenes is therefore kept to a real minimum in performance.

data of Tables 5.1, 5.2, and 5.3 were minimal ones. Correspondingly, the preferred PCDs in the grammatical data of the Greenbergian correlations ((5.11)
and (5.12)) are also minimal ones, as are those in the preferred multiple branching structures of (5.14). This supports PGCH prediction (1.2a): 'If a structure
A is preferred over an A′ of the same structural type in performance, then A
will be more productively grammaticalized, . . .; if A and A′ are more equally
preferred, then A and A′ will both be productive in grammars.' The PCDs for
(5.11a) with [V [P NP]] and for (5.11b) with [[NP P] V] are both minimal,
and these are highly productive grammatical conventions. The corresponding non-minimal PCDs, (5.11c) [V [NP P]] and (5.11d) [[P NP] V], are not
productive.

The center-embedding hierarchy data of Table 5.7 support PGCH prediction (1.2b): 'If there is a preference ranking A>B>C>D among structures of
a common type in performance, then there will be a corresponding hierarchy
of grammatical conventions (with cut-off points and declining frequencies of
languages).' The data of Tables 5.1, 5.2, and 5.3 showed that progressively fewer
structures of the relevant types were selected in performance as PCD sizes
increased, resulting in bigger differences between competitors. Correspondingly, there is a progressive dispreference for larger PCDs in the grammatical
hierarchy of Table 5.7, and this is manifested in the increasing numbers of
grammars that cut off (i.e. that define ungrammatical orderings) at each point
down the hierarchy.

5.4   Multiple preferences for adjacency in grammars

Grammatical conventions also reveal a preference for orderings in proportion
to the number of combinatorial and dependency relations whose processing
domains are minimized, just as the performance data of §5.2 did. Consider
first the positioning of complements and adjuncts.

Complements prefer adjacency to their heads over adjuncts in the basic order
conventions of numerous phrases in English and other languages and are generated adjacent to the head in the phrase structure grammars of Jackendoff
(1977) and Pollard & Sag (1987). Tomlin's (1986) Verb Object Bonding principle provides further cross-linguistic support for this, since he points to
languages in which it is impossible or dispreferred for adjuncts to intervene
between a verbal head and its subcategorized direct object complement. In
fact, Jackendoff's X-bar theory defines varying degrees of adjacency between
heads and their accompanying non-heads. The tightest adjacency is between
the head (X) and its complements, both of which are immediately dominated

by an X with a single bar, X′. The next level of adjacency is between the head and a restrictive adjunct, dominated by X″. And the least adjacency is between the head and an appositive adjunct, dominated by X‴. This is shown in (5.17):

(5.17)

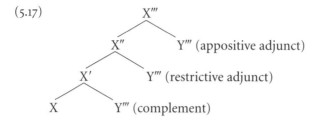

Why should complements be closest to the head? The basic reason I would offer is that complements also prefer head adjacency over adjuncts in perform-ance, in the data of Tables 5.4/5.5 and 5.6, and the explanation I offered for this in turn was that there are more combinatorial and/or dependency relations that link complements to their heads than link adjuncts to their heads. Hence there are more processing domains that can be minimized when complement and head are adjacent.

First, recall that complements are listed in a lexical co-occurrence frame that is defined by, and activated in on-line processing by, a specific head such as a verb. Adjuncts are not so listed and they occur in a wide variety of phrases with which they are semantically compatible (cf. Pollard & Sag 1994). Processing the lexical co-occurrence frame of a verb within a particular sentence therefore favors a minimal Lexical Domain (5.6) linking that verb to the complements or arguments selected. The reality of this preference was seen in the lexical dependency and lexical matching effects observed between intransitive verbs and PPs in the English double PP data of §5.2.1.

Second, there are more productive relations of semantic and syntactic interdependency between heads and complements than between heads and adjuncts—i.e. there are more cases in which the meaning or grammar of one of these categories requires access to the other for its assignment. Processing these interdependencies favors minimal domains.

A direct object, for example, receives its theta-role from the transitive verb, typically a subtype of Dowty's (1991) Proto-Patient role, depending on the particular verb. Adjuncts, by contrast, do not receive theta-roles (cf. Grimshaw 1990). A direct object is also syntactically required by a transitive verb for gram-maticality, whereas adjuncts are not syntactically required sisters. Assigning the appropriate theta-role to the required direct object favors a minimal lexical domain (cf. (5.6)).

Conversely transitive verbs regularly undergo 'function category range reduction' (Keenan 1979) by the direct object NP. Recall the different senses of *run* in *run the race, run the water, run the advertisement,* and so on. The verb is lexically dependent on the direct object for its precise interpretation, but it is not dependent on an accompanying adjunct such as *in the afternoon* (in e.g. *run the race in the afternoon*). Similarly intransitive verbs are frequently dependent on PP complements for their interpretation, as we saw with *count on X*.

Adjuncts may, however, be lexically dependent on a verb by Keenan's principle, as function categories that take verbs as arguments. Compare the different senses of the adverb *smoothly* in *sail smoothly, land smoothly,* and *talk smoothly*. But the number of semantic and syntactic dependencies that link adjuncts to their heads are fewer overall, since adjuncts do not receive theta-roles, they are not grammatically required, and their heads are not lexically dependent on them for their precise interpretation.

A third relevant factor for verb–complement adjacency is EIC. Direct object NPs are shorter on aggregate than PPs, whether complements or adjuncts, and shorter than many other sisters of a transitive verb, and hence phrase structure processing can be more efficient when the NP immediately follows V in head-initial (short-before-long) languages, and immediately precedes it in head-final ones. For example, the aggregate length of the NP in [V NP PP] and [V PP NP] sequences in the English corpus of Hawkins (1994: 183) was 2.5 words, that of the PP 4.6 words, i.e. the PP was almost twice as long. When NP and PP are both complements of V, with verbs like *put* (X *on* Y) and *give* (X *to* Y), the adjacency of the NP will still be preferred by EIC.

Given that adjuncts are not listed in lexical co-occurrence frames and are less interdependent with their heads than complements, the theory proposed here predicts that adjuncts will only intervene between a head and a complement if they are short and can minimize PCDs, thereby speeding up phrase structure processing. Adjuncts adjacent to their heads should therefore be shorter than any accompanying complements, with adjacent single-word adverbials being most favored since they yield the highest EIC ratios. In the corpus of Hawkins (2000) single-word adverbs do regularly precede PPs that are longer, both complements and adjuncts. And there are languages in which Verb Object Bonding has been less strongly grammaticalized than in English, such as French, and in which short adjuncts frequently intervene, as in *j'admire souvent la gloire de mon père* (I admire often the glory of my father).

Summarizing, complements are in a relation of lexical combination and they involve the processing of more syntactic and semantic relations with the head than adjuncts. This results in multiple processing preferences for adjacency. If adjuncts are longer than co-occurring complements there will be no EIC motivation for positioning the adjunct closer to the head, in either head-initial or head-final languages. Only if they are shorter will there be an EIC preference for adjunct adjacency, in proportion to the relative weight difference.

What about the difference between restrictive and appositive adjuncts in (5.17)? Why are restrictives closer to the head? Consider the following example:

(5.18) a. Students that major in mathematics, who must
           of course work hard, ...   R + A
        b. *Students, who must of course work hard, that
           major in mathematics ...   A + R

Both the restrictive and the appositive relative involve similar dependencies on the head noun *students* in terms of co-indexation with it and in terms of various interpretive processes (cf. §6.1.1). But restrictive relatives involve more interdependencies between head and relative overall. For example, the head noun in (5.18a) is referentially reduced by the property in the restrictive clause (the reference is now to that subset of students of which the restrictive clause is true), and the processing of this referential reduction requires access to the relative clause. The appositive relative, by contrast, involves no such reduction, and the head receives its reference independently of the appositive. Restrictives are accordingly predicted to be closer to their heads.[19] A second factor of relevance to the ordering in (5.18) is that there would always be a semantic garden path in the on-line processing of (5.18b). The appositive relative would first be predicated of all students, and would then be predicated only of that subset of which the restrictive clause was true. The ordering in (5.18a) avoids the garden path by placing together all the items that determine the reference of the head, and by positioning them before an appositive property that does not contribute to the head's reference and that would make an erroneous predication on-line if it preceded the restrictive adjunct. An adjacency preference that is motivated by more dependency relations is reinforced in this example by a linear precedence advantage stemming from Maximize On-line Processing (3.16); see further §8.2.4.

The grammatical evidence for phrase structure adjacency conventions such as (5.17) is in accordance with the predictions of the Performance–Grammar Correspondence Hypothesis (PGCH). Prediction (1.2a) states that an ordering will be preferred 'in proportion to its degree of preference'. We have seen a

---

[19] Restrictive relatives also involve more syntactic dependencies on the head noun; see §6.1.1 and Hawkins (1978). Appositive relatives have a more complete clausal structure and greater independent processability.

stronger preference for complement adjacency to a head than for adjunct adjacency, both in performance data (when there are structural choices) and in the basic order conventions of grammars. There is also a stronger preference for restrictive adjuncts closer to their heads than appositive adjuncts. More processing domains prefer adjacency, and an independent (MaOP) preference reinforces the relative ordering preference (in head-initial languages). Prediction (1.2c) states that 'If two preferences P and P' are in (partial) opposition, then there will be grammatical variation, with both P and P' being conventionalized, each in proportion to the degree of motivation for that preference ...' We saw an illustration of this in the contrast between languages that permit short adjuncts to intervene between heads and complements (in accordance with EIC, e.g. French) and those like English that disallow or strongly disprefer this option (in accordance with domain minimization for the processing of lexical dependents).

I have focused in this section on phrase structure data corresponding to (5.17), but I believe there is a general moral here for all grammaticalized adjacency effects. For example, if a category joins with a nominal head to make a compound noun (as in English *paper factory* or *dog biscuit*) there is inevitably adjacency between them, reflecting the interdependency between items that combine to constitute the now complex head. If there is a plurality of prenominal adjectives (*large red balls*) the adjective closest to the noun defines the relevant subset first, relative to which the more distant adjective defines a further subset (i.e. *large* is interpreted relative to the set of *red balls*, and the result can be logically distinct from an interpretation in which *red* applies to the set of *large balls*). The adjacencies here reflect the function–argument relations within the phrase, of the type defined in a Categorial Grammar and in Keenan (1979), each of which prefers adjacency of the respective function-argument pair. *Red* is a function on *balls* as argument in the first combination, and *large* then combines with *red balls*. If *large* combined first with *balls* in *large red balls* there would be non-adjacency between them.

More generally, the inclusion of some category type T within a given mother phrase M in syntactic analysis appears to occur precisely when T contracts some syntactic or semantic relation(s) with the other daughters of M, whether as a complement, an adjunct, a compound, or a sister of an altogether different type. The precise number and nature of the dependencies can vary across languages, even for seemingly identical pairs of categories such as verb and direct object, reflecting lexical and morphological differences between languages and resulting in different bonding and adjacency strengths between them. The whole nature of phrase structure and of sisterhood can be impacted by this, as has been argued by Nichols (1986) when discussing the difference between dependent-marking languages (Russian) and head-marking languages like Abkhaz that have rich agreement marking on the verb (cf. §8.5 below).

For a sisterhood relation of an altogether different type consider grammaticalized focus phrases in head-final languages like Turkish and Korean (Kim 1988) where these phrases are typically adjacent to V and in immediately preverbal position. I have suggested (Hawkins 1994: 373–9) that we can view such adjacencies as involving an extended form of sisterhood between the focus phrase and the higher mother or grandmother node to which the V projects. The focus phrase is understood to be adjacent not just to V but to the higher clause projection, and this latter becomes immediately accessible for on-line syntactic and semantic processing at V. Scope effects for *wh*-phrases adjacent to V are now captured as effectively in the processing of surface syntax as if they were moved to a clause-peripheral position, as in English, since the higher mother or grandmother over which the *wh*-phrase has scope is accessed at V. Whenever there is a relation of projected combination like this, the theory presented here predicts that it should be reflected in the adjacency of the *wh*-phrase and the projecting sister, minimizing the processing domain between them. And more generally, the more syntactic and semantic relations of any type that link A and B, the tighter should be their adjacency.

5.5   Competitions between domains and phrases

The data of Table 5.5 (discussed in §5.2.1) revealed a typical interaction between domain minimization preferences. Sometimes two distinct processing preferences reinforce one another, and the result is consistent ordering and very little variation. This happened when one PP was shorter and in a relation of lexical dependency with the verb (which is assumed here to be a sufficient condition for complement status within a lexical co-occurrence frame). Both the phrasal combination domain (PCD, see (5.2)) and the domain for lexical processing (LD, see (5.6)) are minimized under these conditions. Sometimes one processing operation exerts no preference (when weights are equal) while another does (one of the equal-weight PPs is in a lexical co-occurrence frame, the other is not), and the ordering preferences then follow the active processing operation. On other occasions two processing operations compete. These are the interesting cases, and they arise when the longer PP is in a lexical co-occurrence relation (Pd) and the shorter one is not (Pi). PCDs are minimized by ordering Pi before Pd, LDs are minimized by ordering Pd before Pi. In Tables 5.1 and 5.4 we have seen that each processing domain asserts itself in proportion to its degree of preference, i.e. the relative weight *difference* in the former case, and the degree of separation between V and Pd in the latter as a function of the absolute size of Pi.

In §5.2.3 I proposed a metric for calculating the collective minimization advantage across a plurality of processing domains, in terms of total domain differentials (TDDs) (see (5.7)). This metric predicts different relative strengths and ranking reversals among partially competing preferences in a principled way, and the results when applied to Table 5.5 were encouraging (see (5.10)). In what follows I shall test this relative strength proposal further by giving more examples of variation data in performance and grammars that point clearly to competing processing domains. In §5.5.1 I shall work out a single example in detail and test it on corpus data.

In Hawkins (1990, 1994) I examined numerous competitions between the EIC preferences of different phrases within a sentence. This translates into competing PCDs here. Processing domains for syntactic relations other than phrase structure combination, and for semantic and lexical relations, must now be factored into these calculations. There will still be competitions between PCDs, but there may be more or fewer additional processing operations within each competing phrase, and their number and nature may affect the collective minimization preference for one order over another.

In Hawkins (1994: 198–210) I examined alternations such as those in (5.19) involving relative clause extraposition in German. Sentence (5.19a), *Er hat das Buch das der alte Professor verloren hatte gestern gefunden* (he has the book that the old professor lost had yesterday found), can be translated as 'he found the book yesterday that the old professor had lost'. All of these sentences are grammatical. Sentences (5.19a) and (b) involve no extraposition, (c) and (d) are extraposed. The PCDs for VP and NP processing are shown, and their respective IC-to-word ratios are calculated in the manner illustrated for (5.1) and (5.1′) above:[20]

(5.19) a. Er hat vp[np[das Buch das der alte Professor verloren hatte]
                                       gestern gefunden]

VP PCD:	- -	$3/10 = 30\%$
NP PCD:	- - - - - - - -	$3/3 = 100\%$

[20] The PCDs indicated in (5.19) follow the definition given in (5.2) and they assume that the VP consists of three immediate constituents; the direct object NP, the participial verb *gekauft*, and the adverb *gestern*. The NP also consists of three, the definite article *das*, the head noun *Buch*, and the relative clause following it. This relative clause can be recognized as such on the basis of the relative pronoun following the head, and hence the relative pronoun is the constructor of the relative clause within the NP PCD. An extraposed relative as in (5.19c) and (d) is assumed to be discontinuously attached to NP here, and numerous grammatical and processing arguments are given for this in Hawkins (1994: 197–210).

b. Er hat vp[gestern np[das Buch das der alte Professor verloren
                                    hatte] gefunden]

VP PCD: -   3/10 = 30%
NP PCD: - - - - - - - - - -   3/3 = 100%

c. Er hat vp[np[das Buch] gestern gefunden] np[das der alte P.
                                    verloren hatte]

VP PCD: -   3/4 = 75%
NP PCD: -   3/5 = 60%

d. Er hat vp[gestern np[das Buch] gefunden] np[das der alte P.
                                    verloren hatte]

VP PCD: -   3/4 = 75%
NP PCD: - - - - - - - - - - - - - - - - - - -   3/4 = 75%

Extraposing the relative clause out of the NP in (5.19c) and (d) improves the
VP PCD considerably, since its three immediate constituents (ICs) can be
processed on the basis of just four words rather than ten. This is reflected in
the IC-to-word ratio increases from 30% to 75%. The NP PCD, on the other
hand, which has optimal adjacency of the three categories that constitute or
construct its three daughters in (5.19a) and (b)—the article, the head noun,
and the relative pronoun—is lengthened by an intervening two words in (5.19c)
and by one word in (5.19d), resulting in lower ratios of 60% and 75% compared
with 100% for (5.19ab). Adding up the collective domain differences in words,
(5.19a) and (b) contain thirteen words in the two PCDs, (5.19c) has nine, and
(5.19d) has eight. The TDD theory in (5.8) predicts a degree of preference for
these structures in proportion to their totals. Additional processing domains
will be added in §5.5.1 and their collective predictions will be tested on German
corpus data.

Competitions between PCDs can explain the rearrangements of heavy,
clausal constituents in different language types, and their different directionalities, which were summarized in §5.3.2. In languages with left-peripheral
construction of a clause, by an initial complementizer or relative pronoun, the
preferred rearrangement will be to the right, as in (5.19). This can be seen in
several basic word order types. A VOS language with a clausal object complement and a left-peripheral complementizer, i.e. s[vp[V s'[C S]] NP], will
preferably extrapose it to the right. This structure has a lengthy PCD for the
matrix clause (S), since the VP domain that precedes the subject NP is complex.
The VP itself is efficient in this order, since its two ICs, V and S', are processable
on the basis of two adjacent words, V and C. When the complexity of the S'
exceeds that of the matrix subject, however, as it almost always does, the overall
benefit shifts to a postposed S' structure with an intervening subject NP. It is

for this reason that VOS languages (all of which are complementizer-initial, cf. §7.5.2) obligatorily extrapose their clausal direct objects, to give VSO, as in the following Malagasy example (from Keenan 1976*a*):

(5.20) a. *Mihevitra s'[fa   mitady   ny zaza Rasoa] Rabe (Malagasy)
          thinks   that looks-for the child Rasoa Rabe
          'Rabe thinks that Rasoa is looking for the child'
       b. Mihevitra Rabe s'[fa mitady ny zaza Rasoa]

Languages with basic VSO regularly extrapose a center-embedded clausal sub-ject, for complementary reasons. The basic order is good for matrix clause processing, since the initial V constructs VP and the immediately following complementizer can construct the clausal subject within just a two-word view-ing window. But this center embedding lengthens the domain for verb–object processing, i.e. it lengthens the VP domain (under a discontinuous VP ana-lysis).[21] The postposing of the clausal subject is predicted when an adjacent verb object is better overall, which it almost always is when the subject is clausal and the object simple. Clausal subjects in English (SVO) are also extraposed by a 17–1 margin over their non-extraposed counterparts (Erdmann 1988), thereby improving matrix clause processing but at the possible expense of VP processing (see the quantification below). SOV languages with initial comple-mentizers, like Persian and German, also regularly postpose their heavy clausal complements, shortening both the matrix S and VP domains on this occasion (Hawkins 1994: 299).

SOV languages with final complementizers, by contrast, present us with the mirror image of Malagasy, s[NP [[S C]s' V]vp]. A clausal direct object extends the PCD for the matrix S (from the subject NP to V, the category that constructs the VP) at the same time that the ICs of VP can be processed on the basis of two adjacent words, C and V. Preposing the direct object shortens the S domain, in conjunction with a bottom-up parse, and this generally results in a more efficient sentence overall, even when the VP PCD is lengthened (Hawkins 1994: 66, 80, 300). The frequency of the preposed (5.21b) is predicted to reflect this overall minimization (with longer object clauses, and shorter subject NPs, preferring preposing).

(5.21) a. Mary ga [kinoo   John ga kekkonsi-ta to]s' it-ta (Japanese)
          Mary SU yesterday John SU got-married that said
          Mary said that John got married yesterday.'
       b. [kinoo John ga kekkonsi-ta to]s' Mary ga it-ta

---

[21] Alternatively the various syntactic, semantic, and lexical relations that link (transitive) verb and direct object have longer processing domains in the event that there is no discontinuous VP.

Conversely, when subjects and objects are short and pronominal the respective advantages for VP and S domains are reversed. A heavy clausal object in Malagasy requires VSO order, a lighter object forbids it (and only VOS is used). A light pronominal subject in SVO orders is good for both matrix clause processing and for the VP. A pronominal subject splits the VP in VSO, but not by very much, and is optimal for matrix clause processing (two single words, V and the pronoun, construct VP and the subject NP respectively). VSO will be preferable to VOS when the subject is pronominal, in the event that the direct object is at all complex, since a small disadvantage for VP is better than a large disadvantage for the matrix clause. Preposing of pronominal subjects (to VSO or SVO) can be expected to be productive in the performance of verb-initial languages, therefore, whose grammars permit it (most do). Similarly, while there are *post*posing rules for heavy direct objects in head-initial languages like English, object pronouns are not postposed and they cluster tightly to the verb, either to its left (French) or to the right (English), resulting in motivated exceptions to many rearrangement rules (*I gave it to the generous old lady* ⇏ **I gave the generous old lady it*; see Hawkins 1994: 286).[22]

Some rearrangement rules clearly change the constituency of the item moved, whereas others may or may not depending on the language (and on the linguist's analysis!). The predictions of this section are not generally affected by differences in analysis. When rearrangements do bring about clear differences in attachment, some striking predictions are made based on the resulting changes in phrase structure and their impact on the respective PCDs. Consider clausal subject extraposition in English, which positions the moved clause into the VP (Reinhart 1983), i.e.:

(5.22)   a. s[s′[that their time should not be wasted] vp[is important]]
         b. s[it vp[is important s′[that their time should not be wasted]]]

(5.22a) has an inefficient S domain but an efficient VP (two ICs are processed on the basis of two adjacent words). (5.22b) removes the inefficiency from S (adjacent *it* and *is* construct the two ICs of S); at the same time it either retains the optimality of the VP (when measured in IC-to-word ratios: three adjacent words [*is*, *important* and *that*] constitute or construct the three ICs of VP) or else increases it by only one word (*that*), which suffices to construct the new IC in the VP. Either way, the preference for (5.22b) is substantial, and it is significant that only 5% of these structures are retained in the (a) version in

---

[22] The Celtic languages provide a surprising exception to this regularity: pronouns are productive in rightmost position; see Tallerman (1998).

Erdmann's (1988) English corpus.[23] When the VP contains additional material, however, as in (5.23), there is a big difference in the data.

(5.23) a. s[s'[that their time should not be wasted] vp[is important pp[for us all]]]

   b. s[it vp[is important pp[for us all] s'[that their time should not be wasted]]]

The (a) structure is now found in 24% of Erdmann's data, i.e. in almost five times as many cases.

This can be explained in terms of the competition between S and VP domains. (5.23a) has an inefficient S and an efficient VP (the PCD consists of three adjacent words, *is, important,* and *for* which constructs PP). In (5.23b) the S domain is optimal, but the VP is now less so. Its PCD extends from *is* through *important* and through the PP *for us all* to *that.* In terms of IC-to-words, a 3/3 (100%) VP ratio in (5.23a) has become 4/6 (67%); in terms of words alone a three-word PCD has expanded to six. Extraposition is now predicted when the benefits for S outweigh these disadvantages for VP, i.e. when there is greater collective minimization. Sometimes the unextraposed (5.23a) will be more minimal, when there is less complexity in the clausal subject than in the VP, and in these cases it is preserved. For (5.22), by contrast, extraposition will almost always be preferred, on account of the simpler VP.

A further example of an EIC-predicted constituency change comes from Cantonese. Matthews & Yeung (2001) present the results of an experiment on direct object topicalization out of an s[NP vp[V NP]] structure in this language. The NP in Cantonese is noun-final and it has left-branching relative clauses, i.e. [S N]np, as in (5.24) (from Matthews & Yip 2003):

(5.24) Ngo5 ceng2 go2   di1 pang4jau5
    I   invite those CL friend
    'friends that I invite'

This combination of an early verb in VP and a final noun in NP is typologically quite rare, cf. §8.2.1, and it results in some very long PCDs for VP when the relative clause is complex. Matthews & Yeung (2001) show that object topical-izations into an s[np[S N] s[NP vp[V]]] structure are preferred in proportion to the complexity of this left-branching relative clause, and they argue that top-icalization is motivated in Cantonese not only for pragmatic reasons but for syntactic processing as well. The topicalized NP can be processed bottom-up,

---

[23] Erdmann (1988) uses a corpus of written British English comprising 15 novels, 15 book-length popular scientific writings, 15 editions of the *Daily Telegraph,* and 15 editions of the *Spectator.*

as with np[S N] structures in Japanese, and the result is a processing domain for the highest S that is initiated by the determiner, classifier, or head noun that constructs NP (see §4.4). A topicalized clause is either one, two, or at most three words longer than its non-topicalized counterpart, on these assumptions, whereas a post-verbal direct object NP will include the full contents of the relative clause in the domain for VP, extending from the verb to the head noun. The degree of preference for topicalization here can be predicted to reflect the overall minimization advantage for the topicalized structure.

5.5.1   *Relative clause extrapositions in German*

The four German sentences in (5.19a–d) can be represented structurally as (5.25A–D) respectively:

(5.25) A. vp[np[Det Ni S] XP V]
        B. vp[XP np[Det Ni S] V]
        C. vp[np[Det Ni] XP V] [S]
        D. vp[XP np[Det Ni] V] [S]

In A the relative clause has not undergone extraposition and an XP, the single-word adverb *gestern* 'yesterday', is positioned between the object NP and V. XP could also be a longer adverb phrase or a PP here, like *vor einigen Tagen* 'a few days ago'. In B the XP precedes the NP and there is again no extraposition. C has undergone extraposition and orders the remaining NP elements before XP. D extraposes the relative and orders XP before NP.

A and B both have long PCDs for VP and short PCDs for NP. C and D have the reverse, shorter PCDs for VP and longer ones for NP (see the IC-to-word ratios in (5.19)). In addition, the verb *finden* (past participle *gefunden* 'found') that occurs in (5.19) is transitive and has a lexically listed co-occurrence with a direct object NP, here *das Buch das* ... 'the book which ...'. The lexical domain for processing this co-occurrence is longer in A and C than in B and D, on account of the intervening XP. It is also longer in A and B than in C and D, on account of the unextraposed relative S which intervenes between the head of NP, Ni, and the verb. Both XP and S can add to this lexical co-occurrence domain for V.[24] The domain for theta-role assignment to the object NP proceeds from

---

[24] I shall assume here that this lexical domain for V proceeds from V to the head of NP, Ni. This domain involves the processing of the verb's subcategorization frame (Chomsky 1965) and may also involve selectional restriction processing and greater or lesser polysemy reduction in the verb by the object NP. Since these latter are not consistent across lexical verbs, and were not coded for in Uszkoreit

N*i* to the verb that assigns the relevant role, and is also larger when XP and S intervene. We have three distinct syntactic and semantic relations involving the ICs of the VP that need to be processed in the following domains:

(5.26) *VP domains*
1. Phrasal combination: vp[{NP, XP}, V] defined from Det or the onset of XP to V
2. V's lexical co-occurrence: from V to N*i*
3. NP theta-role assignment: from N*i* to V

Syntactic and semantic relations that are internal to the NP involve phrasal combination first of all. A second relation involves co-indexation between the head N*i* and the position relativized on within S. This co-indexing captures the intuition that there is a form of identity between the head noun and the relevant position, and in German, a language with obligatory relative pronouns, these pronouns are the first items encountered in S to receive the copied index. The relative pronoun will be co-indexed further with some empty position or subcategorizor within S with which it is linked (see Chapter 7), but I regard this as an S-internal processing domain. The co-indexation that links the head noun to the first co-indexed item in the sister S proceeds from N*i* to wh*i*, therefore. A relative clause is also a type of adjunct and receives an adjunct interpretation. The relative is dependent on the head for assignment of this interpretation, and when the relative is restrictive the head noun also undergoes a potential restriction in its semantic range and reference (see §8.3.4). I assume that the whole content of the relative clause must be accessed for full processing of these relations, since any addition or omission can affect truth conditions. We have the following processing domains for ICs of the NP:

(5.27) *NP domains*
1. Phrasal combination: np[Det N*i* ... S] defined from Det to wh*i* in S
2. Co-indexation with N*i*: from N*i* to wh*i* in S
3. S-adjunct interpretation: from N*i* through all of S

Table 5.8 gives an overview of the advantages and disadvantages of the unextraposed A/B v. the extraposed C/D structures with respect to each of these processing domains.

---

et al.'s (1998*a*, *b*) data, I focus here on subcategorization, which is consistently satisfied in the data since all these verbs are transitive. In the quantification of domains in the main text I count verb co-occurrence processing as just one domain, therefore, recognizing that some verbs may involve additional dependencies in processing and a stronger adjacency preference to N*i*.

TABLE 5.8   Relative domain sizes for VP and NP domains in German

	A/B vp[{np[Det, Ni, S], XP}, V]	*C/D* vp[{np[Det, Ni], XP}, V][S]
VP Domains		
1. PCD VP:	longer (by length of S)	shorter
2. V lexical:	longer (by length of S and/or XP)	shorter
3. NP theta role:	longer (by length of S and/or XP)	shorter
NP Domains		
4. PCD NP:	shorter	longer (by length of V and/or XP)
5. Co-index to Ni:	shorter	longer (by length of V and/or XP)
6. S-adjunct:	shorter	longer (by length of V and/or XP)

The challenge is now to assess the overall efficiency of one structure over another, given that different domains are pulling in different directions, and given the different values that can be assigned to XP and S. We must calculate the total domain differentials (TDDs) across the six domains of (5.26) and (5.27), for the different values of XP and S, and our predictions for preferred selections in performance can then be based on these calculations. Table 5.9 presents the TDDs for these structures. The rows give different word assignments to the relative clause (2, 4, 6, etc.) in each A, B, C, and D structure, and the columns give different word assignments to XP (1, 2, 3, etc.). '0' in a given row and column indicates that the relevant structure with the S- and XP-values in question has the most minimal word total for all six processing domains, compared with the other three structures having the same S- and XP-values. '1' in a row and column indicates that the structure has (an average of) one more word per domain, for the same S- and XP-values, than the most minimal structure with these values. '2' indicates (an average of) two more words per domain compared with the most minimal, and so on.

Based on the TDDs given in Table 5.9 we can formulate a number of predictions, given in (5.28):

(5.28) *Predictions for relative clause extraposition*

    a. When only a one-word V (or separable verbal particle) intervenes between Ni and S (i.e. structure D), this extraposition structure is always preferred over non-extraposition (B), and also over A, except for very short relatives (S = 2) which can be equally efficient.

TABLE 5.9   Total domain differentials for structures (5.25 A–D)

	S =	2/4/6/8/10 A	2/4/6/8/10 B	2/4/6/8/10 C	2/4/6/8/10 D
XP =	1	0/1/2/3/4	0/1/2/3/4	0/0/0/0/0	0/0/0/0/0
	2	1/2/3/4/5	0/1/2/3/4	1/1/1/1/1	0/0/0/0/0
	3	1/2/3/4/5	0/1/2/3/4	2/2/2/2/2	0/0/0/0/0
	5	2/3/4/5/6	0/1/2/3/4	4/4/4/4/4	0/0/0/0/0
	7	2/3/4/5/6	0/1/2/3/4/	5/5/5/5/5	0/0/0/0/0

Measured in relative (average) words per domain, 0 = most minimal (i.e. highest
 TDD) of the four structures for the values of S and XP in each row and column
 (or between 0 and 1 word per domain of the most minimal), 1 = between one
 and two words per domain more than the most minimal structure for the values
 of each row and column, 2 = between two and three words more per domain
 more for the same values, etc.
These processing domain calculations assume that: Det constructs NP; the relative
 pronoun constructs S; XP is constructed on its left periphery; and V = 1 word.
Six processing domains are assumed, cf. (5.26) and (5.27).

b. When a one-word XP intervenes between Ni and V (i.e. C), this
extraposition structure is also preferred over non-extraposition
(A), and also over B, except for S = 2, the strength of this
preference being less than for D over A/B when absolute (non-
averaged) word quantities are considered.

c. As XP gains in length, the preference starts to shift from C to the
non-extraposition structures A and B, especially for XP > 3.

d. As S gains in length in the unextraposed A/B, these structures
become increasingly dispreferred compared to the extraposed D
(and also to C); hence more extrapositions in proportion to the
length of S.

These predictions can be tested using the parsed corpus of German developed
by Skut et al. (1997). This corpus consists of 12,000 sentences taken from the
Frankfurter Rundschau newspaper. Uszkoreit et al. (1998a, b) used it in order
to test some of the extraposition predictions made in Hawkins (1994) in terms
of PCDs only. They also used an expanded corpus tagged for parts of speech
only. These corpora can be used here to test the fuller predictions of (5.28).

The strong preference for structure D over B when only a one-word V
potentially intervenes, predicted by (5.28a), is confirmed:

(5.29) *Frankfurter Rundschau* corpus: Uszkoreit et al. (1998a, b) (5.28a)
   Extraposition over a one-word V (D): 95% (219/230)
   Non-extraposition (B):   5%   (11/230)

The (slightly weaker) preference for C over A when XP = 1 is also supported:

(5.30) *Frankfurter Rundschau* corpus: Uszkoreit et al. (1998*a, b*) (5.28b)
    Extraposition over XP(= 1) + V(= 1) (C): 77% (81/105)
    Non-extraposition (A):   23% (24/105)

The increases in NP domains (5.27) are small when a one-word V or XP intervenes between N*i* and S, while the benefits of extraposing S can be significant for the VP domains (5.26). Hence these data strongly prefer VP minimizations over NP minimizations and extraposition is the norm. As XP gains in size, however, the increases in NP domains under extraposition start to outweigh the benefits for the VP domains and the overall preferences shift to non-extraposition (A):[25]

(5.31) *Frankfurter Rundschau* corpus: Uszkoreit et al. (1998*a, b*) (5.28c)

Extraposition distance:	XP(1) + V	XP(2) + V	XP(3–4) + V	XP(5 +) + V
% extraposed (C):	77% (81)	35% (25)	9% (8)	6% (7)
% non-extraposed (A):	23% (24)	65% (47)	91% (81)	94% (118)

For the (5.28d) prediction Uszkoreit et al.'s expanded corpus provides relevant data. Uszkoreit et al. present these data in graph form, which I have converted into aggregated percentages for the relevant rows and columns here. A large relative clause increases VP domains in structures A and B and is predicted to result in more extrapositions in proportion to the size of S. The costs to the NP domains will be progressively outweighed by the benefits to VP of extraposing an S as it expands, and this can be seen clearly in the data of (5.32):

(5.32) Expanded corpus: Uszkoreit et al. (1998*a, b*) (5.28d)

Relative S length =	2–3 words	4–5	6–9	10–15
% extraposed over				
V only (D)	47%	95%	95%	95%
XP(1)+V (C)	34%	52%	62%	82%
XP(2)+V (C)	0%	8%	32%	33%
Average:	27%	52%	63%	70%

These German corpus data provide further support for the TDD performance prediction in (5.8) and for this general approach to competing factors.[26]

---

[25] The data in (5.31) show a 2-to-1 preference for structure A over C when XP = 2 and a 9-to-1 preference when XP = 3. This changeover from the C preference (when XP = 1) happens a little sooner than the calculations in Table 5.9 predict. Table 5.9 predicts a beginning changeover at XP = 3, but the results are close here.

[26] Note that the on-line data in Uszkoreit et al. (1998*a, b*) did not give such clear support for these domain minimization predictions.

6

Minimal Forms in Complements/Adjuncts and Proximity

In this chapter I continue the discussion of domain minimization by examining the impact of reduced formal marking on relative positioning. Researchers working on language universals have long recognized that languages with less morphosyntax, such as Vietnamese and English, have more fixed word orders and tighter adjacency or proximity between categories than languages like Latin and Kalkatungu with richer agreement and case marking, etc (see e.g. Comrie 1989). More recently researchers working on language performance have also shown a striking correlation between the positioning preferences of performance and the degree to which the relevant syntactic and semantic relations are formally marked (see e.g. Rohdenburg 1996, 1998, 1999, 2000). For example, relative clauses in English containing a relative pronoun may occur either close to or far from their nominal heads (*the Danes (…) whom he taught*), while those without relative pronouns (*the Danes he taught*) are only rarely attested at some distance from their heads and prefer adjacency.

We have here a further correspondence between performance and grammars: reduced formal marking favors domain minimization in both. I shall also argue for a descriptive generalization that unites the data of the last chapter with the data to be presented here. In Chapter 5 adjacency was shown to reflect the number of combinatorial and dependency relations linking two categories. When there were lexical-semantic dependencies as well as combinatorial relations between verbs and prepositional phrases there was significantly more adjacency than with combinatorial relations alone. Reduced formal marking increases adjacency as well. Why?

I propose the same answer. A reduction in formal marking makes a phrase less independently processable, and it can then become dependent on some other category for property assignments (see (2.3) in §2.2). The phrase *he taught*, for example, is highly ambiguous: it could be a main clause, a subordinate clause, a relative clause, an intransitive or transitive clause, etc. It becomes an unambiguous relative clause adjunct by accessing the nominal head *Danes*. The direct object co-occurrence requirement of the transitive verb within the relative is also satisfied by accessing this head. By contrast, *whom he taught* is unambiguously subordinate and transitive, and the relative pronoun supplies the verb's direct object within the relative clause itself. There are more dependencies linking *he taught* to the nominal head, therefore, and so by Minimize Domains (3.1) the zero relative is predicted to stand closer to this head.

This chapter also exemplifies the Minimize Forms (3.8) preference. The more that formal marking is reduced, the more processing enrichments are required (see §3.2.3, §§4.5–6). These enrichments will often involve dependency assignments (2.3), and these are easiest to process when the domains linking the interdependent elements are minimal. MiF therefore sets up a corresponding MiD preference, and the degree to which MiF applies to a given structure should be reflected in the degree to which MiD also applies to it.

I first present some data from performance, principally from corpus studies of alternating structures in English (§6.1). I then present corresponding cross-linguistic data from grammars (§6.2) that test the Performance–Grammar Correspondence Hypothesis (1.1). In §6.3 I consider classical morphological typology from the processing perspective of this chapter.

6.1   Minimal formal marking in performance

6.1.1   *Wh, that/zero relativizers*

The selection among alternative relativizers in English relative clauses has been shown in several corpus studies to be correlated with structural features that seem mysterious at first. A description of the combinatorial and dependency relations involved, and of their processing domains, can remove much of the mystery. The basic structure we are dealing with is given in (6.1), with illustrative sentences in (6.2):

(6.1) $np_1[N_i (XP) s[(wh_i) NP_2 vp[V_i ...]]]$

(6.2) a. the Danes whom he taught
  b. the Danes that he taught
  c. the Danes he taught
  d. the Danes from Jutland whom he taught
  e. the Danes from Jutland that he taught
  f. the Danes from Jutland he taught

With regard to processing, the containing NP1 in (6.1) and its immediate constituents have to be constructed within a phrasal combination domain (PCD). This domain will proceed from Ni through whatever category constructs the relative clause. If wh$i$ is present, this relativizer will do so. If not, a finite verb (or auxiliary) will construct S, by Grandmother Node Construction (Hawkins 1994: 361). A further possibility is for a nominative subject pronoun (in NP2) to construct S, again by Grandmother Node Construction. The PCD for NP1 therefore proceeds from Ni through wh$i$ or np2[pronoun] or Vi, whichever comes first.

The processing of the verb within the relative clause, Vi, involves recognition of its lexical co-occurrence (subcategorization) frame and of its semantics relative to the complements selected. When there is a relative pronoun (*the Danes whom/that he taught*) such co-occurrences can be satisfied by accessing nominal or pronominal elements within the relative clause, and this lexical domain (5.6) (§5.2.1) need not extend to the head noun. Similarly in a language like Hebrew in which a resumptive pronoun is retained in the position relativized on (in structures corresponding to *the Danes that he taught them* (cf. §7.2.2)) the pronoun satisfies the co-occurrence requirements of the verb. Both resumptive pronouns and fronted relative pronouns permit the verb's lexical co-occurrence requirements to be satisfied locally within the relative.[1] In an indirect question structure (*I know whom he taught*) we have no hesitation in saying that the *wh* word supplies the direct object required by transitive *taught*. The zero relative (*the Danes he taught*) contains no resumptive or relative pronoun, and the parser has to access the head noun *Danes* in order to assign the intended direct object to *taught*. The domain for processing the lexical co-occurrence frame for Vi accordingly proceeds from Vi to wh$i$ or to Ni, whichever comes first, i.e. this domain is defined on a right-to-left basis.

A third relation that must be processed involves co-indexing the head noun, Ni, with the first item in the relative clause that can bear the index. English is less consistent than German in this respect (see §5.5.1), since relative pronouns are not obligatory. I will assume here that Ni is co-indexed with wh$i$, when present, and with the subcategorizor. Vi (or Pi), when absent, by a direct association between the two, i.e. without postulating empty categories (following Pollard & Sag 1994, Moortgat 1988, Steedman 1987); see the definition of a 'filler–gap

---

[1] The LD linking verb and relative pronouns is generally larger than it is for in situ resumptive pronouns in Hebrew, since the former have been moved into a peripheral complementizer position where they fulfill a dual function as a subordinate clause constructor and as a pronoun that supplies a referent matching the co-occurrence requirements of the subcategorizor; see §5.5.1, §7.2.2.

A preposition can also function as the subcategorizor for the head noun or relative in English (e.g. *the Danes (whom) he gave lectures to*).

domain' in (7.8) of §7.1.[2] This co-indexing formalizes the intuition that the head noun is linked to a certain position in the relative clause, i.e. the 'position relativized on'.

A relative clause is also a type of adjunct to the head and receives an adjunct interpretation. When the adjunct is restrictive, as in the data to be considered here, the head also undergoes a potential restriction in its referential range, and it depends on the relative for assignment of this range (the Danes in question were the ones that he taught, not the ones that anyone else taught, and so on). I assume that the whole content of the relative clause must be accessed for full processing of the adjunct relation and for full processing of the referential restriction of the head, at least as regards the semantics.[3]

These domains are summarized in (6.3):

(6.3) *Domains for Relative Clauses in Structure (6.1)*

1. PCD: NP1: from Ni through wh$i$ or np2[pronoun] or Vi, whichever comes first (L to R)
2. Vi lexical co-occurrence: from Vi to wh$i$ or Ni, whichever comes first (R to L)
3. Co-indexation with Ni: from Ni to wh$i$ or Vi, whichever comes first (L to R)
4. S-adjunct interpretation: from Ni through whole of S
5. Referential restriction of Ni: from Ni through whole of S

The presence or absence of a relative pronoun in (6.2) will affect domain sizes in different ways, and the consequences for each domain are shown in Table 6.1.[4]

The overall efficiency of one relative clause type over another can be calculated in terms of total domain differentials (5.7), as was done for the German

---

[2] The alternative is to assume such empty categories (following Chomsky 1981) and to link Ni directly to them (when wh$i$ is absent). I show in §7.1 that this makes many wrong predictions for domain sizes in 'filler–gap' structures and for their performance and grammatical correlates. Linking fillers to subcategorizors (and to relevant projecting head categories for relativizations on adjunct positions) gives more accurate predictions.

[3] A relative clause in English can be recognized as restrictive based on the sequence (animate) noun + *that*, i.e. considerably in advance of the relative clause-internal material on the basis of which the semantic restriction can be processed; see Hawkins (1978) for summary of the syntactic diagnostics of restrictive versus appositive relatives.

[4] Relativizations on subjects do not generally allow the zero option, *the Danes * (who) taught him*, except in environments such as *there was a man came to see you yesterday*. Deletion of a subject relativizer would result in regular garden paths in the former case (i.e. in on-line 'misassignments' dispreferred by MaOP (3.16)—cf. §3.3). Interestingly, these garden paths are avoided in existential structures in which *there is* introduces the main clause and what follows the NP is necessarily subordinate. See Biber et al. (1999: 619) for usage data on this option.

TABLE 6.1   Relative domain sizes for relative clauses
np1[Ni (XP) s[(wh$i$) NP2 vp[Vi ...]]]

Domains	WH/THAT	ZERO
1. PCD : NP1	same or shorter	same or longer (increasing with NP2)
2. Vi lexical co-occurrence	same or shorter	same or longer (increasing with XP)
3. Co-index to Ni	shorter	longer (increasing with NP2)
4. S-adjunct interpretation	longer (by 1 word)	shorter
5. Refer. restriction of Ni	longer (by 1 word)	shorter

TABLE 6.2   Total domain differentials for relative clauses (cf. 6.2)
np1[Ni (XP) s[(wh$i$) NP2 vp[Vi ...]]]

XP =	0/1/2/3/4 WH/THAT	0/1/2/3/4 ZERO
NP2 = Pronoun	1/0/0/0/0	0/0/1/2/3
Full NP = 2	0/0/0/0/0	2/3/4/5/6
Full NP = 4	0/0/0/0/0	6/7/8/9/10
Full NP = 6	0/0/0/0/0	10/11/12/13/14

Measured in relative words per domain, 0 = the more minimal (i.e. higher TDD) of the two structures being compared for the values of XP and NP2, 1 = one word more than the minimal structure for the values of each row and column, 2 = two words more for the same values, etc. These processing domain calculations assume that: Ni constructs NP; wh$i$ or np[pronoun] or (finite) Vi constructs S; Ni = 1 word, Vi = 1, and vp = 3. Five processing domains are assumed, cf. (6.3).

extraposition structures in Table 5.9. Once again different domains pull in partially different directions, with greater or lesser strength when different values are assigned to a potentially intervening XP and NP2. The overall TDDs for these different value assignments are shown in Table 6.2.

It will be visually apparent that relative clauses with *wh* and *that* are, in general, those with the most minimal overall domains, while those with zero are most minimal only when head and relative are adjacent (XP = 0) and when NP2 is a pronoun.[5] More precisely, this tabulation makes the following

[5] This helps us explain why relative pronouns are not deletable in many languages (French and German). It is far from the case that zero is always simpler.

predictions:

(6.4) *Predictions for relativizers*

     a. When XP = 0, zero is (slightly) preferred for NP2 = pronoun, *wh*/*that* is preferred for NP2 = full; hence either *wh*/*that* or zero can be preferred under adjacency of N*i* and S.

     b. When XP ≥ 1, zero is (equally) preferred only for XP = 1 (when NP2 = pronoun), with *wh*/*that* preferred everywhere else; hence zero is generally dispreferred when N*i* and S are non-adjacent.

     c. As XP gains in size, the preference for *wh*/*that* and the dispreference for zero increases.

     d. When NP2 = pronoun, either *wh*/*that* or zero can be preferred (zero being slightly preferred when XP = 0).

     e. When NP2 = full, *wh*/*that* is always preferred.

These predictions can be tested on various corpora. One of the earliest (and least well-known) corpus studies devoted to subtle aspects of English syntax is Quirk's (1957) 'Relative clauses in educated spoken English'. His quantified data enable us to test the impact of adjacency v. non-adjacency on relativizer selection. The following data show that *wh*, *that*, and zero are indeed all productive under adjacency (XP = 0), as predicted by (6.4a):[6]

(6.5) Quirk's (1957) Corpus
Restrictive (non-subject) relatives adjacent to the head (n = 549)
WH = 28% (154)   THAT = 32%(173)   ZERO = 40% (222)

Under non-adjacency (XP ≥ 1) zero is dispreferred (only 6% of all non-adjacent relatives), while both *wh* and *that* are productive, as predicted by (6.4b):[7]

(6.6) Quirk's (1957) Corpus
Restrictive (non-subject) relatives with intervening material (n = 62)
WH = 50% (31)   THAT = 44% (27)   ZERO = 6% (4)

---

[6] The preferred co-occurrence of a pronominal NP2 subject with zero and of a full NP2 with *wh*/*that* (predicted by (6.4a)) is addressed in (6.8) and (6.9) in the main text (when discussing predictions (6.4de)). Quirk does not give data on the type of NP2 here, and the Longman Corpus, which does so, does not give separate figures for adjacent and non-adjacent relatives, but only a collapsed set of data. It is clear from all these data, however, that a pronominal NP2 is indeed one of the major determinants that leads speakers to choose the zero option over *wh*/*that*. The explanation offered here is that nominative pronouns construct a clause (S) just like *that* and fronted *wh* do. Hence both are not needed simultaneously and zero can be preferred, as long as there is little intervening material to push the overall preference towards *wh*/*that* (see Table 6.2).

[7] The more recent corpus of Guy & Bayley (1995) has very similar figures for the distribution of explicit and zero relativizers in adjacent and non-adjacent environments.

The non-adjacent relatives in Quirk's data could be either NP-internal (with e.g. a PP intervening between the head noun and relative clause) or NP-external as a result of extraposition from NP (e.g. *the Danes came to stay (whom) he taught*), and Quirk's coding does not distinguish between them. Lohse (2000) has accordingly examined these different non-adjacency types and has quantified the distribution of explicit *which* and *that* versus zero using the Brown Corpus. NP-external extraposition generally involves a greater distance between relative clause and head than NP-internal non-adjacency. Hence, the size of XP in (6.1) is generally larger, and by prediction (6.4c) the distribution of zero should be, and is, less.

(6.7) Brown Corpus: Lohse (2000)

    a. *Non-adjacent NP-internal relatives* (n = 196)
       WHICH/THAT = 72% (142)   ZERO = 28% (54)
    b. *Non-adjacent NP-external relatives* (n = 18)
       WHICH/THAT = 94% (17)   ZERO = 6% (1)

Non-adjacent relatives with zero in NP-internal position have a 28% distribution (6.7a), but only one of the eighteen extraposed relatives has zero marking in (6.7b).

The corpus used as the basis for the Longman Grammar of Spoken and Written English (Biber et al. 1999), henceforth the 'Longman Corpus', gives quantified data of relevance to predictions (6.4d) and (e). When the subject (NP2) of the relative is a pronoun (*the Danes (whom) he taught*), both *wh/that* and zero are indeed productively attested, the latter being roughly twice as common as the former, as shown in (6.8):

(6.8) Longman Corpus: Biber et al. (1999: 620)
    Pronominal subjects (NP2) within restrictive relatives: 30–40% have
    WH/THAT; 60–70% ZERO.

Since zero is slightly preferred over *wh/that* under adjacency (XP = 0) in Table 6.2, since pronominal subjects are very common, and since adjacent heads and relatives are significantly more common than non-adjacent ones (compare (6.5) and (6.6)), the greater frequency of zero is to be expected.[8]

---

[8] A more fine-tuned testing of prediction (6.4d) cannot be made using the data reported in Biber et al. (1999), since we are not told how many of these restrictive relatives with pronominal subjects are adjacent or non-adjacent to their heads, and if non-adjacent by what degree (i.e. what is the XP size in each case?). The total domain differentials of Table 6.2 make precise predictions for when *wh/that* or zero will be selected for the different values of NP2 and XP.

When the subject of the relative is a full NP (*the Danes (whom) the professor taught*), *wh/that* is always preferred. This prediction (cf. (6.4e)) is well-supported:

(6.9) Longman Corpus: Biber et al. (1999: 620)
       Full NP subjects (NP2) within restrictive relatives: 80–95% have
       WH/THAT (i.e. only 5–20% ZERO).

When there is a zero relativizer, therefore, a pronominal NP2 subject is much more common than a full NP2 subject.

6.1.2   *Other alternations*

English allows a similar alternation between *that* and zero as complementizers in sentential (non-subject) complements, e.g. *I realized (that) he bothered me.*[9] Parallel to the predictions for the presence or absence of a relativizer in Tables 6.1 and 6.2, the factors that determine the presence or absence of the complementizer are predicted here to include the content of any intervening XP and of the subject NP2 in the complement clause:

(6.10) NP1 vp1[V1 (XP) s[(that) NP2 vp2[V2 . . .]]]

The sooner the subordinate clause can be constructed, by *that*, by a pronominal NP2 subject, or by a finite V2 in VP2, the smaller will be the phrasal combination domain for VP1 (which proceeds from V1 on the left to the first daughter of S that can construct this clause). The processing of the lexical co-occurrence frame and semantics of V1 also prefer a minimal domain. A verb like *realize* can co-occur with a sentential complement, with a simple NP object (*I realized this fact*), or with an empty surface object (*I realized*). The verb *claimed* can co-occur with an infinitival complement in addition to these options (*He claimed that he was a professor, He claimed to be a professor, He claimed immunity, He claimed*). An explicit *that* has the advantage that it immediately constructs the finite sentential complement on its left periphery, thus shortening the lexical domains for these matrix verbs (see (5.6)). It also permits this clause to be immediately recognizable as subordinate, and distinct from a following main clause (*I realized. He was after me.*). As a result, the complement and subordination properties with respect to which zero-clauses are vague or ambiguous can be assigned immediately at *that* and without the need for an additional dependency linking S to V1. The potential shortening of the matrix domains for phrasal and lexical combination, in conjunction with this

---

[9] A sentential complement without *that* in subject position would result in a regular garden path/misassignment, **(that) John was sick surprised me*, and is ungrammatical; see fn. 4 above (Bever 1970, Frazier 1985).

additional dependency of S on V1, result in an increasing dispreference for an intervening XP with zero complementizers, in the same way that zero relatives dispreferred a long XP between the subcategorizing V*i* and the head of the relative (N*i*) in (6.1). On the other hand, the processing domains for certain semantic dependencies, e.g. the assignment of the factive interpretation for sentential complements of *realize*, can be lengthened by the addition of *that*, just as they were for semantic aspects of relative clause interpretation in (6.3), since the whole subordinate clause receives the relevant interpretation and its total content must be accessed for processing of its truth conditions.

Without going into greater detail in the present context, notice how the performance preferences for complementizers are quite similar to those for relativizers. Domains can be shortened or lengthened in both (6.1) and (6.10), depending on the presence or absence of the respective XPs and on their length, and depending on the length of the subordinate subject NP2. This impacts TDDs (cf. e.g. Table 6.2). It also impacts OP-to-UP ratios (3.24) in both structures. This was shown explicitly for the complementizer deletions in §3.3.2. The preferred structures have higher TDDs (i.e. more minimal domains overall) and also higher OP-to-UP ratios (i.e. earlier property assignments on-line).

Rohdenburg (1999: 102) gives the following written corpus data from *The Times* and *Sunday Times* of London (first quarter of 1993) involving the matrix verb *realize*. First, the presence of an intervening adverbial phrase or clause as XP (in (6.10)) results in significantly fewer zero complements, 3% v. 37%.

(6.11) Rohdenburg's (1999: 102) Corpus

 a. *Finite S complements adjacent to V1 (realize)*
   THAT = 63% (294)   ZERO = 37% (172)
 b. *Finite S complements of V1 (realize) with intervening adverbial phrase/clause XP*
   THAT = 97% (62)   ZERO = 3% (2)

Second, in the absence of *that* an S-constructing subject pronoun in NP2 is preferred. The distribution, again for sentences with *realize*, is 73% (personal) pronouns for zero v. 38% for *that*.

(6.12) Rohdenburg's (1999: 102) Corpus: matrix verb *realize*

	ZERO complementizer	THAT complementizer
Personal pronoun NP2	73% (127/174)	38% (137/356)
Full NP2	27% (47/174)	62% (219/356)

With zero complements, additional length in a full NP2 subject delays access to the next available constructor of S on-line, the finite V2, making *that* increasingly preferred for S construction as NP2 gains in length. The figures for *realize*, comparing zero versus *that* in relation to the content and size of NP2, bear this out. They were given in §3.2.3 and are repeated here as (6.13):[10]

(6.13)   Rohdenburg's (1999:102) Corpus: matrix verb *realize*

	ZERO complementizer	THAT complementizer
Personal pronoun	48% (127)	52% (137)
NP2		
1–2 word full NP2	26% (32)	74% (89)
3+ word full NP2	10% (15)	90% (130)

Rohdenburg (1999) gives revealing data on another structural alternation in English involving complements of verbs: between semantically equivalent finite and infinitival complements of the verb *promise*. When the subject of the finite complement is identical to the matrix subject, as in *she promised that she would go to the doctor*, an infinitival complement can be used instead: *she promised to go to the doctor*. In early work in generative grammar the infinitival was derived from the finite complement by Equi-NP Deletion or Identity Erasure (Rosenbaum 1967). More recently the infinitival has been analyzed as a type of 'control' structure (Radford 1997). Correspondingly, the parsing of the infinitival *go* must access the matrix subject *she* in order to assign a subject to it and thereby satisfy the syntactic (and semantic) co-occurrence requirements of this verb. The infinitival complement therefore involves a strong dependency on the matrix subject, and this dependency is processed within a connected domain of surface elements and associated properties that proceeds from the matrix subject to the subordinate verb, i.e. *she promised to go* (see §2.2). The finite complement involves no such dependency, since the co-occurrence requirements of *go* are satisfied within the finite clause

---

[10] Some matrix verbs have higher overall ratios of zero to *that*. For *realize* the overall ratio is 33% to 67%. For *claim* Rohdenburg's (1999) figures are 45% to 55%. All the other relative proportions given in the main text for *realize* (involving XP and the content and size of NP2) hold identically for *claim* in his data, but with higher numbers for zero. Biber et al. (1999: 681) point out that zero is particularly favored with *think* and *say* as matrix verbs in the Longman Corpus. Clearly there is an additional factor that elevates or depresses the occurrence of zero, in addition to the domain minimizations discussed here. Reported speech verbs, *say* and *claim*, and the non-factive *think* have more complementizer omissions than factive *realize*. One obvious motivation for this involves the greater semantic/pragmatic similarity between complements of assertion and of belief predicates and corresponding matrix clauses without *that* (*I claim/Fred claims John is an idiot = John is an idiot [according to me/Fred]*). The precise nature of this descriptive generalization needs to be further investigated and quantified.

itself. The processing of *promise* must select between the finite and non-finite complement options, but the semantics of the verb is not affected by the choice.

Since there are more dependency relations for the less explicit infinitival complements than for finite complements there should be a greater preference for domain minimization, and tighter adjacency is predicted between infinitival complement, matrix subject, and verb. If no other constituent intervenes, the infinitival should be highly preferred. If an adverbial phrase or clause intervenes (*She promised if necessary to .../that ...*) the processing domain will not be minimal and we expect a higher proportion of finite complements, in proportion to the complexity of the intervening constituent.

Rohdenburg (1999: 106) gives the following figures (from *Time Magazine* 1989–94) which show that the presence of an intervening adverbial phrase or clause does increase the proportion of finite complements, from 6% to 27%:

(6.14) Rohdenburg's (1999: 106) Corpus

    a. *Complements adjacent to V (promise)*
        Infin VP = 94% (490)   Finite S = 6% (29)
    b. *Intervening adverbial phrase or clause between V (promise) and*
       complement
        Infin VP = 73% (30)   Finite S = 27% (11)

When the intervening constituent is a finite adverbial clause with a conjunction (i.e. a particularly long clausal constituent headed by e.g. *because* or *although*, of which relatively few occur in this environment in performance), the proportion of finite complements to infinitivals rises dramatically. There appear to be just five instances in the data of (6.14b), four of which (80%) occur with the finite complement. Comparable data reported in Rohdenburg (1996: 167) from the plays of George Bernard Shaw show that 6/6 (100%) of intervening finite adverbial clauses co-occur with finite complements of *promise*, whereas infinitival complements are preferred overall by a 43/50 (86%) margin.

For the verb *pledge* (which, like *promise*, is a commissive verb) Rohdenburg (2000: 28) gives the following figures for *I pledge (AdvP) to ...* v. *I pledge (AdvP) that ...*, taken from a large corpus of several British newspapers. The proportion of finite complements rises from 4% to 20% to 93% as the complexity of intervening constituents increases.

(6.15) Rohdenburg's (2000: 28) Corpus

   a. *Complements adjacent to V (pledge)*
          Infin VP = 96% (3604)   Finite S = 4% (140)
   b. *Intervening adverbial phrase between V (pledge) and complement*
          Infin VP = 80% (220)   Finite S = 20% (55)
   c. *Intervening finite adverbial clause between V (pledge) and*
      complement
          Infin VP = 7% (2)   Finite S = 93% (25)

This supports the domain-minimization prediction for more dependent complements. Rohdenburg also points out that the two instances of intervening adverb clauses that co-occur with the infinitival complement in (6.15c) are actually reduced clauses like *as predicted*, which makes them more like adverbial phrases.

   The verb *promise* also permits a second matrix NP argument, a 'personal object' in Rohdenburg's terms, as in *she promised her mother that she would go to the doctor* and *she promised her mother to go to the doctor*, and *pledge* permits a second PP argument, *I pledge to you that …*, *I pledge to you to … .* The processing of the understood subject in these infinitival complements still involves accessing the matrix subject, and verbs like *promise* are famously different from verbs like *persuade* whose matrix objects are processed as understood subjects of the infinitival verb, as in *she persuaded her mother to go to the doctor*. The processing domain for appropriate subject assignments to an infinitival verb must therefore access both the matrix verb and the controlling subject argument, and since the presence of a personal object necessarily increases that domain in the case of *promise* and *pledge*, we expect a higher proportion of finite complements. In fact, since verbs like *promise* are a distinct minority compared with *persuade*-type verbs, the finite complement could also be motivated by the desire to make clear that the subject of the subordinate verb is not the matrix object, as it usually is. Rohdenburg's (1999: 106) figures for *promise* plus a personal object show 22/26 (85%) finite complements v. 4/26 (15%) infinitival. For *pledge* plus a PP object Rohdenburg (2000: 28) gives a 14/14 (100%) co-occurrence with the finite complement.

   These data involving finite and non-finite complements support the proximity hypothesis of (3.7), which I repeat:

   (3.7) *Proximity Hypothesis*
         Given a structure {A, X, B}, X a variable for a phrase or phrases intervening between A and B, then the more relations of combination or dependency that link B to A, the smaller will be the size and complexity of X.

The verbs in infinitival complements are dependent on the matrix subject and verb for assignment of their subject argument and they prefer a smaller intervening X. The verbs in finite complements can access an explicit subject within the complement itself, they are less dependent on the matrix clause, and a larger intervening X occurs.

There are many such examples of alternating zero and explicit marking in English, and Rohdenburg and his collaborators have shown conclusively that the zero forms prefer less complex and smaller domains. One further case will be summarized briefly, involving the variable use of prepositions in *the police stopped the fans (from) entering the grounds*. The preposition *from* heads a PP complement in the lexical co-occurrence frame for the verb *stop*. Its absence leaves the gerundial phrase *entering the grounds* highly ambiguous with respect to its attachment site and syntactic status, in the same way that the complementizer *that* leaves the clause following *realize* ambiguous. An explicit *from* permits immediate selection of this co-occurrence option for *stop* when processing this verb's subcategorization and semantics. Once again there are more dependencies for zero than for *from*-complements, and greater proximity to the verb is predicted. One prediction that we make here involves the size of the object NP in *the police stopped NP (from)* .... The longer this NP is, the longer these additional processing domains will be for the zero complement, and the more *from*-complements we expect.

Rohdenburg (1999: 107) gives the following data from *The Times* and *Sunday Times* of London:

(6.16)   Rohdenburg's (1999: 107) Corpus: matrix verb *stop* + NP + ...

	ZERO complement	FROM complement
Personal pronoun NP	83% (85)	17% (17)
Full NP	72% (159)	28% (61)
Complex NP with modifying *who*-relative	40% (12)	60% (18)

As the NP gains in size, from a single-word personal pronoun to a full NP to a complex NP containing a *who*-relative, the zero complement option declines and explicit *from* increases.

6.2   Minimal formal marking in grammars

Across languages grammatical rules regularly conventionalize the preferences of performance that we have seen exemplified in English. Zero-marked dependencies may require proximity to their heads or controllers, with non-proximity being completely ungrammatical. Or grammars may conventionalize the zero or the explicit marking option under adjacency and proximity, thereby conventionalizing just one of the possibilities of performance that are strongly or equally preferred. Alternatively both options may be permitted, in languages such as English with frequent alternations whose performance distribution leads to the current prediction for grammars.

Consider the following implicational universal from Moravcsik (1995: 471) for case copying, an agreement device that is common in a number of languages (see Plank 1995):

(6.17) If agreement through case copying applies to NP constituents that are adjacent, it applies to those that are non-adjacent.

In other words, the formal marking of co-constituency signaled by case copying may occur in both adjacent and non-adjacent environments, in non-adjacent environments only, but not in adjacent ones only.

Compare the case marking rules of two Australian languages, Kalkatungu (a 'word-marking' language—see Blake 1987), and Warlpiri (a 'phrase-marking' language, Blake 1987). In Kalkatungu case copying occurs when NP constituents are both adjacent (6.18a) and non-adjacent (6.18b):

(6.18) a. thuku-yu yaun-tu yanyi   itya-mi   (Kalkatungu)
           dog-ERG big-ERG white-man bite-FUT
       b. thuku-yu yanyi   itya-mi   yaun-tu
           dog-ERG white-man bite-FUT big-ERG
           'The big dog will bite the white man.'

In Warlpiri it occurs only under non-adjacency (6.19b). When NP constituents are adjacent in (6.19a) the ergative case marking occurs just once in the NP and is not copied on all constituents:

(6.19)   a. tyarntu wiri-ngki+tyu yarlki-rnu   (Warlpiri)
              dog   big-ERG+me bite-PAST
          b. tyarntu-ngku+tyu yarlku-rnu wiri-ngki
              dog-ERG+me   bite-PAST big-ERG
              'The big dog bit me.'

The distribution of zero and formal marking in these conventionalized data from Kalkatungu and Warlpiri matches the performance preferences of English exactly. Both languages require formal marking in non-adjacent environments, and we saw that this is highly preferred in performance as well, e.g. in the preference for explicit relativizers in the non-adjacent relative clauses of (6.6). Kalkatungu and Warlpiri have each fixed one of the equally preferred options under adjacency–formal marking in the former and zero in the latter–corresponding to the relative clause data of (6.5) in which both explicit and zero relativizers are productive. Grammatical rules have conventionalized the preferences of performance here, eliminating the dispreferred option, and selecting from options that are strongly preferred.

The very possibility of productive non-adjacency in (6.18) and (6.19) appears to be a consequence of formal marking through case copying. In highly inflected languages like Latin, separation of adjective and noun is made possible by rich morphological agreement on the adjective (see Vincent 1987). This is not a possibility of Modern English, which has lost its adjective agreement, but it was a possibility in the earlier Germanic languages with adjective agreement (Sonderegger 1998), though not a requirement, since adjective agreement can still co-occur with NP-internal positioning (as in Modern German). These considerations suggest that if a language permits separation of noun and adjective, then the adjective must agree with the noun in some way.

The presence or absence of explicit case assignment to NPs by verbs has also been conventionalized in a number of languages in a way that reflects domain minimization and adjacency. Consider Kannada, a Dravidian SOV language with morphological case marking on a nominative-accusative basis. Bhat (1991) points out that an accusative-marked *pustaka-vannu* ('book-ACC') can occur without the case marking when it stands adjacent to a transitive verb, giving the structural alternation exemplified in (6.20a) and (6.20b). But there is no zero counterpart to an explicitly marked accusative if the relevant NP has been 'shifted to a position other than the one immediately to the left of the verb' (Bhat 1991: 35), as in (6.20c):

(6.20) a. Avanu   ondu pustaka-vannu bareda.   (Kannada)
         he (NOM) one   book-ACC   wrote
         'He wrote a book'.
    b. Avanu   ondu pustaka bareda.
         he (NOM) onc   book   wrote
    c. A: pustaka-vannu avanu   bareda.
        that book-ACC   he (NOM) wrote
        'That book he wrote'.

Such reorderings can be motivated by pragmatics (e.g. topicalization) or by efficiency in syntactic processing (e.g. EIC) (see §5.5). The important point in the present context is that an accusative NP without explicit case marking becomes dependent on the verb for the assignment of its case, and this additional dependency requires a conventionalized minimal domain for processing. The explicitly marked accusative can be recognized as such without accessing the verb, and is less dependent from this processing perspective.

Corresponding to the minimal domain preferences for infinitival complements, exemplified in the performance data of §6.1.2, the grammar of English has conventionalized what appears to be a universal preference for all control structures that was first captured in Rosenbaum's (1967) Identity Erasure Transformation. In essence, the deleted subject of an infinitival complement is understood to be identical to a matrix NP that stands at a minimal distance from the understood subject, where distance is defined 'in terms of the number of branches in the path connecting them' (Rosenbaum 1967: 6). In *Mary persuaded John to go to the doctor* there are fewer branches connecting the understood subject to *John* than to *Mary*, so *John* controls the deletion.

Rephrasing this insight in terms of lexical subcategorization domains and dependency relations as defined here (see (2.3)), the processing domains for the subordinate verb *go* are more minimal when the processor accesses *John* as the understood subject rather than *Mary*. The Minimal Distance Principle can therefore be viewed as a conventionalization of domain minimization (3.1) in a construction type that involves strong dependencies between a subordinate verb and a matrix argument. This construction type also minimizes forms (cf. MiF (3.8)), since one overt argument is assigned to both a matrix and a subordinate predicate, obviating the need for a subordinate argument. When the subordinate verb is finite (*Mary persuaded John that he should go to the doctor*), the subject of *go* is explicitly present and the matrix clause need not be accessed for this argument assignment. In the infinitival complement there are additional dependencies resulting from form minimization and a conventionalized minimal domain for their processing.

Some infinitival complements, a minority, have non-minimal domains linking controller and controllee, e.g. *Mary promised John to go to the doctor*. Exceptions such as these in English and other languages are discussed in Comrie (1984), who gives a semantic-pragmatic explanation for them. They are found with matrix verbs like *promise* whose meaning involves a commitment on the part of the matrix subject to carry out the action described in the subordinate clause. The preference for minimal processing domains has to be overridden by considerations of meaning in these cases. The reality of the minimization preference can still be seen in performance data involving *promise*, however, when phrases and clauses can potentially intervene between controller and controllee, thereby extending the lexical processing domains for the subordinate verb (see §6.1.2). The longer these intervening constituents are, the more the independently processable finite complement is preferred over the dependent infinitival.

Control structures are extremely efficient, therefore. They employ a single surface argument for the satisfaction of two sets of lexical co-occurrences (for matrix and subordinate verb) and as a result they minimize forms (cf. MiF (3.8)). They also minimize the domain in which the subject argument of the subordinate verb is processed (cf. MiD (3.1)). In addition, they involve no on-line misassignments of the type that arise in many movement structures (cf. MaOP (3.16) and §7.5.1). It is for these reasons that they are extremely productive cross-linguistically, if not completely universal.

'Raising' constructions, by contrast, are far from universal, e.g. *I assume John to have done it* (subject-to-object raising) and *the noise ceased to get on his nerves* (subject-to-subject raising). These structures used to be described in terms of a 'bounded' movement transformation (Postal 1974), the net effect of which was to limit the link between the subordinate verbs *(have) done* and *get* and the matrix objects (*John*) or subjects (*the noise*) to the same minimal domain that we find in control structures. The difference is that the matrix subjects and objects do not now contract an additional argument relation with the matrix predicate, but only with the subordinate one.[11] The result is an unusual structure for processing, since an argument and its immediate predicate are not lexically related, and there are numerous garden paths as a result (*the noise ceased to get on his nerves* is first parsed as 'the noise ceased', etc.); see Hawkins (1986). It is perhaps for these reasons that these structures are cross-linguistically marked (cf. Hawkins 1995, Müller-Gotama 1994). Raising structures displace an argument from its single (subordinate) predicate (contra MiD), and they involve frequent on-line misassignments (contra MaOP).[12]

---

[11] See in this connection the 'Argument Trespassing Generalization' of Hawkins (1986). Hawkins gives a detailed summary of the raising and tough structures of English, contrasts them with their (significantly more restricted) counterparts in German, and compares some different grammatical analyses for their description.

[12] Dwight Bolinger (personal communication) was the first to draw my attention to the potential for on-line misassignments in raising structures, and he ventured the hypothesis that the selection of a raising structure in performance would be preferred just in case the on-line misanalysis could also be true. In many uses of *the noise ceased to get on his nerves* the removal of irritation will result from the noise ceasing rather than from the purchase of earplugs, and Bolinger believed that the former circumstances would favor selection of the raising structure. Similarly, Bolinger found *I believe John to be telling the truth* more natural than *I believe John to be telling a lie*. Bolinger referred to this performance phenomenon as 'consonance'. Whether structural selections do actually favor consonance needs to be investigated empirically. The fact that it exists underscores the point made in the main text that misassignments are frequently possible; and on-line processing efficiency as advocated here would certainly agree with Bolinger's intuition that it is inefficient for a meaning to be assigned on-line that is at variance with the ultimate semantic representation.

Their (limited) efficiency seems to derive from MiF (3.8) and specifically from the fact that more structural types are now assigned to fewer forms (see (3.11)). In the history of English, raising structures 'got a free ride' on the back of control structures at a time when the semantic and theta-role assignments to subjects and objects were being expanded independently; see Hawkins (1986) and §6.3. below.[13]

What these examples from grammars reveal is that many syntactic and semantic relations can either be formally marked, through explicit words or morphemes, or they may not be marked. Adjectives may bear explicit agreement morphology, through case copying or other affixes, and this morphology can signal attachment to the relevant head noun. The absence of such morphology means that the attachment has to be signaled in some other way, principally through positioning. A relative pronoun can make explicit the co-indexation relation with the head, it provides an explicit argument for the subcategorizor within the relative clause, and it can construct the relative clause and signal its onset, while zero relativizers do none of these things. Case marking on NPs can formally signal properties in a verb's argument structure by assigning NPs to their appropriate nominative, accusative, or dative cases, and to the theta-roles or limited sets of theta-roles that are associated with each. The absence of case marking sets up additional dependencies on the verb. And explicit pronouns or other NPs within a finite complement structure, or in relative clauses with resumptive pronouns, provide explicit NPs within the clause on the basis of which lexical subcategorization and dependency relations can be processed locally. The absence of these NPs means that the processor has to access controllers or fillers in a non-local environment.

Zero marking in all these examples results in conventionalized adjacency and proximity effects, i.e. in minimal domains for processing. This can be accounted for by saying that there are stronger dependencies between the relevant categories A and B when syntactic and semantic relations between them are not formally marked. The dependencies are stronger because assigning the relevant properties to category B requires access to category A. An NP whose case morphology renders it unambiguously accusative or dative and whose case is recognizable without accessing the verb permits the relevant morphological, syntactic, and semantic properties to be assigned to NP independently

---

[13] Also relevant here are 'tough movement' and 'tough deletion' structures such as *this book is tough to read* and *John is ugly to look at* (Hawkins 1986). The matrix subject is linked to a subordinate non-subject position in these examples, and the distance between them can now be 'unbounded', i.e. non-minimal (*this book is tough for me to persuade John to read*). Again there is no motivation for these structures in terms of MiD or MaOP (there are frequent on-line misassignments), but they do add extra expressive possibilities to already existing control structures, whence the famous *John is eager to please/John is easy to please* ambiguity in surface structure (Chomsky 1957).

of V (and in advance of V in the parse string; see §8.5). But a bare NP is dependent on access to V for these same property assignments, hence there are more dependency relations between them.[14] And more dependency relations, in this and the other examples we have discussed, means more adjacency and proximity (by MiD (3.1)).

Zero marking involves more dependency assignments, therefore, but it does have a compensating advantage: there is less linguistic form to process phonologically, morphologically, and syntactically. Explicit marking involves fewer dependency assignments, but more processing of linguistic form. One way to quantify this trade-off is to examine its impact on all the domains whose processing is affected by the presence or absence of explicit forms, and to make predictions based on overall domain sizes (i.e. the total domain differentials), as was done for zero and explicit relativizers in Tables 6.1 and 6.2. The zero relativizer shortens some processing domains, while lengthening others. The tabulation reveals, and the performance data of e.g. (6.5) confirm, that within small surface domains (under adjacency of the head and relative clause) language users have a choice, between zero and explicit marking. But in larger domains involving increasing distances between interdependent and combinatorial categories, the balance shifts to explicit marking, which involves fewer dependencies and increasing advantages in terms of total domain differentials. For example, as an intervening XP gains in size between a head and a relative clause in Table 6.2, and as the relative clause subject NP2 gains in size, the overall preference for *wh/that* over zero increases also.

When grammars conventionalize these preferences of performance, they do so in accordance with the predictions of the Performance–Grammar Correspondence Hypothesis (PGCH) (cf. (1.2)). Prediction (1.2a) asserts that if a structure A is preferred over an A′ of the same structural type in performance, then A will be more productively grammaticalized. Formally marked discontinuities between NP constituents are preferred over zero marking, in both performance and grammars. The formal marking of case assignment by verbs is also preferred under non-adjacency to V in grammars, and is predicted to be preferred in performance in languages with both options under non-adjacency. (1.2a) asserts further that if A and A′ are (more) equally preferred (e.g. formally marked and zero-marked adjacent NP constituents, explicitly marked and zero-marked accusative NPs adjacent to V), then both will be productive in performance and grammars. These data also exemplify the variation that is

---

[14] Processing is also aided by default assignments of e.g. nominative and absolutive cases to NPs that are processed in advance of V; cf. Primus's (1999) hierarchies and the discussion in §8.2.2 and §8.5. There are still dependencies of NP on V, even when case-marking and theta-role defaults permit on-line assignments of e.g. nominative and agent to an NP on-line.

predicted by PGCH prediction (1.2c) when different preferences are in partial opposition, involving on this occasion competing preferences for domain minimization, of the kind illustrated in Table 6.1.

6.3   Morphological typology and Sapir's 'drift'

Sapir's (1921) index of synthesis for classical morphological typology is very relevant in the present processing context.[15] This index is intended to measure the degree of morphological richness and complexity in the structure of words within different languages by quantifying the (average) number of morphemes per word in that language. Languages with higher scores and with more agglutinative (Turkish) or inflectional (Latin) morphology will, in general, be those that involve more formal marking of case and agreement and of other syntactic and semantic relations, and that permit more independent processing at each word as it is parsed and produced. Isolating languages like Vietnamese and Modern English, on the other hand, will involve more property assignments through dependency relations between co-occurring words and phrases. Such languages should exhibit strong adjacency and proximity effects, according to the theory proposed here, since there will be more syntactic and semantic processing operations that require access to their interdependent categories, and these operations will favor minimal domains. Morphologically richer languages, by contrast, will permit more independent processing at each word and will require dependent processing for fewer property assignments, resulting in weaker adjacency and proximity effects.

This puts a new perspective on the shift from an inflectional to an isolating language in the history of English and on the general typology that I derived from it in Hawkins (1986, 1995). The 'drift' in English was not just a question of the loss of inflections and of the freezing of SVO word order (see Sapir 1921). There were many concomitant changes that now make sense from this processing perspective. Agreement inflections were lost on adjectives, which became fixed in a position adjacent to the head noun, and case marking was lost on full NPs, which became anchored to the verb in its new basic (SVO) position. In the process these adjectives and full NPs became dependent on their respective sister categories for the assignment of properties that had been independently processable hitherto. In earlier stages of English, accusative and dative case could be recognized on the basis of the NP itself, and the associated patient and recipient proto-roles could be assigned without accessing the verb.

---

[15] See Comrie (1989) for a summary of the major differences between isolating, agglutinating, inflectional, and polysynthetic languages, and for a summary of Sapir's indices of synthesis and fusion.

But the zero-marked NPs of Middle English required access to the verb for case and theta-role assignment. And once this extreme dependency on the verb was conventionalized, the stage was set for a broader set of theta-role assignment possibilities, sensitive to the idiosyncrasies of different verb classes, within the new SVO structure in which S and O were guaranteed to be adjacent to V. Thus, Modern English transitive clauses with locative and instrumental subjects emerged, such as *this tent sleeps four, my lute broke a string,* and *a penny once bought several pins,* and these are without parallel in Old English and in Modern German (Rohdenburg 1974). Locative and instrumental theta-roles are normally assigned to PPs (*four can sleep in this tent,* etc.), but they can be assigned to a grammatical subject that is adjacent to its theta-role assigner, while the corresponding (and occasionally agent-like!) theta-role of the direct object can also be assigned under adjacency to the verb.

Relative pronouns and complementizers also became deletable in the history of English, resulting in the structural alternations that we saw in §6.1. Independent processability again gave way to dependent processing for the assignment of numerous syntactic and semantic properties to clauses that could now be highly vague and ambiguous in their zero-marked versions. Many verbs and nouns also became category-ambiguous which had been lexically or morphologically unambiguous hitherto and which now required co-occurring articles or infinitival *to* for disambiguation (e.g. *I want the run/to run*). One of the motivations for the emergence and expansion of definite (and also indefinite) articles in Middle English can be argued to be a processing one, in terms of category construction and disambiguation (see §4.4.2).

More generally, Modern English has significantly more ambiguity and vagueness in its syntactic, lexical, and morphological categories than it once did, and it relies to a much greater extent on co-occurring categories for the assignment of the relevant (disambiguating) properties. This results in the typological contrasts between Modern English and Modern German that were discussed at length in Hawkins (1986, 1995). What I would add to this typology in the present context is that conventionalized adjacency and proximity appear to be required for these sweeping changes, since the processing domains for the increased dependency assignments are then guaranteed to be minimal.

7

Relative Clause and *Wh*-movement Universals

This chapter is concerned with relative clauses and *Wh*-movement structures across languages, which I shall examine from the perspective of Minimize Domains (3.1), Minimize Forms (3.8), and Maximize On-line Processing (3.16). A primary focus will be the 'filler–gap dependency' relationship exemplified in the following sentences of English:

(7.1) a. The person who you think that John saw is Mary.
      b. Who do you think that John saw?

In many analyses, a filler is matched with a co-indexed empty position, or gap, as shown in (7.1′):

(7.1′) a. the person$i$ [who$i$ you think [that John saw Oi]]
       b. Who$i$ [do you think [that John saw Oi]]?

The filler *who$i$* is also co-indexed with the head noun *person$i$* in (7.1′a).

    There are severe restrictions on grammaticality in these constructions. Ross (1967) was the first to define constraints of generality, and in the years since then there has been a lot of further cross-linguistic research. The constraints and principles that have been proposed now lie at the core of 'UG' (or Universal Grammar in the Chomskyan sense). There has also been important work in the typological tradition, exemplified by Keenan & Comrie's (1977) 'Accessibility Hierarchy'. More recently there has been a growing interest in the processing of filler–gap dependencies, and some key insights have been gained as a result of psycholinguistic experiments that will be incorporated into this chapter. I will argue that these insights, in conjunction with the general principles proposed here, can help us explain a number of facts about the grammar of relative clauses and *wh*-movement.

    For example, quite a few languages are counterexamples to Ross's 'Complex NP Constraint' and to subsequent reformulations in terms of subjacency (Chomsky 1981) and barriers (Chomsky 1986). The ungrammaticality of (7.2) reveals the operation of this constraint in English, but corresponding sentences in Swedish, Japanese and Akan are not ungrammatical (see §7.4.1):

(7.2) *Which bone*i* [did you see np[the dog s[that was biting O*i*]]]?

If constraints like this are intended to be universal, they are too strong. They are also too weak. There are languages that make a distinction between the relative clause of (7.1a) and the *wh*-question of (7.1b). In many dialects of German, including the standard language, the direct translation of (7.1a) is ungrammatical, the direct translation of (7.1b) is not (Kvam 1983):[1]

(7.3) a. *die Person*i* [die*i* du   glaubst [dass Johan O*i* gesehen hat]]   (German)
            the person who you think   that John   seen   has
            'the person who you think that John saw'
        b. Wen*i* [glaubst du [dass Johan O*i* gesehen hat]]
            who think   you that John   seen   has
            'Who do you think that John saw?'

The same distinction has been noted for Russian in Comrie (1973). Most current models assume a single parameter setting for a given language, and do not predict this kind of construction-specific difference. Keenan & Comrie's Accessibility Hierarchy data also do not follow readily from current principles in terms of parameterized bounding nodes (IP[S] and NP, etc). And there are many other cross-linguistic patterns that are either not being predicted or are not well understood.

There is also a lot of stipulation. Why should complex NPs be less hospitable environments for gaps than other structures? Why are there so-called *wh*-islands? Why are resumptive pronouns found in place of gaps in some syntactic positions and not others? We are simply told that this is the way things are. It is also apparent that numerous factors contribute to well-formedness—syntactic, semantic, and lexical—yet no unifying principle has been proposed for why they combine together in the ways they do to give us the variation we observe.

In this chapter I pursue a different approach to these questions, following the research program of this book. I will argue that the grammatical variation is highly correlated with processing ease and efficiency, in accordance with the Performance–Grammar Correspondence Hypothesis (1.1). Structures that are preferred in the performance of one language are the only ones grammatical-ized in another, and when there is a preference ranking A > B > C > D in performance, there is a corresponding hierarchy of grammatical conventions,

---

[1] The southern German dialects permit more extensive filler–gap dependencies than the northern dialects. The distinction between (7.3a) and (7.3b) is based, inter alia, on native-speaker judgments by Germans who are considered by Kvam (1983) to be speakers of Standard German.

with cut-off points in increasing numbers of grammars down the hierarchy (see (1.2b)).

The order of presentation is as follows. In §7.1 I introduce background assumptions and details. §7.2 examines the Keenan–Comrie Accessibility Hierarchy from the perspective of MiD and MiF. §7.3 links the *wh*-fronting option to basic word order types, specifically to verb position, and accounts for the quantitative regularities in terms of MiD. In §7.4 numerous other increasing complexity hierarchies are proposed and tested, derived from MiD and MiF. §7.5 examines MaOP effects in *wh*-questions and relative clauses. And §7.6 summarizes some apparent grammatical mysteries that make sense from a processing perspective, such as the '*that*-trace' effect in English and subjacency violations in Japanese.

7.1   The grammar and processing of filler–gap dependencies

In standard transformational grammar (Chomsky 1965), and in much work derived from it, it has been assumed that the *wh*-phrase in questions, relative clauses and similar constructions is moved from a grammatically determined original position into the leftmost position of the relevant clause. In Government-Binding theory (Chomsky 1981), movement leaves a 'trace' which is co-indexed with the *wh*-phrase, as shown in (7.1'). Other models, such as Generalized Phrase Structure Grammar (Gazdar et al. 1985) assume no actual movement of the *wh*-phrase, but maintain the notion of a trace.

In psycholinguistics the terms 'filler' and 'gap' have been used for the moved element and its trace respectively (following J. D. Fodor 1978, 1989), and it is assumed that an association is set up between these items in on-line processing. Some processing theories assume instead that an association is made between the *wh*-phrase and the actual word that subcategorizes for it (Pickering et al. 1994), as shown in (7.4):

(7.4) Who$i$ [do you think [that John saw$i$]]?

These 'direct association' theories are based on trace-free models of grammar such as Categorial Grammar (Moortgat 1988, Steedman 1987) and Head-Driven Phrase Structure Grammar (Pollard & Sag 1994).

Filler–subcategorizor theories capture two important insights in the present context. First, the co-indexation that links the filler to the position questioned or relativized on, and that makes explicit the filler's role within the relevant clause, is defined from filler to subcategorizor rather than from filler to gap. In terms of processing, the size of a 'filler–gap domain' will crucially involve the distance between the filler and the subcategorizor, according to this theory. Second, and conversely, the lexical co-occurrence requirements of the subcategorizor will need to access the filler, not the gap. The lexical co-occurrences of the transitive *saw*i are processed by accessing the local subject *John* in (7.4) and the displaced object *who*i, and the major difference between a 'filler–gap' structure and a basic ordering with a minimal lexical domain lies in its added size.

Co-indexation and lexical co-occurrence processing both make crucial reference to subcategorizors, in these structures with gaps. But in some languages and structures the two processes are dissociated. In the event that the filler corresponds to an adjunct, for which there is no subcategorizor, there will be co-indexation between the filler and some position within the clause, but the filler will not be involved in any simultaneous lexical processing domain (e.g. in *How*i *[do you think [that John wrote the paper Oi]]?*). Similarly, in languages like Hebrew in which the gap is replaced by a resumptive pronoun (giving structures corresponding to *the person*i *[that you think [that John saw her*i]]—see (7.14)–(7.15) below) there will be co-indexation between the coreferential items, but the lexical processing of *saw* can take place locally, with the subject *John* and the object *her*i immediately adjacent to *saw*. The link between the filler and the position questioned or relativized on can involve more or fewer relations of combination and dependency, therefore, and this should have consequences for adjacency and proximity, in the same way that more such relations minimized domains in §§5 and 6.

In what follows I shall still refer to gap positions. When the gap has a subcategorizor, the filler–gap domain will proceed from filler to subcategorizor, with some limited additional items that will be defined below. When the gap has no subcategorizor, the filler–gap domain will proceed from the filler to the head of phrase that actually constructs the mother node containing the gap and to which the gap must be attached. As a result, the processing domains for filler–gap identification may not need to extend to the gap site itself, but only to the subcategorizor or relevant head, and they can generally be shorter and more efficient as a result. In fact, to define these domains from filler to gap results in some implausible predictions for both performance and grammars.

Consider a VOS language like Malagasy, which has head-initial relative clauses, and which only allows relativizations on a subject (Keenan & Comrie 1977). If we assume that the head of the relative is linked to the empty subject position in the relative clause, within a filler–gap domain so defined, then the only allowable domain in this language is the largest possible one, in which

the (clause-final) gap is furthest from the head noun filler.[2] Clearly a coun-
terintuitive result! But if the filler is connected to the subcategorizor of the
gap, the verb, then the path from the head of the relative to the (clause-initial)
verb is short and efficient. The same applies to the mirror-image situation in
SOV languages with prenominal relatives, such as Japanese. Subject relatives
would again have the largest possible filler–gap domains if these were defined
from the (clause-initial) gap to the (head noun) filler, whereas the clause-final
verb is adjacent to the head. Most relativization types in English, an SVO
language, will also have smaller filler–gap domains when defined from filler
to subcategorizor.[3]

It is not significant here whether movement or base generation of the *wh*-
phrase is involved. In both cases a filler in surface structure must be matched
with a subcategorizor or head at some distance from the filler.

With regard to the on-line processing of filler–gap structures, there appears
to be a consensus on the following basic point in the psycholinguistic literature. Filler–gap dependencies are hard to process, and they are characterized
by a heightened processing load and a constant effort to relate the filler to
the appropriate gap site or subcategorizor. Doing so is not easy. There is no
surface manifestation of the position in the parse string to which the filler
must be attached, as there is in resumptive pronoun structures, and making the attachment requires recognition of the intended subcategorizor or
head. At the same time the filler must be held in working memory, all the
other material on the path from filler to gap/subcategorizor must be processed
simultaneously, and the latter must be correctly identified and co-indexed.
This insight has been central to psycholinguistic theorizing ever since Wanner
& Maratsos (1978) provided experimental evidence for a measurable processing load within a filler–gap domain. Numerous subsequent experiments

---

[2] There are no relative pronouns in Malagasy that can constitute the immediate filler for the filler–
gap relationship. In fact, languages with relative pronouns are a minority type among head-initial
languages and do not occur in head-final languages: see C. Lehmann (1984), Maxwell (1979), and §7.5.1.
The head noun itself is therefore the filler for filler–gap co-indexation in these languages, and for lexical
co-occurrence processing.

[3] In some structures and languages (a minority) a filler–gap domain will be lengthened by a direct
association with the subcategorizor, for example if the filler precedes the gap which in turn precedes its
subcategorizor. Such a situation arises in Dutch, for which Frazier (1987) and Frazier & Flores d'Arcais
(1989) have presented evidence that subject–object gap ambiguities can be resolved in favor of subject
assignments to the gap prior to a clause-final lexical verb. But the theta-roles assigned to NP sequences
in Dutch and their precise thematic entailments are determined by the verb and admit of various
combinatorial possibilities (see Primus 1999 for illustration from numerous languages), whether these
NPs are overt or not, so that processing of the verb is still required for full gap interpretation, which
supports the definition in (7.8).

have refined it, and there has also been neurolinguistic support using event-related brain potentials or ERPs (Kluender & Kutas 1993*a*, *b*, King & Kutas 1992, 1993).

One significant finding is that there appears to be a 'first resort strategy' in parsing. A gap/subcategorizor is postulated as soon as it can be and is linked with the filler, thereby relieving structural uncertainty and demands on working memory. Consider (7.5):

(7.5) Which student did you ask John about?
(7.5′) Which student*i* [did you ask(*i*) John about*i*]?

There are two possible attachment sites for *which student* in the on-line parse: to *ask* and to *about*. A slow reading of (7.5) confirms that *which student* is first interpreted as the direct object of *ask*, i.e. it is assigned to the first subcategorizor encountered. This interpretation is then revised as soon as *John* is parsed, since *John* has to be understood as the direct object, and *which student* is returned to its unfilled filler status until the preposition *about* is encountered, to which it can be assigned as a complement. Clifton and Frazier (1989) define this parsing process as the 'Active Filler Hypothesis':

(7.6) *Active Filler Hypothesis*
When a filler of category XP has been identified in a non-argument position, such as COMP, rank the option of assigning its corresponding gap to the sentence over the option of identifying a lexical phrase of category XP. (Clifton & Frazier 1989: 292)

As an illustration of the kinds of processing effects that this predicts in on-line experiments, consider the following sentences from Stowe (1986):

(7.7) a. My brother wanted to know if Ruth will bring us home to Mom at Christmas.
b. My brother wanted to know who*i* will bring*i* us home to Mom at Christmas.
c. My brother wanted to know who*i* Ruth will bring(*i*) us home to*i* at Christmas.

Stowe found that subjects took significantly longer to process *us* in (7.7c) than in (7.7a) or (7.7b). This is explained as follows. The parser makes an on-line assignment of *who*i to *bring* as a direct object in (7.7c), in accordance with (7.6). This attachment is then immediately contradicted by the presence of the overt pronoun *us*, leading to a reanalysis and longer processing times. (7.7a) and (7.7b) involve no such reanalysis.

Filler–gap dependencies are complex structures to process, therefore, and the effect of the Active Filler Hypothesis is to minimize the domains in which they are processed by postulating a subcategorizor or gap as soon as possible. Positioning the filler before the subcategorizor/gap has also been argued (by J.D. Fodor 1983) to have processing advantages over gap (/subcategorizor)-before-filler orders, for reasons that accord well with the MaOP preference (§7.5.1). And the presence of a gap minimizes forms compared with an explicit argument in the gap position (see §3.2), though overall efficiency will not be improved when co-indexing and lexical co-occurrences must be processed over large domains.

The question of interest for grammatical analysis is this. Have grammars responded to the processing complexity of matching a filler with a sub-categorizor/gap, and if so, what structural properties might we expect them to conventionalize in order to do so? I will argue that we see clear evidence in cross-linguistic grammatical conventions for properties that reflect the three major processing preferences of this book. Domain minimization effects have been conventionalized in the permitted distances between filler and subcategorizor/gap. As distances increase, the number of attested grammars declines (see §§7.2–4). Some of these increases are captured in increasing complexity hierarchies, like the Keenan–Comrie Accessibility Hierarchy or in subjacency parameters. At the same time, form minimization is reflected in the gap structure itself and in the complementarity between gaps and resumptive pronouns, with the former preferring simpler and the latter more complex domains for processing (see §7.2). MaOP effects are reflected in leftward rather than rightward movements, and in numerous other syntactic and morphosyntactic properties that facilitate on-line processing (see §7.5).

Let us define a filler–gap domain as follows:

(7.8) *Filler–Gap Domain* (FGD)

An FGD consists of the smallest set of terminal and non-terminal nodes dominated by the mother of a filler and on a connected path that must be accessed for gap identification and processing; for subcategorized gaps the path connects the filler to a co-indexed subcategorizor and includes, or is extended to include, any additional arguments of the subcategorizor on which the gap depends for its processing; for non-subcategorized gaps the path connects the filler to the head category that constructs the mother node containing the co-indexed gap; all constituency relations and co-occurrence requirements holding between these nodes belong in the description of the FGD.

There are circumstances in which the FGD extends beyond the minimal path connecting the filler to its co-indexed subcategorizer, namely when the processor requires access to an additional argument of this subcategorizor in order to process the gap. This can happen in two cases.

First, if the gap is in a position that requires the co-occurrence of another argument, then that argument must be in the FGD as well. A direct object requires the co-occurrence of a subject; an indirect object is assumed here to require both; a subcategorized PP complement requires at least a co-occurring subject. These required co-occurrences are added to an FGD, if they are not already in it, in order to include categories on whose interpretation the gap can depend. A direct object not only requires the co-occurrence of a subject, it can be asymmetrically dependent on it syntactically and semantically (Dowty 1991, Primus 1999; cf. §4.6). A subject, by contrast, does not require a co-occurring direct object, and it is not dependent on a direct object when there is one. In English the SVO word order guarantees that the subject will always be in the FGD for an object gap, whereas an overt object will not be in the FGD for a subject gap. Compare *papers*i *[that students write*i*]* with *students*i *[that write*i *books]* (FGDs in bold). In a VSO language, however, the FGD for the object gap will be extended to include the overt subject, *papers*i *[that write*i *students]*, whereas the FGD for the subject gap need not include the overt object, i.e. *students*i *[that write*i *books]*.[4] The intuition behind this is that the FGD in the latter case is complete and processable, even when the subcategorizor is transitive and takes an object. The head, *students,* is recognizable as the subject and agent of *write* within the relative clause. By contrast, although *papers* is recognizable as the object and patient of *write* in *papers*i *that write*i, the processing of the object is incomplete without the subject, and one is left wondering who performed this action and brought the papers into existence (on account of the required co-occurrence of the subject and the thematic dependence of the patient on the agent).

Second, there are circumstances in which additional arguments may also be included in the FGD, namely when filler and subcategorizor alone are ambiguous between a subject gap and an object gap interpretation. Depending on case marking and verb agreement in the language in question the sequence *cats that saw mice* in a VSO language could be assigned a subject relative interpretation (i.e. 'cats that saw mice') or an object interpretation ('cats that mice saw'). In such cases the FGD for both interpretations will include the overt NP in the

---

[4] Notice how the domains for filler–gap processing (7.8) diverge from those for lexical co-occurrence processing (see (5.6) in §5.2.1) in these examples. Both subject and object arguments of *write* must always be accessed within the domains for lexical co-occurrence processing, but the FGDs for subject relatives are smaller than for object relatives, for the reasons given.

relative, [N*i* [V*i* NP]], in the event that the latter is needed for disambiguation. In the mirror-image verb-final structure of Japanese, [[NP V*i*] N*i*], the FGD will similarly include a disambiguating lower NP.

The definition in (7.8) states that all constituency relations and co-occurrence requirements holding between nodes belong to the description of the domain, as is the case for all processing domains (all the properties conventionally associated with terminal elements are part of a domain—see (2.4)). Constituency relations can be stated in terms of immediate domination, from which further structural relations such as sisterhood and c-command can be derived. Co-occurrence requirements (abbreviated here as B RQ A) will principally be those defined by verbs and prepositions/postpositions and may be syntactic (subcategorization), morphosyntactic (e.g. case assignment), or semantic (e.g. theta-role assignment).

7.2   The Keenan–Comrie Accessibility Hierarchy

Keenan & Comrie (1977, 1979) proposed that relativization becomes more difficult down an Accessibility Hierarchy (AH), and that certain languages 'cut off' at each of the implicationally permitted points:[5]

(7.9) Accessibility Hierarchy (AH): SU > DO > IO/OBL > GEN

Their precise predictions were formulated as a set of hierarchy constraints, defined in terms of relative clause 'strategies'. I have argued (in Hawkins 1994: 37–42, 1999) that their data can be explained in terms of the increasing complexity of the processing domains for different relativizable positions.[6]

The complexity claim is not straightforward, given the differences between languages with respect to case marking, linear ordering, syntactic configuration, etc. Nonetheless there is a clear general correlation between the number

---

[5] The original formulation of the AH was: SU > DO > IO > OBL > GEN > OCOMP. The version given here is the one used by Comrie (1989), with IO and OBL positions collapsed. This collapsing is supported by the complexity metric of (7.11), which does not distinguish between them. OCOMP has also been excluded on account of its highly variable coding (Stassen 1985), and since Keenan & Comrie do not have systematic data for it. Illustrative sentences (from English) for the four relativizable positions on the current hierarchy are:

  (i) SU *the student [who worked hard]*
  (ii) DO *the book [which the professor wrote]*
  (iii) IO/OBL *the course [which the professor wrote the book for]*
  (iv) GEN *the professor [whose book the student read]*

[6] The reader is referred to Hawkins (1994, 1999) for many details that are omitted here. The key generalizations are summarized in this context in order to integrate them within the broader theory of this book and in order to present some recent findings that are relevant, especially from performance.

of dominating and co-occurring nodes required for these relativizable positions and their AH ranking. Subjects generally occupy the highest argument position in a tree and c-command other NP positions (generally asymmetrically; see §4.6). A direct object requires the co-occurrence of a (c-commanding) subject and contracts a tight bond with the verb (Tomlin 1986) which motivates a dominating VP in addition to S. FGDs for object gaps will always contain the subcategorizor's subject, as discussed in §7.1, whereas FGDs for subject gaps need not contain overt objects. An indirect object is regarded in models of Relational Grammar (Blake 1990) as the third argument of a three-place predicate, requiring the co-occurrence of both subject and object, and in this context I will assume that overt subjects and objects are required in FGDs with indirect object gaps. Indirect objects are not distinguishable from obliques in terms of the complexity metric proposed here. Oblique NPs are often embedded within a PP, which gives them extra depth, but they differ from indirect objects in not generally requiring a direct object, though they do require a subject. Finally, a genitive NP is dominated by a possessive phrase within a higher dominating NP in a variety of structural positions, the aggregated complexity of which puts the genitive at the bottom of the hierarchy.

In (7.11) I calculate the minimal FGD sizes for (gap) relativizations on each of the AH positions, given these assumptions. The configurational structure for the different relativizations can be summarized in a single tree representation, with unordered ICs of each phrase ('s' identifies the constituents of a subject NP within the relative, 'o' the constituents of an object NP, 'g' identifies the genitive NP within the relevant NPs, NPo, etc.):

(7.10)

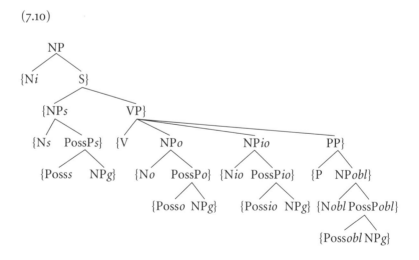

The minimal FGD for each relativizable position will include: the filler Ni (and NP); the co-indexed subcategorizor of Ni's gap (Vi, Pi or Poss$i$, and their projected VP, PP or PossP); any overt arguments (NP and head N) that are required by the gap position (DO RQ SU, etc); (for genitives) the NP and/or PP dominating the subcategorizor Poss$i$ and PossP plus the heads N and/or P that project to NP and PP; and the verb in the relative clause (and dominating VP and S).[7] Items beyond these minima may also be in the FGD for particular languages if they are necessarily present in the domain connecting Ni to its subcategorizor. For relativizations on a genitive I assume that the NP containing the genitive gap exhibits the same asymmetrical co-occurrence requirements that I have discussed for gaps, so that a containing direct object requires a subject (NPs and Ns), etc. (GEN-SU stands for relativization on a genitive within a subject NP, GEN-DO for relativization on a genitive within a direct object, and so on).

(7.11)   *Minimal FGDs for relativizations on:*

SU $= 5$	{Ni, NP, Vi, VP, S}
DO $= 7$	{Ni, NP, Vi, VP, NPs, Ns, S} (RQ SU)
IO $= 9$	{Ni, NP, Vi, VP, NPs, Ns, NPo, No, S} (RQ DO & SU)
OBL $= 9$	{Ni, NP, Pi, PP, NPs, Ns, V, VP, S} (RQ SU)
GEN-SU $= 9$	{Ni, NP, Posssi, PossPs, NPs, Ns, V, VP, S}
GEN-DO $= 11$	{Ni, NP, Possoi, PossPo, NPs, Ns, NPo, No, V, VP,S} (RQ SU)
GEN-IO $= 13$	{Ni, NP, Possioi, PossPio, NPs, Ns, NPo, No, NPio, Nio, V, VP, S} (RQ DO & SU)
GEN-OBL $= 13$	{Ni, NP, Poss$obli$, PossPobl, NPs, Ns, NPobl, Nobl, PP, P, V, VP, S} (RQ SU)

The total number of nodes in the minimal FGD increases down (7.11). As these nodes increase there are more structural relations and co-occurrence requirements to compute, and more morphosyntactic and semantic dependencies. There will also be more terminal elements in larger domains, with more words to access and process. Node quantity is just one index of the relative complexity of an FGD, therefore, but it is a fundamental one, with numerous correlating properties that involve additional processing operations.

FGDs going beyond these minima will arise when relative clauses contain optional elements in the path from filler to subcategorizor. The consistent

---

[7] The dominating NP or PP nodes over genitive (PossP) gaps are included in these FGDs since otherwise there is no attachment site for the Poss subcategorizor. The verb in the relative clause is also included, in the event that it is not the subcategorizor, since otherwise the clause is unprocessable.

addition of an optional element to all the relative clauses of (7.11) should not, in general, affect the relative ranking based on obligatorily present elements.[8] Different word order conventions in different languages will also not change the ranking, in most cases. If the verb is peripheral to the relative clause and the head noun is adjacent to the verb (i.e. Ni [V ...] and [... V] Ni), in VSO and many SOV languages, then FGDs will expand down the AH to include categories to the right and left of V respectively, in accordance with (7.11). So they will too in SVO languages, with Ni [Vi ...] for subject relatives, Ni [NPs Vi ...] for object relatives, and with expanding domains to the right of V for the lower positions.

There are two interesting word order types. For the (rare) SVO type in which the relative clause precedes the head, exemplified by Chinese, the subcategorizing verb can be closer to the head when relativizing on a direct object than on the subject of a transitive verb, i.e. [NPs Vi] Ni (DO relative) v. [Vi NPo] Ni (SU relative). By the criteria in (7.8) these relativizations have equally minimal FGDs, since the DO relative must include the required NPs in the FGD, while the SU relative includes the NPo that stands on the path from Vi to Ni. As lower positions on the AH are relativized, however, there will be progressively more categories in the path from V(i) to Ni, and FGDs will increase in accordance with (7.11). Similarly for the mirror-image German type with SOV order in the relative clause and head-initial fillers, Ni [...V(i)], the FGD proceeds from Ni to V(i) and there will be larger FGDs on relativizations down the AH.[9]

7.2.1   *Performance support for the FGD complexity ranking*

There is extensive evidence from psycholinguistic experiments on English that support the SU > DO ranking of (7.9) and (7.11). Wanner & Maratsos (1978)

---

[8] For illustration of this point, see Hawkins (1994: 38–9).

[9] One interesting difference between Chinese and German v. other word order types, according to (7.11), is the following. For relative clauses containing one and the same verb, e.g. ditransitive 'give', relativizations on SU, DO and IO positions will have identical FGDs. The domains proceed from Ni to V and they will include all three arguments in Chinese and German, whichever position is being relativized on. When different verbs are compared, however, FGDs can be, and generally will be, larger or smaller in accordance with (7.11). A SU relative with an intransitive verb in German (Ni [Vi]) can have a smaller FGD than a DO relative with a transitive (Ni [NPs Vi), and this can be smaller than an IO relative with a ditransitive (Ni [NPs NPo Vi]). The same applies to Chinese ([Vi] Ni vs [NPs Vi] Ni vs [NPs Vi NPo] Ni). In all other word order types the complexity differences defined by (7.11) will apply both to one and the same verb and to different verbs. It remains to be seen whether there is a difference between Chinese/German and other languages in this regard. One confounding factor here will be the greater frequency of subjects compared with direct objects, and of direct compared with indirect objects, which will result in default gap-filling preferences of the type reported for Dutch in Frazier (1987) and Frazier & Flores d'Arcais (1989). On the other hand, the data from Chinese discussed in §7.2.1 support the relevance of FGD size as a determinant of the presence or avoidance of a gap structure, and also point to a significant difference between Chinese and other languages with respect to subject relative and object relative processing.

were the first to argue for the greater processing load of object relatives compared with subject relatives. Since then Ford (1983) has pointed to longer lexical decision times in object relatives compared to subject relatives. King & Just (1991) found lower comprehension accuracy and longer reading times in self-paced reading experiments. Pickering & Shillcock (1992) also found significant reaction time differences between the two positions in self-paced reading experiments, both within and across clause boundaries. Neurolinguistic support using event-related brain potentials or ERPs has also been presented in King & Kutas (1992, 1993).

There is also evidence for SU > DO from a language with identical surface word orders for relatives on the two positions. Frauenfelder et al. (1980) and Holmes & O'Regan (1981) compared subject relatives with stylistically inverted object relatives in French, e.g. *la femme [qui connaît ma mère]* ('the woman who knows my mother') and *la femme [que connaît ma mère]* ('the woman that my mother knows'). These constructions use the same RelPro-V-NP order and differ only in the form of the relative pronoun (*qui* v. *que*) and in the grammatical relations assigned to the identical string (SVO v. OVS). They found that the subject relatives were still easier to process than the object relatives. According to (7.11) the DO relatives contain a required subject in their FGDs, whereas the SU relatives do not contain the direct object.[10]

Performance support for the remaining ranked positions of the AH (7.9) has been offered by Keenan & S. Hawkins (1987) on the basis of a repetition experiment conducted on English-speaking children and adults. They predicted that repetition accuracy would correlate with AH position. Their data, summarized in (7.12), bear this out.

(7.12) Repetition accuracies for relativization (%)

	SU	DO	IO	OBL	GEN-SU	GEN-DO
Adults	64	62.5	57	52	31	36
Children	63	51	50	35	21	18

---

[10] Another possible explanation for the SU relative preference here, which Maryellen MacDonald has reminded me of (personal communication), is that it is a reflection of the greater frequency of SVO v. (inverted) OVS order. It is certainly true that SVO orders are more frequent in French overall, including in relative clauses, but it is not obvious that this should be relevant for the processing of a uniquely distinctive DO relative clause constructed by the unambiguous relative pronoun *que*. The FGDs for these relatives contain an extra (subject) argument, according to the theory proposed here, and this makes their processing domain more complex and comparable to the object relatives of English. The choice between stylistically inverted RelPro-V-NPs and RelPro-NPs-V is predicted here to reflect the length and complexity of NPs. A long NPs delays access to V and VP and lengthens the Phrasal Combination Domain for the relative clause (see (5.2) in §5.1.1). So-called 'stylistic inversion' is therefore an EIC effect in this context (FGDs for the basic and inverted orders can be equally long since both contain V and NPs).

Keenan (1975) also quantified relativization frequencies in a corpus of written English and showed that they followed the AH ranking. Keenan's aggregates were: SU = 46%; DO = 24%; IO/OBL = 15%; GEN = 5%.

These corpus data are interesting, but their interpretation is complicated (as Keenan acknowledges) by correlating differences in frequency for many of the AH positions, irrespective of any relativization. The repetition experiment controlled for word frequency and sentence length, but relative frequencies of the AH positions, in relativizations and quite generally, could have been a factor here too. In addition, the interpretation of this experiment is complicated by the syntactic details of English and their impact on FGDs as defined in (7.8). Relativizations on a genitive involve co-indexing the head Ni with a relative pronoun *whose$i$*, pied piping the NP (and/or PP) containing *whose$i$* (Ross 1967), and setting up a further FGD between the pied piped phrase and the relevant subcategorizor or head with which it is co-indexed. An example is given in (7.13):

(7.13) the professor$i$ [[whose$i$ book]k the student read$k$]

A potentially long and complex FGD (cf. the GEN-DO position in (7.11)) is broken up in this way into two shorter domains, a head-pronoun co-indexing domain linking *professor$i$* to the immediately adjacent *whose$i$*, and a filler–gap domain linking the displaced [*whose$i$ book*]k to *read$k$*. This latter FGD is no more complex than it is for a DO relative like *the book$i$ [which$i$ the student read$i$]*. Two domains involve more processing than a single domain, but both are fairly small, and their combined processing is clearly preferred to the (essentially ungrammatical) alternative with a longer single domain: *the professor$i$ [that the student read the book of$i$]*. The data of (7.12) support the AH ranking, therefore, but in order to derive these results from domain complexity we would need to calculate total domain differentials in the manner of (5.7) in §5.2.3 and collect performance data accordingly.[11]

A more direct test of FGD size as a determinant of complexity can come from languages in which the gap structure alternates with a resumptive pronoun in the position relativized on, i.e. structures corresponding to *the professor$i$ [that the student knows$i$]* and *the professor$i$ [that the student knows him$i$]*. We shall see in the next section that the choice between the two is generally fixed by grammatical convention, with gaps preferring smaller domains and higher

---

[11] A similar issue arises for IO and OBL relativizations, which can involve either pied piping of the PP (*the student$i$ [to whom$i$]k the professor gave$k$ the book*) or stranding of the preposition (*the student$i$ [that the professor gave the book to$i$]*). The former involves two shorter domains: a domain for co-indexation of *student$i$* with *whom$i$* and an FGD linking the moved PP [*to whom$i$*]k to its verbal subcategorizor *gave$k$*. The latter involves one longer FGD linking *student$i$* directly to its prepositional subcategorizor *to$i$*.

positions on the AH, and pronouns more complex and lower ones. Evidently, having explicit pronouns in lieu of gaps makes processing easier and the pronouns are used in the harder-to-relativize positions. But if this is so, languages with choices should provide evidence for the same preferences in performance. Hebrew and Chinese can provide relevant data.

Before we consider these languages, we need to ask the basic question. Why exactly is the pronoun preferred in harder-to-relativize positions? How does the explicit argument aid processing? The intuitive answer is that the pronoun provides a local argument for lexical processing of the subcategorizor. The verb *know* can be assigned its direct object in an immediately adjacent position in . . . *knows him*$_i$, and the more distant head noun *professor*$_i$ does not need to be accessed.

This explanation may be on the right track, but we must also consider the other processing relations involved in relative clauses (see §5.5.1 and §6.1.1), especially co-indexation between the head and the position relativized on, either the subcategorizor or the pronoun. In §3.1 I formulated the following proximity hypothesis:

(3.7) *Proximity Hypothesis*
Given a structure {A, X, B}, X a variable for a phrase or phrases intervening between A and B, then the more relations of combination or dependency that link B to A, the smaller will be the size and complexity of X.

In the gap structure, filler (A) and subcategorizor (B) are linked by co-indexation within an FGD (7.8) and by lexical co-occurrence processing within a lexical domain ((5.6) in §5.2.1). In the resumptive pronoun structure, the subcategorizor has a local pronominal argument for lexical processing, so the head noun does not need to be accessed for this purpose, and only co-indexation links the head (A) to an item B (the pronoun) in the relevant clause. Hence, there are more relations of combination and dependency linking the filler to the subcategorizor in the gap structure than link a corresponding head to the resumptive pronoun, and a smaller intervening X and a smaller FGD are predicted for gaps as a result.

Hebrew is a language in which resumptive pronouns are obligatory in lower positions of the AH such as the indirect object position exemplified in (7.14) (Keenan & Comrie 1977):

(7.14) ha-isha*i*   [she-Yoav natan la*i*   et   ha-sefer]
the-woman that-Yoav gave   to-her ACC the-book
'the woman that Yoav gave the book to'

But when relativizing on direct objects speakers must choose between the gap and the pronoun, and one of the factors determining the selection, according to Ariel (1990), is the distance between the head and the position relativized on. She gives the following pair (p. 149) and she states that the pronoun is preferred and more 'acceptable' in (7.15b), with a large X intervening between head and pronoun, than it is in (7.15a) with a small X.

(7.15) a. ?Shoshana hi ha-isaha*i*   [she-nili   ohevet ota*i*]
Shoshana is the-woman that-Nilly loves   her
'Shoshana is the woman that Nilly loves'
    b. Shoshana hi ha-isha*i*   [she-dani   siper she-moshe rixel
Shoshana is the-woman that-Danny said that Moshe gossiped
she-nili   ohevet ota*i*]
that Nilly loves   her
'Shoshana is the woman that Danny said that Moshe gossiped that Nilly loves'

Correspondingly, the gap structure in (7.16a) (without *otai* and with co-indexation between *ha-ishai* and *oheveti*) is preferred to (7.15a).

(7.16) a. Shoshana hi ha-isha*i* [she-nili ohevet*i*]
    b. Shoshana hi ha-isha*i* [she-dani siper she-moshe rixel she-nili ohevet*i*]

Acceptability judgments are not always reliable in alternations such as this. Corpus data and experimental data are needed in order to test these preferences. The predictions made by the current theory do support Ariel's judgments, however, and this can be illustrated using total domain differentials (5.7), measured in word numbers. The FGD links the filler *ha-ishai* to its co-indexed subcategorizor *oheveti*. A corresponding head–pronoun domain (HPD) links *ha-ishai* to *otai*. And the lexical domain (LD) for the verb *ohevet* extends to its subject and object arguments, *Nilly* and *ha-ishai* or *otai* when the latter is present. (The complementizer *she* and NP subject *nili*, etc, are counted as separate words here.)

(7.15′a)   Shoshana hi ha-isha*i* [she-nili ohevet ota*i*]
HPD: - - - - - - - - - - - - - - - - - - -
                1   2   3   4   5
LD:*ohevet*   - - - - - - - - -
                           1   2   3   TOTAL = 8

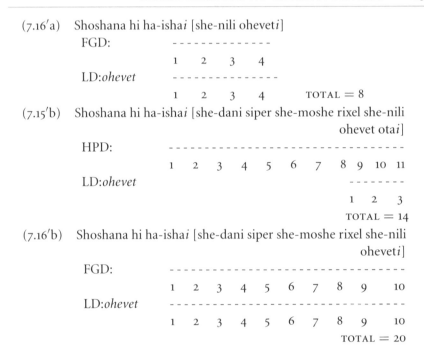

(7.16′a)   Shoshana hi ha-isha*i* [she-nili ohevet*i*]
  FGD: – – – – – – – – – – – – –
                1   2   3   4
  LD:*ohevet*   – – – – – – – – – – – – –
                1   2   3   4   TOTAL = 8

(7.15′b)   Shoshana hi ha-isha*i* [she-dani siper she-moshe rixel she-nili
                                                    ohevet ota*i*]
  HPD: –
                1   2   3   4   5   6   7   8   9   10   11
  LD:*ohevet*   – – – – – – – –
                                                1   2   3
                                                TOTAL = 14

(7.16′b)   Shoshana hi ha-isha*i* [she-dani siper she-moshe rixel she-nili
                                                    ohevet*i*]
  FGD: –
                1   2   3   4   5   6   7   8   9   10
  LD:*ohevet*   –
                1   2   3   4   5   6   7   8   9   10
                                                TOTAL = 20

The gap structure (7.16′a) has the same domain total (8) as (7.15′a) with a resumptive pronoun. By Minimize Domains (3.1) the two structures are equivalent, therefore. There is one less word to process overall in the np[N S] of (7.16′a), 4 v. 5, and this means that Minimize Forms (3.8) and Maximize On-line Processing (3.16) both define a small preference for the gap in this simple structure. The complex relative (7.15′b) with a pronoun has a significantly smaller domain total (14) than (7.16′b) with a gap (20), and is strongly preferred by MiD. The extra word in the overall np[N S] (11 v. 10) still results in a weak preference for the gap by MiF and MaOP, but the total domain differential is now so strongly in favor of the pronoun that this small benefit for the gap is outweighed. The total domain differential results from the significantly reduced LD:*ohevet* in (7.15′b), which is made possible by the co-indexed pronoun supplying the object argument locally. These figures illustrate the basis for the Proximity Hypothesis prediction that gaps will be preferred in smaller domains, and pronouns in larger ones.

  Cantonese provides a variant of this same preference. Yip & Matthews (2001: 123) and Matthews & Yip (2003) point out that resumptive pronouns are not used for direct object relativizations in simple clauses like (7.17a), but can be used in more complex structures such as (7.17b) in which there is a (purpose) clause separating the subcategorizing verb *ceng2i* ('invite') from the head noun:

(7.17) a. [Ngo5 ceng2i (*keoi5dei6i)] go2   di1 pang4jau5i   (Cantonese)
          I   invite (*them)   those CL friend
          'friends that I invite'
       b. [Ngo5 ceng2i (keoi5dei6i) sik6-faan6] go2   di1 pang4jau5i
          I   invite (them)   eat-rice   those CL friend
          'friends that I invite to have dinner'

The gap is obligatory when there is a small distance between Vi and Ni in the structure [NPs Vi ...] Ni, but the pronoun is optional when the distance is larger. Lexical processing can then be local, and head–pronoun domains can be relatively short too in (7.17b). The clear prediction made here is that the frequency of the pronoun in Cantonese performance should correlate with the size of the corresponding FGD and of the lexical processing domain for the subcategorizing verb.

7.2.2   *Grammatical support for the FGD complexity ranking*

The Proximity Hypothesis (3.7) leads to complementary predictions for the distribution of gaps and resumptive pronouns down the AH, given the proposed complexity ranking of (7.11). These predictions were defined in (3.5) and (3.6) of §3.1:

(3.5) *Filler–Gap Complexity Hypothesis*
      If an FGD of complexity n on a complexity hierarchy H is grammatical, then FGDs for all less complex variables on H ($n - 1$) will also be grammatical; if an FGD of complexity n is ungrammatical, then FGDs for all more complex variables on H ($n + 1$) will also be ungrammatical.

(3.6) *Resumptive Pronoun Hierarchy Prediction*
      If a resumptive pronoun is grammatical in position P on a complexity hierarchy H, then resumptive pronouns will be grammatical in all lower and more complex positions that can be relativized at all.

These predictions can be tested using Keenan & Comrie's (1977, 1979) 50-language sample.

Keenan & Comrie classified relative clauses on the basis of their position (postnominal, prenominal, or head-internal) and in terms of 'case-coding'. A relative clause strategy was assigned [+Case] if it contains a nominal element indicating unequivocally which NP position is being relativized on. This 'nominal element' was interpreted rather liberally to mean that the relative clause has a resumptive pronoun (as in Hebrew and Chinese), or a case-coded relative pronoun (Latin and Russian), or a preposition governing the position relativized on (e.g. *the course that I wrote the book for* in English). Relative clauses containing no such nominal elements were assigned [−Case] (e.g. *the course that I wrote*). Languages with this strategy typically employ a subordinating complementizer or nominalizor (e.g. English *that*), a participial verb form (Basque, Tamil, Korean), or else no special subordination marking apart from adjacency of the relative clause to the head (Japanese); cf. C. Lehmann (1984).[12]

[+Case] languages with resumptive pronouns are clearly relevant for prediction (3.6).[13] The [−Case] languages employ a consistent gap strategy whereby the gap/subcategorizor or head of phrase in the relative clause must be linked directly with the filler (head noun or relative pronoun, if there is one—see fn. 12) in order to process the relevant lexical and syntactic relations between them. The Proximity Hypothesis (3.7) and the Filler-Gap Complexity Hypothesis (3.6) make clear predictions for permitted variation in grammaticalized gap positions in these languages.

I counted forty languages with [−Case] gap strategies in Keenan & Comrie's sample and they support prediction (3.6) without exception. Gaps are found in all and only the implicationally permitted relativization positions of (7.18):

(7.18) *Languages with [−Case] relative clause gaps in Keenan & Comrie's data*

SU only: Aoban, Arabic (Classical), German, Gilbertese, Iban, Javanese, Kera, Malagasy, Maori, Minang-Kabau, Tagalog, Toba Batak

SU & DO only: Chinese (Pekingese), Dutch, English, Finnish, Fulani, Genoese, Greek, Hebrew, Italian, Malay, Persian, Swedish, Tongan, Welsh, Yoruba, Zurich German

SU & DO & IO/OBL only: Basque, Catalan, Korean, North Frisian, Hausa, Roviana, Shona, Sinhala, Spanish, Tamil, Turkish

SU & DO & IO/OBL & GEN: Japanese

---

[12] Sometimes a [−Case] strategy can contain what is often categorized as a 'relative pronoun', but it must be case-invariant (such as *die* in Dutch or *who* in dialects of English): see Maxwell (1979) for discussion.

[13] [+Case] languages with relative pronouns involve both a (displaced) pronoun within the relative clause and a gap (or subcategorizor) co-indexed with that pronoun. As a result both predictions, for gaps and for retained (relative-clause-internal) pronouns, are relevant here: see Hawkins (1999: 260–61) for discussion and testing using Maxwell's (1979) classification of relative pronoun types.

Keenan & Comrie's sample is a convenience one, which does not control for genetic or areal bias. We cannot draw reliable conclusions about relative frequencies from it, therefore. But it does contain enough languages to illustrate all the predicted cut-off points, and since any single language is a potential counterexample it is interesting that no language shows an unpredicted combination of gap positions (such as DO & GEN or SU & IO/OBL).

Twenty-seven of Keenan & Comrie's languages are classified as having a resumptive pronoun strategy and these languages support prediction (3.6) without exception:

> (7.19) *Pronoun-retaining languages in Keenan & Comrie's data*
>   GEN only: Japanese, Javanese, Korean, Malay, Roviana, Turkish, Yoruba
>   IO/OBL & GEN only: Fulani, Greek, Hausa, Minang-Kabau, Shona, Toba Batak, Welsh, Zurich German
>   DO & IO/OBL & GEN only: Aoban, Arabic, Chinese (Pekingese), Czech, Genoese, Gilbertese, Hebrew, Kera, Persian, Slovenian, Tongan
>   SU & DO & IO/OBL & GEN: Urhobo

Prediction (3.6) allows pronoun retention not to go down to the bottom of the hierarchy, in the event that relativization is completely ungrammatical on the lowest positions. For this (clause-internal) hierarchy all twenty-seven languages do go all the way down (in contrast to languages that we will consider when discussing the clause-embedding hierarchies of §7.4, involving potentially greater complexity).

We clearly have two implicational patterns going in opposite directions in these relative clause data: gaps from low to high, resumptive pronouns from high to low. The gaps cut off in more complex environments with large FGDs (and large lexical processing domains), while the pronouns cut off in simpler environments and are replaced by gaps. This can be seen vividly when we examine twenty-four languages in the Keenan–Comrie sample that have both gaps and pronouns, like Hebrew and Chinese. The two strategies are largely complementary to each other, with overlapping options only at the points of transition, as shown in Table 7.1. The distribution of gaps to pronouns decreases down AH (100% to 65% to 25% to 4%) while that of pronouns to gaps increases (0% to 35% to 75% to 96%).

This reverse implicational structuring and the distribution of the two strategies in Table 7.1 support the proposed complexity ranking of AH positions in terms of FGDs. But a relevant question to ask is why gaps are preferred

TABLE 7.1   Languages combining [−Case] gaps with [+Case] resumptive pronouns

	SU	DO	IO/OBL	GEN
Aoban	gap	pro	pro	pro
Arabic	gap	pro	pro	pro
Gilbertese	gap	pro	pro	pro
Kera	gap	pro	pro	pro
Chinese (Peking)	gap	gap/pro	pro	pro
Genoese	gap	gap/pro	pro	pro
Hebrew	gap	gap/pro	pro	pro
Persian	gap	gap/pro	pro	pro
Tongan	gap	gap/pro	pro	pro
Fulani	gap	gap	pro	pro
Greek	gap	gap	pro	pro
Welsh	gap	gap	pro	pro
Zurich German	gap	gap	pro	pro
Toba Batak	gap	*	pro	pro
Hausa	gap	gap	gap/pro	pro
Shona	gap	gap	gap/pro	pro
Minang-Kabau	gap	*	*/pro	pro
Korean	gap	gap	gap	pro
Roviana	gap	gap	gap	pro
Turkish	gap	gap	gap	pro
Yoruba	gap	gap	O	pro
Malay	gap	gap	RP	pro
Javanese	gap	*	*	pro
Japanese	gap	gap	gap	gap/pro
Gaps =	24 [100%]	17 [65%]	6 [25%]	1 [4%]
Pros =	0 [0%]	9 [35%]	18 [75%]	24 [96%]

gap = [−Case] strategy
pro = copy pronoun retained (as a subinstance of [+Case]).
* = obligatory passivization to a higher position prior to relativization.
O = position does not exist as such.
RP = relative pronoun plus gap (as a subinstance of [+Case]).
These gap ([−Case]) and copy pronoun classifications are all from Keenan & Comrie (1977; 1979).
   [−Case] gap languages may employ a general subordination marker within the relative clause, no
   subordination marking, a participial verb form, or a fronted case-invariant relative pronoun. For
   Tongan, an ergative language, the top two positions of AH are Absolutive and Ergative respectively,
   not SU and DO; cf. Primus (1999).

at all in the higher positions, given that filler–gap structures are hard to process
(see §7.1). Why does pronoun retention not regularly extend all the way up?

An answer can be given in terms of the resulting domains for syntactic and
semantic processing. The gap has the advantage of less form processing. There
is an accessible category, the filler, on the basis of which relevant properties

can be assigned to the gap or subcategorizor or head of phrase in the relative clause (see §4.6). In high positions on the AH, the total size of these processing domains is smaller than it is for corresponding structures with pronouns. For direct object relatives in Hebrew, the gap will be preferred in small domains (see (7.15) and (7.16)). For subject relatives, domains will be even smaller, especially in languages with subject agreement markers on verbs (like Hebrew: see Ariel 1990) that can reduce lexical processing domains to the limit (see §8.5). As FGDs gain in size, resumptive pronouns become more efficient overall, largely because lexical processing domains for the subcategorizor have a local argument and do not need to access the head. This variation in grammars, with gaps predominating in small FGDs, pronouns in larger (head–pronoun) domains, and both in domains of intermediate complexity, reflects the shifting degrees of overall preference from gaps to pronouns.

The benefit of form minimization in this structure is that it introduces greater efficiency in certain instances. The cost is that it sets up an additional dependency on the filler for lexical processing (and for syntactic processing in the event that the filler supplies an adjunct to a phrase), and these dependencies, like others, prefer minimal domains for processing. The result is a stronger domain minimization preference, of the same type that we saw in the adjacency and proximity effects of §§6.1–2. More combinatorial and dependency relations now prefer minimization, and as distances increase the preferences shift to an alternative structure with more explicit forms and more local processing (cf. e.g. the English relative pronoun data in Tables 6.1 and 6.2).

Notice finally that gap processing can be facilitated not just by smaller domains but also by parallel function effects between the matrix filler and the position relativized on. Cole (1976: 244–5) points out that the gap strategy in Hebrew can in fact extend to indirect objects and oblique NPs, just in case the matrix position is parallel to that of the position relativized on. Aldai (2003) discusses similar parallel function effects in Basque, and Kirby (1999) gives a detailed discussion of the interaction between domain minimization and parallel function as facilitators of gap processing.

7.3   *Wh*-fronting and basic word order

MiD (3.1) and the Proximity Hypothesis (3.7) also appear to be part of the explanation for another cross-linguistic pattern involving *wh*-fronting and basic verb position. There are languages like English that regularly front *wh*-question words, thereby forming a filler–gap dependency, as in (7.1b). Approximately 40% of the world's languages have this option, according to

Dryer's (1991) figures given in (7.20) below. Alternative strategies for forming *wh*-questions include keeping the *wh*-word 'in situ', i.e. in its original position, or some form of adjacency and attachment to the verb (see §5.4 and Hawkins 1994: 373–9). The fronting option is highly correlated with basic verb position, and is especially favored in V-initial languages. The adjacency and attachment option is especially favored in SOV languages (Kim 1988).

Two questions arise from this. First, why is the displacement of *wh* asymmetric? In almost all languages *wh* moves to the left and not to the right, i.e. it moves to sentence-initial position. I return to this question in the discussion of 'Fillers First' in §7.5.1. Second, why is *wh*-fronting correlated with basic verb position?

The correlations can be seen in different language samples. Greenberg (1963) and Ultan (1978) give partially overlapping data on *wh*-fronting and basic verb position, and in (7.20) I have combined their two samples. Dryer (1991) gives similar data from his genetically and areally controlled sample, in terms of genera.

(7.20) *Wh-fronting and basic verb position*
   Greenberg/Ultan (Hawkins 1999: 274) Dryer (1991)
   V-initial: 17/20 lgs = 85%   23/29 genera = 79%
   SVO: 25/34 lgs = 73.5%   21/52 genera = 40%
   SOV: 7/33 lgs = 21%   26/82 genera = 32%

The two sets of figures show a strong preference for *wh*-fronting in V-initial languages (85% and 79%). They also show that this option is not preferred in SOV languages: 79% and 68% of SOV languages/genera do not have it. They agree in the relative frequency ranking of V-initial > SVO > SOV for *wh*-fronting. The major difference concerns the absolute numbers for SVO languages. 73.5% have *wh*-fronting in the language sample v. 40% in the genera sample.

Why should verb position be correlated with the existence of a filler–gap dependency in *wh*-question structures? The definition of an FGD in (7.8) suggests an answer. The verb is the subcategorizer for all *wh*-words that are verbal arguments and that must be linked to the verb in the relevant domains for lexical processing (see (5.6) in §5.2.1). The verb is also the head category that constructs the VP and/or S nodes containing the gap sites for most adjunct *wh*-words. As a result FGDs linking *wh* to the verb will be most minimal in verb-early languages and will become larger as the verb occurs further to the right. Domains for lexical processing and for the syntactic processing of adjunct relations will become larger as well. A leftward *wh*-word (predicted independently by MaOP (3.16)—see §7.5) accordingly sets up an

MiD prediction that co-occurring verb positions will be progressively dis-preferred as FGDs and other domains linking the filler to the verb become larger. The filler–gap structure is increasingly not selected, and in situ or attachment structures are used instead, in the same way that gaps give way to resumptive pronouns in relative clauses with increasing FGD size. In one case it is independently motivated form minimization that results in greater prox-imity between filler and subcategorizor or head, in the other it is independently motivated *wh*-fronting (§ 7.5.1).

The distinction between rigid and non-rigid SOV languages is also relev-ant here. *Wh*-fronting should be more productive with non-rigid than with rigid SOV, according to this theory, since the distance between Wh_i and V_i in $Wh_i[SOV_iX]$ languages will be smaller than in it is in $Wh_i[SXOV_i]$. Con-versely, in situ and V-attached *wh* phrases should be more frequent in rigid than in non-rigid SOV languages. Dryer's sample does not distinguish between the two SOV types, unfortunately, and Greenberg's and Ultan's SOV language numbers are too small to permit reliable testing.

7.4   Other complexity hierarchies

Ross's (1967) original constraints blocked movements out of complex NPs such as (7.2) and (7.21):

(7.21) the bone$_i$ [which$_i$ you saw np[the dog s[that was biting$_i$]]]

His Complex NP Constraint was defined as follows:

(7.22) *CNPC*
         No element contained in an S dominated by an NP with a lexical head noun may be moved out of that NP by a transformation.

Subsequent reformulations in terms of subjacency (Chomsky 1981, 1986) pre-vented movements out of all environments that involved crossing more than one bounding node, e.g. IP or NP, with the selection of such nodes being subject to parametric variation (Rizzi 1982). The precise predictions of subjacency for cross-linguistic variation depend on a number of theory-internal assumptions, some of which are quite controversial, such as the successive cyclic movement of *wh* (Bach 1977). What is significant for our purposes is that general con-straints on grammars have been proposed that block filler–gap dependencies in environments with large FGDs, while smaller FGDs can be unconstrained and allowed to run free. In fact, we can set up numerous complexity hierarchies involving FGDs that contain increasing numbers of syntactic and semantic properties, on which we can test the filler–gap complexity hypothesis (3.5) and the resumptive pronoun prediction (3.6). A number of traditional puzzles now appear in a new light, and some new predictions are made for cross-linguistic variation.

7.4.1 A clause-embedding hierarchy

Notice first that some languages permit violations of Ross's CNPC. The Scandinavian languages provide convincing examples, such as (7.23) from Allwood (1982):

(7.23) ett ben$i$ [som$i$ jag ser np[en hund s[som   gnager   påi]]] (Swedish)
         a   bone which I   see   a   dog   which is-gnawing on

Productive counterexamples are also found in Japanese, as discussed by Kuno (1973b: 239–40), e.g. (7.24):

(7.24) [[[osiete-ita$i$]s seito   ga]np rakudaisita] sensei$i$
         teaching-was   student NOM flunked   teacher
         'the teacher who the students that (he) was teaching flunked'

And CNPC violations are permitted in Akan (Saah & Goodluck 1995). There has been no quantification, to my knowledge, of the languages permitting such violations, though Maxwell (1979) gives an initial classification and cites Korean and Tamil as further counterexamples. Impressionistically CNPC-violating languages are a minority, and their productivity in performance is often restricted and attests to their complexity.[14]

Conversely, many languages impose grammatical constraints on FGDs that are stronger and more restrictive than those of English. The ungrammatical relative clause gap in the German finite subordinate clause of (7.3a) contrasts with its grammatical English counterpart (7.1'a), both of which are repeated

---

[14] Kvam (1983: 125) mentions that the heads of complex NPs in CNPC-violating extractions in Norwegian are typically indefinite (see §7.4.3 for discussion of the significance of this point). A detailed discussion of performance factors that influence acceptability in Swedish CNPC violations can be found in Allwood (1982), Andersson (1982), and Engdahl (1982). Gaps in complex NPs in Akan are less acceptable than in simple finite complements of the verb (Saah & Goodluck 1995). For Japanese, Kuno (1973b: 239–40, 244–60) discussed acceptability in terms of the appropriateness or otherwise of a theme interpretation for the filler of the relative clause whose gap is within the complex NP. Haig (1996), Matsumoto (1997), and Comrie (1998) provide a more general discussion of the pragmatic and semantic factors that facilitate acceptability in this language: see §7.6.

here (assuming direct association between filler and subcategorizor):

(7.3a) *die Person$i$ [die$i$ du glaubst s[dass Johan gesehen$i$ hat]]
        the person who you think   that   John   seen   has

(7.1'a) the person$i$ [who$i$ you think s[that John saw$i$]]

Relative clause gaps in finite subordinate clauses are also ungrammatical in Russian, as shown in (7.25) from Comrie (1973: 297):

(7.25) *Vot   ogurcy$i$ [kotorye$i$ ja obeščal   s[čto prinesu$i$]]
         here are the cucumbers which   I   promised that I'd bring

Both German and Russian permit relative clause gaps in infinitival embeddings, however. Corresponding to (7.3a) German has the grammatical (7.26) with an infinitival complement of *glauben* 'believe':

(7.26) die Person$i$ [die$i$ du glaubst vp[zu sehen$i$]]
        the person who you think to   see
        'the person who you think you are seeing'

And corresponding to the ungrammatical (7.25), Russian permits (7.27):

(7.27) Vot   ogurcy$i$ [kotorye$i$ ja obeščal   vp[prinesti$i$]]
        here are the cucumbers which   I   promised to-bring

Relative clause gaps are possible in both finite and infinitival complements in English, as seen in these translations, and so they are in French:

(7.28) a. la femme$i$ [que$i$ j'espère s[que j'épouserai$i$]]
            the woman who I hope that I will marry

        b. la femme$i$ [que$i$ j'espère vp[épouser$i$]]
            the woman who I-hope to-marry

This distribution of grammaticality facts suggests the following hierarchy of increasingly complex FGDs in embedding environments (with > interpreted as 'simpler than', as in the AH (7.9)):

(7.29) *Clause-embedding hierarchy for gaps*
        infinitival (VP) complement > finite (S) complement > S within a complex NP

An infinitival complement involves fewer terminal elements for processing than a finite complement and a correspondingly smaller FGD. Compare (the ungrammatical) (7.3a) in German with (the grammatical) (7.26). The finite complement contains an overt subject (*Johan*), finiteness marking (*gesehen hat*), and a complementizer (*dass*). The infinitival contains no overt subject and no finite verb forms, though it does contain an infinitival complement-izer *zu*. The FGD for (7.3a) contains more nodes, therefore, and so does the lexical domain for processing the co-occurrences of the verb *sehen*. Complex NP environments such as (7.23) and (7.24) have the largest domains link-ing filler and subcategorizer, since they have an additional dominating NP over the S that contains the gap and an additional lexical head noun as sister to this S.

These differences in FGD sizes motivate the ranking in (7.29). As with the AH (7.9) there are more nodes to process down the hierarchy, and these additional nodes involve phonological, morphological, lexical, syntactic, and semantic processing operations that apply simultaneously with gap processing. Performance support for the greater processing difficulty of complex NP envir-onments compared with finite complement environments comes from Akan, a language that permits both grammatically, in a controlled acceptability experiment conducted by Saah & Goodluck (1995). Gaps in complex NPs were judged significantly less acceptable than those in simpler environments. Saah & Goodluck tested the same sentence types on speakers of English and found, predictably, that English CNPC violations were completely unacceptable, on account of their conventionalized ungrammaticality. The processing difficulty posed by gaps in complex NPs can also be seen in Swedish and Norwegian. These structures are made as easy as possible in performance by minimizing all other complexity factors in the FGD (see the references in fn. 14). I have not seen experimental results of relevance to the infinitival/finite complement distinction, but independent support for this ranking comes from acceptability judgments involving *wh*-island violations in English (§7.4.2). Impressionistic-ally infinitival gaps are also more frequent in English performance than finite gaps.[15]

Representative grammars supporting hierarchy (7.29), on the basis of relat-ive clause gaps, are those illustrated in the examples of this section. They are summarized in (7.30). All these languages permit gaps in infinitival comple-ments: Russian and German cut off at finite complements (but see §7.4.2 for *Wh-questions*), while English and French cut off at the complex NP position.

---

[15] Further support for positioning infinitival complements above finite ones comes from co-indexation domains involving reflexive anaphors. There are languages such as Russian in which long-distance reflexives are grammatical in infinitival embeddings, but not in finite complements: see Huang (2000: 93) and Rappaport (1986).

(7.30)   *Permitted relative clause gaps*

Infinitival (VP) complement:	Swedish, Japanese, English, French, Russian, German
Finite (S) complement:	Swedish, Japanese, English, French
S within complex NP:	Swedish, Japanese

Notice that English gaps in complex NPs can sometimes be rescued by resumptive pronouns. (7.31) is not too bad:

(7.31)   I met the woman*i* [who*i* I had almost forgotten [the fact that you once introduced me to her*i*]]

But sometimes even retained pronouns are ungrammatical. Erteschik-Shir (1992: 90) stars (7.32), with a pronoun in a complex NP in subject position (her example, not mine!):

(7.32)   *This is the girl*i* [who*i* [the man who raped her*i*] had escaped from prison]

There are several factors that make (7.32) worse than (7.31). A relative clause complex NP involves more processing complexity than a 'fact that' complex NP since it introduces an additional filler–gap dependency relation into the structure (see §7.4.2). Adding a relative clause to the subject NP *the man* (rather than to an object NP) also extends the phrasal combination domain for the clause in which *the man* is the subject. Resumptive pronouns are preferred to gaps in English environments of intermediate complexity, it seems, but even pronouns are ungrammatical when overall complexity is greatest.

The resumptive pronoun prediction of (3.6) is as relevant for clause-embeddings as it is for the AH (7.9). A pronoun in situ is easier to process than a gap, since lexical relations with the subcategorizor can be processed locally. The anaphoric relation between pronoun and head noun, formalized by co-indexation, means that there is still a processing domain linking the two, and the longer this domain, the more complex it is. Complexity was not strained in the single clause relatives of the AH, so pronoun retention could go all the way down in languages that had it all (see (7.19)). But in the multi-clause hierarchy of (7.30) a low position like a complex NP may not be relativizable at all, especially when expressiveness demands are minimal. When pronoun retention is grammatical, therefore, it should still obey a high-to-low prediction, but only for as long as relativization is possible at all. If the pronoun is ungrammatical, at a low hierarchy point, then no further relativization should be possible down the hierarchy, since pronoun retention is the most efficient strategy there is.[16]

Consider Hebrew again. In this language resumptive pronouns are regularly possible in complex NPs such as (7.33) from Keenan (1972*a*):

(7.33) Ani roa et   ha-ish*i*   [she-Sally ma'amina np[la-shmoa s[she-Miriam
        hikta oto*i*]]
     I   see ACC the-man that-Sally believes   the rumor   that-Mary
     hit   him
     'I see the man that Sally believes the rumor that Mary hit him' (Hebrew)

In Toba Batak, on the other hand, resumptive pronouns are not possible in complex NPs such as this, even though they are possible in finite subordinate clauses, and on IO/OBL and GEN within clauses (see Table 7.1). Keenan (1972*b*) gives the following example of a grammatical resumptive pronoun in a finite subordinate clause:

(7.34) boruborui i   [ima   na dirippu si Bissar s[na manussi abit   ibana*i*]]
      woman   the namely that thought by Bissar that washes   clothes she
      'the woman who Bissar thought that she washed the clothes' (Toba Batak)

Pronouns do not go all the way down the clause-embedding hierarchy (7.29) in Toba Batak, therefore, though they do go down the AH.

Languages like Hebrew led Ross (1967) to exclude resumptive pronoun relatives from his CNPC, limiting it to gap strategies only. But pronouns in complex NPs are ungrammatical in Toba Batak, suggesting that the CNPC (and subjacency) are operative here too. All of this crosslinguistic variation is predicted by processing complexity. The fully ungrammatical structures are those at the lower ends of complexity hierarchies, with ungrammaticality at a higher point generally implying ungrammaticality all the way down using any strategy. Pronoun retention is grammatical from high to low positions for as long as relativization is possible at all. And gaps are grammatical from low to high all the way up to the highest position.

7.4.2   *Reduce additional syntactic processing*

FGDs of the same or similar size reveal subtle preferences that provide further support for domain minimization and for the filler–gap complexity hypothesis (3.5). *Wh*-island effects, first formulated in Chomsky (1973), provide

---

[16] Any relative clause has to define the relationship between the head and the position relativized on, since the two positions can be quite distinct from one another, and this is what the resumptive pronoun makes explicit.

relevant examples. An embedded clause that has undergone *wh*-fronting and co-indexation with a subcategorizor or gap, e.g. in indirect questions, is more difficult to extract out of than a simple (declarative) *that*-clause in English.

(7.35) a. What$i$ did you hope s[that you would bake$i$]
      b. *What$i$ did you wonder s[how$k$ you would bake$i$ Ok]

Having an additional filler–gap dependency to resolve in the subordinate clause evidently makes it harder to process the link between the matrix filler *what*i and its subcategorizor or gap in the subordinate clause. The additional filler–gap dependency adds to the simultaneous processing load required for items in the FGD of the matrix filler, and hence adds to the complexity of this FGD. We can propose the following, therefore:

(7.36) *The additional gap hierarchy*
      If a matrix filler can be co-indexed with a subcategorizor/gap in an embedded clause of complexity n containing an additional sub-categorizor/gap, then it can be co-indexed into an embedded clause of complexity *n* containing no other (or fewer) gaps.

When we convert the finite embedded clauses of (7.35) to their infinit-ival counterparts, an interesting (and grammatically unpredicted) difference emerges. The indirect question infinitival is no longer a *wh*-island, and both the declarative and the indirect question complement can contain a subcategorizor/gap co-indexed with the matrix *what*i:

(7.37) a. What$i$ did you hope vp[to bake$i$]
      b. What$i$ did you wonder vp[how$k$ to bake$i$ Ok]

Other infinitival complements do constitute a *wh*-island (e.g. *what$i$ did you ask vp[why$k$ to bake$i$ Ok]*), but infinitival complements permit more *wh*-island violations than finite complements. We have already seen that infinitival com-plements permit more (relative clause) gaps than finite embeddings in Russian and German (§7.4.1) and I have argued that the added complexity of the latter is responsible for its lower ranking on the clause-embedding hierarchy (7.29). What we see now is that the relative simplicity of the infinitival complement can compensate for the complexity of the additional gap and render (7.37b) grammatical.

More generally, the difference between (7.37b) and (7.35b) is explained by the combinatorial effect of our two hierarchies: the clause-embedding hier-archy (7.29) and the additional gap hierarchy (7.36). English has limited its extractions from additional gap clauses to infinitival complements, i.e. to the highest position on the clause-embedding hierarchy, and these extractions cut off at the finite complement position. Extractions from clauses without additional gaps go down lower, and include both finite and infinitival environments ((7.35a) and (7.37a)). Other languages have conventionalized the combinatorial options differently. Swedish and Norwegian are more liberal than English, and permit extractions from structures corresponding to both (7.35b) and (7.37b), (see Engdahl (1982)). German is more restrictive, and permits them in neither, (see Kvam (1983)). In all these languages both hierarchies are respected and the grammatical conventions fall within a limited set at the intersection of each. No language can exist, for example, in which extractions are more productive from additional gap clauses than from corresponding clauses with no additional gap, or more productive from finite clauses than from infinitival clauses.

Hierarchy (7.36) makes a further prediction in combination with (7.29). Movement out of relative clause complex NPs should be worse than out of an NP complement (*fact that* and *rumor that*) complex NP, since the latter does not contain a second filler–gap dependency in the FGD for the matrix filler and gap. Compare (7.38a) and (b):

(7.38) a. *Who$i$ [do you know np[the professor$k$ s[that taughtki]]]?
        b. ?*What$i$ [do you regret np[the fact s[that he stole$i$]]]?

The (b) sentence is indeed more acceptable than (a) and even borders on grammaticality. Certain lexicalized phrases like *make the claim* permit gaps quite productively, as Ross (1967) originally pointed out.

Consider now the difference between relative clauses and *wh*-questions in Russian and German. In both languages relative clause gaps are not productive in finite clause embeddings (cf. (7.3a) and (7.25)), but *wh*-question gaps are possible here. (7.3a) and (b) from German are repeated:

(7.3) a. *die Person$i$ [die$i$ du glaubst s[dass Johan gesehen$i$ hat]]
           'the person who you think that John saw'
        b. Wen$i$ [glaubst du s[dass Johan gesehen$i$ hat]]?
           'who do you think that John saw?'

What could explain the difference? A plausible answer is that the FGD for the relative clause contains more syntactic and semantic properties for processing than the *wh*-question. Both structures must link a filler to the relevant subcategorizer or gap. But the immediate filler of the relative clause gap, i.e. the relative pronoun, is also co-indexed with the nominal head, and this head is the ultimate antecedent for the 'chain' of co-indexed items, *Person$i$*, *die$i$*, and *gesehen$i$*. Aspects of the lexical processing of the verb *gesehen* require access to this ultimate filler, just as they do in relative clause structures without relative pronouns (see §6.1.1), and the relative pronoun is in turn dependent on the head. Hence, the full co-indexation domain linking the nominal head to its subcategorizer or gap is larger in (7.3a) than it is in (7.3b). The head is also a constituent of the matrix clause and it undergoes all the rules and processes that apply to matrix NP constituents; case assignment, theta-role assignment, positioning, and so on. When the head and relative pronoun are matched with their subcategorizer or gap, these matrix properties must often be systematically undone, since the case, theta-role and positioning of the item relativized on can be quite different. By contrast, a *wh*-question word is not co-indexed with a higher filler, it receives one set of grammatical properties only, namely those that are appropriate for its gap site, and it does not receive all the additional properties that are characteristic of the relative clause head. The co-indexation domains for relative clauses contain more properties than those for *wh*-questions, and it is on this basis that we can set up the following prediction:

(7.39) *Relative clause and* Wh-*question hierarchy*
In languages that have filler–gap structures for both relative clauses and *wh*-questions, if a gap is grammatical for a relative clause filler in an FGD of complexity n, then a gap will be grammatical for a *wh*-question filler in an FGD of complexity *n*.

(7.39) permits relative clauses and *wh*-questions to be equally productive, in languages with filler–gap structures for both, and it permits relative clauses to be less productive. English exhibits the former (in the finite complement environment), German the latter. The reverse of German, in which relative clauses are more productive than *wh*-questions, is predicted not to occur.

We can now return to the 'parallel function' effects of §4.5. Recall that when head and gap are both subjects or both objects, processing is easier (Sheldon 1974, MacWhinney 1982, Clancy et al. 1986). When this happens, the relative clause head noun filler is, in effect, similar to the *wh*-question filler, whose properties are identical to those of its gap. There is independent evidence (from e.g. co-ordinate deletions) for saying that parallelism facilitates the copying of target material onto minimal forms. But we now see a second motivation for these effects. The total FGD contains more distinct properties (cases, theta-roles, etc.) when the filler is a (non-parallel) relative clause head than when it is a *wh*-question word or a parallel relative clause head (the filler can be nominative and agent, the gap accusative and patient, etc.).

Note that prediction (7.39) applies only to languages that actually have a filler–gap structure for both types of fillers. Many languages will not have a fronted *wh*-word, on account of their basic word order, e.g. Japanese (see §7.3). In such languages relative clauses will be more productive by default. But in languages that do have both types of fillers and gaps, the relative clauses are predicted to be less or equally productive.

7.4.3   *Reduce additional semantic processing*

In addition to the preference for reduced syntactic processing in FGDs there is substantial evidence for less semantic processing as well. Kluender (1992) ties together a number of semantic generalizations about the material that can stand in the path from filler to gap, and he proposes that the more semantic processing that is required within the domain, the more unacceptable and/or ungrammatical the filler–gap dependency becomes.

Consider the so-called 'bridging' verbs that permit their clausal complements to contain gaps. Across languages, the bridging verbs that are grammatical seem always to include semantically weak verbs like *say* rather than *whisper,* or non-factives (*think/believe*) more productively than factives (*realize/regret*). For English Kluender gives the following examples, adapted from Culicover & Wilkins (1984) (where > means 'better than'):

(7.40) a. How angry$i$ [did Mary *say* that John was$i$]?   >
       b. How angry$i$ [did Mary *say softly* that John was$i$]?   =
       c. How angry$i$ [did Mary *whisper* that John was$i$]?

Even in a language with extensive extractions, like Norwegian, long-distance FGDs exhibit the same preference for semantically weak bridging verbs (Kvam 1983). This can be captured in hierarchy (7.41):

(7.41) *Bridging verb hierarchy*
       If a bridging verb or verb complex of semantic specificity n is grammatical in an FGD, then verbs or verb complexes V' with less semantic specificity will also be grammatical.

Degrees of specificity could be defined in terms of semantic components or features. *Whispers* combines components of meaning associated with both *say* and *softly,* and is accordingly semantically richer and more specific. Specificity could also be defined by entailment: *whisper* entails *say,* but not vice versa. Entailment would also define a specificity difference between factive and non-factive verbs, since factives (*John realizes that he is sick*) entail corresponding sentences with non-factives (*John believes that he is sick*), whereas the converse fails. Factives are more difficult to extract out of in English and in many other languages and exhibit so-called 'weak island' effects (Kiparsky & Kiparsky 1970, Hukari & Levine 1995; see §7.5.3).

Another clear example of semantically based complexity can be seen in the declining acceptability/grammaticality down (7.42), cited in Kluender (1992) and adapted from Chomsky (1973) and Erteschik-Shir & Lappin (1979):

(7.42) a. Who*i* [did you see *a* picture of*i*]?   >
       b. Who*i* [did you see *the* picture of*i*]?   >
       c. Who*i* [did you see *John's* picture of*i*]?

An NP with an indefinite head permits a gap readily in the *of*-complement. The definite head (7.42b) is worse, since it adds a uniqueness claim to the existential claim of the indefinite, as well as pragmatic appropriateness conditions guaranteeing the satisfaction of uniqueness within some portion of the universe of discourse, see §4.4.1 and Hawkins (1991). A possessive modifier (7.42c) makes the filler–gap structure worst of all. This modifier contains an additional referring expression (*John*) and there is a relation of possession or association between this referent and the head's referent (*picture*). The amount of semantic processing increases down (7.42), therefore, and as it does so the filler–gap structure becomes increasingly dispreferred. Neurolinguistic support for this increase, using ERP measurements, has been given in Kluender & Kutas (1993*b*) and in Neville et al. (1991). Parallel to (7.41), therefore, is hierarchy (7.43):

(7.43) *Containing NP hierarchy*
       If a containing NP with a determiner phrase of semantic specificity n is grammatical in an FGD, then determiner phrases with less semantic specificity will also be grammatical.

Further evidence for (7.43) comes from complex NP gaps in Swedish and Norwegian. In performance they generally involve indefinite heads, as in (7.23) above.

Kluender (1992) proposes a similar hierarchy for the complementizers of (7.44):

(7.44) What*i* [did John doubt (a) *that* she would win*i*]?   >
                            (b) *if* she would win*i*]?   >
                            (c) *whether* she would win*i*]?

He justifies this hierarchy as follows: 'The complementizer *that* merely signals that a proposition follows, while *if* indexes a possible state of affairs from among an infinite set of such possible states, and *whether* indexes one of only two possible (alternative) states of affairs, and can thus in a way be said to be more referentially specific in character' (Kluender 1992: 240). Neuro-linguistic support for the heightened processing load down (7.44), using ERP measurements, is given in Kluender & Kutas (1993*a*, *b*).

Notice how these semantic hierarchies interact in principled ways with the syntactic hierarchies of §§7.4.1–2 to constrain the permitted variation in a way that respects each relevant hierarchy. If gaps are permitted at all in finite (S) complements, and if there are restrictions in this environment involving semantic types of permitted bridging verbs, then the restricted verb types will be the semantically more specific ones. In this way both the clause-embedding hierarchy (7.29) and the bridging verb hierarchy (7.41) are respected. Similarly, any restrictions on the determiner phrase in complex NPs containing gaps will respect hierarchy (7.29) and (7.43).

7.5   MaOP effects

The cross-linguistic data of §§7.2–4 revealed principled degrees of domain minimization and of form minimization in performance preferences and grammatical conventions. There are also patterns in the grammar of rela-tivization and *wh*-movement that exemplify the Maximize On-line Processing preference of (3.16). There are ways of making a gap structure easier to process, other than by converting it to a resumptive pronoun. One of these, which I shall call 'Fillers First', has already been seen in the *wh*-fronting data of §7.3, and I shall argue that MaOP is the causative principle (§7.5.1). The principled interaction between MaOP and MiD in predicting relative clause orders in dif-ferent basic word order types is discussed in §7.5.2. Various syntactic (as well as morphological and phonological) peculiarities of filler–gap structures that make little sense from a narrowly grammatical perspective will then be argued to be explainable by on-line processing efficiency and MaOP in §7.5.3.

7.5.1   *Fillers First*

Displaced *wh*-words across languages move to the left of the clause over which they have scope and within which they are co-indexed, and this asym-metry is almost exceptionless. Polinsky (2002) and Petronio & Lillo-Martin (1997) mention American Sign Language as exceptional, and Polinsky adds the (Tibeto-Burman) language Meithei. The regular pattern can be seen in English questions such as *Who did you say came to the party?* and *How did you say John came to the party?* (as opposed to *Did you say came to the party who?*, etc.). Alternative in situ strategies are discussed in §5.4 and §7.3.

Why should *wh* be displaced to the left with such consistency, when it is displaced at all? An early idea proposed by J. D. Fodor (1983) is that it is easier to process the filler before the gap than gap before filler. A gap is simply the absence of something. Its very existence must be inferred. But a filler has both form and content which can be used to initiate an FGD and activate the search for the gap, checking for the appropriateness of a co-indexation when each possible subcategorizor or gap site is encountered. If the gap comes first, it will be harder to recognize and there may be considerable backtracking when the filler is encountered. Fodor's principle was initially proposed for English, but it has even more force in languages with more scrambling and argument deletions than English. It is summarized in (7.45):

(7.45) *Fillers First*
The human processor prefers to process fillers before their co-indexed subcategorizors or gaps.

We can represent the positioning alternatives as in (7.46), where X stands either for the subcategorizor or for the gap site from which *wh* has been displaced.

(7.46)   a. Whi s[... Xi ...]
          b. s[... Xi ...] Whi

From the perspective of MaOP (3.16), Fodor's insight can be motivated as follows. Structure (7.46b) would be associated with significant unassignments on-line, requiring backtracking and recovery of the appropriate gap or subcategorizor once *wh* is encountered. There could also be significant misassignments of prior and accessible discourse referents to a subcategorizor that precedes a *wh*-phrase, thereby pre-empting this argument for *wh* especially in languages with rich verb agreement. Either way, (7.46b) is a regular unassignment or misassignment structure.

(7.46a) avoids these unassignments and misassignments by positioning *wh* first. This filler activates the search for its subcategorizor or gap, and experiments have shown that the parser then tries to make the match between filler and subcategorizor/gap as rapidly as possible, cf. §7.1. In the process, however, (7.46a) does introduce the potential for misassigning *wh* to subcategorizors or gaps on-line that will subsequently be abandoned by the parser. Example (7.5), (*Which student$i$ [did you ask(i) John about$i$]?*), was a case in point. This misassignment is avoided in languages that disallow preposition stranding and that permit only verbs to be subcategorizors for gaps, forcing other subcategorizors to 'pied pipe' with *wh* (Ross 1967): [*About which student*]i *did John ask*i?

Preposition stranding is outlawed in the vast majority of languages (Van Riemsdijk 1978), and this constraint can be explained by MaOP. Limiting the permitted subcategorizors syntactically (to verbs only) precludes assignment of the filler to 'competing' and ultimately erroneous subcategorizors on-line.[17] As a result of this and of other grammatical restrictions and conventions (§§7.5.2–3) the potential for on-line misassignment and unassignment in (7.46a) is reduced. And (7.46b) with its systematic unassignments and possible misassignments becomes a much less preferred on-line option than (7.46a).

Wh-question-word fronting reflects this preference for (7.46a). Relative pronouns, in languages that have them, also reflect it. These pronouns are, in effect, displaced copies of the head noun filler within a relative clause. They are found invariably to the left of their subcategorizors or gaps, never to the right, and they occur exclusively in postnominal relatives. In this way they can both be adjacent to the filler (minimizing the co-indexation domain) and obey Fillers First (7.45), thereby maximizing on-line processing.

7.5.2   *Relative clause ordering asymmetries*

We can quantify the disadvantages of gap-before-filler processing (7.46b) using the unassignment and misassignment criteria of (3.18) and (3.21) in §3.3.1. We can also use MaOP to explain an asymmetry in the positioning of relative clauses in languages with different basic word orders, and we can motivate an interesting difference between relative clauses and *wh*-questions with respect to this asymmetry.

The post-nominal relative clause type of English, exemplified in (7.47), is good for domain minimization:

(7.47) I vp[saw np[professors*i* s[that wrote*i* books]]]

With the head noun *professors* adjacent to *saw*, the phrasal combination domain for VP is an optimal two words (*saw professors*), giving a $2/2 = 100\%$ IC-to-word ratio (see (5.2) in §5.1.1). The domains for processing the various lexical relations of co-occurrence with the verb are also minimal (see (5.6) in §5.2.1). If the relative clause were to precede *professors*, as in (7.48), these domains would be larger.

---

[17] See Hawkins (1999: 276–7) for further discussion of preposition stranding and for an 'Avoid Competing Subcategorizors' principle. Notice also that sentences like *Which students*i *[did you ask*(i) *John about*i*]* result in the assignment of an 'additional gap' in on-line processing. We saw in §7.4.2 that additional gaps increase complexity and reduce acceptability and grammaticality quite generally (see (7.36)).

(7.48) I vp[saw np[s{books, wrote*i*, that} professors*i*]]

Regardless of the internal ordering of relative clause constituents, a four-word viewing window would be required for the PCD and for lexical processing.

(7.47) is also optimal for MaOP. It avoids misassignments of relative clause constituents to the matrix VP, or their unassignment in the event that the co-occurrence requirements of the matrix verb are not met. For example, if *books* is the first relative clause constituent to be parsed in (7.48) it will be misassigned to the matrix VP as a direct object of *saw*; if the complementizer *that* occurs first, a clausal complement of V can be misassigned to VP, instead of a relative clause attached to NP (see Hawkins 1994: 327). If the matrix verb were *greeted* rather than *saw* (i.e. *I [greeted [[books wrotei that] professorsi]]* and *I [greeted [[that wrotei books] professorsi]]*), then *books* and *that* would be unassigned to their dominating nodes on-line rather than misassigned, since it is not normal to ?*greet books*. Either way, misassignments or unassignments would be extensive for RelN in phrases that contain it in an otherwise head-initial language.[18]

Hence NRel is optimal both for MiD and for MaOP in verb-early languages, and it is to this that I attribute its almost exceptionless co-occurrence with VO in typological samples (C. Lehmann 1984, Dryer 1992).

Languages with containing head-final phrases, however, cannot satisfy both MiD and MaOP simultaneously, since the two preferences conflict in this language type. Consider a misassignment structure in Japanese that has been shown by Clancy et al. (1986) to result in processing difficulty (see also Antinucci et al. 1979):

(7.49) Zoo-ga   kirin-o   taoshi-ta(*i*)   shika-o*i* nade-ta
        elephant-NOM giraffe-ACC knocked down deer-ACC patted
        The elephant patted the deer that knocked down the giraffe.

The on-line parse first misrecognizes *Zoo-ga* as the nominative subject of *taoshi-ta* within a simple main-clause analysis of *Zoo-ga kirin-o taoshi-ta* (with the meaning 'the elephant knocked down the giraffe'), and then reassigns

---

[18] (7.47) is optimal for syntactic parsing within the NP as well. An initial complementizer or relative pronoun can construct S immediately after N, giving a 2/2 = 100% IC-to-word ratio for NP. Having the verb early within the relative clause also places the subcategorizor of a subcategorized gap close to the head noun filler of that gap and results in a small and potentially optimal FGD (7.8). All parsing domains for VP- and NP-internal relations are small and potentially minimal, therefore. They are larger and less efficient for the VP in (7.48). And depending on the relative clause-internal orderings chosen, they may be inefficient for NP as well. For example, if the complementizer is initial in the relative clause of (7.48), np[s[*that*, {*books*, *wrote*}] professors], this creates a long PCD for the two ICs of NP (S and N). An early verb, np[s[*wrote*, {*books*, *that*}] *professors*], would create a long FGD linking *professors* with its subcategorizor *wrote*.

words and phrases in accordance with the tree structure in (7.50). The on-line misassignments are quite severe in this example, as shown, by the criteria from (3.21):

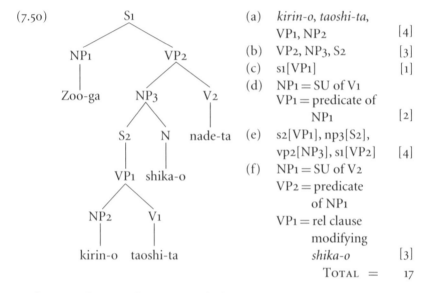

(7.50)

(a)	*kirin-o, taoshi-ta,* VP1, NP2 [4]
(b)	VP2, NP3, S2 [3]
(c)	s1[VP1] [1]
(d)	NP1 = SU of V1 VP1 = predicate of NP1 [2]
(e)	s2[VP1], np3[S2], vp2[NP3], s1[VP2] [4]
(f)	NP1 = SU of V2 VP2 = predicate of NP1 VP1 = rel clause modifying *shika-o* [3]
	TOTAL = 17

In the event that NP1 does not match the co-occurrence requirements of V1, then the words, phrases, and relations that are misassigned by (3.21) will be temporarily unassigned, in accordance with (3.18). Either way misassignments or unassignments are extensive for RelN in this structural position, and indeed in all head-final phrases that contain NP3. But (7.50) is optimal for MiD. The PCD for VP2 permits processing of its two ICs (NP3 and V2) in the same two-word viewing window that renders the mirror-image head-initial VP optimal in (7.47): *shika-o nade-ta* (2/2 = 100%). The lexical relations between V2 and NP3 can be recognized in this same optimal viewing window.

By contrast, if Japanese were to have a NRel construction co-occurring with OV (as in German relative clauses), as shown in (7.51), the PCD for VP2 would be as inefficient as RelN is with VO in (7.48): *shika-o kirin-o taoshi-ta nade-ta* (2/4 = 50%). The domains for processing the lexical relations between V2 (*nade-ta*) and NP3 would be larger as well, since the head of NP3 (*shika-o*) is significantly further from V2 than in (7.50).[19]

(7.51) Zoo-ga vp2[np3[shika-o*i* s2[kirin-o taoshi-ta*i*]] nade-ta]

---

[19] (7.50) also provides minimal domains for NP-internal processing. (7.51), with NRel, separates the head noun from its clause-final subcategorizor, expanding the FGD, and producing longer PCDs for VP2 and NP3 (on the assumption that *taoshi-ta* ultimately constructs the relative clause S2.

On the other hand, the misassignments and unassignments of the RelN structure in (7.49)/(7.50) would be avoided by the early positioning of the head noun in this NRel structure. The early construction of the appropriate NP (NP3) and S to which *kirin-o* and *taoshi-ta* are to be attached means that these words can be correctly attached as they are processed, and this improves their On-line Property to Ultimate Property ratios (see (3.24) in §3.3.2), making their on-line processing more efficient.

Hence whereas MiD & MaOP define the same preferences for head-initial (VO) lgs, resulting in almost exceptionless NRel, head-final languages must choose (for their basic word orders at least) either minimal domains at the expense of mis/unassignments, or mis/unassignment avoidance at the expense of minimal domains. This is shown in (7.52).

(7.52)	MiD	MaOP
VO & NRel	+	+
VO & RelN	−	−
OV & RelN	+	−
OV & NRel	−	+

A processing approach to this distribution can motivate the absence of the VO & RelN co-occurrence, and the co-occurrence of either RelN or NRel with OV. As a result it can explain the asymmetric absence of RelN in VO languages. It also defines some more fine-tuned predictions that merit further testing.

First, the more rigidly head-final a language is (see Greenberg 1963), the more containing phrases there will be that are head-final and that dominate NP. Consequently there will be more containing phrases whose IC-to-word ratios are improved by having a head-final NP as well, i.e. by RelN. RelN is therefore strongly motivated for rigid OV languages like Japanese, but less so for non-rigid OV languages like German, in which the verb often precedes NP and prefers NRel. This prediction appears to be correct, but systematic investigation is needed.

Second, if a given preference is conventionalized in a basic order, then non-basic orders, morphosyntactic devices, or other structural responses should be conventionalized that can realize the suppressed preference in proportion to its degree. In other words, these are universal preferences, and even though a given basic word order cannot incorporate both simultaneously in OV lgs, neither one can be ignored altogether. In German, Extraposition from NP and other rules postposing material to the right of the verb (Hawkins 1986) can reduce lengthy domains in the basic orders of VP. Similarly, RelN languages, motivated by MiD, tolerate misassignments and unassignments only to a certain extent, allowing MaOP to assert itself in the form of numerous otherwise unexplained typological properties. Christian Lehmann (1984: 168–73) points out that the syntactic form and content of prenominal relatives is much more restricted than that of their postnominal counterparts. Prenominal relatives are more strongly nominalized, with more participial and non-finite verb forms (as in Dravidian: C. Lehmann 1984: 50–52), with more deletion of arguments, and more obligatory removal of modal, tense and aspect markers, and so on. All of this makes them shorter, and reduces on-line unassignments by the criteria in (3.18), as well as misassignments, since subordinate status is explicitly signaled on-line within the relative clause.

Third, we make predictions for performance selections, and these predictions are particularly interesting for languages with negative values for MiD or MaOP in their basic word orders (see (7.52)). The worse the relevant structures are by the associated quantitative metrics, the less frequently they should be selected, etc. The basic NRel & OV orders of German, motivated by MaOP, tolerate a lengthy VP PCD only to a limited degree, and beyond that degree MiD asserts itself through extrapositions from NP (cf. §5.5.1). Cantonese preposes a RelN in its VO structure in proportion to the complexity of the relative and the strain on the PCD for VP (see §5.5, §7.2.1, and Matthews & Yeung 2001). Degrees of misassignment and unassignment in OV languages should also correlate with selection dispreferences.

The explanation proposed here for the asymmetry in head noun and relative clause orderings across languages can be supported by a very similar asymmetry in the positioning of complementizers and their sister clauses. VO languages are exceptionlessly complementizer-initial, as in English (*I believe [that the boy knows the answer]*). OV languages are either complementizer-initial (Persian) or complementizer-final (Japanese), and the same general explanation can be given for this as I have given for relative clauses.[20] I give the summary chart in (7.53):

(7.53)	MiD	MaOP
VO & CompS	+	+
VO & SComp	−	−
OV & SComp	+	−
OV & CompS	−	+

A major difference remains to be explained between relative clauses and *wh*-questions. *Wh* fillers to the right, as in (7.46b), are largely unattested. Head noun fillers to the right, i.e. RelN, are productive, but limited to (primarily rigid) OV languages. Why the difference?

---

[20] The reader is referred to Hawkins (2002*a*) for details.

I offer the following. An NP can be contained in numerous mother phrases (PP, VP, NP, etc) that will favor head-finality for this NP by MiD (3.1). *Wh*-phrases, by contrast, typically occur in the highest, matrix clause, and there is generally no dominating phrase, head-final or otherwise, to exert a preference for a consistent positioning of the *wh*-word either to the right or left of its sister clause. The MaOP preference for Fillers First (7.45) is therefore unopposed by MiD, whereas the corresponding preference for NRel is systematically opposed in all head-final phrases containing NP. Indirect questions (*I wonder who John saw*) do embed the questioned clause within a matrix clause, but their frequency appears to be limited compared with direct questions and their impact on a grammaticalized ordering should be correspondingly small. The variation in relative clause filler–gap ordering is therefore the result of a competition between MaOP and MiD, whereas for *wh* filler–gaps the preferences of MaOP are generally unopposed and favor Fillers First.

7.5.3 *Grammatical conventions that facilitate filler–gap processing*

I referred in §7.5.1 to the avoidance of competing subcategorizors as a plausible motive for the absence of preposition stranding in most languages. Limiting co-indexed subcategorizors to verbs facilitates on-line processing. There are many other grammatical conventions that point in the same direction.

Consider the 'Valency Completeness' preference (Hawkins 1999):

(7.54) *Valency Completeness*
      The human processor prefers FGDs to include the subcategorizor for all phrases within the domain that contain the gap.

In a sentential subject extraction like (7.55a) the FGD would proceed from *Who$i$* to the subcategorizor (*disliked$i$*) and the subcategorizor for the sentential subject, *surprise*, would be outside the domain. The FGD in the corresponding extraposition structure, (7.55b), contains this higher subcategorizor:

(7.55) a. *Who$i$ [did s[that Mary disliked$i$] vp[surprise Sue]]?
      b. Who$i$ [did it vp[surprise Sue s[that Mary disliked$i$]]]?

Valency completeness makes it clear how the sentential subject (containing the verb *disliked$i$*) fits into the overall structure of the FGD. The extended combination domain linking the subcategorizor/gap to the filler is complete (see (4.24) in §4.6), and this makes the processing of the filler's role in the FGD easier. This in turn reduces the likelihood of unassignments and of misassignments on-line. It is to this that I attribute the existence of Ross's (1967) sentential subject constraint, and other subject–object extraction asymmetries like (7.56).

(7.56) a. *What*i* [did np[the title of*i*] vp[amuse John]]?
      b. What*i* [did John vp[read np[the title of*i*]]]?

The SSC does not apply in a VOS language like Malagasy, whose basic ordering for sentential subjects corresponds to what is in effect the extraposition order of English and already contains the higher subcategorizing verb (see Keenan 1972*b*):[21]

(7.57) ny vehivavy*i* [izay noheverin-dRakoto   s[fa nividy*i* vary]] (Malagasy)
      the woman   that (was) thought-by-Rakoto that bought rice
      'the woman who was thought by Rakoto that (she) bought rice'

The languages in which sentential subject constraints should be productive (but not actually necessary—see the discussion below) are those like English, therefore, whose basic word order excludes the subcategorizor of the sentential subject from the minimal FGD.

Notice that the FGD in (7.55b) is longer than that of (7.55a), which goes against the normal domain minimization preference. But the extra material in(7.55b) includes the subcategorizor for the containing clause, and this sub-categorizor facilitates processing by clarifying the structural relations in the path from filler to gap. Extra length is therefore tolerated when it directly aids the processing of structural relations, in the same way that extra material in the form of a resumptive pronoun is welcome when it clarifies the filler's role in the dependent sentence (see §7.2.2 and §7.4.1). Domain minimization applies in the normal case, unless it is in competition with independently motivated processing preferences such as (7.54). This means that constituents and operations that add to the processing load of filler–gap dependencies will always be minimized, whereas those that facilitate processing may not be.

In (7.55a) and in corresponding infinitival complement structures in English the minimal domain is ungrammatical:

(7.58) a. *What*i* [did vp[to read*i*] [fascinate Fred]]?
      b. What*i* [did it [fascinate Fred vp[to read*i*]]]?

---

[21] Notice that there is also no sentential subject constraint in Japanese, in which the subcategorizor of the subject would be included in the FGD, in the reverse gap before filler order. The following example, from Kuno (1973*b*: 241) illustrates this (but see §7.6 for a more general explanation):

[[kare ga   kaita*i* koto]s ga   yoku sirarete-iru] bun*i*   (Japanese)
 he NOM wrote that   NOM well known-is   article
 'The article which that he has written (it) is well known'

But in some structures and languages we see variation between minimal and harder-to-process FGDs and less minimal and easier-to-process counterparts. Consider the following German pair with gaps in infinitival object complements:

> (7.59) a. Wem*i*   [hast du vp[zu helfen*i*] versucht]?
>   Who-DAT have you   to help   tried?
>
>   b. Wem*i*   [hast du versucht vp[zu helfen*i*]]?
>   Who-DAT have you tried   to help?
>   'Who have you tried to help?'

(7.59a) has the more minimal FGD without the higher subcategorizor *versucht*, (7.59b) has the longer FGD with it, and both are grammatical.[22]

Gaps are also easier to identify and process when they correspond to argument phrases as opposed to adjunct phrases. In environments in which complexity is strained, e.g. in clausal embeddings (§7.4.1) with semantically specific bridging verbs (§7.4.3), we see the advantage of argument gaps quite clearly. The adjunct extraction of *why*i in (7.61b) is worse than the argument extraction of *what*i in (7.60b), with factive bridging verbs in English:

> (7.60) a. What*i* [does Fred think s[that Mary ate*i*]]?
>   b. What*i* [does Fred regret s[that Mary ate*i*]]?
> (7.61) a. Why*i* [does Fred think s[that Mary refused the offer O*i*]]?
>   b. *Why*i* [does Fred regret s[that Mary refused the offer O*i*]]?

An explanation that can be given for this is as follows. If a lexically required argument is missing from an FGD, the gap can be postulated readily on the basis of the relevant subcategorizor and its lexical co-occurrence frame. An adjunct is generally an optional constituent that is compatible with attachment to a mother phrase, but it is not actually predictable based on constrained grammatical requirements, and there are many heads constructing mother

---

[22] Notice that sentences corresponding to the English (7.58a), in which the infinitival is the subject of *fascinate*, are also ungrammatical in German: see (ia):

> (i) a. *Was*i* [hat vp[zu lesen*i*] [Fritz fasziniert]]
>   b. Was*i* [hat es [Fritz fasziniert vp[zu lesen*i*]]]

The greater processability of (7.59a) may reflect the fact that the argument structure for the subordinate subcategorizor *helfen* is complete and fully processable at *helfen* (its required nominative *du* and dative *wem* have both been processed prior to *helfen*), and the on-line sequence *Wem*i hast du zu helfen*i is also an independently processable sentence with the meaning 'Who do you have to help'. Neither of these conditions is met in (7.58a) and in (ia).

phrases that could potentially contain the relevant gap site in the FGD. The search space for the gap is larger than it is when there is some conventionalized lexical knowledge that actually requires an argument corresponding to the filler, and unassignments and misassignments can be reduced on the basis of conventionalized knowledge.

Extraction from adjunct phrases is also more limited than from argument phrases. The ungrammaticality of (7.62) in English contrasts with finite object complement extractions such as (7.1) and (7.35a) above:

(7.62) *Which film$i$ [did John go to the movies s[even though he disliked$i$]]?

A resumptive pronoun has to be used here, ... *even though he disliked it*i. Interestingly, English does allow extractions out of some infinitival adjunct phrases:

(7.63) Which film$i$ [did John go to the movies vp[in order to see$i$]]?

The lesser complexity of infinitival embedding is compatible with adjunct clause extraction, and this provides further support for the ranking in hierarchy (7.29) of §7.4.1. Such extractions are more limited in German than in English (see Hawkins 1986: 91), while in Scandinavian they are more productive (see the references in fn. 14). In all these languages, extractions out of adjunct clauses are less common than out of argument clauses. What differs is the precise cut-off point in grammaticality.

The explanation for the greater restrictiveness of adjunct-containing phrases is similar to that for the adjunct gaps themselves. There is less conventionalized linguistic knowledge to make clear how the categories in the FGD fit together, and hence there is less grammatical information to clarify the filler's role in the FGD. This rationale is similar to that for valency completeness (7.54). Filler–gap dependencies are easier to process when the path connecting them contains more grammatical information for the processing of structural relations whose processing is a prerequisite for gap identification.

We can summarize these facts in (7.64)

(7.64) *Conventionalized gap sites easier than non-conventionalized*
        Gap sites and nodes containing them that are predictable on the basis of the conventionalized co-occurrences of their subcategorizors are easier to process than adjunct gaps and adjunct clauses containing gaps.

and we can add another hierarchy prediction to those of this chapter:

(7.65) *Argument–adjunct hierarchy*
      If an adjunct position can be, or contain, a gap in an FGD of com-
      plexity *n* on a hierarchy H, then an argument position can be, or
      contain, a gap respectively in the FGD of complexity n.

Notice another parallel to valency completeness (7.54). An FGD that contains more argument phrases and lexical domains for their processing is a
more complex and less minimal FGD than one with adjuncts, since lexical as
well as phrasal relations need to be processed. But the added complexity eases
processing by clarifying structural relations in the path from filler to gap. Extra
complexity is again beneficial when it eases processing. Domain minimization
gives way in these cases, but not when the added complexity increases processing load in a way that does not facilitate filler–gap processing (as in the
hierarchies of §7.4).

A further way to facilitate gap identification and reduce unassignments
and misassignments is to assign special surface structure properties to FGDs.
The extent of the FGD can then be signaled explicitly, and the processor can
be guided to the gap.

Irish exhibits an interesting alternation between complementizers that are
within an FGD and those that are not. McCloskey (1979: 150–51) discusses the
contrast in (7.66):

(7.66) a. Shíl   mé [goN mbeadh sé ann]   (Irish)
            thought I   COMP would-be he there
            'I thought that he would be there'
        b. an fear*i* [aL   shíl   mé [aL bdeadh*i* ann]]
            the man COMP thought I   that would-be there
            'the man that I thought that (he) would be there'

In the path from filler to gap in (7.66b) a special complementizer is used,
aL (where L indicates lenition), as opposed to the normal complementizer
with nasal mutation (*goN*) shown in (7.66a). The *aL* complementizer serves
as a signal to the processor that the FGD is still ongoing and that the sub-
categorizor/gap has not yet been encountered. As soon as it is encountered, any
complementizers to the right of the FGD must revert to *goN*, as shown in (7.67):

(7.67) an fear*i* [aL   shíl*i*   [goN mbeadh sé ann]]   (Irish)
       the man COMP thought that   would-be he there
       'the man that (he) thought that he would be there'

Having alternating complementizers like this indicates which clause the gap is in.

Another type of morphological response can be seen in Chamorro, which employs special verb marking on all verbs in the path from filler to sub-categorizor/gap (Chung 1982, 1994). The explicit marking of FGDs through phonological means has been documented in Kikuyu. Clements et al. (1983) point out that FGDs are distinguished from corresponding domains without gaps by suppression of the tonal downstep. When the *wh*-word is left in situ, the downstep reappears.

A common syntactic strategy for signaling FGDs is through verb fronting, as in (7.68), a German example from Grewendorf (1991: 75):

(7.68) Was*i* [sagte Hans [glaubte Karl [fürchtete Maria [werde Peter tun*i*]]]]
       what said   Hans believed Karl feared   Maria would Peter do
       'What did Hans say Karl believed Maria feared Peter would do'

The fronting of the verb in each embedded clause signals that this clause is in the FGD. Other languages with similar verb fronting rules in FGDs are Yiddish (Diesing 1990), Spanish (Torrego 1984), and French (Kayne & Pollock 1978).

7.6 *That*-trace in English and processing enrichments in Japanese

A property of English, much discussed since Chomsky (1973), is the ungram-maticality of *that*-trace sequences when extracting subjects out of embedded clauses (i.e. sequences of *that* immediately before a co-indexed subcategorizor in direct association theories). Contrast (7.69a) and (b):

(7.69) a. *the person*i* who*i* you think [that committed*i* the crime]
        b. the person*i* who*i* you think [committed*i* the crime]

Embedded object extractions are grammatical both with and without *that* (*the person who*i *you think [(that) the criminal saw*i*]*). The greater restrictiveness of subjects is surprising at first, since unembedded subjects are generally easiest to relativize on (cf. §7.2).

The *that*-trace condition is not universal.[23] But other languages do show a similar dispreference for embedded subject relativizations. For example,

---

[23] The following *that*-trace violation is grammatical in German (Kvam 1983):

(i) Was*i* glaubst du [dass geschehen*i* ist]?
   what think   you that happened has
   'What do you think has happened?'

Comrie (1989: 162) points out that whereas embedded objects are freely relativizable in Hungarian, there is native-speaker uncertainty over embedded
subjects:

(7.70) ?a fiú*i* aki*i* mondtam [hogy elvette*i*   a   pénzt]
       the boy who I-said   that took-away the money-ACC
       'the boy who I said took away the money'

What could explain these *that*-trace effects? There would appear to be two
possibilities. Either the subject gap is responsible, and the ungrammatical-
ities or dispreferences are a reflection of this grammatical position in some
way. Or we are dealing with some property of the complementizer. The
former is unlikely, since subjects are generally easier to relativize on than
objects (§7.2). Pickering & Shillcock (1992) have also shown in their self-
paced reading experiments on English that embedded subjects are easier to
process than embedded objects in sentences in which *that* is consistently
deleted. So what is it about the presence of *that* in (7.69a) that produces
the ungrammaticality?

Notice that the FGD linking *who*i to *committed*i is longer in (7.69a) than in
(7.69b) by one word, namely *that*. So is the lexical domain (LD) for processing
the arguments of *committed*. The complementizer is not needed for early
phrase structure processing in (7.69a), according to the clause construction
principles of Hawkins (1994: 381–7). A complementizer constructs (i.e. projects
to) a subordinate clause, and thereby introduces this category into the syntactic
tree and indicates its onset. The finite verb *committed* also constructs a clause,
and in this environment following the matrix verb *think* the constructed clause
must be subordinate.[24] Hence the two structures are functionally equivalent
with respect to their phrasal combination domains for the containing VP
(PCD : vp—see (5.2) in §5.1.1). Both are minimal. The lexical domains for
processing the matrix verb *think* and its co-occurrences are also minimal in
both, and extend from the subject *you* through *think* through either *that* or
committed. Hence (7.69b) is more efficient overall, with a shorter FGD and
a shorter LD:*committed*, and we can hypothesize that English, a language
with an optional complementizer rule, has conventionalized the performance
preference for the more minimal structure with zero by disallowing the less
minimal (7.69a) altogether, whence the *that*-trace condition.

---

[24] It is this clause-constructing property of finite verbs that ultimately explains why there are verb-
fronting rules in Germanic and Celtic languages, positioning these items at the onsets of the clauses
they construct. These rules are limited to finite verbs, which bear a morphological property unique to
the clause, rather than non-finite verbs which project only to VP: see Hawkins (1994: 381–7).

Total domain differentials for (7.69a) and (b) are shown in (7.69'):

(7.69') a. the person*i* who*i* you vp[think s[**that** committed*i* the crime]]

FGD	----------------------	5 words
LD : *committed*	--------------------------------	7 words
PCD : vp	-------	2 words
LD : *think*	------------	3 words
		TOTAL=17

   b. the person*i* who*i* you vp[think s[committed*i* the crime]]

FGD	-------------------	4 words
LD : *committed*	----------------------------	6 words
PCD : vp	-------	2 words
LD : *think*	-------------	3 words
		TOTAL=15

This kind of theory will be unappealing to those who are used to grammar-only accounts of this phenomenon, so it is important to find some independent evidence that might support it. Recall first that one of the determinants of the presence or absence of *that* in sentence complements without gaps is the nature of the subordinate subject (see §6.1.2). When the subordinate subject in a clausal complement of *realize* is a personal pronoun, both zero and *that* are productive, especially the former (*I realized (that) he wrote the paper*— see (6.12)). When the subject is a full NP (*I realize (that) the student wrote the paper*), zero is dispreferred in proportion to the subject's length. The explanation that was given for this distribution appealed to the construction potential of *that*, of finite verbs, and of nominative pronouns, all of which are unique to and can construct a clause. The longer the full NP subjects are, the less minimal the phrasal combination domains for the containing VP will be (and the lower their OP-to-UP ratios—see §3.3.2). These same minimization and on-line processing advantages should hold for complements of *realize* in which there is an object gap, and this theory predicts a greater preference for zero in *the paper*i *which I realize (that) he wrote*i than in *the paper*i *which I realize (that) the hard-working student wrote*i.

   Now the crucial prediction. In a subject gap sentence, the distribution of zero to *that* cannot reflect the nature or size of any overt subject, but it can still be correlated with the size of phrasal combination and lexical domains linking predicates such as *realize* to the first of the two remaining constructors of the clause, namely *that* and finiteness. This size will vary in the event that material is preposed within the subordinate clause so as to precede the finite verb. In such cases *that* should be preferred to zero in proportion to the length of the preposed material. Culicover (1993) discusses some relevant evidence. He points out that *that*-trace structures are indeed much improved, and even well-formed, when additional material intervenes between *that* and the gap or subcategorizor:

> (7.71) John is the kind of person$i$ who$i$ I suspect [that after a few drinks would be$i$ unable to walk straight]

This follows from the account given here. The finite verb *would* is not in clause-initial position and cannot construct the subordinate clause at its onset. Hence *that* is not redundant, and its presence can introduce constructed properties earlier and minimize phrasal and lexical combination domains involving the verb *suspect* and its projected phrase (VP).

We can illustrate this by adding a preposed *after a few drinks* to the subordinate clause of (7.69) to yield (7.72). The additional word in the FGD and LD : *committed* is now outweighed by significant reductions in PCD : vp and in LD : *think* that are brought about by the presence of *that*. The more minimal structure overall is (7.72a), with *that*.

(7.72) a. the person$i$ who$i$ you vp[think s[**that** after a few drinks committed$i$ the crime]]
FGD	- -	9 words
LD : *committed*	- -	11 words
PCD : vp	- - - - - - -	2 words
LD : *think*	- - - - - - - - - - - -	3 words
		TOTAL=25

b. the person$i$ who$i$ you vp[think s[after a few drinks committed$i$ the crime]]
FGD	- -	8 words
LD : *committed*	- -	10 words
PCD : vp	- -	6 words
LD : *think*	- -	7 words
		TOTAL=31

Numerous predictions remain to be tested, but Culicover's data support the account given here in terms of processing domains. They are surprising from a purely grammatical point of view.

Let me end this chapter with some comments about the analysis of relative clauses in Japanese. There has been a growing research literature on this language questioning whether Japanese actually has a relative clause construction as such. Kuno (1973*b*) observed that the translation equivalents of English relative clauses in Japanese were superficially similar to other noun-modifying constructions. Since then Matsumoto (1997), Comrie (1998), and most recently

Comrie (2003) have argued that there is a common surface syntax to all of (7.73)–(7.75), and that Japanese has no relative clause construction as such.

(7.73) [gakusei ga   katta] hon   (Japanese)
       student   NOM bought book
       'the book that the student bought'

(7.74) [gakusei ga   hon o   katta] zizitu
       student   NOM book ACC bought fact
       'the fact that the student bought the book'

(7.75) [dareka   ga   doa o   tataku] oto
       someone NOM door ACC knock   sound
       'the sound of someone knocking at the door'

The different relationships between the modifier and the head, and the contextual appropriateness of these relationships, can be described in semantic and pragmatic terms, according to these authors, and even apparently 'syntactic' constraints such as subjacency have been recast along these lines, following Haig (1996).

The efficiency principles of this book support this general analysis and enable us to see it in a wider context. The modifier (nominal) head structure of Japanese is a minimal form, as this term was discussed in §3.2, involving structural vagueness and considerable processing enrichment in performance (§3.2.3). The enrichments come about through the factors that were enumerated in (3.15) and are partly pragmatic (relevance implicatures, accessibility of the entity referred to by the NP, etc.) and partly structural. Since pragmatic aspects have been much discussed in the cited literature, let me say a word about the structural.

Assume that Japanese has no relative clause construction. What would this mean for a formal analysis of [S N]np structures like (7.73)–(7.75)? Since this general structure is, by hypothesis, vague with respect to different relationships between the clausal modifier and the head, the grammar of Japanese has not conventionalized any properties that are special to, and unique to, relative clauses. In particular, since many instances of this structure can have interpretations in which the nominal head is not a filler for some co-indexed gap or subcategorizor (e.g. (7.74) and (7.75)), Japanese has not conventionalized a filler–gap dependency relationship in this structure, in the way that English has in its relative clause construction (and also in *wh*-movement structures). So how does the appearance of such a structure come about?

Recall that there is a close relationship between a filler–gap domain as defined in (7.8) and the lexical co-occurrence relations holding between subcategorizors and their subcategorized elements. The two relations and their processing domains can be dissociated when the filler is co-indexed with a resumptive pronoun and when lexical co-occurrence processing accesses this (local) pronoun rather than the filler itself (§7.2.1), and also when the filler is an adjunct and is co-indexed with a position in the relative that is not subcategorized. I suggest now that they can also be dissociated in languages like Japanese, in which there are clear lexical co-occurrence relations but no conventionalized relative clause structure with a filler–gap dependency.

The difference between the 'relative-clause-like' (7.73) and the others comes about because the lexical co-occurrence requirements of *katta* ('bought') are met by *hon* ('book') in the head noun position. In (7.74) these co-occurrences are satisfied within the modifying clause and do not extend to the head *zizitu* ('fact'), and in (7.75) the co-occurrence requirements of *tataku* ('knock') are also complete within the modifier. The common structure of (7.73)–(7.75) requires enrichment in processing, therefore, and the particular enrichments that lead to the relative-clause-like interpretation are made on the basis of lexical co-occurrence information. One of the required arguments of *katta* in (7.73) is in an accessible and (asymmetrically) c-commanding position (§4.6), and this makes it look like a relative clause filler–gap structure as defined in §7.8, with grammaticalized co-indexation between $katta_i$ and hon_i. But if [S N]np is neutral between numerous interpretations, there can be no such grammatical analysis, and a processing enrichment account has to be given that exploits independently motivated relations of lexical co-occurrence.

Two pieces of grammatical evidence support this. First, there are no obvious and uniquely distinctive surface properties of the different subtypes of [S N]np, as there are between, say, the relative pronouns of English (*the book which the student bought*) and *that*-complementizers in *the fact that the student bought the book*. Second, if there is no relative clause filler–gap convention, there can be no grammatical constraints on filler–gap relations either, and the absence of subjacency and of other constraints is automatically accounted for.

Instead, the acceptability differences between different relative-clause-like structures will be entirely a function of the kinds of processing factors considered in this chapter, whose relative degrees of difficulty have been conventionalized in other languages (in proportion to their degree), but not in Japanese.

So, as domains for lexical processing become increasingly non-minimal, e.g. in 'subjacency-violating' structures, acceptability and frequency decline and contextual help is often needed. (7.76) is fully acceptable, since it is widely known in Japan that it refers to the loyal dog Hachiko who continued to go to the railway station until his own death to meet his master, even after his master died (see Comrie 2003: 33):

(7.76) [[Kawaigatte ita] hito   ga   nakunatta inu] ga   maiban
           keeping   was person NOM died   dog NOM each-evening
           eki   made   kainusi o   mukae ni kita   (Japanese)
           station to   master ACC greet   to came
       'The dog$_i$ [that the person$_k$ [who$_k$ was keeping$_{ki}$] died] came to the station every evening to greet his master.'

The performance preferences of Japanese accordingly reveal the same complexity distinctions that can be found in the grammars of languages that have clear relative clause constructions with conventionalized cut-off points down the hierarchies of §7.2, §7.4, and §7.5.3, i.e. clause-embedding effects (§7.4.1), parallel function effects (§7.4.2), head as argument rather than adjunct in the modifier (§7.5.3), and so on. But they are not conventionalized in Japanese, and the processing of the general noun-modifier structure reveals preferences according to domain size and complexity in performance, and reflects the degree of enrichment from pragmatic accessibility and relevance, etc. When there are independent lexical clues to supply the role of the head within the modifier, there will be less need for enrichment.

8

Symmetries, Asymmetric Dependencies, and Earliness Effects

In this chapter I continue the discussion of Maximize On-line Processing (MaOP—see §3.3 and §7.5). My goal will be to focus on the distinction between symmetry and asymmetry in cross-linguistic variation. Symmetry is observed when two categories A and B are found productively in A + B and B + A orders: both VO and OV are productive across languages, as are NRel and RelN. Asymmetry occurs when only A + B is attested or is significantly preferred, either in all languages or in a subset for which independent evidence suggests that symmetry could have occurred. We saw in §7.3 that displaced *Wh*-words almost always stand to the left of their clauses, rather than to the right (A + B/*B + A). And whereas NRel and RelN is symmetrical in OV languages, it is almost exceptionless in VO languages, making this an asymmetry within this subset (see §7.5.2).

Can we predict which pairs of categories will be symmetrical and which asymmetrical? Most of the research hitherto has been of a purely grammatical nature, much of it influenced by Kayne (1994). A different theory is proposed here, derived from processing. I begin with a summary of some major symmetries and asymmetries (§8.1). Some of the asymmetries were discussed in §7.5. §8.2 examines asymmetric orders that appear to reflect asymmetries in the dependency relations between the categories in question. §8.3 considers symmetrical dependencies and orders. My central hypothesis for the distribution of symmetries and asymmetries is summarized in §8.4. §8.5 tests some predictions deriving from this hypothesis for morphosyntactic asymmetries, principally verb agreement and case marking, and in §8.6 I discuss the processing approach presented here in relation to Kayne's (1994) antisymmetry theory.

8.1   Some cross-linguistic generalizations

8.1.1   *Symmetries*

The relative ordering of a verb and a full NP direct object is symmetrical across languages. Both VO and OV basic orders are productive, as shown in the figures in (8.1) which are taken from five samples of languages, families, and genera. The top three samples are convenience samples, the bottom two are areally and genetically controlled:

(8.1) *VO and OV basic orders* (VO = SVO,VSO,VOS; OV = SOV,OVS)
      VO/OV ratio: 55%/45% (78/64)   Greenberg's (1963) Appendix II
                                    (lgs and families)
               48%/52% (162/174)   Hawkins's (1983) Expanded
                                      Sample (lgs and fams)
               54%/46% (217/185)   Tomlin (1986) (lgs)
               42%/58% (79/111)   Dryer (1989) (genera)
               39%/61% (50/78)   Nichols (1992) (lgs)

The 'Greenbergian correlations' (Greenberg 1963, Dryer 1992) provide numerous examples of symmetry: both head-initial and head-final orders are productive, with numerous intercorrelations (§5.3). Languages with verb-initial ordering in VP or S (SVO, VSO, VOS) are preferably prepositional within PP, while those with verb-final ordering (SOV, OVS) are preferably postpositional. The data in (8.2), repeated from (5.11), are taken from Dryer's (1992) sample (using languages rather than genera; see Hawkins 1994: 257). V + PP and PP + V, and P + NP and NP + P are all productive.

(8.2) *Head-initial and head-final correlations: V and P*
     (a) [V pp[P NP]] = 161 (41%)   (b) [[NP P]pp V] = 204 (52%)
     (c) [V [NP P]pp] = 18 (5%)   (d) [pp[P NP] V] = 6 (2%)

Within the NP, a genitive (Possp) sister to N is productive both after and before N. Once again there is a correlation between the positioning of N and the positioning of P within a PP that contains NP. The data in (8.3), repeated from (5.12), are taken from Hawkins's (1983) Expanded Sample.

(8.3) *Head-initial and head-final correlations: P and N*
     (a) pp[P np[N Possp]]   (b) [[Possp N]np P]pp
        = 134 (40%)   = 177 (53%)
     (c) pp[P [Possp N]np]   (d) [np[N Possp] P]pp
        = 14 (4%)   = 11 (3%)

Recall also the directionality of rearrangement for 'heavy' NPs and clauses across languages. In head-initial languages like English, heavy phrases are positioned to the right, by operations that are standardly referred to as Heavy NP Shift, Extraposition, and Extraposition from NP (Ross 1967, Hawkins 1990, 1994, Wasow 1997, 2002; see §5.1.1). In head-final languages like Japanese the clear preference is for heavy phrases to be positioned to the left (Hawkins 1994, Yamashita & Chang 2001; see §5.1.2). Light + Heavy and Heavy + Light orderings are both productive, making this another symmetry.

8.1.2 *Asymmetries*

Contrasting with these symmetries are asymmetries of varying degrees of preference or strength. We do not yet have reliable assessments of whether a given asymmetry is exceptionless or just significantly preferred. In what follows I shall give my best estimate, based on language samples and studies that I am familiar with. Eight syntactic examples are summarized in (8.4)–(8.11). The first three were discussed in the last chapter, the remaining five will be discussed here. Further asymmetries, of a morphosyntactic nature, are given in §8.5.

(8.4) *Displaced WH positioned to the left* (almost exceptionless; Hawkins 1999, Polinsky 2003; see §7.3, §7.5.1)
e.g. English **Who** *did you say came to the party/* You said came to the party* **who**

(8.5) *Head noun to the left of a relative clause sister*
If a lg has basic VO, then NRel (almost exceptionless; Hawkins 1999, Polinsky 2003; see §7.5.2)

VO	OV
NRel (English)	NRel (German)
*RelN	RelN (Japanese)

(8.6) *Complementizer to the left of its clausal sister*
If a lg has basic VO, then CompS (exceptionless: Hawkins 1990, 2002*a,b*, Dryer 1992; see §7.5.2)

VO	OV
CompS (English)	CompS (German)
*SComp	SComp (Japanese)

(8.7) *Antecedent precedes anaphor* (highly preferred cross-linguistically)
e.g. **John** *washed* **himself** (SVO), *Washed* **John** *himself* (VSO), **John** *himself washed* (SOV) all highly preferred over e.g. *Washed* **himself** *John* (VOS)

(8.8) *Subjects precede direct objects* (highly preferred cross-linguistically)
SOV, SVO and VSO basic orders are much more common than VOS, OVS and OSV (Greenberg 1963, Tomlin 1986)

(8.9) *Wide scope quantifier/operator precedes narrow scope Qu/Op* (preferred)
e.g. *Every student a book* read (SOV lgs)   ∀∃ preferred
     A book every student read   ∃∀ preferred

(8.10) *Topic to the left of a dependent predication* (exceptionless for some dependencies, highly preferred for others)
e.g. Japanese *John wa gakusei desu* "Speaking of John, he is a student" (Kuno 1973*b*)

(8.11) *Restrictive relative precedes appositive relative*
If NRel, then restrictive before appositive rel (exceptionless?)
e.g. *Students that major in mathematics, who must work very hard* (R + A)
     Students, who must work very hard, that major in mathematics (A + R)

8.2   Asymmetric dependencies

A productive cause of linear precedence asymmetries in grammars can be traced to an asymmetry in the dependency relations between two categories A and B. I repeat, for convenience, the definition of 'dependency' given in (2.2) of §2.2:

(2.2) *Dependency*
Two categories A and B are in a relation of dependency iff the parsing of B requires access to A for the assignment of syntactic or semantic properties to B with respect to which B is zero-specified or ambiguously or polysemously specified.

Dependency asymmetries result in regular unassignments and misassignments if the dependent category precedes the category on which it depends for property assignments, and it is to this that I attribute many asymmetric orderings. I shall consider several examples in which dependencies between A and B are either fully or predominantly asymmetric; i.e. property assignments to B require prior access to A, but property assignments to A require no or significantly less access to B. We will see that the order B + A is systematically dispreferred in these cases.

8.2.1 *Antecedent precedes anaphor*

The index assigned to an anaphor is determined by the antecedent with which it is co-indexed. Less technically, *himself* in *John washed himself* refers to the same individual that *John* refers to, and assigning this individual to the anaphor requires access to the antecedent. The antecedent, on the other hand, is referentially independent: no property assignments to the antecedent require access to the anaphor. This dependency between anaphor and antecedent is fully asymmetric. If the antecedent precedes the anaphor, the appropriate index can be assigned to the anaphor immediately as it is parsed, along with its other properties such as category type, syntactic phrasal type, and morphosyntactic features. But if the anaphor precedes, co-indexation is delayed and must be assigned retrospectively once the antecedent is encountered. The result is an unassignment structure with a lower On-line Property-to-Ultimate Property ratio (see (3.24) in §3.3.2 for definition of the 'OP-to-UP' metric).

This is shown in (8.12)–(8.14). In (8.12) the antecedent precedes the anaphor in an arbitrary VSO language with a proper name subject as antecedent, and the object as a reflexive pronoun (R-pronoun) anaphor. There is an even distribution of properties to words in this subset of the parse string. In (8.13) the anaphor precedes the antecedent in an arbitrary VOS language and the distribution is no longer even: one less property is assigned at word 1 and one more at word 2. The Unassignment Difference is shown in (8.14).

(8.12)	Antecedent (*John*) +	Reflexive Anaphor (*himself*)
		VSO lg
Category	Name	R-Pronoun
Phrase	NP	NP
Features	+ Masc	+ Masc
Indexation	Index i	Co-index i
	4	4
OP-to-UP Ratio:	4/8 = 50%	8/8 = 100%

(8.13)	Reflexive Anaphor (himself) +	Antecedent (John)
		VOS lg
Category	R-pronoun	Name
Phrase	NP	NP
Features	+ Masc	+ Masc
Indexation		Index i
	<-------------------------------	Co-index i
	3	5
OP-to-UP Ratio:	3/8 = 38%	8/8 = 100%

(8.14) Unassignment Difference: Word 1   2

		Word 1	2
(8.12)	Ant + Anaph	50%	100%
(8.13)	Anaph + Ant	38%	100%
		−12	0

i.e. Ant + Anaph preferred by 12

Empirically, antecedent before anaphor is highly preferred cross-linguistically. Antecedents and anaphors are commonly subjects and non-subjects respectively and this asymmetric dependency is one of the correlates of subjecthood and non-subjecthood that Primus (1999) has broken down into asymmetric c(onstituent)-command, asymmetric theta-roles, and asymmetric cases in her generalized hierarchy approach to grammatical relations and their typology, cf. §8.2.2. The dependency of an anaphor on its antecedent is what motivates its assignment to a non-subject and dependent syntactic position, theta-role, or case in her approach. MaOP then provides an explanation for the asymmetric ordering: if a dependent NP precedes another on which it depends, for e.g. anaphor co-indexing, there will be an unassignment in on-line processing and a lower OP-to-UP ratio. For those languages that actually have an explicit reflexive anaphor (many do, but some do not; see König & Siemund 2000), positioning it after the antecedent is preferred. For languages whose pronouns are ambiguous between reflexive and non-reflexive values, positioning these pronouns first will result not just in unassignment of the (co-)index, but in frequent misassignments as well (assigning e.g. *him* in structures corresponding to *near him John saw a snake* (see Reinhart 1983) to a previous discourse referent rather than to *John*, when this latter is the intended antecedent).

8.2.2   *Subjects precede direct objects*

The subject before object ordering preference in grammars was observed by Greenberg (1963) and has been quantified in the larger sample of Tomlin (1986): just 4% of languages have OS as a basic order in Tomlin's sample, as opposed to 96% SO. This is shown in Table 8.1.

OS ordering is also rare in the performance of languages like Japanese that permit both SO and OS prior to the verb: only 4–5% of sentences had OSV as opposed to SOV in the written corpus of Hawkins (1994: 145), while the object-initial figures reported for other corpora of written and spoken Japanese are even smaller (e.g. Yamashita & Chang 2001, Yamashita in press).

Primus's (1999) decomposition of 'subjects' and 'objects' into more primitive c-command, theta-role, and case relations provides a cross-linguistically

TABLE 8.1   Relative frequencies of basic word orders in
Tomlin's (1986) sample (402 languages)

SOV (168)			OVS (5)
	> VSO (37) > VOS (12) >		
SVO (180)			OSV (0)
87%	9%	3%	1%

motivated and precise grammatical framework that we can use here to explain
the linear ordering asymmetry. She argues (in Primus 1999 and 2002) that
these relations are hierarchically organized, and that many of them involve
a dependency asymmetry that is compatible with the theory of dependency in (2.2) and with the MaOP prediction for linear precedence. For
example, building on Dowty's (1991) theory of proto-roles, she argues that
lower theta-roles on her thematic hierarchies (e.g. Agent > Recipient > Patient;
Possessor > Possessed; Experiencer > Stimulus) involve different forms of
semantic dependency on higher positions. The patient's involvement in the
event depends on the agent and on his/her actions, rather than vice versa; if
something is possessed, there must be a possessor; and so on. The assignment of these dependencies cannot be made immediately if NPs with lower
theta-roles precede those with higher ones, and Primus cites several neurolinguistic studies showing that the preferred agent before patient roles are
indeed assigned on-line and prior to the verb in verb-final structures of
German.[1]

When subjects and objects are quantified NPs, as in *All the students read a
book,* the subject generally has wide scope and the object narrow scope and
we see a further reflection of the asymmetric dependency between them. The
appropriate interpretation for *a book* depends on the reference of the preceding
subject *all the students,* and this latter must be accessed when interpreting the
narrow scope direct object. Compare *Some students read a book* and *Three
students read a book,* in which the number of books referred to is less, because
the subject NPs with these quantifiers refer to fewer students than universally
quantified subjects, and the interpretation of the existentially quantified object
depends on that of the subject. At the same time the interpretation of these
subject NPs is generally independent of the quantity of books referred to in

---

[1] See Bornkessel (2002) and Bornkessel et al. (2003) for supporting neurolinguistic experimental
results and discussion.

the object NP.[2] These scope differences contribute further to the subject before object-ordering preference.

When the direct object is, contrary to the normal case, not dependent on the subject for its scope interpretation, then it can be, and in some languages must be, positioned prior to the subject (giving *A book all the students read*). This makes sense from the current perspective, since *all the students* is not yet accessible to the parser at the time that *a book* is parsed, resulting in its wide scope and specific interpretation. This linear rearrangement precludes the quantifier scope dependency in on-line processing that holds in the normal case.

For structural c-command, Primus (1999) assumes, as I do (see §4.6), that dependent elements must be c-commanded by the items on which they depend. The linear precedence correlate of c-command proposed by Primus, and also by Kayne (1994), whereby c-commanding items precede c-commanded ones can be motivated in the present context as a parsing preference with conventionalized grammatical effects. When the ordering is reversed and c-commanded items precede, there is structural unassignment on-line (and often misassignment—see §7.5.2) resulting from the absence of dominating nodes to which the c-commanded items can be attached at that stage in the parse string (cf. the unassignment factors of (3.18), and the misassignment factors of (3.21) in §3.3.1). The linear precedence preference for (subject) antecedents, wide-scope quantifiers and agents all preceding (non-subject) anaphors, narrow-scope quantifiers, and patients respectively can be motivated both on the basis of their semantic dependency asymmetries and on the basis of asymmetric c-command, therefore, both of which contribute to improved OP-to-UP ratios in the preferred order. See §8.6 for further discussion of this point.

Let me illustrate what MaOP now predicts, in conjunction with MiD (3.1), for the relative frequencies of {S, V, O} in the world's languages, since the ranking is slightly different from the one proposed in Hawkins (1994: 328–339).

---

[2] The preference for wide scope quantifiers or operators to the left of narrow scope quantifiers or operators (as in *All the students read a book* (preferred ∀∃) v. *A book was read by all the students* (preferred ∃∀)) has been noticed ever since logicians and linguists began looking at the surface structure correlates of logical scope. It soon became apparent that it is not just linear precedence that is relevant here: for example some quantifiers are inherently more capable of taking wide scope than others, e.g. *each* v. *all* in English. And languages appear to differ in their tolerances for structures that go against the preference for wide scope elements to the left (English being more tolerant than most, e.g. *All that glitters is not gold*). Nonetheless, there is a clear linear precedence preference for wide scope before narrow scope.

TABLE 8.2   Efficiency ratios for basic word orders

		IC-to-word ratios (aggregate)	OP-to-UP ratios
$mS[VmO]$	IP CRD: $2/3 = 67\%$ VP CRD: $2/2 = 100\%$	84%	high
$[V]mS[mO]$	IP CRD: $2/2 = 100\%$ VP CRD: $2/4 = 50\%$	75%	high
$[VmO]mS$	IP CRD: $2/4 = 50\%$ VP CRD: $2/2 = 100\%$	75%	lower
$Sm[OmV]$	IP CRD: $2/3 = 67\%$ VP CRD: $2/2 = 100\%$	84%	high
$[OmV]Sm$	IP CRD: $2/4 = 50\%$ VP CRD: $2/2 = 100\%$	75%	lowest
$[Om]Sm[V]$	IP CRD: $2/3 = 67\%$ VP CRD: $2/4 = 50\%$	59%	lower

Assumptions (cf. Hawkins 1994: 328–39):
Subjects and objects are assigned left-peripheral constructing categories for mother nodes in head-initial (VO) languages, i.e. mS, mO; and right-peripheral constructing categories in head-final (OV) languages, i.e. Sm, Om.
VP dominates V and O (even when discontinuous), these VP constituents being placed within square brackets [...]; IP dominates S and VP.
S = 2 words, O = 2, V = 1.
V or O constructs VP, whichever comes first (if O, then VP is constructed at the point m which projects to O by Mother Node Construction and to VP by Grandmother Node Construction; cf. Hawkins 1994).

MiD defines the ranking shown in (8.15), assuming a VP that immediately dominates V and O (in any order), and an IP that dominates S and VP (again in any order):

(8.15) MiD: SOV, SVO   > VSO, VOS, OVS   > OSV
             1   2   3

The justification for this, using IC-to-word ratios within VP- and IP-phrasal combination domains, is set out in Table 8.2, which incorporates many of the assumptions made in Hawkins (1994: 328–39). The aggregate efficiency ratio for the first group of basic orders is 84%, for those in the second group 75%, and for OSV in the third 59%.

MaOP defines the ranking shown in (8.16):

(8.16) MaOP: SOV, SVO, VSO   > VOS, OSV   > OVS
              1   2   3

The orders in the first group all have S before O, those in the second group have O immediately before S, while OVS in the third group has an intervening V. Property assignments to O that depend on S can be made immediately at O when O follows S, and this results in optimal OP-to-UP ratios for the first group. There will be a small delay for property assignments to O in the second group, and correspondingly lower ratios, and a larger delay and the lowest ratio for OVS, in which the distance between O and S is greater. This is also shown in Table 8.2.

Now, let us combine these rankings by adding up the relative score for each basic order in (8.15) and (8.16). The result is (8.17).[3] The smaller the total, the greater the combined preference.

(8.17) SOV, SVO   > VSO   > VOS   > OVS, OSV
          2   3   4   5

This combined ranking matches the relative frequencies of the languages in Tomlin's sample (with 87% > 9% > 3% > 1% corresponding to 2 > 3 > 4 > 5 for these four groups). There is just one difference between (8.17) and that of Hawkins (1994: 328–39). The OVS order now belongs in the bottom group rather than in third position. Tomlin (1986) mentions that the VOS > OVS distribution is indeed statistically significant, despite the small numbers of each in his sample, and so is VOS > OSV.

It is instructive to compare the processing explanation for subject before object ordering given here in terms of MaOP with the rather different account proposed by Gibson (1998). For Gibson, what is crucial is the fact that a direct object requires and predicts the co-occurrence of a subject, whereas a subject does not require and predict an object. An initial object involves more working memory load in on-line processing, therefore, as reflected in his 'memory cost function'. His theory, like mine, defines a locality preference for the processing of combinatorial and dependency relations (his 'integration cost function', my MiD (3.1)). But the two theories differ over so-called 'predictions' in processing and over 'memory cost'.

Gibson (1998: 59) gives the following explanation for the processing preference for SVO over OVS in languages such as German and Finnish with both:

OVS ... orders are more complex at the initial nouns because it is necessary to retain the prediction of a subject noun at this location. ... SVO sentences are expected to be more frequent than OVS ..., because they require less memory to produce and comprehend.

---

[3] Notice that this combination of rankings assumes that MiD and MaOP each count equally. This assumption is probably incorrect, but it is a reasonable initial hypothesis.

I agree with Gibson that an initial direct object that is clearly recognizable as such (through e.g. case marking) probably does activate the expectation of a subject. To that extent there is greater memory cost in object before subject orders. But this cannot be the explanation for the subject–object ordering preference.

Notice first that there are many SOV and VSO languages that have ergatively case marked transitive subjects (see Dixon 1994, Primus 1999). In the great majority of these the subject agent precedes the object patient, even though the ergative subject is now the predicting and working-memory-load-increasing category (an ergative case always requires the co-occurrence of an absolutive, just as an accusative requires a nominative in nominative–accusative systems).[4] The following basic orders are typical in Avar (see Comrie 1978) and Hindi (see Primus 1999), two languages with ergative case marking:

(8.18) Vas-as: jas   j-ec:ula.   (Avar)
       boy-ERG girl-ABS SG.FEM.ABS-praise,
       'The boy praises the girl'

(8.19) Laṛke ne   kitaab   paṛhh-ii.   (Hindi)
       boy   ERG book-ABS read-PERF.FEM.3SG,
       'The boy read the book'

Second, it is not in general the case that X + Y is preferred over Y + X when Y predicts X and not vice versa. In the asymmetries of this chapter, sometimes the non-predicting X is initial (English subjects before objects). Sometimes the predictive Y is preferred initially, as in (8.18) and (8.19). Topic-marked phrases, e.g. Japanese *wa* (Kuno 1973*b*), predict a predication and are also generally initial (see §8.2.3). Complementizers are preferred *before* the

---

4 Primus (1999) shows that a significant number of the rare language types with OSV and OVS orders (see Table 8.1) have ergative case marking and hence position the (non-predicting) absolutive before the (predicting) ergative. But this correlation does not salvage the memory cost explanation, since the great majority of ergative languages position the ergative agent before the absolutive patient. The issue that does need to be explained here is why Primus's case hierarchy (absolutive > ergative) should be so much weaker than the theta-role hierarchy (agent > patient) (and the c-command hierarchy) and less capable of bringing about asymmetric linear orderings favoring absolutives first. A possible explanation can be given in terms of MaOP. While an ergative or accusative case requires (and possibly predicts) the co-occurrence of an absolutive and a nominative respectively, these lower cases are generally clearly marked morphologically and can be recognized in on-line processing without accessing their higher cases. Each is processable as it is encountered, therefore. But Primus's point about dependent theta-roles (and lower c-commanded structural positions) is that many of the relevant semantic and syntactic properties are not assignable to lower hierarchy positions in isolation from (and in advance of) the higher positions. Hence there is a stronger MaOP motivation for positioning agents before patients than absolutive case before ergative case.

subordinate clauses sisters that they generally predict (see (8.6) above). On other occasions neither X nor Y predicts the other, as in restrictive before appositive relative clauses (§8.2.4). There is no consistent correlation between ordering asymmetries across languages and memory cost, therefore.

In place of Gibson's memory load for predictions ahead, the theory of MaOP focuses on the (un)assignability of properties to each item X as it is processed and on the resulting OP-to-UP ratios for alternative X + Y and Y + X orders. MaOP is repeated for convenience:

(3.16) *Maximize On-line Processing* (MaOP)
The human processor prefers to maximize the set of properties that are assignable to each item X as X is processed, thereby increasing O(n-line) P(roperty) to U(ltimate) P(roperty) ratios. The maximization difference between competing orders and structures will be a function of the number of properties that are unassigned or misassigned to X in a structure/sequence S, compared with the number in an alternative.

What explains the OS dispreference is the fact that numerous semantic and syntactic properties, referential indices, lower theta-roles, narrow scope, and phrasal attachment sites, cannot be assigned to O as O is processed, whereas they can be assigned immediately in the SO order, given the semantic and syntactic asymmetries between S and O. The predictiveness of O, when it exists, is irrelevant.

This example reveals an important general point about the role of working memory in theories of processing complexity. Structures can be preferred even when there is *greater* working memory load, as currently defined. These and other preferences reflect efficiencies, of the type I am trying to define in this book, and sometimes these efficiencies will correlate with reductions in working-memory load (generally when domain minimization is implicated), but sometimes they correlate with increases, as in this case.

This example also reveals that efficiency and complexity in on-line processing are a function of the amount of processing that can be undertaken at each item X as it is processed. Whatever global predictions can be made in on-line processing are irrelevant to linear ordering. But if there are significant delays in property assignments to X that can be avoided by positioning X to the right of Y on which it depends, then this positioning will be preferred.

More generally, these considerations cast doubt on the whole 'memory cost' proposal (which goes back at least to Yngve 1960). The notion of a 'prediction' in processing is problematic. Many or most 'predictions' involve possible, rather than required, co-occurrences with different degrees of probability of co-occurrence. A theory that limits itself to 100% guaranteed co-occurrences is too narrow. Other activated co-occurrences are surely adding to the storage in working memory and facilitating the processing of activated constituents once encountered. Such activations are not quantified in Gibson's theory, and for an understandable reason. The manner in which they should be quantified is not clear. Do more such activations increase working-memory load, making e.g. lexical entries with multiple co-occurrences harder to process? If not, why not, given the increases in working-memory load? These are some of the issues that arise in a prediction-based complexity model. The alternative proposed here, in terms of MaOP and OP-to-UP ratios, avoids a lot of these problems, as well as the vagueness inherent in the very notion of an on-line prediction, and appears to be the more general theory for ordering asymmetries at least.

8.2.3   *Topic to the left of a dependent predication*

In languages that have a well-defined topic phrase as sister to a clausal predication, such as Mandarin Chinese and Japanese, the topic generally precedes the predication (Gundel 1988, Primus 1999). This is often motivated in terms of the pragmatic givenness of the topic (Givón 1983), along with the Prague School claim that given generally precedes new information (Firbas 1966). Unfortunately, topics in these languages are not always given, given before new is not universal (Givón 1988, Hawkins 1994), and there are additional semantic dimensions to the topic–comment relation (cf. e.g. Jacobs 2001 for a particularly clear discussion) that are highly relevant for linear ordering.

I want to propose here, following Primus (1999), that the primary reason for the asymmetric ordering is that there are numerous dependency relations holding between a topic and its predication, and that it is predominantly the predication that depends on the topic, rather than vice versa. Ordering the topic first permits the parser to assign the dependent properties to the predication immediately as it is parsed, whereas ordering the predication first would delay assignment of these properties until the following topic is encountered, and would produce low OP-to-UP ratios for the matrix clause.

Chinese- and Japanese-style topics have independent reference (Keenan 1976b), when they are noun phrases. They are not just pragmatically given, they are semantically definite or universal or generic (Tsao 1978, Kuno 1973b) and they lack the kind of structural dependence that is characteristic of indefinite expressions and that results in regular narrow scope interpretations (cf. §8.2.2). An initial topic permits the parser to access its definite or universal or generic referent in advance of the predication, and the parser would generally assign the same reference to it if it followed the predication. But the predication does not have such independence from the topic. Reinhart (1982) proposed that predications stand in a relation of 'aboutness' to their topics (Jacobs 2001 refers to it as 'addressation'), and aboutness is a form of dependency with far-reaching consequences for semantic interpretations. Predications are zero-specified or ambiguously or polysemously specified with respect to numerous properties that topics provide (see (2.2)). Consider some examples from (Mandarin) Chinese, taken from the detailed study of topic–predication structures in this language by Tsao (1978).

First, the predication may depend on a topic to provide an argument with respect to which the subcategorizor in the predication is specified, as illustrated in (8.20). The argument structure of the verb *lai* ('come') is not satisfied within the predication here, and the parser needs access to the topic NP *Jang San* in order to assign a subject and thereby recognize a property that is zero-specified within the predication. The regular polysemy or ambiguity of verbal predicates is also resolved by the topic in such cases, along the lines discussed for *the boy ran/the water ran/the stocking ran/the advertisement ran* in English by Keenan (1979). These lexical property assignments would remain unassigned in a predication + topic ordering until the topic was encountered, and there could also be misassignments on-line depending on discourse context and on frequency effects in assigning meanings to predicates (i.e. the meanings preferred by discourse and frequency would often not be those required by the topic). But when the topic precedes, these dependent properties can be assigned to the predication simultaneously with the processing of its non-dependent properties.

(8.20) **Jang San (a)**, dzwo-tyan lai kan wo.   (argument assignment:
        Jang San (Topic Part), yesterday (he) came (to) see me.   subcategorizor specification)

Second, the semantic interpretation of an explicit noun phrase within the predication is often enriched by reference to the topic. The topic may provide the possessor for which this NP is understood as a possessee, even though explicit possessive marking is completely absent, as shown in (8.21). If the predication preceded the topic here, the link to the possessor would be delayed and it would be unclear on-line whose mind was being talked about. Positioning the possessor first removes the indeterminacy and permits the possession relationship to be assigned immediately as the possessee is processed.

(8.21) **Jei-ge ren** (a), tounau jyandan.   (argument enrichment:
      This-Classif man (Topic Part), (his) mind (is) simple.   possessor-possessed)

The topic may also provide the reference class or the total set of entities relative to which a quantified expression in the predication is interpreted, as in the examples of (8.22). Unassignments ('two of what?', etc.) and possible misassignments to the quantified expression on-line are again avoided by positioning the topic first.

(8.22) a. **Wu-ge pinggwo** (a), lyang-ge hwai-le.   (argument enrichment:
        Rice-Classif apples (Topic Part), two-Classif (are) spoiled.   class-member)
    b. **Ta-de san-ge haidz** (a), yi-ge dang lyushr.   (argument enrichment:
        His three-Classif children (Topic Part), one-Classif serve-as lawyer.   set-member)

A further case of argument enrichment is found in examples where the topic provides a phrase that would correspond to a restrictive adjunct to some argument within the predication, as in (8.23). The claim made by the predication in isolation, 'my experience is very rich', may not be true here, whereas the restrictively modified 'my experience in this matter is very rich' is asserted as true. Positioning the topic first avoids the misassignment of an overly general interpretation on-line (or at least an unassignment of the intended restrictive interpretation).

(8.23) **Jei-jyan shr** (a), wo-de jingyan tai dwo-le.   (argument enrichment:
      This-Classif matter (Topic Part), my experience too many-Asp.   restrictive adjunct)
      i.e. (With regard to) this matter (topic), my experience is very rich.

Third, the predication may be semantically enriched by the topic in ways that would correspond to various adverbial expressions or PPs, if these were explicit. Tsao (1978) gives numerous examples of 'understood' locative, temporal, and even causal meanings whose assignment to the predication depends crucially on the topic. I will refer to these as 'predicate enrichments', since the relevant expressions when explicit are most closely linked to the verbal (or adjectival) predicate within the predication. Examples are given in (8.24):

(8.24) a. **Nei kwai tyan (a)**, daudz jang de hen da.   (predicate enrichment:
   That piece land (Topic Part), rice grows Part very big (in it)   location)
  b. **Dzwo-tyan (a)**, Jang San lai kan wo.   (predicate enrichment:
   Yesterday (Topic Part), Jang San came (to) see me.   time)
  c. **Weile jei-ge haidz**, wo bu jr chr-le dwoshau ku.   (predicate enrichment:
   For this-Classif child, I not know eat-Asp how-much hardship.   cause)
   i.e. For this child (topic), I have endured a lot of hardship (on account of him/her).

By positioning the topic first the predicate enrichments can be made to the predication as it is being processed. These examples are reminiscent of Jacobs's, 'frame-setting' generalization for topics: 'In (X, Y), X is the *frame* for Y if X specifies a domain of (possible) reality to which the proposition expressed by Y is restricted' (Jacobs 2001: 656). If Y preceded the frame X here, the relevant restriction would not be made on-line and there would be semantic misassignments or unassignments. The topic may also provide the frame or domain relative to which a superlative expression is interpreted, as in (8.25). In this example the expensiveness of tuna is interpreted relative to fish, the topic, not to meat or other items, and these more general interpretations are precluded and the intended interpretation is immediately assignable when the topic precedes.

(8.25) **Yu (a)**, wei-yu syandzai dzwei gwei.   (predicate enrichment:
   Fish (Topic Part), tuna is now the most expensive. superlative domain)

These productive dependency asymmetries predict an asymmetric topic + predication ordering, in order to avoid temporary unassignments or misassignments of the relevant properties on-line. Gundel (1988: 226) claims that dependencies of the type I am calling 'argument enrichments' (8.21)–(8.23), and 'predicate enrichments' (8.24) and (8.25) (both of which are sometimes referred to, rather misleadingly, as 'double-subject' constructions) do not occur in the order predication + topic across languages and are exclusively topic-first. Argument assignment dependencies involving empty argument positions or gaps, as in (8.20), can be found in both orders, though topic + predication is again preferred (see Primus 1999). The argument and predicate enrichment dependencies are fully asymmetric, as they were for antecedent and anaphor (§8.3.1): arguments and predicates within the predication depend on the topic for the relevant property assignments, whereas the topic does not depend on the predication for any such enrichments. But *Jang San* in (8.20) does receive a theta-role from the following verb *lai* and is dependent on this latter for selection of the appropriate one, while the predication is dependent on the topic for argument assignment and for ambiguity and polysemy reduction. The dependencies go in both directions in this case, and so do the relative orderings. Gundel (1988) cites e.g. Lisu for topic + predication (as in Chinese), and Ojibwe for predication + topic (following Tomlin & Rhodes's 1979 analysis). But the great majority of dependent property assignments go from predication to topic, and the topic is quite independent of the predication with respect to its reference, and this can explain the preference for topic + predication overall.

When the predication contains an explicit pronoun co-referential with the topic, in so-called 'dislocation' structures, then both topic orderings are productive across languages. English examples are *Bill, he worked hard* (left dislocation) and *He worked hard, Bill* (right dislocation). Since the predication is now a complete clause, the subcategorizing verb (e.g. *worked*) is no longer dependent on the topic for argument assignment and for recognition of its appropriate co-occurrence frame and semantic interpretation, since it can satisfy these dependencies by reference to the local pronoun *he* within the predication (just as a resumptive pronoun satisfies these lexical subcategorizations locally within relative clauses). Enrichment dependencies are also replaced in dislocation structures by explicit phrases that are co-referential with the topic, e.g. *This man, his mind is simple* corresponding to (8.21) in Chinese, and *That piece of land, rice grows very big in it* corresponding to (8.24a). Either ordering, topic + predication and predication + topic, is then good for such structures, since the predication dependencies on the topic are now eliminated, apart from co-reference, which favors topic before pronoun. For the topic itself, final positioning has the advantage that a theta-role is immediately assignable since the subcategorizor precedes. When the topic precedes, theta-role assignment is delayed but co-reference assignment can be immediate at the processing of the pronoun. If the reference of the pronoun is already contextually accessible, e.g. if the discourse is already about Bill, then *He worked hard, Bill* is an optimal structure, since the pronoun can receive its referential index on-line and avoid a forward-looking co-reference dependency on *Bill, Bill* can receive its theta-role immediately as it is processed, and the co-occurrence and semantic properties of *worked* can be assigned immediately on-line as well.

The prediction made by the current parsing approach is that predication + topic structures should only be productive in languages in which the predication contains (a) an explicit pronoun or (b) a verb agreement affix or clitic that is sufficient to activate the argument structure of a verb and resolve its co-occurrence frame and semantic interpretation on-line (cf. §8.5). And any co-referential positions within the predication that go beyond the structural options licensed by these verb agreement devices should be expressed by explicit pronouns when the topic follows. The relevant structures should then be preferred in performance when the relevant pronouns, affixes, or clitics have accessible referents in context (see Ariel 1990).

Notice finally in this section that the explanation given here for topic-initial positioning extends to other structures that have been claimed to be 'topic-like', such as the antecedent clauses of conditional constructions (Haiman 1978, Diessel 2001). There are obvious asymmetric dependencies in meaning between the consequent clauses of conditionals and their antecedents, and this provides an MaOP motivation for the preferred initial positioning of the antecedent. This preference interacts with MiD's predictions for efficient phrase structure processing (i.e. EIC) based on the head-initial or head-final positioning of the 'adverbial subordinator' that constructs the antecedent clause (*if* etc.—see Dryer 1992, Diessel 2001). This MaOP–MiD interaction provides a framework for analyzing the other adverbial clause asymmetries (involving e.g. temporal and purpose clauses) in Diessel's cross-language sample.

8.2.4   *Restrictive before appositive relatives*

The ordering of restrictive before appositive relative clauses appears to be widespread in head-initial languages, and is exemplified in (8.26) from English:

(8.26) a. Students that major in mathematics, who must of course work
            hard, …   R + A
        b. *Students, who must of course work hard, that major in math-
            ematics …   A + R

If (8.26b) were grammatical, there would be a regular semantic misassignment on-line. The appositive relative would first be predicated of all students, and would then be predicated only of that subset of which the restrictive is true, once the latter was parsed. R + A in (8.26a) avoids the misassignment. The ungrammaticality of (8.26b) is motivated by MaOP, therefore.

The definition of dependency given in (2.2) can clarify why the misassignment arises. A nominal head and a restrictive relative are in a relationship of symmetrical dependency. The relative depends on the head for co-indexation between filler and gap/subcategorizor, for providing the semantic domain within which the relative clause proposition is interpreted as an adjunct, and for various polysemy and ambiguity reductions within the relative clause itself (recall *the water that ran/the stocking that ran*, etc.—see §6.1.1). At the same time the head noun, *students* in (8.26), is quantitatively and referentially reduced by the property in the restrictive relative and requires access to this latter for the reduction. An appositive relative is also dependent on its head for the same property assignments as restrictives, but the head is not dependent on the relative for any referential reduction: the appositive predicates a proposition of whatever entities the head refers to independently, possibly including a set of head referents that are restricted by an adjunct as in (8.26a). In short, the reference of the head is established independently of an appositive relative, and the dependencies between them are fully asymmetric. There are more dependency relations linking head and restrictive relative than head and appositive, therefore, on account of their symmetry, and this is a reinforcing factor that motivates their adjacency by MiD. But by positioning the appositive to the right, the parser can have prior access to head (and adjunct) properties on which the appositive interpretation is dependent, and can avoid erroneous commitments on-line. Hence: N + R + A.

Head-final noun phrases, by this logic, are predicted to disprefer both A + R + N and R + A + N, i.e. with a prenominal appositive relative, and to prefer R + N + A, with the same rightward positioning of the appositive as in English. Since this results in a conflict with the NP-final syntactic positioning of the nominal head (preferred by MiD), then either appositive relatives are predicted to be less productive in these languages, or postnominal relatives are predicted to co-occur with prenominal ones, with appositives favoring the postnominal position. Christian Lehmann (1984: 277–80) gives cross-linguistic support for both predictions. He shows that the prenominal relatives of Basque, Tamil, Chinese, and Japanese permit significantly fewer appositive interpretations than are found in languages with postnominal relatives.[5] He also cites Basque, Lahu, and Turkish as languages with R + N + A orders, and he mentions that languages with head-internal relatives seem to exclude appositive interpretations altogether. The English preference for appositive relatives to the right of head noun and restrictive adjunct is visible in head-final languages as well, therefore, though the independent motivation for RelN in SOV languages (by MiD—see §7.5.2) may position some appositives to the left of the head. Head-initial languages are independently

---

[5] For an analysis of prenominal relatives in Chinese according to which they can receive only a restrictive and not an appositive interpretation, see Del Gobbo (2003). Her grammatical analysis confirms the typological dispreference for prenominal appositives noticed by C. Lehmann (1984), and the processing explanation for this offered here.

predicted to have NRel, and their relative ordering of R and A can reflect their asymmetric dependency in a straightforward way. Only if appositives were significantly shorter and less internally complex than restrictives in grammar and performance would there be a contrary motivation for N + A + R by MiD, but in fact appositives are generally more complete and clause-like than restrictives.[6]

8.3   Symmetrical dependencies

In contrast to the asymmetric dependencies of §8.2, dependencies between a verb and e.g. an NP direct object are symmetrical by (2.2). The NP may depend on V for its case- and theta-role assignments, and also for construction of the VP mother to which NP is attached, while V depends on NP for selection of the intended syntactic and semantic co-occurrence frame (e.g. transitive v. intransitive *run* (*John ran/John ran the race*), and for the intended semantics of V from among ambiguous or polysemous alternatives (*ran the race/the water/the advertisement/the stocking*). These symmetrical dependencies are reflected in mirror-image orderings across languages, VO and OV. Both orders introduce potential unassignments and misassignments. If the verb precedes, then decisions that are dependent on the direct object can be delayed or misassigned, and if the direct object precedes, then case and theta-role assignments and VP attachment are potentially delayed or misassigned. This potential for delay and misassignment is eliminated to a considerable extent by verb agreement in the former case, and case marking in the latter (see §9.1).

The dependencies between a verb and a complement PP can be similarly symmetrical, and so is the relative ordering of V and PP (see (8.2) above). The dependencies between V and PP were discussed in §5.2.1 and were defined in terms of various entailments. *John counted on his father* does not entail *John counted*, and nor does it entail *John did something on his father*. The processing of *count* requires access to *on* for its meaning assignment, and the processing of *on* requires access to *count*, and that is why the meanings assigned to corresponding sentences without the PP and with a general proverb in lieu of *count* are different from, and not entailed by, *John counted on his father*. The V and the PP are dependent on each other in this example.

---

[6] For example, relative pronouns are not deletable in appositive relatives in English, and numerous parenthetical expressions and question tags can appear in them that are blocked in restrictives; see Hawkins 1978: 282–9).

Other V–PP pairs may involve an asymmetric dependency (of PP on V or of V on PP) by these tests, or no dependency at all. The dependencies can be productive in both directions here, and across languages their orderings are symmetrical.

The dependencies between an adposition (preposition or postposition) and its sister NP are also symmetrical, and so is their relative ordering (see (8.3) above). An adposition is a subcategorizor and a function category (Keenan 1979), and the selection of its co-occurrence frame and semantic interpretation can depend on an accompanying NP, if any. Compare *I went in/in the boat/in the afternoon* in English, in which the relevant NP selections involve very different semantic assignments to *in* through forward-looking dependencies. But NPs can receive different theta-roles, and in some languages different cases, from adpositions, and are also dependent on the P category for construction of the mother PP to which NP is attached. These NP properties can be assigned immediately by backward-looking dependencies in the on-line processing of English. Each ordering, P-NP and NP-P, can avoid some forward-looking dependencies and can provide immediate property assignments through backward-looking dependencies.

Contrasting with the regular asymmetry of topic before predications containing gaps (see §8.2.3), we have seen symmetry for the 'dislocation' structures in which the predication is a complete clause containing an overt pronoun or agreement clitic or affix, e.g. *Bill, he worked hard* (left dislocation) and *He worked hard, Bill* (right dislocation). These dislocation structures do not involve the argument and predicate enrichment dependencies that motivate (backward-looking) topic + predication orders, and nor is the predication dependent on the topic phrase for argument assignment. Explicit arguments within the predicate clause permit lexical processing to take place locally and without accessing the topic. Both orderings of the topic can occur, therefore, and each has potential advantages. Topic first permits immediate and correct co-reference assignment to the pronoun, predication first permits immediate and correct theta-assignment to the topic. Most of the asymmetric dependencies characteristic of predication structures without pronouns or without verb agreement morphology are removed in dislocation structures, and such dependencies as remain are potentially symmetrical and are reflected in symmetrical orderings across and within languages.

The dependencies between a head noun and a restrictive relative are also symmetrical, and both orderings are productive, whereas NRel is preferred for appositive relatives, which are asymmetrically dependent on the head noun (§8.2.4).

8.4   A hypothesis for symmetries and asymmetries

The parsing approach proposed here leads to a general hypothesis about the distribution of symmetrical versus asymmetric linear orderings across grammars. The asymmetries are characterized by the conjunction of properties given in (8.27).

(8.27) *Asymmetries*
    a. one ordering, A + B, avoids regular unassignments or misassignments of properties that would arise in *B + A and is motivated by MaOP (and possibly MiD); and
    b. there is no or significantly less motivation for *B + A, by MaOP or MiD.

When dependencies between A and B are fully or predominantly asymmetric (§8.2) rather than symmetrical (§8.3), there will be no motivation for *B+A in terms of dependency relations, since all or most dependencies can be backward-looking in their A + B orders, in accordance with MaOP. If *B + A results in on-line structural misassignments or unassignments of the types discussed for relative clauses and *Wh*-questions in §7.5, there will be no MaOP motivation for it in terms of these (more combinatorial) aspects of processing either. If *B + A is also not motivated by MiD, for the processing of any relations, then A + B will be the only order that is preferred. We except asymmetric orderings in these cases, and the evidence of §8.2 suggests that we get them. Similarly, when MaOP's preference for NRel joins MiD's preference for this same order in VO languages (§7.5.2), there is no contrary MiD preference for RelN, as there is in OV languages. NRel in VO languages satisfies condition (8.27a), and neither MiD nor MaOP motivate VO & RelN, in accordance with (8.27b). The order A + B will be strongly preferred in performance in all these cases and should be the one that is conventionalized in grammars.

Symmetries arise when condition (8.27b) fails and when each order is potentially motivated by at least one principle.

(8.28) *Symmetries*
    Each ordering, A + B and B + A, is potentially motivated, by either MaOP or MiD.

For example, when dependency relations are symmetrical (§8.2), A + B guarantees backward-looking dependencies for some properties (i.e. immediate property assignments to B by reference to a preceding A), but a delay in those property assignments for which A is dependent on B. B + A has the reverse advantages and disadvantages. Hence each ordering is motivated by

MaOP, for at least some property assignments. Similarly, in the mirror-image Greenbergian correlations (§5.3.1) MiD guarantees minimal domains for syntactic and semantic processing in both optimal orders, [V [P NP]] and [[NP P] V]. NRel is motivated by MaOP in OV languages, and RelN in these languages by MiD (§7.5.2). And so on. Both orders have their respective efficiencies, and both can be conventionalized in grammars, in accordance with the predictions of the Performance–Grammar Correspondence Hypothesis, cf. (1.2a) (in §1.2) '. . . if (structures) A and A' are . . . equally preferred, then A and A' will both be productive in grammars', and (1.2c) 'If two preferences P and P' are in (partial) opposition, then there will be variation in performance and grammars, with both P and P' being realized, each in proportion to its degree of motivation …'.

The potential motivation for A + B and B + A in the case of symmetries means that a grammar has to choose one set of ordering preferences at the expense of another. This gave rise to the prediction (in §7.5.2) that the benefits of the suppressed order would assert themselves in proportion to their degree of motivation, in transformations of the basic order, morphosyntactic devices, or other structural responses. The co-occurrence NRel with OV (good for MaOP, bad for MiD) results in numerous extrapositions from NP (good for MiD); while the co-occurrence of RelN with OV (good for MiD, bad for MaOP) results in numerous structural and semantic limitations in RelN (good for MaOP).

For the symmetrical dependencies between a verb and its arguments we now make a similar prediction. If the arguments follow the verb, then argument-processing decisions dependent on the verb (case and theta-role assignments, attachment to VP) can be made immediately as arguments are processed, by backward-looking dependencies (good for MaOP), whereas verb-processing decisions dependent on their arguments are potentially delayed (bad for MaOP). When arguments precede verbs, the benefits and disadvantages are reversed. Depending on which basic order is conventionalized, we can expect any suppressed preferences of MaOP to assert themselves, even in symmetries, by minimizing the forward-looking dependencies in the relevant order (associated with unassignments and misassignments). One productive way of doing this is through rich verb agreement and rich case marking, and the result is a predicted set of asymmetries in which morphosyntactic marking is skewed to the left of the clause. This and other morphosyntactic asymmetries across grammars predicted by MaOP will be taken up in the next section.

A crucial assumption in this whole processing approach to grammatical variation and typology is that certain orderings of categories involve misassignments or unassignments and do not maximize on-line processing, compared with other orderings or structures. The extent of these misassignments or unassignments can be quantified (see (3.18), (3.21), and (3.24)). It is the orders/structures with potential property assignment delays that result in regular asymmetries across grammars. The preferences predicted by MaOP must be viewed in conjunction with domain minimization preferences predicted by MiD, however. Asymmetry arises when an ordering is favored by MaOP, and when the reverse ordering is not motivated, either by MiD or by MaOP (see (8.27)). Symmetries are found when both orders are potentially motivated, by MiD or by MaOP (see (8.28)). Depending on the basic order selected, NRel vs RelN, or verb-early v. verb-late, grammars will then incorporate transformed orders, morphosyntactic devices, or other structural responses that reinstate the preferences of the suppressed order in proportion to their degree.

The field of psycholinguistics has focussed, since its inception, on garden paths (/misassignments) and on the processing difficulties they cause. The evidence considered here suggests that unassignments are also strongly dispreferred in parsing, and that both can determine asymmetries versus symmetries. Misassignments arise when the co-occurrence requirements of relevant items in the parse string are compatible with a garden path analysis. When they are not, there are regular unassignments. It is quite regularly the case that a language will possess unassignment structures that are identical to misassignment structures but without the actual misanalysis, as was illustrated in §3.3.1 (e.g. *I realize the boy knows the answer* v. *I believe the boy knows the answer*). The challenge for any theory of unassignments is to properly compare relevant alternatives and to quantify the overall distribution of properties to words online. A metric for doing this using OP-to-UP ratios has been proposed here that yields an Unassignment Difference between two structures, and this difference can be used to quantify the severity of the unassignment and make predictions for degrees of dispreference (§3.3.2). The performance testing of these predictions should preferably focus on (head-final) structures in which MaOP and MiD effects are dissociated, in contrast to languages like English in which these preferences often reinforce one another. Other factors such as discourse context and frequency must also be controlled for, in addition to syntactic and semantic property assignments, for the reasons discussed in MacDonald et al. (1994) (see §3.3.2).

8.5   Morphosyntactic asymmetries

In the last section I formulated a prediction for the distribution of rich verb agreement and rich case marking in languages with different verb positions. If the arguments of a verb follow that verb, then verb-processing decisions dependent on the arguments are potentially delayed. Agreement affixes can avoid forward-looking dependencies by, in effect, copying these arguments onto the verb itself. We expect such affixes to be productive in verb-before-argument languages. If the arguments precede the verb, then argument-processing decisions dependent on the verb are possibly delayed. Case marking can signal differences in thematic proto-roles prior to the verb, again reducing forward-looking dependencies, and their presence is predicted to be productive in argument before verb languages.

These earliness effects must be seen alongside other processing motivations of relevance to agreement and case marking. Even in verb-final languages, both agreement and case marking can play a disambiguating role, distinguishing one argument from another, and so too in verb-initial languages. Such disambiguation is also motivated by MaOP, since unassignments and misassignments of verb–argument relations are avoided, not just in on-line processing but in the final representation of the argument-predicate structure as well. Verb agreement is also efficient by MiF (3.8), since affixes reduce the formal complexity of free-standing arguments and generally make it possible for corresponding full NPs to be absent altogether. Gilligan (1987) has shown that so-called 'pro-drop' phenomena involve not just the omission of subject NPs but of other NPs as well, and that such omissions are highly correlated with rich verb agreement. Du Bois (1987) has quantified these omissions in Sacapultec.

What we expect to see in cross-language samples is, therefore, the following. Both morphological types can be present in verb-initial and verb-final languages, for reasons of disambiguation. Verb-initial languages should favor agreement over case marking, and verb-final languages case marking over agreement, for reasons of on-line efficiency. This is summarized in (8.29) and (8.30), in which 'R-agr' and 'R-case' stand for rich verb agreement and rich case marking respectively.

(8.29) V-initial lgs: R-agr > R-case

(8.30) V-final lgs: R-case > R-agr

Languages with basic SVO use verb position as a disambiguator, so there should be less morphological marking overall in these languages, since there is less need for it. In fact, I shall argue below that verb agreement is more advantageous than case marking in SVO, and that we should still see a preference for it in these languages too.

(8.31) SVO lgs: R-agr > R-case

'Rich' verb agreement will be defined here to mean that the verb has verbal affixes or cliticized morphemes that index at least two argument positions in a clause, e.g. a nominative and an accusative NP or an absolute and an ergative one. This definition follows the ('head-marking') classification of Nichols (1986, 1992). Indo-European languages with single-argument (subject-) agreeing verbs do not have rich verb agreement by this definition. A language that does is Kambera, as shown in (8.32) (from Tallerman 1998):

> (8.32) **na-kei-ya**
>   3Sg:Nom-buy-3Sg:Acc
>   'he buys it'

Rich verb agreement provides an immediate syntactic and semantic co-occurrence frame for the verb as it is parsed. Any choices that need to be made between intransitive, transitive, and (for three-argument agreement systems) ditransitive frames can be made immediately, and the parser does not need to wait for subsequent arguments. Semantic disambiguation and polysemy reduction are accomplished immediately as well. When the verb follows its arguments, these latter have already been processed when the verb is processed and the motivation for verb agreement is less.

I shall understand 'rich case marking' to mean that lexical NPs have case affixes that distinguish at least two argument positions in a clause, e.g. nominative and accusative, or absolutive and ergative. A clear example of a language with rich case marking is Japanese, as shown in (8.33) (from Kuno 1973*b*).

> (8.33) John **ga**   tegami **o**   yonda (Japanese)
>   John **Nom**   letter **Acc**   wrote

Rich case marking permits the parser to immediately assign thematic proto-roles to NPs prior to the verb. Nominative *ga* in Japanese is closely associated with the agent of a transitive verb and *o* with the patient. More precisely, *ga* is compatible with both an agent and a patient for following intransitive verbs, and the parser does not know at first whether a transitive or intransitive verb is to follow. But as soon as *o* is encountered, both agent and patient can be assigned in advance of the verb. The case marking avoids unassignments and possible misassignments of case and thematic-role information on-line.[7]

Notice here how a parsing definition of dependency (see (2.2)) diverges from, and makes different predictions from, a definition in purely grammatical

---

[7] The direct object case marker *o* can also be argued to construct a VP by Grandmother Node Construction (Hawkins 1994), thereby avoiding a forward-looking dependency on V for VP construction at the same time that the phrasal combination domain for subject NP and VP processing within S is shortened. Alternatively, rich case-marking languages may reduce forward-looking attachment dependencies on V by not having a VP phrase at all and by relying, in effect, on sisterhood relations such as case, rather than mother–daughter relations, as a way of signaling the word grouping information that is conveyed by rich phrase structure in (head-initial) languages like English.

TABLE 8.3   Rich agreement and rich case-marking correlations with V position

	R-agr		R-case	
	Dryer (2002)	Nichols (1986)	Dryer (2002)	Nichols (1986)
V-initial				
Languages	56% (48/86)	77% (10/13)	47% (28/59)	38% (5/13)
Genera	62% (29/47)		41% (15/37)	
V-final				
Languages	49% (140/283)	46% (13/28)	72% (181/253)	89% (25/28)
Genera	54% (80/147)		62% (85/138)	
SVO				
Languages	44% (94/213)		14% (26/190)	
Genera	47% (49/104)		20% (16/82)	

Notice that some languages have both R-agr and R-case, and that the set of languages and genera for which Dryer has R-agr information is not identical to the set for which he has R-case information. The percentages reflect the proportions of languages/genera having each basic verb position and for which he has relevant information that they have R-agr and R-case respectively.

terms. The case particles of Japanese are lexically dependent on co-occurring verbs for their selection. But they are not dependent on the verb for their assignment in parsing, when they are morphologically well-differentiated and precede the verb, and it is the absence of a forward-looking dependency in parsing that enables me to predict the case marking preference in verb-final languages.[8]

In Table 8.3 I present figures for rich verb agreement and rich case marking (as defined above) in V-initial, V-final, and SVO languages. These figures are taken from two samples, Nichols (1986) and Dryer (2002). Dryer quantifies both languages and genera, so both are reproduced here, and Nichols gives language quantities.[9] Prediction (8.29) is supported: the percentages for R-agr

[8] If forward-looking dependencies on the verb are to be avoided in SOV structures it is important, first, that cases should be clearly differentiated (e.g. Nom from Acc or Abs from Erg) so that they are not confused with one another on-line, resulting in unassignments or misassignments. Failing this, there should be clear default assignments that can be made based on performance frequencies, e.g. the first NP in the parse string should regularly be Nom. Second, the set of theta-roles that are assignable to surface cases should be narrow and predictable, e.g. Nom = Agent and Acc = Patient, so that these theta-roles can be assigned with confidence prior to the verb. Cross-linguistic evidence provides clear support for narrow theta-role assignments to case-marked NPs in SOV languages; see Müller-Gotama (1994), Hawkins (1995).

[9] The larger data base of Nichols (1992) appears to give similar results to those presented here (based on Nichols 1986), but her method for coding argument positions (discriminating between pronouns and full NPs) now makes it less clear whether a verb agrees with just one argument position (subject), two (subject and object), or three (subject and direct and indirect object). For this reason

in V-initial languages (56%, 77%, and 62%) all exceed those for R-case (47%, 38%, and 41%). Prediction (8.30) is also supported: the percentages for R-case in V-final languages (72%, 89%, and 62%) all exceed those for R-agr (49%, 46%, and 54%). Derivatively, the proportions for R-agr in V-initial languages exceed those in V-final languages, and the proportions of R-case in V-final languages exceed those in V-initial languages.[10]

(8.31) is also supported: the percentages for R-agr in SVO languages (44% and 47%) exceed those for R-case (14% and 20%). I pointed out above that there is no disambiguation motive for rich morphosyntax in SVO languages, since the medial verb position distinguishes the two arguments. Form minimization still supports verb agreement, however, since it results in regular 'pro-drops' of full arguments (Gilligan 1987). There is also (limited) MaOP support for case marking a nominative subject prior to the verb, and for verb agreement with postverbal arguments. Overall there is greater motivation for R-agr in SVO languages than for R-case, and this is supported in Dryer's sample.

The general logic of these morphosyntactic predictions can be extended to the typological distinction between 'verb-coding' and 'noun-coding' languages. Polinsky (1997) points out that detransitivization strategies such as passives and antipassives are especially productive in both the performance and grammars of verb-initial languages. The rich passive voices of Malagasy (Keenan 1985) and Tagalog (Schachter and Otanes 1972) code for patient and instrument subjects, etc. on a verb whose transitivity status is also signaled by the coding. By positioning the verb initially in these languages the parser gets early access to this argument structure information, in advance of the NP arguments themselves. We can expect less verb coding in verb-final languages, therefore. Conversely, the rich coding of thematic role information on NPs in languages with many so-called cases and without productive adpositions (Tsunoda et al. 1995, Blake 2001) should correlate with verb-finality and be less productive in verb-early languages.

her earlier data were used instead. The languages quantified in Table 8.3 are those for which she gives a single basic verb position, namely V-initial, SVO or SOV. There are only five SVO languages in her sample, however (three of which have R-agr and three R-case), which is too small to permit any reliable quantitative inferences to be drawn, so the data for SVO in Table 8.3 rely only on Dryer (2002).

[10] In Hawkins (2002*a*) I focussed primarily on these predictions for the occurrence of R-agr across different verb positions and similarly for R-case. It now seems to me that the primary prediction we need to make here should be in terms of each basic verb position, as reflected in (8.29)–(8.31). If the verb is initial, what is the optimal co-occurring morphology, etc.? The derivative predictions, R-agr and V-initial > R-agr and V-final, and R-case and V-final > R-case and V-initial, are examined by Dryer (2002) and found to hold. But the primary predictions should be relative to each basic verb position, V-initial and R-agr > V-initial and R-case.

8.6   Processing in relation to antisymmetry in formal grammar

It is instructive to consider some consequences of the present approach for theories of formal grammar that try to capture the difference between symmetries and asymmetries. The most influential approach has been Kayne's (1994) antisymmetry theory. This theory rests on the ultimately stipulated assumption that c-commanding nodes consistently precede c-commanded ones in all language types and that all grammars are underlyingly SVO. Kayne (pp. 5–6) proposes his *Linear Correspondence Axiom*, as follows:

consider the set A of ordered pairs $<Xj, Yj>$ such that for each j, Xj asymmetrically c-commands Yj. . . . Then . . . for a given phrase marker P, with T the set of terminal elements and A as just given . . . d(A) is a linear ordering of T.

This relation d is a many-to-many mapping from non-terminals to terminals, and Kayne proposes further (p. 33) that it maps asymmetric c-command onto *linear precedence* rather than subsequence:

Let X, Y be nonterminals and x, y terminals such that X dominates x and Y dominates y. Then if X asymmetrically c-commands Y, x precedes y.

There are numerous prima facie problems for this theory, including the productivity of SOV languages and the existence of many structures in which apparently asymmetrically c-command*ed* nodes precede c-command*ing* ones. But it is interesting that Kayne's Linear Correspondence Axiom plus precedence is in accordance with some of MaOP's predictions. When an asymmetrically c-commanded relative clause precedes its nominal head in a head-final language, for example, there are regular unassignments and misassignments resulting from the late attachment of the clause to its immediately dominating NP in on-line processing (§7.5.2). In the reverse ordering, when the head noun precedes, the NP is immediately available for attachment since it has been constructed by the noun. More generally, when sentential or NP complements precede their heads, there is a period of structural uncertainty on-line, i.e. of unassignment or even misassignment, during which items being processed are not attachable to their higher dominating nodes. In head-initial, c-commanding before c-commanded orders, the head constructs the mother in advance of the c-commanded nodes and these latter can be immediately attached without any unassignment delay as they are parsed (see the criteria in (3.18)). And when there are asymmetric dependencies between antecedent and anaphor (§8.2.1) or between wide scope and narrow scope quantifiers (§8.2.2), with the dependent in a c-commanded structural position, processing the c-commanding item first permits immediate assignment of the dependent property to the c-commanded item. The reverse positioning results in unassignment and misassignment delays.

The problem for *anti*symmetry, however, is that MaOP can also motivate symmetrical orderings, namely when there are symmetrical dependencies (§8.3) in what are most plausibly symmetrical c-command relationships (§4.6).[11] Processing also motivates a second general principle, MiD (3.1), that sometimes reinforces linear precedence and sometimes opposes it, by preferring what are most plausibly c-commanded phrasal nodes to the left of c-commanding ones, as we saw also in the relative clause discussion (§7.5.2). And it is the empirical effects of MiD that render Kayne's theory most problematic.

Let us pursue this interface between performance and formal grammar in more detail, since there may be a general moral here about the way in which processing can reduce stipulation and guide theory construction in formal grammar. Kayne argues (1994: 35) that only two relative orderings of specifier, head, and complement are compatible with his Linear Correspondence Axiom, (8.34a) and (8.34b), while just one is compatible with precedence (8.34a):

(8.34) a. [Specifier [Head Complement]]
        b. [[Complement Head] Specifier]

But in terms of processing, a grammar with consistent orders of both types can be efficient for MiD (3.1), and this was illustrated for the head–complement orders of vp{V, pp{P, NP}} and pp{P, np{N, Possp}} in §5.3.1. Consistent head adjacency produces minimal domains for phrasal combination and for the processing of other syntactic and semantic relations, whether higher heads precede or follow lower ones, and hence MiD supports (8.34a) and (b), not just the former.[12] MaOP also supports both.

---

[11] The symmetrical dependencies of §8.3 motivate both VO and OV, and also P-NP and NP-P, etc. Each ordering is compatible with some forward-looking and some backward-looking dependencies, and the structural and morphosyntactic correlates of each are predicted to minimize the forward-looking ones, resulting in verb agreement and case marking preferences (§8.5). Symmetrical dependencies reinforce EIC-type effects in ultimately explaining the existence of symmetrical orderings, therefore, and any asymmetries within symmetries should assert themselves in proportion to MaOP's preference.

Notice that these symmetrical dependencies motivate a definition of c-command in terms of 'first branching node up' (as in Reinhart 1983) rather than 'first node up', as in Kayne (1994: 7).

[12] It is also interesting to note that the left-branching specifier and adjunct categories in a head-initial language like English generally result in short and minimal phrasal combination domains. This serves to minimize the period of attachment uncertainty prior to the head, as well as the PCD for the phrase immediately containing the head's maximal projection. See Hawkins (1994: 282–93) for illustration of the grammatical limitations on specifiers (and preceding) adjuncts within VP, NP (and DP). For subject specifiers of an IP (or S) dominating VP, the clausal node can either be postulated immediately at the outset of a matrix clause, or else the subject will regularly be a case-marked pronoun (or preceded by a complementizer in subordinate position), all of which have the effect of constructing an S early to which the subject can be attached.

For head-final languages in which relative clauses, complement clauses, and NPs precede their respective heads, Kayne is forced to postulate upward movement of the relevant phrase into an asymmetrically c-commanding specifier position. This salvages the Linear Correspondence Axiom plus precedence, since these left-branching structures, RelN, SComp, and NP-Po, are now analysed as c-commanding phrases before c-commanded heads. But it is controversial because complements are c-command*ed* by their heads in SVO languages, and it is far from clear empirically that SOV languages should be analysed differently, in this respect at least.

The questionable upward movements into c-commanding positions are not needed in the present account. The traditional analysis of complements as c-commanded items in VO and OV languages provides structures that are optimally efficient by MiD, and both VO and OV languages, more generally head-initial and head-final structures, are correctly predicted to be productive. Orderings that are genuinely asymmetric, namely those summarized in §8.1.2, are predicted to be so by MaOP. The interaction between these two principles gives us the principled difference between VO and OV languages, whereby the former are consistently (and asymmetrically) NRel and CompS, while the latter have symmetrical NRel/RelN and CompS/SComp (see §7.5.2). Both principles converge in combination with VO, but diverge in OV languages, with MiD preferring RelN and SComp and MaOP the reverse.

The conversion of RelN to NRel and of SComp to CompS in many head-final languages follows on this account from the fact that unassignments and misassignments are more severe for complex left-branching phrases like RelN and SComp than for shorter phrases such as NP before P, and as a result the former are less productive than NP-P in combination with OV and are frequently reduced in expressiveness and/or replaced. RelN and OV is in turn associated with more misassignments and unassignments than SComp and OV, on account of its missing argument position (i.e. the gap), and it is the least productive structure of all. There is a principled reduction in MiD-motivated head-finality, therefore, in proportion to the degree of MaOP's preference for unassignment/misassignment avoidance, resulting in the following relative frequencies across languages: NP-P > SComp > RelN.

(8.35) *OV languages*[13]
NP-P = 93%	P-NP = 7%	(Hawkins 1983: 288)
SComp = 69%	CompS = 31%	(Hawkins 1994: 326)
RelN = 41%	NRel = 59%	(Hawkins 1994: 326)

---

[13] The figures given here and in Hawkins (1994: 326) are based on figures taken from Dryer's (1992) sample.

NP-P structures (i.e. postpositions) are also less productive in head-final languages than their P-NP counterparts (i.e. prepositions) in head-initial languages. Numerous languages that are typologically head-final have few or no postpositions (see Tsunoda et al. 1995 for quantification) and the conversion of adpositions into affixes is much more productive in head-final languages and contributes to the overall 'suffixing preference' (Greenberg 1957, Hawkins & Gilligan 1988, Hall 1992). The avoidance of left-branching NPs and the affixal attachment of adpositions both reduce the unassignment (and misassignment) period in on-line processing.

Processing efficiency makes fine-tuned predictions for degrees of asymmetry in these cases, and for property co-occurrences which are either not predicted or which are stipulated in Kayne's grammar-only theory. At the same time processing supports *rightward* movements such as Heavy NP Shift and Extraposition from NP in head-initial languages, all of which are outlawed by Kayne. This is because alternations like *I gave [the book that was expensive] [to Mary]* and *I gave [to Mary] [the book that was expensive]* reinstate the same domain minimization advantages for heavy phrases that normally hold for lighter counterparts in their more basic leftward positions, according to EIC (§5.3). Postverbal NPs are normally less internally complex and shorter than PPs and are normally complements of V, and so they are adjacent to V in their basic orders. When they are heavier they shift to the right of PP with a frequency that is proportional to the relative weight difference (§5.1.1). Hence such rightward movements are actually required on this account in order to maintain the optimal efficiency of head-initial structures for MiD (see §5.5 for further examples).

9

Conclusions

It is a truism of scientific reasoning that you cannot prove a theory right, you can only prove it wrong. One can, however, offer a lot of supporting evidence and show that the evidence is predicted by a given theory, and that it is not predicted by alternative theories. This is what I have tried to do in this book, and in this final chapter I give an overview of what I am arguing for and draw attention to some of the issues that it raises.

I began in §1.1 by formulating the PGCH:

(1.1) *Performance–Grammar Correspondence Hypothesis* (PGCH)
   Grammars have conventionalized syntactic structures in proportion to their degree of preference in performance, as evidenced by patterns of selection in corpora and by ease of processing in psycholinguistic experiments.

This hypothesis predicts a correspondence between preferences in performance, in languages with choices and variants, and preferences in the grammatical conventions of languages with fewer choices and variants. In Chapters 2 and 3 I formulated three general principles of efficiency, with associated quantitative metrics, as a way of structuring and defining the predictions, Minimize Domains (§3.1), Minimize Forms (§3.2), and Maximize On-line Processing (§3.3). Chapters 4–8 tested these predictions on comparative data from performance and grammars, involving several types of structures. The data reveal some quite striking parallels between performance and grammars, and I have argued that these patterns support the PGCH. They are not predicted by a theory in which grammars are autonomous from performance, i.e. they are not predicted by models such as Chomsky (1965) in which grammars are constantly accessed in processing, yet processing gives nothing back. And if the PGCH is on the right track, there are some radical consequences for grammatical theory that we need to make explicit.

I shall first summarize some of the data supporting the PGCH (§9.1). I then draw attention to grammatical generalizations that are either not predicted or heavily stipulated and for which the principles proposed here offer an explanation (§9.2). The next section (§9.3) raises questions about the ultimate causality of these performance–grammar preferences and argues for multiple factors, of which working memory load is just one. §9.4 discusses some further issues that are raised by this research program and its conclusions. And §9.5 outlines some of the consequences for acquisition and learnability.

9.1   Support for the PGCH

The general predictions made by the PGCH for grammars were formulated as follows in §1.2:

(1.2)   *Grammatical predictions of the PGCH*

(a)   If a structure A is preferred over an A′ of the same structural type in performance, then A will be more productively grammatical-ized, in proportion to its degree of preference; if A and A′ are more equally preferred, then A and A′ will both be productive in grammars.

(b)   If there is a preference ranking A > B > C > D among structures of a common type in performance, then there will be a correspond-ing hierarchy of grammatical conventions (with cut-off points and declining frequencies of languages).

(c)   If two preferences P and P′ are in (partial) opposition, then there will be variation in performance and grammars, with both P and P′ being realized, each in proportion to its degree of motivation in a given language structure.

Consider (1.2a). In §5.1 I summarized performance data from English, Hungarian, and Japanese showing clear preferences for minimal domains rel-evant for phrase structure production and recognition (EIC effects in my earlier work). Ordering variants in which one structure (short constituent before long constituent, or long before short) had a smaller domain than another exhibited preferences that were highly correlated with the degree of minimization in the respective order; orderings that were equally minimal were all productive.[1] These same preferences can be seen in the Greenber-gian head-ordering correlations (§5.3.1), i.e. in the grammatical preference for minimal phrasal combination domains with adjacent heads. A V-initial VP co-occurring with a P-initial PP is significantly more frequent than V-initial

---

[1] See Tables 5.1, 5.2, 5.3, 5.6, and other performance data summarized in §5.1 plus the references therein.

with P-final. A V-final VP co-occurring with a P-final PP is just as minimal as V-initial co-occurring with P-initial, and both head orderings are highly productive in grammars.[2] Domain minimizations can also be seen in universal ordering preferences for noun-phrase-internal constituents ((5.14) in §5.3.2) and in the different directionalities of rearrangement rules, to the right or left as a function of the position of the constructing or head category within the rearranged constituent (§5.3.2 and §5.5).

Performance data from English also showed a clear preference for complement PPs to be closer to their verbal heads than adjunct PPs (§5.2.1), a preference that was derived from MiD as formulated in (3.1). This same preference for complement adjacency can be seen in grammatical models and in cross-linguistic ordering preferences (§5.4).[3]

Data from English involving minimal formal marking in adjunct and complement clauses revealed another performance pattern of direct relevance for (1.2a) (§6.1). Under conditions of adjacency to the head, both minimal forms and explicit forms (e.g. relative clauses with zero relativizers and those with relative pronouns) are productive, whereas under non-adjacency formal marking is preferred and zero is dispreferred in proportion to the distance from the head (§6.1.1).[4] Similarly, in grammars that have conventionalized the presence or absence of morphosyntactic marking on noun phrase constituents according to their adjacency to one another, it is the zero option that is systematically disallowed under non-adjacency.[5] And under adjacency either formal marking or zero or both (as in English) can be conventionalized. The dispreferred performance option is the first to be eliminated in grammars, while productive performance options are also productive across grammars.

In §8.2.2 I referred to data from Japanese, German, and Finnish supporting the asymmetric preference for subjects before objects in performance (SOV and OSV, or SVO and OVS, are grammatical in these languages). Correspondingly, a clear asymmetric preference for subjects before objects can be found in the basic ordering conventions of grammars, again in accordance with (1.2a).[6]

With respect to (1.2b) I have argued that many hierarchies structuring grammatical conventions are correlated with preference patterns and ease of processing in performance. Greenberg's (1966) feature hierarchies involve both performance and grammar (§4.1). Declining performance frequencies are matched by increases in formal marking in morphological paradigms

---

[2] See the quantities in (5.11) of §5.3.1.

[3] For example, verb complement adjacency can be seen in the data supporting Tomlin's (1986) Verb Object Bonding principle.

[4] See Tables 6.1 and 6.2 and the data of (6.5), (6.6), and (6.7) in §6.1.1.

[5] See implicational universal (6.17) and the data of (6.18) and (6.19) in §6.2.

[6] See Table 8.1 in §8.2.2.

(e.g. by non-zero v. zero forms). They are also matched by decreases in the very existence of uniquely distinctive morphemes (duals and datives, etc.) and by declining feature combinations (plural *and* gender, etc.).[7]

There are hierarchies of permitted center-embedded constituents in grammatical conventions, and I have argued (in §5.3.2) that these hierarchies are structured by degrees of minimization in phrasal combination domains: a more complex center-embedded constituent implies the grammaticality of less complex constituents (whose presence in the respective phrases is independently motivated).[8]

In §7.2 I discussed Keenan & Comrie's Accessibility Hierarchy from the perspective of (1.2b), building on their intuition that this grammatical hierarchy is ultimately structured by complexity and declining ease of processing. Performance data were summarized from various languages (including English, French, Hebrew, and Cantonese) supporting the declining preferences for gaps in filler–gap domains of increasing size, and the complementary preference for resumptive pronouns in languages possessing this grammatical option (§7.2.1). These data then enabled me to predict that there would be reverse hierarchies for gaps and resumptive pronouns across grammars, with gaps declining in increasingly large domains, and pronouns declining in smaller domains (§7.2.2). The Keenan–Comrie language sample supported this prediction exceptionlessly.[9]

Other complexity hierarchies were discussed in §7.4, involving clause embedding and reduced additional processing simultaneously with gap identification and filling. Performance data supporting the hierarchies were summarized from different languages (including English, Akan, and Scandinavian) and the grammatical cut-offs and conversions from gaps to resumptive pronouns were then supported by grammatical data from representative languages.[10]

Prediction (1.2c) links the variation that results from competing preferences in performance to variation across grammars. For example, in the English double PP data of Table 5.5 (§5.2.1 and §5.2.3) there is sometimes a competition between domain minimization for lexical dependency processing and minimization for phrasal combination processing, namely when the longer PP is in

---

[7] See the Sanskrit performance data of (4.2), the grammatical principles of (4.3)–(4.5), and supporting synchronic and diachronic data in §§4.1–2.

[8] See Table 5.7 and the data of (5.15) and (5.16) in §5.3.2. See also Hawkins (1994: 315–21) for further center-embedding hierarchies in grammars.

[9] See Table 7.1 and the data of (7.18) and (7.19) in §7.2.2.

[10] See the grammatical hierarchies in (7.29) (clause embeddings), (7.36) (additional gaps), (7.39) (relative clauses and *Wh*-questions), (7.41)(bridging verbs), and (7.43) (containing NPs). Relevant grammatical and performance evidence are summarized in §§7.4.1–3.

a lexical dependency relation with the verb. The short-before-long preference conflicts here with the preferred adjacency of lexical dependents. Numerous minimization competitions between different processing domains, and between different phrases, were illustrated in §5.5, with predicted consequences for structural variants in performance and grammars.

The typology of relative clause ordering exhibits variation in OV grammars (productive RelN and NRel) and unity in VO languages (almost all are NRel). This was attributed to the conflicting demands of MiD and MaOP in OV languages, and to their mutual reinforcement in VO (§7.5.2). More generally, asymmetric ordering preferences in performance and grammars were argued in §8.4 to be those in which different preferences converge on a single order, whereas symmetries (VO and OV) have complementary preferences and dispreferences in each order. Whichever order is selected in a grammar conventionalizes one preference at the expense of another, and compensating syntactic and morphosyntactic properties are predicted as a consequence. Examples are the relative clause extrapositions of NRel in OV languages (good for MiD in an MaOP-motivated structure that conflicts with MiD—see §5.5.1), reduced expressiveness of RelN with OV (good for MaOP in an MiD-motivated structure—see §7.5.2), more verb agreement in verb-early languages (good for on-line verb processing in a structure that optimizes on-line argument processing, cf. §8.5), and more case morphology in verb-late languages (good for on-line argument processing in a structure that optimizes on-line verb processing, cf. §8.5).

Both performance (corpus data and processing experiments) and grammars provide support for the efficiency principles that have structured these predictions, MiD, MiF, and MaOP. In many cases I could point to closely matched data from usage and grammar, as in several of the examples just summarized, and these provide the strongest support for the PGCH. In other cases I have given data from performance or from grammars only supporting the general principles.

9.2 The performance basis of grammatical generalizations

At several points I have contrasted the grammatical generalizations and universals proposed in this book with those formulated in purely grammatical models. I have argued that in a significant number of cases these models do not do full justice to the grammatical facts, because their ultimate explanation is of a performance nature and does not follow from grammatical considerations alone. When predictions are made, they rely heavily on stipulated assumptions, and the most descriptively adequate stipulations are those that conventionalize performance preferences in some way.

For example, in §5.3.1 I discussed the head ordering parameter of generative grammar in relation to the Greenbergian correlations, and I referred to Dryer's (1992) finding that there are systematic exceptions when the non-head category is a non-branching category like a single-word adjective. The single-word/multi-word distinction involves what is most plausibly a difference in terminal elements among items of the same category type (e.g. adjective phrases). To the extent that single-word and multi-word phrases have different positionings, with one being regularly subsumed under head ordering and the other not, their common category type precludes a straightforward grammatical generalization distinguishing them. And even if some difference in grammatical (sub)type could be justified, it would need to be shown why one (sub)type should regularly follow head ordering, whereas the other may or may not.

Performance data, and the principle of MiD, provide us with an explanation. When one phrasal combination domain competes with another in performance and involves a difference of only a single word (e.g. in the data of Table 5.1—see §5.1.1) the preference for the more minimal domain is very small, since there is little gain, and both orders are productive (see (1.2a)). But when multiple words are potentially added to a domain, there is a much stronger preference for minimization. Similarly in grammars. The difference between vp[V np[N Adj]] and vp[V np[Adj N]] (with a single-word adjective) is small, and cross-linguistic variation can be expected, destroying the generality of a head ordering parameter that favors V-initial in VP and N-initial in NP. The difference between vp[V np[N AdjP]] and vp[V np[AdjP N]] (containing a multi-word adjective phrase) is much greater, and consistent head ordering is predicted. More generally, the head ordering parameter is a quantitative preference, not an absolute universal, and the degree of consistency for different pairs of categories is predicted by MiD to be proportional to the (aggregate) complexity of the potentially intervening non-heads. This results in the prediction that single-word adjectives can precede nouns more readily than adjective phrases in head-initial languages (§5.3.1). It results in the center-embedding hierarchy for NP constituents ((5.15) in §5.3.2) whereby single-word adjectives can precede nouns more readily than (the typically longer) possessive phrases in head-initial languages, while these latter can precede nouns more readily than relative clauses (which are typically longer still).[11] The important point here is that there is a principled performance basis for consistent head ordering

---

[11] For head-final languages, exceptional non-heads following their heads (e.g. vp[np[N Adj] V] and vp[np[N Rel] V]) are predicted either by domain minimization (favoring e.g. single-word adjectives

and for the different levels of consistency that can be expected with different pairs of categories, as a function of their terminal content. Grammars do not predict this. They can stipulate a head ordering parameter, but the stipulation is partly right, partly wrong, and above all it is unexplained and hence unexplanatory. Performance preferences and principles such as MiD can predict the degrees of adherence to consistent head ordering, and they provide us with an independent motivation and explanation for this fundamental property of grammars.

We have seen various examples in this book of zero marking in morphosyntax and in morphological paradigms alternating with non-zero and explicit forms. In §6.2 it was shown that agreement marking on noun phrase constituents could be zero under adjacency, alternating with explicit marking when there were discontinuities (as in Warlpiri case copying). This mirrored the strong preference for explicit relativizers in English under non-adjacency (§6.1.1). In §4.1 the distribution of zero forms on Greenberg's markedness hierarchies was shown to be systematically skewed to the higher positions of these hierarchies, i.e. to those that are most frequent in performance and easiest to access and process.[12]

The clear generalization that emerges from these facts is that zero is associated with greater processing ease, i.e. with smaller domains linking the zero-marked constituents to others, and with greater frequency and accessibility permitting the assignment of default values like nominative (rather than accusative and dative), singularity (rather than plurality and duality), etc. This association between zero and ease of processing enrichment follows from MiF (see §3.2.3), hence declining zeros down the hierarchies. But the greater efficiency of more minimal forms then sets up dependencies on neighboring items for the processing of syntactic and semantic relations, and these additional dependencies favor more minimal domains, by MiD.[13] Once again, there appears to be no grammatical explanation for these hierarchies and for the respective environments favoring zero and non-zero forms. Grammars have conventionalized the preferences of performance, and to explain

---

over adjective phrases in an exceptional order, as in head-initial languages) or by MaOP, favoring e.g. NRel (cf. §7.5.2). Single-word postnominal adjectives and postnominal relatives are indeed significantly more frequent than the consistent GenN order in head-final languages; see Hawkins (1983).

[12] See the quantitative formal marking prediction (4.3) and the performance frequency data of §4.1.

[13] For example, explicitly agreeing adjectives or other noun phrase constituents are independently processable as NP-dominated by virtue of their morphology; corresponding items with zero must access the head noun for NP attachment (§2.2). Predicates that are ambiguous between noun and verb must access a neighboring function category for syntactic category assignment (§4.4.2). For a quantification of domain size differences between zero-marked relatives in English and relatives with explicit relative pronouns, see Tables 6.1, 6.2 and §6.1.1.

grammars you have to explain performance and provide a theory of ease of processing.

The Keenan–Comrie Accessibility Hierarchy has been one of the most discussed empirical generalizations about relative clause formation across languages, since it was first proposed in the 1970s. It has received very little attention in the formal grammatical literature. Hierarchies of relativizable positions within a clause do not fit well with a parameterized theory of Universal Grammar when they do not involve the kinds of bounding nodes (IP, NP, etc.) that generative grammarians normally invoke for filler–gap dependencies. Yet there is a growing body of psycholinguistic evidence to support Keenan & Comrie's original intuition of increasing processing complexity down the hierarchy, and I have tried to quantify it (§7.2) and to subsume it under the efficiency principles proposed here. Once again, gaps (i.e. zero marking of the position relativized on) favor the easier-to-process and higher positions on the hierarchy, i.e. those with more minimal domains. The gaps themselves are efficient by MiF since a nominal head is already available and accessible in this structure (§4.6). As the size of filler–gap domains increases, this benefit is outweighed by the increasing non-minimality of both co-indexing and lexical processing domains for the subcategorizor, and gaps are replaced by resumptive pronouns. The pronouns provide local domains for lexical co-occurrence processing and for adjunct processing in the event that the filler is an adjunct, and only co-indexing with the filler needs a larger processing domain. The result is systematic and reverse implicational statements in these grammatical universals, with gaps going from low to high positions, and resumptive pronouns from high to low.[14]

This reverse structuring is not predicted by any grammatical theory I know of, and for good reason. It is not fundamentally a reflection of any deep grammatical principles. It reflects the processing architecture of language users and the interaction between efficiency benefits deriving from less form processing and from the increasing strain on those benefits in non-minimal filler-gap and lexical domains. This interaction is reflected in performance (§7.2.1) and in the variation patterns and preferences that have been 'frozen' in grammars.

But having reached this conclusion for relativizations within a clause, we can look afresh at relativizations and other movements and dependencies across clause boundaries, which have dominated formal grammatical research since Chomsky (1957). Again we find hierarchies of increasing complexity, like the clause-embedding hierarchy of §7.4.1, and again we see a similar distribution of

---

[14] See §7.2.2 and §7.4.1.

gaps in easier positions and pronouns in more complex ones. Generative grammarians are to be credited with the discovery of many of these patterns, but general principles like subjacency that have been proposed for their description have the same weaknesses that the head ordering principle has. They are stipulated, and no attempt is made to provide an explanation for their existence, or for one version rather than another (apart from the usual unsupportable appeal to innateness—see §1.4 and §9.3). And descriptively they are partly right and partly wrong. They are partly right because there are minimal domain preferences for gap structures, and many grammars conventionalize these preferences in a way that corresponds to subjacency formulations. But several do not, and there is no reason why they all should.[15] The hierarchies of §7.4, like the Accessibility Hierarchy, involve quantifiable degrees of processing complexity, and we expect declining language numbers in proportion to these degrees. Hence we have an explanation for grammatical variation here, based on performance data and performance principles, and these data and principles give us a reason for formulating grammars one way rather than another, and for choosing between different models.

I have also given an explanation for adjacency effects in phrase structure (§5.4), which are again essentially stipulated in different grammatical models. Why should complements be closer to their heads than adjuncts, and restrictive adjuncts closer than appositive ones? Performance data reveal adjacency preferences in proportion to the number of processing relations between heads and their sisters. Complements (being lexically listed co-occurrences with frequent dependencies in processing) exhibit many more such relations and dependencies than adjuncts. Restrictive adjuncts in turn involve more mutual dependencies than appositive adjuncts. Basic orders in grammars conventionalize these preferences of performance. The more processing domains there are to exert a minimization preference, the tighter the adjacency.

In §8.6 I discussed Kayne's antisymmetry theory. The Linear Correspondence Axiom, whereby asymmetric c-command maps onto linear precedence in surface structure, is a very interesting proposal in relation to the efficiency principles of this book, especially MaOP. It is still a stipulation, however, and like the other stipulations discussed in this section it appears to be partly right and partly wrong. What is right about it follows from MaOP. When c-commanding nodes precede c-commanded ones, property assignments to the latter can proceed more efficiently. Constituents can be assigned

---

[15] See the counterexamples to Ross's (1967) Complex NP Constraint and to subsequent reformulations in terms of subjacency, in §7.4.1.

immediately to their dominating nodes, many dependencies can be processed immediately, and on-line unassignments (and misassignments) can
be avoided. What is wrong with it also follows from MaOP and especially from
MiD. There are symmetrical dependencies, and most plausibly symmetrical
c-command relations, between pairs such as V and O, and the symmetrical
orderings between these categories are explained here in terms of these symmetrical relations and in terms of MiD effects (such as the optimal efficiency
of both head-initial and head-final structures for many categories). MiD and
MaOP make predictions for degrees of asymmetry in different structural types
(§8.4), and MiD provides a clear motivation for rightward movements of
heavy constituents in head-initial languages. The most plausible basic order
for a (normally quite short) direct object complement in English is immediately after the verb. The rearrangement of a heavy direct object to the
right reinstates minimal domains for phrase structure processing (§5.1.1) and
provides a principled reason for rejecting a theory that disallows rightward
movements.

In §4.6 I offered an explanation for the c-command constraint on so many
dependencies in grammars. I argued that independent relations of phrasal
combination rendered the antecedents of anaphors and the fillers of gaps
'grammatically accessible', and that asymmetries in these (extended) combination relations corresponded to asymmetries in possible dependencies.
A principle of conventionalized dependency was formulated (4.26) according
to which all dependencies of B on A had to involve the grammatical accessibility of A through some independent structural relation, in conjunction with
ease of processing. The hierarchies of filler–gap domains and antecedent–
anaphor environments across languages are grammatical counterparts of the
degrees of accessibility and relative ease of processing enrichment involving
non-grammatical factors (§3.2.3).

The main point I wish to make with these examples is that performance
principles, and the performance data that motivate them, give us an explanation for many fundamental properties of grammars for which there are either
no current principles, or else stipulations with varying degrees of adequacy.
To the extent that the PGCH is supported, a theory that accounts only for
grammars misses significant generalizations. It also fails to incorporate the
principles that can lead to more adequate grammars. Formal models that
stand the greatest chance of being descriptively adequate, according to this
view, are those variants of Optimality Theory that incorporate performance
preferences and hierarchies directly and that seek some functional grounding and explanation for the constraints themselves; see Haspelmath (1999*a*),
Bresnan et al. (2001), and Bresnan & Aissen (2002). Formalization can make

explicit how functional generalizations have been conventionalized in grammars, and it can define all and only the predicted outputs of grammars (the 'factorial typology') with greater precision.

We still need a theory for why the basic hierarchies and functional principles reflected in grammars are the way they are, and this is the major issue I have been dealing with here. All kinds of questions remain to be answered, but it is surprising to me that there has been such a lack of curiosity in formal grammar concerning the ultimate explanation for basic principles. Why is there a subjacency constraint? Why are some categories adjacent and others not? Why are gaps and zero forms found in some environments and not others? Why are some categories asymmetrically ordered and others not? What we have seen is a succession of formal models and principles, each of which has been proposed in an explanatory vacuum. Principles are motivated by descriptive details from particular languages, and it is rare to find grammarians who feel the need to give a reason for why some basic principle should exist and for why it should be formulated in the precise way that it is. Even if one believes in grammatical innateness, why this particular formulation? This has impeded progress, in my opinion, because you don't know which descriptive details to examine unless you have a general theory that can lead you to some data sets rather than others, as a way of refining the general theory. Compounding the problem has been the indifference of most formal linguists to performance data, i.e. to the very data that can provide a principled choice between models and lead to greater descriptive adequacy.[16]

9.3 The ultimate causality of the performance–grammar preferences

If there are profound correspondences between performance patterns and grammars, then one thing seems clear. An innate grammar cannot explain both. Grammars define possible and impossible structures; principles of performance are concerned with selection and processing in real-time language use. Principles of innate grammar determine (in part) the structures available for use, and these principles in combination with language-particular details are, quite plausibly, constantly accessed in production and comprehension. But grammatical principles have not, in general, been shaped by performance, according to Chomsky.[17]

---

[16] See Wasow's (2002) methodological critique of the indifference of formal grammarians to performance data, with which I concur of course.

[17] One possibility that Chomsky does allow for is that processing explanations might be relevant at the level of the evolution of the species (see Chomsky & Lasnik 1977). Performance could have shaped

Yet there are common patterns in grammar and usage, so we do need a more general explanation. We can get one, I have argued, from processing. I have proposed principles of efficiency and complexity that predict the performance selections of different language types. These same principles explain grammars, in conjunction with a theory of language change and adaptation according to which grammars have conventionalized the preferences of performance in proportion to the same degrees that we see in performance data. These conventionalizations have come about through the kinds of diachronic processes described in Haspelmath (1999a) and modeled in the computer simulations of Kirby (1999). Processing plus grammatical evolution give us a framework for the more general explanation that we need.

The details of this explanation will require a model of the human processing architecture. The preferences in different types of performance data in different languages will have to be derivable from this architecture. General organizing principles like MiD (3.1), MiF (3.8), and MaOP (3.16) will also need to be derived from it. We do not currently have a single architecture that psycholinguists are agreed on.[18] But the independent domain from which we draw the ultimate explanation for grammars is now, in contrast to the innateness hypothesis, an empirical one and issues of uncertainty can be resolved. Degrees of complexity in filler–gap domains can be measured in the performance of different languages (including subjacency-violating languages like Akan—see Saah & Goodluck 1995), and theories of their processing can be refined. For the innate grammar there is no such independent evidence apart from learnability arguments, and these are weakened by parallel arguments for which there is no UG solution (§1.4).

Data from grammars can also be of direct relevance for psycholinguistic theorizing, according to the PGCH (cf. §1.2). Grammars are not just bits of conventionalized knowledge that are activated in processing. They reflect the same preferences that performance data do, in relativizable positions, mirror-image weight effects in head-initial and head-final languages, and so on. Grammars can therefore suggest hypotheses for performance testing when

the human language faculty in its evolution, favoring some innate universals of grammar over others. This argument presupposes that there are innate universals of head ordering and subjacency, etc. But I have argued here that these universals are not empirically adequate, so they can scarcely be innate (see §9.2). And this view of the possible connection between performance and grammar does not explain the range of variation and the hierarchies in grammars that are predicted by the PGCH (1.2). See Hawkins (1994: 12–13) for further discussion.

[18] There are profound differences between connectionist and symbolic models in psycholinguistics, there are unresolved issues involving the similarities and differences between production and comprehension, and there are different approaches to working memory, to name just a few bones of current contention.

there are variants, precisely because the conventions are shaped by these same preferences.

My principal goal in this book is not, and cannot be, to define a model of the human processing architecture. I leave that to professional psychologists. What I am trying to do is to correct a view of the performance–grammar relationship that has been very widely accepted since Chomsky (1965) and that is, in my opinion, simply wrong. Many linguists will be reluctant to accept my conclusions about the deep interconnectedness of performance and grammar, but it would be uncharitable to deny that performance has shaped at least some grammatical rules in some languages, and there have been several arguments to this effect since Bever (1970) (cf. §1.1). Even this limited feedback is excluded by the asymmetric relationship between grammar and performance advocated in Chomsky (1965). Chomsky made a very strong claim, based on very little evidence, and many have accepted his philosophizing. This has held back empirical and theoretical research into many fundamental properties of grammatical conventions and their evolution. And it has given to psycholinguists and cognitive scientists a misleading view of grammar according to which grammatical generalizations are orthogonal to the kinds of processing generalizations and acquisition generalizations that these fields are primarily interested in. They are not. There are profound correspondences between them.

The technical machinery that Chomsky gave us has undoubtedly improved grammar-writing. But there comes a point, after many reformulations and notational variants, when it is unclear how we get to the next stage of descriptive adequacy and how we choose between different formalisms. I attribute this to the increasing disconnect between formalization and the search for explanatory principles. Grammatical formalizations can and should incorporate the potentially explanatory principles derived from performance data, and psycholinguists should pay more attention to conventionalized grammatical variation than they currently do.

I assume that much of processing is innately determined ultimately, and I suspect that the innateness of human language resides primarily in the 'architectural innateness' of Elman (1998). Whether and to what extent grammars are also determined by 'representational innateness' of the Chomskyan kind will depend on how far the PGCH can be taken, and on the relationship between architectural and representational features of innateness. I believe that many more features of UG, possibly all, will be derivable from efficiency and complexity considerations of the kind discussed here. But this is speculation, and in the meantime I have focussed on those areas of grammar and performance for which I have some systematic data and some general organizing principles that apply to both.

Many of the preference patterns documented in this book have been discussed in the psycholinguistic literature in terms of working memory load, e.g. by Bever (1970), Frazier & Fodor (1978), Frazier (1979, 1985) and Gibson (1998). In other words, the properties of the innate human processing architecture that have been causally implicated are those that involve the recruitment and computation of different knowledge sources in on-line processing, for which Just & Carpenter (1992) and Gibson (1998) have offered quantified models of capacity constraints in working memory. In Hawkins (1994, 2001) I gave an explanation for EIC and MiD effects in these terms, building on the central insight that there is a gain in simultaneous processing load as domains for the processing of syntactic and semantic relations increase.

I still think that working memory has an explanatory role to play. But there are two issues that arise from the data of this book. First, how exactly do preferences emerge from a theory that sets limits on overall capacity, when many preferences are nowhere close to exceeding the proposed limits? And second, preference data point to the reality of multiple possible causes, not just working memory load, and there has been a tendency in psycholinguistics to ignore these and to subsume everything under working memory.

With regard to the first point, any proposed constraints on working memory capacity are important for grammars since they can potentially explain limits on grammatical variation. Frazier (1985) used the two-stage parsing architecture of Frazier & Fodor (1978) (in which the first stage has a limited viewing window of five or six adjacent words) to explain head adjacency effects in grammatical universals, such as the Greenbergian correlations (§5.3.1). The problem with this and with other explanations of this type is that they are too strong and too weak. They are too strong in that there are exceptional grammars (e.g. those with non-head-adjacent phrases in §§5.3.1–2, whose properties have been linked here to degrees of domain minimization in phrase structure processing). And they are too weak in that the universals they try to explain involve preferences, not absolute structural prohibitions, and the preferences are in the form of patterns that fall within the proposed constraints. Since the constraints are the primary explanatory features of these models, and since they are not exceeded, the preferences are not explained.[19] The same issue arises in relation to the performance data themselves. It is at best unclear how constrained capacity theories can account for structured preferences like those of Chapter 5 when most of the data fall within the proposed capacities.

The second issue is related to the first. What explains the preferences of performance and grammars appears to go well beyond working memory. The

---

[19] See Hawkins (1994: 7–9, 265–8) for elaboration of this point.

MiD principle lends itself most readily to a working memory explanation (if the first problem can be solved), but even here one could appeal to the general speed of processing (everyone is agreed it is fast), and to less processing effort in smaller processing domains, irrespective of whatever capacity constraints there might be. Actual communication is also faster when processing dependencies are resolved in small domains—disambiguating the verb *count* and other lexical co-occurrence ambiguities rapidly, assigning referential indexes and matching fillers with gaps with minimal delays, etc.

MiF involves less articulatory effort on the part of the speaker, and a corresponding reduction in processing effort for the hearer. It also involves less duplication in processing, through fine-tuning to other knowledge sources, to frequency, and to both discourse and grammatical accessibility. All of this makes structures with minimal forms more efficient and less complex than corresponding structures with more duplication.

MaOP reduces on-line processing errors (misassignments) and incomplete property assignments on-line (unassignments). It can also be motivated by general speed of processing and of communication, and (in the case of misassignments) by an avoidance of repairs.

There are several causes here, and a theory of the human processing architecture must incorporate the general properties from which minimal domains, minimal forms, and maximal on-line property assignments can be shown to follow. There are presumably some overall limits on, and architectural properties of, working memory. But there are also efficiencies like MiD, MiF, and MaOP that operate within these limits, that follow from the general architecture, and that are arguably distinct from working memory as such. Even if some efficiency factor (domain minimization) reduces on-line working memory load, this does not necessarily mean that working memory *per se* is the ultimate cause. It could be general processing load or speed, irrespective of the ultimate capacity. We need to tease apart these different causalities, therefore, within a broader theory of the processing architecture, and not throw everything into the working memory basket.

This conclusion is reinforced by the discussion of §8.2.2 in which I argued that some preferences (predicted by MaOP) actually increase working-memory load, as defined in Gibson's (1998) theory. Subject-before-object orderings have lower memory costs than objects before subjects in nominative–accusative languages (German and Finnish), but higher memory costs in ergative–absolutive languages like Avar and Hindi, yet the more costly orders are still preferred in the latter. So they are too in topic before predication structures (§8.2.3) and in complementizer-initial subordinate clauses (§7.5.2). The efficiencies proposed in this book sometimes reduce, but sometimes increase, working memory load, and this underscores the need for a more general processing architecture from which these efficiencies can be derived.[20]

9.4   Some further issues

Many further issues are raised by the PGCH and by the supporting data discussed here. Many linguists and psychologists will not want to accept it, given their current commitments, and they will find fault with various details and indeed with the whole picture, or else they will just ignore it.

I am sure that many of the faults will be justified. There are reasons why research groups band together and pursue a common agenda with common assumptions and methodologies, and the work described here breaks away from this tradition. It is deliberately interdisciplinary, or intersubdisciplinary, drawing on language typology, formal grammar, psycholinguistics, and also historical linguistics, and this kind of attempted synthesis is not easy and runs the risk of appealing to no one and of offending everyone. On the other hand, it also holds out the possibility of connecting some of the better ideas, generalizations, and methodological practices from different fields into a more adequate whole, and I hope that people will view it in that light. You can shoot the postman, therefore, but most of his mail has been written by others, and at some point it is going to be opened, read, and acted on.

Typologists have often been puzzled by my interest in formal grammar, and some even regard me as a formal grammarian. I can assure them that no MIT grammarian does! I just believe that you need an adequate description of the structures whose cross-linguistic distribution you are documenting, and generative grammars often provide one. The performance explanation for typological variation proposed here fits right into the tradition of functional explanations pioneered by Greenberg and continued by other typologists, and there is now a rich body of work in psycholinguistics that is of direct relevance for principles such as 'economy'. Linguists need to know about this, and the cross-linguistic evidence for these principles should, in turn, be of interest to psychologists.[21] Formal grammars and processing theories can contribute to

---

[20] The discussion in this section should make it clear why this book has been structured around the organizing principles of MiD, MiF, and MaOP. Psycholinguistic discussions of syntax have been too focused on working memory, and grammatical models have been largely autonomous of performance. I have made extensive use of descriptive details from psycholinguistic and grammatical models, but none of them gives me the general framework that I think we need. I approve of functionally based Optimality Theories for grammars, though their basic constraints do need to be motivated and not stipulated, for the reasons discussed here and in Haspelmath (1999a).

[21] See Croft (2003) for an overview of these functional principles in language typology.

the descriptive and the explanatory goals of the typological enterprise, as I have tried to show here.

Many formal grammarians take exception to my critique of the innateness hypothesis and of the proposed immunity of grammars to performance. Yet it is these very general points that result in the failure to predict many universal patterns and in numerous stipulations (§9.2). There is no reason why we can't have formal precision and explicitness, and also a more descriptively and explanatorily adequate basis to our formal generalizations, as certain versions of Optimality Theory have shown. The best of generative grammar merges with typological insights here, and processing principles can also motivate the constraints and constraint interactions that form the axioms of these theories.

Psycholinguists have, thank goodness, introduced some scientific rigor and precision into the methods of data collection, and they give linguists like me a hard time over the data we use, and over elicitation techniques, appropriate statistics, etc.—and so they should. But this preoccupation with method comes at a price. Processing theorists do not, in general, know enough languages, and what linguistics they know is often limited to some now-defunct version of a formal model. The PGCH proposal will be rather remote if you are not aware of the typology side of the variation patterns.

The performance data of this book rely too heavily on corpus frequencies for some psycholinguists. In my defense I would point out that I have also drawn extensively on the results of processing experiments, some of them conducted by students and close collaborators (e.g. Stallings 1998, Wasow 2002). The principle of MiD, for example, makes very similar predictions to Gibson's (1998) locality preference in integration domains, and the considerable experimental support that he cites for his theory carries over into mine. Students and collaborators have also helped me with different statistical tests in relation to a lot of my performance data (see Hawkins 2000, Wasow 2002). And for grammatical correlations I have made extensive use of Dryer's (1992) sophisticated sampling and statistical techniques.

Psycholinguists will also want greater clarity on the respective benefits for the producer and for the comprehender of the efficiency principles proposed here, and I wish that I could provide it! Sometimes I have formulated these benefits in terms of comprehension alone, sometimes in terms of both production and comprehension. This is a matter on which there is currently intense debate, and it would be unreasonable to expect me to be the one who has to solve it. What I can do is draw attention to relevant issues that emerge from my data and principles, for example in the discussion of dependencies in processing (§2.2) and when discussing weight effects in different language types (§§5.1.1–2) and I can suggest some conclusions.

The principles of this book provide a partial solution at least to the criticisms that Newmeyer (1998) has leveled against all multiple constraint theories (§1.5). One of these involves the relative strengths of principles. Independent support for relative strengths can come, according to the PGCH, from performance data in languages with choices. These in turn are predicted by the quantitative metrics proposed here. The relative strengths in performance of e.g. phrase structure processing demands and lexical co-occurrence processing in §5.2.1 are predicted by their respective degrees of domain minimization in individual sentences and by the total domain differential metric of §5.2.3. This is a performance theory of relative strength, with wide applicability to other structural alternations in which multiple processing domains are exerting partially competing preferences (see e.g. §5.5.1, §6.1.1, and §7.2.2). The performance variation reflects properties of the relevant sentences in performance. Grammatical rankings with stipulated intervals, as in Stochastic OT, appear to be explainable and the explanation involves properties of individual sentences in performance.

The nature of the interaction between MiD, MiF, and MaOP proceeds in accordance with the definitions given for each. Greater application of MiF results in tighter adjacency and proximity for zero-marked elements by MiD as defined (Chapter 6), for the same reason ultimately that more semantically and grammatically interdependent elements are adjacent and proximate (Chapter 5). The predictions of MiD and MaOP converge on NRel and CompS in head-initial languages, but diverge in head-final languages to give asymmetry in head-initial and symmetry in head-final languages (§7.5.2). MaOP leads to the prediction for more formal marking on NPs and less on verbs in verb-final languages, and to the reverse preference in verb-initial languages (§8.5). And so on.

9.5   Acquisition and learnability

Finally some remarks about a major area of language study for which the efficiency and complexity factors of this book are of direct relevance and about which I have said relatively little: first and second language acquisition and learnability. The precise role of these factors within the 'complex adaptive system' (Gell-Mann 1992) of language acquisition requires a separate study in order to do it justice; here I shall merely raise some issues that specialists in these areas may want to consider.

First, the learnability issue. If a whole range of current UG principles, such as head ordering and subjacency (§9.2), are not in fact innate, then these parameters and constraints will not be available to the learner. The architecture of the human processor can be innate. So can certain general learning procedures of the kind discussed by Braine (1971), Berman (1984), Bowerman (1988), and Slobin (1973). But innate grammatical knowledge about head orderings within phrases and about permitted gap locations for fillers will not be known in advance, according to the theory of this book. Instead, the grammatical universals, hierarchies and preferences are explained now as conventionalizations of performance preferences that can be seen in languages that do not have the relevant grammatical rules and that have evolved into grammatical conventions in proportion to the degree of (performance) motivation for them in the relevant language types.

This conclusion will be unwelcome to learnability theorists. Constraints such as subjacency have always been a prime example of how innateness makes available grammatical restrictions that (it is claimed) cannot be learned from positive evidence alone; see e.g. Hoekstra & Kooij (1988). My approach suggests a different solution to the negative evidence problem, which is a genuine problem regardless of one's theoretical position on innateness since one does have to explain how the child learns the limits on the set of possible sentences that go beyond the positive data to which he or she has been exposed (see Bowerman 1988). The empirical evidence from cross-linguistic universals of head ordering and subjacency do not support proposed grammatical formulations, let alone innateness (see §5.3 and §7.4). And parallel learnability puzzles involving language-particular data further weaken this solution to the negative evidence problem (see §1.4 and Culicover 1999).

Instead, we can propose that learners will comprehend their input and will construct grammars in accordance with innate processing and learning mechanisms. With regard to the former, we can hypothesize that acquisition data will reflect ease of processing, just as adult performance does and just as grammars do. Smaller domains will precede larger ones in grammar acquisition, domains with fewer simultaneous processing demands will precede those with more, parallel function filler–gap structures will come before non-parallel function ones, and so on, all in accordance with Minimize Domains (3.1). In this way the simplest environments on each hierarchy are postulated first, on account of their processing ease, and any extension beyond them to lower hierarchy positions will be forced on the learner by positive evidence from the relevant language. I have argued (in Hawkins 1987) that hierarchies of complexity make predictions for the order of first and second language acquisition. I propose now that the processing complexity that motivates these hierarchies may also explain the negative evidence problem by structuring initial hypotheses and by requiring extensions beyond these to be justified by the data of experience. A similar sequence of events has been proposed in Berwick's (1985) 'subset principle', for which processing can be argued to provide the motivation. Saah & Goodluck (1995) reach a similar conclusion in their discussion of filler–gap processing in English and Akan. It is also possible that learning is facilitated by encountering grammatical instances of a low hierarchy position gap, whereupon the grammaticality of all simpler instances of that construction type can be inferred. All these issues require further theoretical and especially empirical research.

Consider some brief data illustrating the correspondences that one finds between grammars, adult performance, and acquisition. Data from second language acquisition are particularly intriguing from a grammatical and typological perspective, since they involve interlanguage stages that combine the properties of two languages.[22] The manner in which L1 and L2 properties are combined, the relative timing of their acquisition, the error types and avoidance phenomena, etc. all point to the need for a multi-factor predictive model, within which processing complexity is one major factor. In §7.2 I gave some grammatical and performance data supporting the Keenan–Comrie (1977) Accessibility Hierarchy (SU>DO>IO/OBL>GEN), and in particular I showed how the distribution of gaps to resumptive pronouns was very precisely correlated with the simplicity versus complexity of FGDs, in performance and in grammars, see especially Table 7.1. Acquisition data on gaps versus pronoun retention in relative clauses have been collected by Hyltenstam (1984) for different L1 speakers (Persian, Greek, Spanish, and Finnish) learning Swedish as L2, and these data enable us to test whether patterns of acquisition also follow the patterns of grammar and performance.

Swedish has a productive (relative pronoun plus) gap strategy, and does not use resumptive pronouns when relativizing on main clause positions. The L1 grammars in Hyltenstam's study differ according to whether they do (Persian, Greek) or do not (Spanish, Finnish) employ pronouns. Hyltenstam shows that the interlanguage data for the L1/L2 pairs all contain at least some retained pronouns, with their occurrence being especially favored when the L1 also has them. This shows that the transfer of L1 properties is a relevant and contributing factor, but that it is not on its own sufficient to explain the interlanguage data. What is most important in the present context is that the distribution of gaps to pronouns in Hyltenstam's data is systematically correlated with the grammatical data of Table 7.1, i.e. with gaps always more or equally preferred

---

[22] See Gass & Selinker (2001) for a recent summary of the state of the art in second language acquisition research.

in the higher positions and pronouns always more or equally preferred in the lower positions.

In (9.1) and (9.2) I have quantified the distribution of gaps to pronouns for all the subjects listed in Hyltenstam's study (Persians learning Swedish, Greeks learning Swedish, etc.) and for all grammatical positions on the AH (as defined in (7.9) of §7.2 and in Comrie 1989).[23]

(9.1)	*Gaps* (%)	SU	DO	IO/OBL	GEN
	Persian–Swedish	100	42	25	8
	Greek–Swedish	100	58	42	8
	Spanish–Swedish	100	83	62	8
	Finnish–Swedish	100	100	100	33
(9.2)	*Pronouns* (%)	SU	DO	IO/OBL	GEN
	Persian–Swedish	0	58	75	92
	Greek–Swedish	0	42	58	92
	Spanish–Swedish	0	17	38	92
	Finnish–Swedish	0	0	0	67

These data support the general correspondence between conventionalized grammatical data and acquisition data for which I argued in Hawkins (1987). They also suggest that L1 transfer, where it is relevant, operates relative to the same distributional preferences that can be found in grammars and performance, increasing the absolute values for retained pronouns in interlanguages in which the L1 also has such pronouns, but retaining the same relative distribution throughout. It is important to find out whether other factors that facilitate second language acquisition, namely frequency effects, L1–L2 similarity, etc. also operate within the hierarchies and constraints that are motivated by processing, or whether they result in partial mismatches with these.

An interesting case to look at here is the Minimize Forms principle defined in (3.8). In adult processing there is clear evidence for minimal forms of the different types discussed in §3.2 and Chapters 4 and 6. These minimizations result in greater ambiguity, vagueness, and zero specification (cf. §3.2.1), and in the greater exploitation of grammatical dependencies (§4.6) and of other processing enrichments (§3.2.3). In both first and second language acquisition,

---

[23] Hyltenstam (1984) used the original Keenan–Comrie (1977) formulation of the AH with a separate IO and OBL and with an OCOMP. This has been revised to the SU > DO > IO/OBL > GEN hierarchy used here and in Comrie (1989), for the reasons summarized in fn. 5 of §7. Hyltenstam's data provide further support for this revision, since there were some partial exceptions to the AH as originally formulated, yet these data are now highly regular and precisely correlated with the distribution of gaps to pronouns in Table 7.1, as (9.1) and (9.2) show. The figures for IO/OBL collapse the two separate sets of figures given in Hyltenstam (1984).

however, there is clear evidence that a unique one-to-one form–property pairing aids the recognition and learning of the property in question (see Slobin 1973, 1997, E. S. Andersen 1992, R. W. Andersen 1984). One can hypothesize that we are dealing with a general learning mechanism here that asserts itself, especially at the early stages of language acquisition. But once the properties of the adult or L2 grammar have been identified, the general processing preference for minimal unique $F_1 : P_1$ pairs, with concomitant reductions in processing effort and greater exploitation of processing enrichments, should gradually take over, and we should see later acquisition stages that are more in accordance with adult processing and with grammatical conventions.

This, and a whole host of other issues in this fascinating area, requires a separate monograph and will very likely be the topic of a future study.

References

Abney, S. P. (1987), 'The English Noun Phrase in its Sentential Aspect', Ph.D. dissertation, MIT.

Aissen, J. (1999), 'Markedness and Subject Choice in Optimality Theory', *Natural Language and Linguistic Theory* 17: 673–711.

Aldai, G. (2003), 'The Prenominal [−Case] Relativization Strategy of Basque: Conventionalization, Processing and Frame Semantics', MS, Departments of Linguistics, University of Southern California and University of California Los Angeles.

Allwood, J. (1982), 'The Complex NP Constraint in Swedish', in E. Engdahl and E. Ejerhed (eds.), *Readings on Unbounded Dependencies in Scandinavian Languages* (Stockholm: Almqvist & Wiksell).

——Andersson, L.-G., and Dahl, Ö. (1977), *Logic in Linguistics* (Cambridge: Cambridge University Press).

Andersen, E. S. (1992), 'Complexity and Language Acquisition: Influences on the Development of Morphological Systems in Children', in J. A. Hawkins and M. Gell-Mann (eds.), *The Evolution of Human Languages* (Redwood City, Calif.: Addison-Wesley), 241–71.

Andersen, R. W. (1984), 'The One-to-One Principle of Interlanguage Construction', *Language Learning* 34: 77–95.

Anderson, S. R., and Keenan, E. L. (1985), 'Deixis', in T. Shopen (ed.), *Language Typology and Syntactic Description*, vol. 3: *Grammatical Categories and the Lexicon* (Cambridge: Cambridge University Press), 259–308.

Andersson, L.-G. (1982), 'What is Swedish an Exception to? Extractions and Island Constraints', in E. Engdahl and E. Ejerhed (eds.), *Readings on Unbounded Dependencies in Scandinavian Languages* (Stockholm: Almqvist & Wiksell).

Antinucci, F., Duranti, A., and Gebert, L. (1979), 'Relative Clause Structure, Relative Clause Perception and the Change from SOV to SVO', *Cognition* 7: 145–76.

Anward, J., Moravcsik, E., and Stassen, L. (1997), 'Parts of Speech: A Challenge for Typology', *Linguistic Typology* 1: 167–83.

Arbib, M. A., and Hill, J. C. (1988), 'Language Acquisition: Schemas Replace Universal Grammar', in J. A. Hawkins (ed.), *Explaining Language Universals* (Oxford: Blackwell), 56–72.

Ariel, M. (1990), *Accessing Noun-Phrase Antecedents* (London: Routledge).

Arnold, J. E., Wasow, T., Losongco, A., and Ginstrom, R. (2000), 'Heaviness vs. Newness: The Effects of Structural Complexity and Discourse Status on Constituent Ordering', *Language* 76: 28–55.

Bach, E. (1977), 'Comments on the Paper by Chomsky', in P. W. Culicover, T. Wasow, and A. Akmajian (eds.), *Formal Syntax* (New York: Academic Press), 133–55.

BAUER, W. (1993), *Maori* (London: Routledge).

BERMAN, R. A. (1984), 'Cross-Linguistic First Language Perspectives on Second Language Acquisition Research', in R. W. Andersen (ed.), *Second Languages: A Cross-Linguistic Perspective* (Rowley, Mass.: Newbury House), 13–36.

BERWICK, R. (1985), *The Acquisition of Syntactic Knowledge* (Cambridge, Mass.: MIT Press).

BEVER, T. G. (1970), 'The Cognitive Basis for Linguistic Structures', in J. R. Hayes (ed.), *Cognition and the Development of Language* (New York: Wiley), 279–362.

BHAT, D. N. S. (1991), *Grammatical Relations: The Evidence against their Necessity and Universality* (London: Routledge).

BIBER, D., JOHANSSON, S., LEECH, G., CONRAD, S., and FINEGAN, E. (1999), *Longman Grammar of Spoken and Written English* (London: Longman).

BIRNER, B. J., and WARD, G. (1994), 'Uniqueness, Familiarity, and the Definite Article in English', *Berkeley Linguistics Society* 20: 93–102.

BLAKE, B. (1987), *Australian Aboriginal Grammar* (London: Croom Helm).

—— (1990), *Relational Grammar* (London: Routledge).

—— (2001), *Case*, 2nd edn. (Cambridge: Cambridge University Press).

BÖRJARS, K. (1994), 'Swedish Double Determination in a European Typological Perspective', *Nordic Journal of Linguistics* 17: 219–52.

BORNKESSEL, I. (2002), 'The Argument Dependency Model: A Neurocognitive Approach to Incremental Interpretation', Ph.D. dissertation, University of Potsdam.

—— SCHLESEWSKY, M., and FRIEDERICI, A. D. (2003), 'Eliciting Thematic Reanalysis Effects: The Role of Syntax-Independent Information during Parsing', *Language and Cognitive Processes* 18: 269–98.

BOWERMAN, M. (1988), 'The "No Negative Evidence" Problem: How Do Children Avoid Constructing an Overly General Grammar?', in J. A. Hawkins (ed.), *Explaining Language Universals* (Oxford: Blackwell), 73–101.

BRAINE, M. D. S. (1971), 'On Two Types of Models of the Internalization of Grammars', in D. I. Slobin (ed.), *The Ontogenesis of Grammar* (New York: Academic Press).

BRESNAN, J., and AISSEN, J. (2002), 'Optimality and Functionality: Objections and Refutations', *Natural Language and Linguistic Theory* 20: 81–95.

—— DINGARE, S., and MANNING, C. D. (2001), 'Soft Constraints Mirror Hard Constraints: Voice and Person in English and Lummi', in M. Butt and T. H. King (eds.), *Proceedings of the LFG OI Conference* (Stanford, Calif.: CSLI Publications), on-line.

BRIZUELA, M. (1999), 'Definiteness Types in Spanish: A Study of Natural Discourse', Ph.D. dissertation, University of Southern California.

BROSCHART, J. (1997), 'Why Tongan Does it Differently: Categorial Distinctions in a Language without Nouns and Verbs', *Linguistic Typology* 1: 123–65.

BROWN, K., and MILLER, J. (1996), *Concise Encyclopedia of Syntactic Theories* (Oxford: Elsevier Science).

BUECHEL, E. (1939), *A Grammar of Lakhota: The Language of the Teton Sioux Indians* (Rosebud, South Dakota: Rosebud Educational Society).

BYBEE, J. (1985), *Morphology: A Study of the Relation between Meaning and Form* (Amsterdam: Benjamins).

—— and HOPPER, P. (eds.) (2001), *Frequency and the Emergence of Linguistic Structure* (Amsterdam: Benjamins).

CAMPBELL, L. (1998), *Historical Linguistics* (Edinburgh: Edinburgh University Press).

CHOMSKY, N. (1957), *Syntactic Structures* (The Hague: Mouton).

—— (1965), *Aspects of the Theory of Syntax* (Cambridge, Mass.: MIT Press).

—— (1968), *Language and Mind* (New York: Harcourt, Brace & World).

—— (1973), 'Conditions on Transformations', in S. R. Anderson and P. Kiparsky (eds.), *Festschrift for Morris Halle* (New York: Holt, Rinehart & Winston), 232–86.

—— (1975), *Reflections on Language* (New York: Pantheon).

—— (1981), *Lectures on Government and Binding* (Dordrecht: Foris).

—— (1986), *Barriers* (Cambridge, Mass.: MIT Press).

—— and LASNIK, H. (1977), 'Filters and Control', *Linguistic Inquiry* 8: 425–504.

CHRISTOPHERSEN, P. (1939), *The Articles: A Study of their Theory and Use in English* (Copenhagen: Munksgaard).

CHUNG, S. (1982), 'Unbounded Dependencies in Chamorro Grammar', *Linguistic Inquiry* 13: 39–77.

—— (1994), 'WH-Agreement and "Referentiality" in Chamorro', *Linguistic Inquiry* 25: 1–44.

CLANCY, P. M., LEE, H., and ZOH, M. (1986), 'Processing Strategies in the Acquisition of Relative Clauses', *Cognition* 14: 225–62.

CLARK, H. H., and HAVILAND, S. (1977), 'Comprehension and the Given–New Contract', in R. Freedle (ed.), *Discourse Production and Comprehension* (Hillsdale, NJ: Erlbaum), 1–40.

—— and MARSHALL, C. R. (1981), 'Definite Reference and Mutual Knowledge', in A. Joshi, B. Webber, and I. Sag (eds.), *Elements of Discourse Understanding* (Cambridge: Cambridge University Press), 10–63.

CLEMENTS, G. N., McCLOSKEY, J., MALING, J., and ZAENEN, A. (1983), 'String-Vacuous Rule Application', *Linguistic Inquiry* 14: 1–17.

CLIFTON, C., and FRAZIER, L. (1989), 'Comprehending Sentences with Long-Distance Dependencies', in G. N. Carlson and M. K. Tannenhaus (eds.), *Linguistic Structure in Language Processing* (Dordrecht: Kluwer).

COLE, P. (1976), 'An Apparent Asymmetry in the Formation of Relative Clauses in Modern Hebrew', in P. Cole (ed.), *Studies in Modern Hebrew Syntax and Semantics* (Amsterdam: North-Holland), 231–47.

COMRIE, B. (1973), 'Clause Structure and Movement Constraints in Russian', in C. Corum, T. C. Smith-Stark, and A. Weiser (eds.), *You Take the High Road and I'll Take the Low Node* (Chicago: Chicago Linguistic Society), 291–304.

—— (1978), 'Ergativity', in W. P. Lehmann (ed.), *Syntactic Typology: Studies in the Phenomenology of Language* (Austin: University of Texas Press).

—— (1984), 'Form and Function in Explaining Language Universals', in B. Butterworth, B. Comrie, and Ö. Dahl (eds.), *Explanations for Language Universals* (New York: Mouton), 87–103.

—— (1989), *Language Universals and Linguistic Typology*, 2nd edn. (Chicago: University of Chicago Press).

COMRIE, B. (1998), 'Rethinking the Typology of Relative Clauses', *Language Design* 1: 59–86.

—— (2003), 'Typology and Language Acquisition: The Case of Relative Clauses', in A. G. Ramat (ed.), *Typology and Second Language Acquisition* (Berlin: de Gruyter), 19–37.

CORBETT, G. G. (1991), *Gender* (Cambridge: Cambridge University Press).

—— (2000), *Number* (Cambridge: Cambridge University Press).

—— and HAYWARD, R. J. (1987), 'Gender and Number in Bayso', *Lingua* 73: 1–28.

—— FRASER, N. M., and McGLASHAN, S. (eds.) (1993), *Heads in Grammatical Theory* (Cambridge: Cambridge University Press).

CROFT, W. (1990), *Typology and Universals* (Cambridge: Cambridge University Press).

—— (2001), *Radical Construction Grammar: Syntactic Theory in Typological Perspective* (Oxford: Oxford University Press).

—— (2003), *Typology and Universals*, 2nd edn. (Cambridge: Cambridge University Press).

CULICOVER, P. W. (1993), 'Evidence against ECP Accounts of the That-t Effect', *Linguistic Inquiry* 26: 249–75.

—— (1999), *Syntactic Nuts: Hard Cases, Syntactic Theory and Language Acquisition* (Oxford: Oxford University Press).

—— and WILKINS, W. K. (1984), *Locality in Linguistic Theory* (Orlando, Fla.: Academic Press).

DE SMEDT, K. J. M. J. (1994), 'Parallelism in Incremental Sentence Generation', in G. Adriaens and U. Hahn (eds.), *Parallelism in Natural Language Processing* (Norwood, NJ: Ablex).

DEL GOBBO, F. (2003), 'Appositives and Chinese Relative Clauses', in *Papers from the 38th Meeting of the Chicago Linguistic Society*, vol. 1 (Chicago: Chicago Linguistic Society), 175–90.

DIESING, M. (1990), 'Verb Movement and the Subject Position in Yiddish', *Natural Language and Linguistic Theory* 8: 41–79.

DIESSEL, H. (1999a), 'The Morphosyntax of Demonstratives in Synchrony and Diachrony', *Linguistic Typology* 3: 1–49.

—— (1999b), *Demonstratives: Form, Function and Grammaticalization* (Amsterdam: John Benjamins).

—— (2001), 'The Ordering Distribution of Main and Subordinate Clauses: A Typological Study', *Language* 77: 433–55.

DIXON, R. M. W. (1994), *Ergativity* (Cambridge: Cambridge University Press).

—— (1999), 'Arawá', in R. M. W. Dixon and A. Y. Aikhenvald (eds.), *The Amazonian Languages* (Cambridge: Cambridge University Press), 293–306.

DOWTY, D. R. (1991), 'Thematic Proto-Roles and Argument Selection', *Language* 67: 547–619.

DRYER, M. S. (1980), 'The Positional Tendencies of Sentential Noun Phrases in Universal Grammar', *Canadian Journal of Linguistics* 25: 123–95.

—— (1989), 'Large Linguistic Areas and Language Sampling', *Studies in Language* 13: 257–92.

—— (1991), 'SVO languages and the OV : VO Typology', *Journal of Linguistics* 27: 443–82.

—— (1992), 'The Greenbergian Word Order Correlations', *Language* 68: 81–138.

—— (1993), 'Modifying Hawkins' Prepositional Noun Modifier Hierarchy', Paper presented at the Linguistic Society of America Annual Meeting, Los Angeles.

—— (2002), 'Case Distinctions, Rich Verb Agreement, and Word Order Type', *Theoretical Linguistics* 28: 151–7.

Du Bois, J. W. (1987), 'The Discourse Basis of Ergativity', *Language* 63: 805–55.

Ebert, K. H. (1971a), *Referenz, Sprechsituation und die bestimmten Artikel in einem nordfriesischen Dialekt (Fering)* (Bredstedt: Nordfriisk Instituut).

—— (1971b), 'Zwei Formen des bestimmten Artikels', in D. Wunderlich (ed.), *Probleme und Fortschritte der Transformationsgrammatik* (Munich: Hueber), 159–74.

Elman, J. (1998), *Rethinking Innateness: A Connectionist Perspective on Development* (Cambridge, Mass.: MIT Press).

Engdahl, E. (1982), 'Restrictions on Unbounded Dependencies in Swedish', in E. Engdahl and E. Ejerhed (eds.), *Readings on Unbounded Dependencies in Scandinavian Languages* (Stockholm: Almqvist & Wiksell), 151–74.

Erdmann, P. (1988), 'On the Principle of "Weight" in English', in C. Duncan-Rose and T. Vennemann (eds.), *On Language, Rhetorica, Phonologica, Syntactica: A Festschrift for Robert P. Stockwell from his Friends and Colleagues* (London: Routledge), 325–39.

Erteschik-Shir, N. (1992), 'Resumptive Pronouns in Islands', in H. Goodluck and M. Rochemont (eds.), *Island Constraints: Theory, Acquisition and Processing* (Dordrecht: Kluwer), 89–108.

—— and Lappin, S. (1979), 'Dominance and the Functional Explanation of Island Phenomena', *Theoretical Linguistics* 6: 41–86.

Fillmore, C. J. (1968), 'The Case for Case', in E. Bach and R. T. Harms (eds.), *Universals of Linguistic Theory* (New York: Holt, Rinehart & Winston).

Firbas, J. (1966), 'On the Concept of Communicative Dynamism in the Theory of Functional Sentence Perspective', *Sbornik Praci Filosoficke Fakulty Brnenske University*, A-19: 135–44.

Fodor, J. A. (1983), *The Modularity of Mind* (Cambridge, Mass.: MIT Press).

—— Bever, T. G., and Garrett, M. F. (1974), *The Psychology of Language* (New York: McGraw-Hill).

Fodor, J. D. (1978), 'Parsing Strategies and Constraints on Transformations', *Linguistic Inquiry* 8: 425–504.

—— (1983), 'Phrase Structure Parsing and the Island Constraints', *Linguistics and Philosophy* 6: 163–223.

—— (1984), 'Constraints on Gaps: Is the Parser a Significant Influence?', in B. Butterworth, B. Comrie, and Ö. Dahl (eds.), *Explanations for Language Universals* (Berlin: Mouton), 9–34.

FODOR, J. D. (1989), 'Empty Categories in Sentence Processing', *Language and Cognitive Processes* 3: 155–209.

FOLEY, W. (1980), 'Toward a Universal Typology of the Noun Phrase', *Studies in Language* 4: 171–99.

FORD, M. (1983), 'A Method of Obtaining Measures of Local Parsing Complexity throughout Sentences', *Journal of Verbal Learning and Verbal Behavior* 22: 203–18.

FRANCIS, W. N., and KUČERA, H. (1982), *Frequency Analysis of English Usage: Lexicon and Grammar* (Boston: Houghton Mifflin).

FRAUENFELDER, U., SEGUI, J., and MEHLER, J. (1980), 'Monitoring around the Relative Clause', *Journal of Verbal Learning and Verbal Behavior* 19: 328–37.

FRAZIER, L. (1979), 'On Comprehending Sentences: Syntactic Parsing Strategies' (Bloomington: Indiana University Linguistics Club).

—— (1985), 'Syntactic Complexity', in D. Dowty, L. Karttunen, and A. Zwicky (eds.), *Natural Language Parsing* (Cambridge: Cambridge University Press), 129–89.

—— (1987), 'Syntactic Processing: Evidence from Dutch', *Natural Language and Linguistic Theory* 5: 519–59.

—— and FLORES D'ARCAIS, G. B. (1989), 'Filler Driven Parsing: A Study of Gap Filling in Dutch', *Journal of Memory and Language* 28: 331–44.

—— and FODOR, J. D. (1978), 'The Sausage Machine: A New Two-Stage Parsing Model', *Cognition* 6: 291–326.

GASS, S. M., and SELINKER, L. (2001), *Second Language Acquisition: An Introductory Course*, 2nd edn. (London: Erlbaum).

GAZDAR, G., KLEIN, E., PULLUM, G. K., and SAG, I. (1985), *Generalized Phrase Structure Grammar* (Cambridge, Mass.: Harvard University Press).

GELL-MANN, M. (1992), 'Complexity and Complex Adaptive Systems', in J. A. Hawkins and M. Gell-Mann (eds.), *The Evolution of Human Languages* (Redwood City, Calif.: Addison-Wesley), 3–18.

GERNSBACHER, M. A. (1990), *Language Comprehension as Structure Building* (Hillsdale, NJ: Erlbaum).

GIBSON, E. (1998), 'Linguistic Complexity: Locality of Syntactic Dependencies', *Cognition* 68: 1–76.

GILLIGAN, G. M. (1987), 'A Cross-Linguistic Approach to the Pro-Drop Parameter', Ph.D. dissertation, University of Southern California.

GIVÓN, T. (1979), *On Understanding Grammar* (New York: Academic Press).

—— (ed.) (1983), *Topic Continuity in Discourse: A Quantitative Cross-Language Study* (Amsterdam: Benjamins).

—— (1988), 'The Pragmatics of Word Order: Predictability, Importance and Attention', in M. Hammond, E. Moravcsik, and J. R. Wirth (eds.), *Studies in Syntactic Typology* (Amsterdam: Benjamins), 243–84.

—— (1995), *Functionalism and Grammar* (Amsterdam: Benjamins).

GOLDBERG, A. E. (1995), *Constructions: A Construction Grammar Approach to Argument Structure* (Chicago: University of Chicago Press).

GREENBERG, J. H. (1957), 'Order of Affixing: A Study in General Linguistics', in J. H. Greenberg, *Essays in Linguistics* (Chicago: Chicago University Press), 86–94.

—— (1963), 'Some Universals of Grammar with Particular Reference to the Order of Meaningful Elements', in J. H. Greenberg (ed.), *Universals of Language* (Cambridge, Mass.: MIT Press), 73–113.

—— (1966), *Language Universals, with Special Reference to Feature Hierarchies* (The Hague: Mouton).

—— (1978), 'How Does a Language Acquire Gender Markers?', in J. H. Greenberg, C. A. Ferguson, and E. A. Moravcsik (eds.), *Universals of Human Language*, vol. 3: *Word Structure* (Stanford, Calif.: Stanford University Press), 47–82.

GREWENDORF, G. (1991), *Aspekte der deutschen Syntax* (Tübingen: Narr).

GRICE, H. P. (1975), 'Logic and Conversation', in P. Cole and J. Morgan (eds.), *Speech Acts* (New York: Academic Press), 41–58.

GRIMSHAW, J. (1990), *Argument Structure* (Cambridge, Mass.: MIT Press).

—— (1997), 'Projection, Heads, and Optimality', *Linguistic Inquiry* 28: 373–422.

GUNDEL, J. K. (1988), 'Universals of Topic-Comment Structure', in M. Hammond, E. Moravcsik, and J. R. Wirth (eds.), *Studies in Syntactic Typology* (Amsterdam: Benjamins), 209–39.

GUY, G., and BAYLEY, R. (1995), 'Relative Pronouns in English', *American Speech* 70: 148–62.

HAIG, J. H. (1996), 'Subjacency and Japanese Grammar: A Functional Account', *Studies in Language* 20: 53–92.

HAIMAN, J. (1978), 'Conditionals are Topics', *Language* 59: 564–89.

—— (1983), 'Iconic and Economic Motivation', *Language* 59: 781–819.

—— (1985), *Natural Syntax* (Cambridge: Cambridge University Press).

HALL, C. J. (1992), *Morphology and Mind* (London: Routledge).

HANKAMER, J., and SAG, I. (1976), 'Deep and Surface Anaphora', *Linguistic Inquiry* 7: 391–428.

HASPELMATH, M. (1999a), 'Optimality and Diachronic Adaptation', *Zeitschrift für Sprachwissenschaft* 18: 180–205.

—— (1999b), 'Explaining Article–Possessor Complementarity: Economic Motivation in Noun Phrase Syntax', *Language* 75: 227–43.

—— (2002), *Morphology* (London: Arnold).

HAWKINS, J. A. (1978), *Definiteness and Indefiniteness: A Study in Reference and Grammaticality Prediction* (London: Croom Helm).

—— (1983), *Word Order Universals* (New York: Academic Press).

—— (1986), *A Comparative Typology of English and German: Unifying the Contrasts* (Austin: University of Texas Press).

—— (1987), 'Implicational Universals as Predictors of Language Acquisition', *Linguistics* 25: 453–73.

—— (1988), 'Explaining Language Universals', in J. A. Hawkins (ed.), *Explaining Language Universals* (Oxford: Blackwell), 3–28.

—— (1990), 'A Parsing Theory of Word Order Universals', *Linguistic Inquiry* 21: 223–61.

—— (1991), 'On (In)definite Articles: Implicatures and (Un)grammaticality Prediction', *Journal of Linguistics* 27: 405–42.

HAWKINS, J. A. (1993), 'Heads, Parsing, and Word Order Universals', in Corbett et al. (1993: 231–65).

—— (1994), *A Performance Theory of Order and Constituency* (Cambridge: Cambridge University Press).

—— (1995), 'Argument–Predicate Structure in Grammar and Performance: A Comparison of English and German', in I. Rauch and G. F. Carr (eds.), *Insights in Germanic Linguistics*, vol. 1 (Berlin: de Gruyter), 127–144.

—— (1998*a*), 'Some Issues in a Performance Theory of Word Order', in A. Siewierska (ed.), *Constituent Order in the Languages of Europe* (Berlin: de Gruyter), 729–81.

—— (1998*b*), 'Morphological Hierarchies in the History of Germanic', *International Journal of Germanic Linguistics and Semiotic Analysis* 3: 197–217.

—— (1998*c*), 'A Typological Approach to Germanic Morphology', in J. O. Askedal (ed.), *Historische Germanische und Deutsche Syntax* (Frankfurt am Main: Lang), 49–68.

—— (1999), 'Processing Complexity and Filler–Gap Dependencies', *Language* 75: 244–85.

—— (2000), 'The Relative Order of Prepositional Phrases in English: Going beyond Manner–Place–Time', *Language Variation and Change* 11: 231–66.

—— (2001), 'Why are Categories Adjacent?', *Journal of Linguistics* 37: 1–34.

—— (2002*a*), 'Symmetries and Asymmetries: Their Grammar, Typology and Parsing', *Theoretical Linguistics* 28: 95–149.

—— (2002*b*), 'Issues at the Performance–Grammar Interface: Some Comments on the Commentaries', *Theoretical Linguistics* 28: 211–27.

—— and CUTLER, A. (1988), 'Psycholinguistic Factors in Morphological Asymmetry', in J. A. Hawkins (ed.), *Explaining Language Universals* (Oxford: Blackwell), 280–317.

—— and GILLIGAN, G. M. (1988), 'Prefixing and Suffixing Universals in Relation to Basic Word Order', in J. A. Hawkins and H. K. Holmback (eds.), *Papers in Universal Grammar: Generative and Typological Approaches*, Lingua Special Issue, 74(2/3): 219–59.

HAYS, D. G. (1964), 'Dependency Theory: A Formalism and Some Observations', *Language* 40: 511–25.

HEINE, B., and KUTEVA, T. (2002), *World Lexicon of Grammaticalization* (Cambridge: Cambridge University Press).

—— and REH, M. (1984), *Grammaticalisation and Reanalysis in African Languages* (Hamburg: Buske).

HEINRICHS, H. M. (1954), *Studien zum bestimmten Artikel in den germanischen Sprachen* (Giessen: Schmitz).

HENGEVELD, K. (1992), 'Parts of Speech', in M. Fortescue, P. Harder, and L. Kristoffersen (eds.), *Layered Structure and Reference in a Functional Perspective* (Amsterdam: Benjamins), 29–56.

HIMMELMANN, N. P. (1998), 'Regularity in Irregularity: Article Use in Adpositional Phrases', *Linguistic Typology* 2: 315–53.

HODLER, W. (1954), *Grundzüge einer germanischen Artikellehre* (Heidelberg: Winter).

HOEKSTRA, T., and KOOIJ, J. G. (1988), 'The Innateness Hypothesis', in J. A. Hawkins (ed.), *Explaining Language Universals* (Oxford: Blackwell), 31–55.

HOLMES, V. M., and O'REGAN, J. K. (1981), 'Eye Fixation Patterns during the Reading of Relative Clause Sentences', *Journal of Verbal Learning and Verbal Behavior* 20: 417–30.

HOPPER, P. J., and TRAUGOTT, E. C. (1993), *Grammaticalization* (Cambridge: Cambridge University Press).

HUANG, Y. (2000), *Anaphora: A Cross-Linguistic Approach* (Oxford: Oxford University Press).

HUKARI, T. E., and LEVINE, R. D. (1995), 'Adjunct Extraction', *Journal of Linguistics* 31: 195–226.

HURFORD, J. (2000), 'Social Transmission Favors Linguistic Generalization', in C. Knight, M. Studdert-Kennedy, and J. R. Hurford (eds.), *Approaches to the Evolution of Language: The Emergence of Phonology and Syntax* (Cambridge: Cambridge University Press), 324–52.

HYLTENSTAM, K. (1984), 'The Use of Typological Markedness Conditions as Predictors in Second Language Acquisition: The Case of Pronominal Copies in Relative Clauses', in R. W. Andersen (ed.), *Second Languages: A Cross-Linguistic Perspective* (Rowley, Mass.: Newbury House), 39–58.

JACKENDOFF, R. (1977), *X-bar Syntax: A Study of Phrase Structure* (Cambridge, Mass.: MIT Press).

JACOBS, J. (2001), 'The Dimensions of Topic-Comment', *Linguistics* 39: 641–81.

JAGGER, P. J. (1985), 'Factors Governing the Morphological Coding of Referents in Hausa Narrative Discourse', Ph.D. dissertation, University of California Los Angeles.

JELINEK, E., and DEMERS, R. (1983), 'The Agent Hierarchy and Voice in some Coast Salish Languages', *International Journal of American Linguistics* 49: 167–85.

————— (1994), 'Predicates and Pronominal Arguments in Straits Salish', *Language* 70: 697–736.

JOSEPH, B., and PHILIPPAKI-WARBURTON, I. (1987), *Modern Greek* (London: Croom Helm).

JUST, M. A., and CARPENTER, P. A. (1992), 'A Capacity Theory of Comprehension: Individual Differences in Working Memory', *Psychological Review* 99:122–49.

KAYNE, R. S. (1994), *The Antisymmetry of Syntax* (Cambridge, Mass.: MIT Press).

—— and POLLOCK, J.-Y. (1978), 'Stylistic Inversion, Successive Cyclicity, and Move NP', *Linguistic Inquiry* 9: 595–621.

KEENAN, E. L. (1972a), 'The Logical Status of Deep Structures', in L. Heilmann (ed.), *Proceedings of the Eleventh International Congress of Linguists* (Bologna: il Mulino), 477–95. Reprinted in Keenan (1987: 337–60).

—— (1972b), 'Relative Clause Formation in Malagasy (and Some Related and not so Related Languages)', in P. M. Peranteau, J. N. Levi, and G. C. Phares (eds.), *The Chicago Which Hunt* (Chicago: Chicago Linguistic Society), 169–90.

—— (1975), 'Variation in Universal Grammar', in R. Fasold and R. Shuy (eds.), *Analyzing Variation in English* (Washington, DC: Georgetown University Press), 136–48. Repr. in Keenan (1987: 46–59).

KEENAN, E. L. (1976a), 'Remarkable Subjects in Malagasy', in C. N. Li (ed.), *Subject and Topic* (New York: Academic Press).

—— (1976b), 'Towards a Universal Definition of "Subject of"', in C. N. Li (ed.), *Subject and Topic* (New York: Academic Press). Repr. in Keenan (1987: 89–120).

—— (1979), 'On Surface Form and Logical Form', *Studies in the Linguistic Sciences* 8: 163–203. Repr. in Keenan (1987: 375–428).

—— (1985), 'Passive in the World's Languages', in T. Shopen (ed.), *Language Typology and Syntactic Description*, vol. 1 *Clause Structure* (Cambridge: Cambridge University Press), 243–81.

—— (1987), *Universal Grammar: 15 Essays* (London: Croom Helm).

—— and COMRIE, B. (1977), 'Noun Phrase Accessibility and Universal Grammar', *Linguistic Inquiry* 8: 63–99. Repr. in Keenan (1987: 3–45).

—— —— (1979), 'Data on the Noun Phrase Accessibility Hierarchy', *Language* 55: 333–51.

—— and HAWKINS, S. (1987), 'The Psychological Validity of the Accessibility Hierarchy', in Keenan (1987: 60–85).

KEMPEN, G. (2003), 'Cognitive Architectures for Human Grammatical Encoding and Decoding', MS, Max-Planck-Institute for Psycholinguistics, Nijmegen.

KEMPSON, R. M. (1977), *Semantic Theory* (Cambridge: Cambridge University Press).

KIM, A. H. (1988), 'Preverbal Focusing and Type XXIII Languages', in M. Hammond, E. Moravcsik, and J. R. Wirth (eds.), *Studies in Syntactic Typology* (Amsterdam: Benjamins), 147–69.

KIMBALL, J. (1973), 'Seven Principles of Surface Structure Parsing in Natural Language', *Cognition* 2: 15–47.

KING, J., and JUST, M. A. (1991), 'Individual Differences in Syntactic Processing: The Role of Working Memory', *Journal of Memory and Language* 30: 580–602.

—— and KUTAS, M. (1992), 'ERP Responses to Sentences That Vary in Syntactic Complexity: Differences between Good and Poor Comprehenders', poster presented at the Annual Conference of the Society for Psychophysiological Research, San Diego, Calif.

—— —— (1993), 'Bridging Gaps with Longer Spans: Enhancing ERP Studies of Parsing', poster presented at the Sixth Annual CUNY Sentence Processing Conference, University of Massachusetts, Amherst.

KIPARSKY, P., and KIPARSKY, C. (1970), 'Fact', in M. Bierwisch and K. E. Heidolph (eds.), *Progress in Linguistics* (The Hague: Mouton), 143–73.

KIRBY, S. (1999), *Function, Selection and Innateness* (Oxford: Oxford University Press).

KISS, K. E. (1987), *Configurationality in Hungarian* (Dordrecht: Reidel).

—— (2002), *The Syntax of Hungarian* (Cambridge: Cambridge University Press).

KLUENDER, R. (1992), 'Deriving Island Constraints from Principles of Predication', in H. Goodluck and M. Rochemont (eds.), *Island Constraints: Theory, Acquisition and Processing* (Dordrecht: Kluwer), 223–58.

—— and KUTAS, M. (1993a), 'Subjacency as a Processing Phenomenon', *Language and Cognitive Processes* 8: 573–633.

————(1993*b*), 'Bridging the Gap: Evidence from ERPs on the Processing of Unbounded Dependencies', *Journal of Cognitive Neuroscience* 5: 196–214.

König, E., and van der Auwera, J. (1994), *The Germanic Languages* (London: Routledge).

—— and Siemund, P. (2000), 'Intensifiers and Reflexives: A Typological Perspective', in Z. Frajzyngier and T. S. Curl (eds.), *Reflexives: Forms and Functions* (Amsterdam: Benjamins), 41–74.

Kuno, S. (1973*a*), 'Constraints on Internal Clauses and Sentential Subjects', *Linguistic Inquiry* 4: 363–85.

—— (1973*b*), *The Structure of the Japanese Language* (Cambridge, Mass.: MIT Press).

—— (1974), 'The Position of Relative Clauses and Conjunctions', *Linguistic Inquiry* 5: 117–36.

Kvam, S. (1983), *Linksverschachtelung im Deutschen und Norwegischen* (Tübingen: Niemeyer).

Lehmann, C. (1984), *Der Relativsatz* (Tübingen: Narr).

—— (1995), *Thoughts on Grammaticalization* (Munich: Lincom Europa).

Lehmann, W. P. (1978), 'The Great Underlying Ground-Plans', in W. P. Lehmann (ed.), *Syntactic Typology: Studies in the Phenomenology of Language* (Austin: University of Texas Press), 3–55.

Levelt, W. J. M. (1989), *Speaking: From Intention to Articulation* (Cambridge, Mass.: MIT Press).

Levi, J. N. (1978), *The Syntax and Semantics of Complex Nominals* (New York: Academic Press).

Levinson, S. C. (1983), *Pragmatics* (Cambridge: Cambridge University Press).

—— (2000), *Presumptive Meanings: The Theory of Generalized Conversational Implicature* (Cambridge, Mass.: MIT Press).

Li, C. N., and Thompson, S. A. (1981), *A Functional Reference Grammar of Mandarin Chinese* (Berkeley: University of California Press).

Lichtenberk, F. (1983), *A Grammar of Manam* (Honolulu: University of Hawaii Press).

Lindblom, B., and Maddieson, I. (1988), 'Phonetic Universals in Consonant Systems', in L. M. Hyman and C. N. Li (eds.), *Language, Speech and Mind: Studies in Honour of Victoria A. Fromkin* (London: Routledge).

—— MacNeilage, P., and Studdert-Kennedy, M. (1984), 'Self-Organizing Processes and the Explanation of Phonological Universals', in B. Butterworth, B. Comrie, and Ö. Dahl (eds.), *Explanations for Language Universals* (New York: Mouton).

Lohse, B. (2000), 'Zero versus Explicit Marking in Relative Clauses', MS, Department of Linguistics, University of Southern California.

Lyons, C. (1999), *Definiteness* (Cambridge: Cambridge University Press).

Lyons, J. (1968), *Introduction to Theoretical Linguistics* (Cambridge: Cambridge University Press).

—— (1977), *Semantics* (2 vols., Cambridge: Cambridge University Press).

—— (1995), *Linguistic Semantics* (Cambridge: Cambridge University Press).

McCloskey, J. (1979), *Transformational Syntax and Model-Theoretic Semantics: A Case Study in Modern Irish* (Dordrecht: Reidel).

MacDonald, M. C., and Christiansen, M. (2002), 'Reassessing Working Memory: Comment on Just and Carpenter (1992) and Waters and Caplan (1996)', *Psychological Review* 109: 35–54.

—— Pearlmutter, N. J., and Seidenberg, M. S. (1994), 'The Lexical Nature of Syntactic Ambiguity Resolution', *Psychological Review* 101: 676–703.

MacWhinney, B. (1982), 'Basic Syntactic Processes', in S. Kuczaj (ed.), *Language Acquisition: Syntax and Semantics* (Mahwah, NJ: Erlbaum).

Mallinson, G. (1986), *Rumanian* (London: Croom Helm).

Manning, C. D. (2003), 'Probabilistic Syntax', in R. Bod, J. Hay, and S. Jannedy (eds.), *Probability Theory in Linguistics* (Cambridge, Mass.: MIT Press), 289–341.

Marcus, M. (1980), *A Theory of Syntactic Recognition for Natural Language* (Cambridge, Mass.: MIT Press).

Marslen-Wilson, W. D. (1989), 'Access and Integration: Projecting Sound onto Meaning', in W. D. Marslen-Wilson (ed.), *Lexical Representation and Process* (Cambridge: Cambridge University Press), 3–24.

—— and Tyler, L. K. (1980), 'The Temporal Structure of Spoken Language Understanding', *Cognition* 8: 1–71.

—— —— (1987), 'Against Modularity', in J. L. Garfield (ed.), *Modularity in Knowledge Representation and Natural Language Understanding* (Cambridge, Mass.: MIT Press).

Mater, E. (1971), *Deutsche Verben* (Leipzig: VEB Bibliographisches Institut).

Matsui, T. (2000), *Bridging and Relevance* (Amsterdam: Benjamins).

Matsumoto, Y. (1997), *Noun-Modifying Constructions in Japanese: A Frame Semantic Approach* (Amsterdam: Benjamins).

Matthews, S., and Yeung, L. Y. Y. (2001), 'Processing Motivations for Topicalization in Cantonese', in K. Horie and S. Sato (eds.), *Cognitive-Functional Linguistics in an East Asian Context* (Tokyo: Kurosio), 81–102.

—— and Yip, V. (1994), *Cantonese: A Comprehensive Grammar* (London: Routledge).

—— —— (2003), 'Relative Clauses in Early Bilingual Development: Transfer and Universals', in A. G. Ramat (ed.), *Typology and Second Language Acquisition* (Berlin: de Gruyter).

Maxwell, D. N. (1979), 'Strategies of Relativization and NP Accessibility', *Language* 55: 352–71.

Meillet, A. (1912), 'L'Évolution des formes grammaticales', *Scientia* 12–26 (Milan). Repr. in *Linguistique historique et linguistique générale* (Paris: Champion, 1948), 130–148.

Miller, G. A., and Chomsky, N. (1963), 'Finitary Models of Language Users', in R. D. Luce, R. Bush, and E. Galanter (eds.), *Handbook of Mathematical Psychology*, vol. 2 (New York: Wiley), 419–92.

Minsky, M. (1975), 'A Framework for Representing Knowledge', in P. Winston (ed.), *The Psychology of Computer Vision* (New York: McGraw-Hill), 211–77.

Moravcsik, E. (1995), 'Summing up Suffixaufnahme', in Plank (1995: 451–84).

MOORTGAT, M. (1988), *Categorial Investigations: Logical and Linguistic Aspects of the Lambek Calculus* (Dordrecht: Foris).

MÜLLER-GOTAMA, F. (1994), *Grammatical Relations: A Cross-Linguistic Perspective on their Syntax and Semantics* (Berlin: de Gruyter).

NEVILLE, H. J., NICHOL, J. L., BARSS, A., FORSTER, K. I., and GARRETT, M. F. (1991), 'Syntactically Based Sentence Processing Classes: Evidence from Event-Related Brain Potentials', *Journal of Cognitive Neuroscience* 3: 151–65.

NEWMEYER, F. J. (1998), *Language Form and Language Function* (Cambridge, Mass.: MIT Press).

—— (2002), 'Optimality and Functionality: A Critique of Functionally Based Optimality-Theoretic Syntax', *Natural Language and Linguistic Theory* 20: 43–80.

NICHOLS, J. (1986), 'Head-Marking and Dependent-Marking Grammar', *Language* 62: 56–119.

—— (1992), *Linguistic Diversity in Space and Time* (Chicago: University of Chicago Press).

O'GRADY, W., ARCHIBALD, J., ARONOFF, M., and REES-MILLER, J. (2001), *Contemporary Linguistics: An Introduction*, 4th edn. (New York: St. Martin's Press).

VAN OIRSOUW, R. A. (1987), *The Syntax of Coordination* (London: Croom Helm).

PETRONIO, K., and LILLO-MARTIN, D. (1997), 'WH-movement and the Position of Spec-CP: Evidence from American Sign Language', *Language* 73: 18–57.

PICKERING, M., and SHILLCOCK, R. (1992), 'Processing Subject Extractions', in H. Goodluck and M. Rochemont (eds.), *Island Constraints: Theory, Acquisition and Processing* (Dordrecht: Kluwer), 295–320.

—— BARTON, S., and SHILLCOCK, R. (1994), 'Unbounded Dependencies, Island Constraints and Processing Complexity', in C. Clifton, L. Frazier, and K. Rayner (eds.), *Perspectives on Sentence Processing* (Hillsdale, NJ: Erlbaum), 199–224.

PLANK, F. (ed.) (1995), *Double Case: Agreement by Suffixaufnahme* (Oxford: Oxford University Press).

POLINSKY, M. (1997), 'Dominance in Precedence: SO/OS Languages', in *Papers from the 33rd Regional Meeting of the Chicago Linguistic Society*.

—— (2002), 'Efficiency Preferences: Refinements, Rankings, and Unresolved Questions', *Theoretical Linguistics* 28: 177–202.

POLLARD, C., and SAG, I. A. (1987), *Information-Based Syntax and Semantics*, vol. 1: *Fundamentals*, CSLI Lecture Notes No. 13 (Stanford, Calif.: CSLI).

—— —— (1994), *Head-Driven Phrase Structure Grammar* (Chicago: University of Chicago Press).

POSTAL, P. (1974), *On Raising* (Cambridge, Mass.: MIT Press).

PRINCE, E. F. (1981), 'Toward a Taxonomy of Given/New Information', in P. Cole (ed.), *Radical Pragmatics* (New York: Academic Press), 223–55.

PRIMUS, B. (1993), 'Syntactic Relations', in J. Jacobs, A. von Stechow, W. Sternefeld, and T. Vennemann (eds.), *Syntax: An International Handbook of Contemporary Research*, vol. 1 (Berlin: de Gruyter), 686–705.

PRIMUS, B. (1995), 'Relational Typology', in J. Jacobs, A. von Stechow, W. Sternefeld, and T. Vennemann (eds.), *Syntax: An International Handbook of Contemporary Research*, vol. 2 (Berlin: de Gruyter), 1076–1109.

—— (1999), *Cases and Thematic Roles: Ergative, Accusative and Active* (Tuebingen: Niemeyer).

—— (2002), 'How Good is Hawkins' Performance of Performance?', *Theoretical Linguistics* 28: 203–9.

QUIRK, R. (1957), 'Relative Clauses in Educated Spoken English', *English Studies* 38: 97–109.

—— GREENBAUM, S., LEECH, G., and SVARTVIK, J. (1985), *A Comprehensive Grammar of the English Language* (London: Longman).

RADFORD, A. (1997), *Syntactic Theory and the Structure of English* (Cambridge: Cambridge University Press).

RAPPAPORT, G. C. (1986), 'On Anaphor Binding in Russian', *Natural Language and Linguistic Theory* 4: 97–120.

REINHART, T. (1982), 'Pragmatics and Linguistics: An Analysis of Sentence Topics', *Philosophica* 27: 53–94.

—— (1983), *Anaphora and Semantic Interpretation* (London: Croom Helm).

RIZZI, L. (1982), 'Violations of the WH-island Constraint and the Subjacency Condition', in L. Rizzi (ed.), *Issues in Italian Syntax* (Dordrecht: Foris), 49–76.

ROHDENBURG, G. (1974), *Sekundäre Subjektivierungen im Englischen und Deutschen* (Bielefeld: Cornelson-Velhagen & Klasing).

—— (1996), 'Cognitive Complexity and Grammatical Explicitness in English', *Cognitive Linguistics* 7: 149–82.

—— (1998), 'Clarifying Structural Relationships in Cases of Increased Complexity in English', in R. Schulze (ed.), *Making Meaningful Choices in English: On Dimensions, Perspectives, Methodology and Evidence* (Tübingen: Narr).

—— (1999), 'Clausal Complementation and Cognitive Complexity in English', in F.-W. Neumann and S. Schülting (eds.), *Anglistentag 1998: Erfurt* (Trier: Wissenschaftlicher Verlag), 101–12.

—— (2000), 'The Complexity Principle as a Factor Determining Grammatical Variation and Change in English', in I. Plag and K. P. Schneider (eds.), *Language Use, Language Acquisition and Language History* (Trier: Wissenschaftlicher Verlag), 25–44.

ROSCH, E. (1978), 'Principles of Categorization', in E. Rosch and L. L. Lloyd (eds.), *Cognition and Categorization* (Hillsdale, NJ: Erlbaum), 27–48.

ROSENBAUM, P. S. (1967), *The Grammar of English Predicate Complement Constructions* (Englewood Cliffs, NJ: Prentice-Hall).

ROSS, J. R. (1967), 'Constraints on Variables in Syntax', Ph.D. dissertation, MIT.

RUSS, C. V. J. (ed.) (1990), *The Dialects of Modern German: A Linguistic Survey* (London: Routledge).

RUSSELL, B. (1905), 'On Denoting', *Mind* 14: 479–93.

SAAH, K. K., and Goodluck, H. (1995), 'Island Effects in Parsing and Grammar: Evidence from Akan', *Linguistic Review* 12: 381–409.

SADOCK, J., and ZWICKY, A. (1985), 'Speech Act Distinctions in Syntax', in T. Shopen (ed.), *Language Typology and Syntactic Description*, vol. 1: *Clause Structure* (Cambridge: Cambridge University Press).

SANFORD, A. J., and GARROD, S. C. (1981), *Understanding Written Language* (Chichester: Wiley).

SAPIR, E. (1921), *Language: An Introduction to the Study of Speech* (New York: Harcourt Brace).

SASSE, H.-J. (1988), 'Der irokesische Sprachtyp', *Zeitschrift für Sprachwissenschaft* 7: 173–213.

—— (1993), 'Das Nomen—eine universale Kategorie?', *Sprachtypologie und Universalienforschung* 46: 187–221.

SCHACHTER, P. (1985), 'Parts-of-Speech Systems', in T. Shopen (ed.), *Language Typology and Syntactic Description*, vol. 1: *Clause Structure* (Cambridge: Cambridge University Press), 3–61.

—— and OTANES, F. T. (1972), *Tagalog Reference Grammar* (Berkeley: University of California Press).

SCHUH, R. G. (1983), 'The Evolution of Determiners in Chadic', in E. Wolff and H. Meyer-Bahlburg (eds.), *Studies in Chadic and Afroasiatic Linguistics* (Hamburg: Buske Verlag), 157–210.

SCHÜTZE, C. T., and GIBSON, E. (1999), 'Argumenthood and English Prepositional Phrase Attachment', *Journal of Memory and Language* 40: 409–31.

SHELDON, A. (1974), 'On the Role of Parallel Function in the Acquisition of Relative Clauses in English', *Journal of Verbal Learning and Verbal Behavior* 13: 272–81.

SHIBATANI, M. (1976), *The Grammar of Causative Constructions* (New York: Academic Press).

SKUT, W., KRENN, B., BRANTS, T., and USZKOREIT, H. (1997), 'An Annotation Scheme for Free Word Order Languages', in *Proceedings of ANLP-97* (Washington, DC.).

SLOBIN, D. I. (1973), 'Cognitive Prerequisites for the Development of Grammar', in C. Ferguson and D. I. Slobin (eds.), *Studies of Child Language Development* (New York: Holt, Rinehart & Winston), 175–208.

—— (1997), 'The Universal, the Typological, and the Particular in Acquisition', in D. I. Slobin (ed.), *The Crosslinguistic Study of Language Acquisition*, vol. 5: *Expanding the Contexts* (London: Erlbaum), 1–39.

SONDEREGGER, S. (1998), 'Dichterische Wortstellungstypen im Altgermanischen und ihr Nachleben im älteren Deutsch', in J. O. Askedal (ed.), *Historische Germanische und Deutsche Syntax* (Frankfurt am Main: Lang), 25–47.

SPEAS, M. (1997), 'Optimality Theory and Syntax: Null Pronouns and Control', in D. Archangeli and T. Langendoen (eds.), *Optimality Theory* (Oxford: Blackwell).

SPERBER, D., and WILSON, D. (1995), *Relevance: Communication and Cognition*, 2nd edn. (Oxford: Blackwell). 1st edn. 1986.

STALLINGS, L. M. (1998), 'Evaluating Heaviness: Relative Weight in the Spoken Production of Heavy-NP Shift', Ph.D. dissertation, University of Southern California.

STASSEN, L. (1985), *Comparison and Universal Grammar* (Oxford: Blackwell).

STEEDMAN, M. (1987), 'Combinatory Grammars and Parasitic Gaps', *Natural Language and Linguistic Theory* 5: 403–39.

STOWE, L. A. (1986), 'Parsing WH-Constructions: Evidence from On-line Gap Location', *Language and Cognitive Processes* 1: 227–45.

SVENONIUS, P. (2000), 'Introduction', in P. Svenonius (ed.), *The Derivation of VO and OV* (Amsterdam: Benjamins), 1–26.

SWINNEY, D. A. (1979), 'Lexical Access during Sentence Comprehension: (Re)consideration of Context Effects', *Journal of Verbal Learning and Verbal Behavior* 18: 645–60.

TALLERMAN, M. (1998), *Understanding Syntax* (London: Arnold).

TESNIÈRE, L. (1959), *Éléments de syntaxe structurale* (Paris: Klincksieck).

TOMLIN, R. S. (1986), *Basic Word Order: Functional Principles* (London: CroomHelm).

—— and RHODES, R. (1979), 'An Introduction to Information Distribution in Ojibwa', *Papers from the 15th Regional Meeting of the Chicago Linguistic Society*, 307–20.

TORREGO, E. (1984), 'On Inversion in Spanish and Some of its Effects', *Linguistic Inquiry* 15: 103–30.

TOSCO, M. (1998), 'A Parsing View on Inconsistent Word Order: Articles in Tigre and its Relatives', *Linguistic Typology* 2: 355–80.

TRAUGOTT, E. C., and HEINE, B. (eds.) (1991), *Approaches to Grammaticalization* (Amsterdam: Benjamins).

—— and KÖNIG, E. (1991), 'The Semantics-Pragmatics of Grammaticalization Revisited', in Traugott and Heine (1991: 189–218).

TRAVIS, L. (1984), 'Parameters and Effects of Word Order Variation', Ph.D. dissertation, MIT.

—— (1989), 'Parameters of Phrase Structure', in M. R. Baltin and A. S. Kroch (eds.), *Alternative Conceptions of Phrase Structure* (Chicago: University of Chicago Press).

TSAO, F.-F. (1978), *A Functional Study of Topic in Chinese* (Taipei: Student Book Company).

TSUNODA, T., UEDA, S., and ITOH, Y. (1995), 'Adpositions in Word-Order Typology', *Linguistics* 33: 741–61.

TYLER, L. K. (1989), 'The Role of Lexical Representation in Language Comprehension', in W. Marslen-Wilson (ed.), *Lexical Representation and Process* (Cambridge: Cambridge University Press), 439–62.

ULTAN, R. (1978), 'Some General Characteristics of Interrogative Systems', in J. H. Greenberg (ed.), *Universals of Human Language* (Stanford, Calif.: Stanford University Press), 211–48.

USZKOREIT, H., BRANTS, T., DUCHIER, D., KRENN, B., KONIECZNY, OEPEN, S., and SKUT, W. (1998*a*), 'Studien zur performanzorientierten Linguistik: Aspekte der Relativsatzextraposition im Deutschen', *Kognitionswissenschaft* 7: 129–33.

———— ———— ———— ———— ———— ———— (1998*b*), 'Studien zur performanzorientierten Linguistik: Aspekte der Relativsatzextraposition in Deutschen', in CLAUS Report No. 99 (Saarbrücken: Universität des Saarlandes, Computerlinguistik), 1–14.

VAN RIEMSDIJK, H. (1978), *A Case Study in Syntactic Markedness: The Binding Nature of Prepositional Phrases* (Dordrecht: Foris).

VASISHTH, S. (2002), 'Working Memory in Sentence Comprehension: Processing Hindi Center Embeddings', Ph.D. dissertation, Ohio State University.

VENNEMANN, T. (1974), 'Theoretical Word Order Studies: Results and Problems', *Papiere zur Linguistik* 7: 5–25.

VINCENT, N. B. (1987), 'Latin', in M. B. Harris and N. B. Vincent (eds.), *The Romance Languages* (Oxford: Oxford University Press), 26–78.

WALKER, A. G. H. (1990), 'Frisian', in C. V. J. Russ (ed.), *The Dialects of Modern German* (London: Routledge), 1–30.

WANNER, E., and MARATSOS, M. (1978), 'An ATN Approach to Comprehension', in M. Halle, J. Bresnan, and G. A. Miller (eds.), *Linguistic Theory and Psychological Reality* (Cambridge, Mass.: MIT Press), 119–61.

WASOW, T. (1997), 'Remarks on Grammatical Weight', *Language Variation and Change* 9: 81–105.

—— (2002), *Postverbal Behavior* (Stanford, Calif.: CSLI Publications).

YAMASHITA, H. (in press), 'Scrambled Sentences in Japanese: Linguistic Properties and Motivation for Production', *Text*.

—— and CHANG, F. (2001), '"Long before Short" Preference in the Production of a Head-Final Language', *Cognition* 81: B45–B55.

YIP, V., and MATTHEWS, S. (2001), *Intermediate Cantonese: A Grammar and Workbook* (London: Routledge).

YNGVE, V. H. (1960), 'A Model and an Hypothesis for Language Structure', *Proceedings of the American Philosophical Society* 104: 444–66.

ZIPF, G. (1949), *Human Behavior and the Principle of Least Effort* (New York: Hafner).

Author Index

Language Index

Subject Index